# A Brilliant Little Victory

*The 48th (South Midlands) Division on the Western and Italian Fronts during the First World War*

Lt Col (Retd) Derek A Plews, BA(Hons), MA, VR

Helion & Company

Helion & Company Limited
Unit 8 Amherst Business Centre
Budbrooke Road
Warwick
CV34 5WE
England
Tel. 01926 499 619
Email: info@helion.co.uk
Website: www.helion.co.uk
Twitter: @helionbooks
Visit our blog at blog.helion.co.uk

Published by Helion & Company 2024
Designed and typeset by Mach 3 Solutions (www.mach3solutions.co.uk)
Cover designed by Paul Hewitt, Battlefield Design (www.battlefield-design.co.uk)

Text © Lt. Col. Derek Plews 2024
Images © as per individually credited
Maps drawn by George Anderson © Helion & Company Ltd 2024

Every reasonable effort has been made to trace copyright holders and to obtain their permission for the use of copyright material. The author and publisher apologize for any errors or omissions in this work and would be grateful if notified of any corrections that should be incorporated in future reprints or editions of this book.

ISBN 978-1-804514-29-0

British Library Cataloguing-in-Publication Data.
A catalogue record for this book is available from the British Library.

All rights reserved. No part of this publication may be reproduced, stored in a retrieval system, or transmitted, in any form, or by any means, electronic, mechanical, photocopying, recording or otherwise, without the express written consent of Helion & Company Limited.

For details of other military history titles published by Helion & Company Limited contact the above address or visit our website: http://www.helion.co.uk.

We always welcome receipt of book proposals from prospective authors.

# Contents

| | | |
|---|---|---|
| List of Photographs | | iv |
| List of Maps | | vi |
| Introduction | | vii |
| 1 | Birth of a Territorial Force Division | 9 |
| 2 | War and Mobilisation | 20 |
| 3 | Learning the Ropes | 26 |
| 4 | Somme Offensive | 37 |
| 5 | From Peronne to Passchendaele | 82 |
| 6 | Road to Caporetto | 115 |
| 7 | From Flanders Mud To Italian Sun | 156 |
| 8 | Battle of Asiago Origins | 173 |
| 9 | Battle of Asiago: 15–16th June 1918 | 198 |
| 10 | Fanshawe 'Degummed' | 231 |
| 11 | From Asiago to Austria | 269 |
| Select Bibliography | | 278 |
| Index | | 283 |

# List of Photographs

| | |
|---|---|
| Warwick Barracks. (Author) | 133 |
| The 1/1st Buckinghamshire Battalion enjoying Christmas day dinner, Chelmsford December 1914. (BMMT) | 133 |
| 1/1st Bucks Battalion 1914: A rifle platoon of 1/1st Buckinghamshire Battalio marches past Aylesbury courthouse, August 1914. (BMMT) | 134 |
| Men of the 1/1st Buckinghamshire Battalion in a breastwork trench at Ploegsteert Wood, April 1915. (BMMT) | 134 |
| Final resting place of Pte William Holland, 48th Division's first fatality. Killed near Ploegsteert Wood on 8th April 1915, his remains were originally buried in a small wartime cemetery near Le Bizet Convent. They were subsequently re-interred at Strand Military Cemetery by Ploegsteert village. (Author) | 135 |
| Lt W Cloutman grave. He died whilst attempting to rescue his sergeant during the Somme offensive. Cloutman was responsible for detonating the mines at the Bird Cage during the 48th Division's time at Ploegsteert Wood. (Author) | 136 |
| Lt R Leighton gravesite. Engaged to be married to Vera Brittain, author of the celebrated memoir Testament of Youth, he died of wounds at Louvencourt on 23rd December 1915. (Author) | 137 |
| General view from Poziéres towards Albert depicting the ground over which 48th Division fought during July and August 1916. (Author) | 138 |
| The medal group belonging to Capt Lionel Crouch of 1/1st Buckinghamshire Battalion. The medals include (L to R) the 1914-15 Star, War Medal, Victory Medal and George V Coronation Medal. (Author) | 138 |
| Capt. L Crouch gravesite. He was killed near Poziéres on 21st July 1916. (Author) | 139 |
| Lt R G Norwood gravesite at Poziéres Military Cemetery. His remains were uncovered during post-war battlefield clearance. (Author) | 140 |
| Maj Gen R Fanshawe c. 1907. (Open source) | 141 |
| Lt Gen the Earl of Cavan. (Open Source) | 141 |
| 1/1st Bucks Bn Lewis Gunners, Italy 1918. (BMMT) | 141 |
| Austrian trench remnants on Mt Zebio. (Author) | 142 |
| 1/1st Bucks and 1/4th OBLI battalion officers sight-seeing in Venice 1918. (BMMT) | 142 |
| Remains of British trench systems. (Author) | 143 |
| Maj E A M Bindloss gravesite Magnaboschi Military Cemetery. (Author) | 144 |
| British ferro-concrete dressing station situated between Grenezza and Pria del Acqua. (Author) | 145 |
| British lines from Mt Zebio. (Author) | 145 |
| Carriola base site. (Author) | 146 |

| | |
|---|---|
| Clo, short for Casello, a small structure situated astride the light railway running from Asiago to Cesuna. (Author) | 146 |
| Ghelphac Stream which ran opposite the British lines. (Author) | 147 |
| British machine gun post situated above the light railway that extended from Asiago to Cesuna. This portion of the line was held by 1/4th OBLI on the morning of 15 June 1918. (Author) | 147 |
| British dugout, Pria del Acqua. (Author) | 148 |
| Pelly Cross site. (Author) | 148 |
| Grenezza base site. (Author) | 149 |
| Handley Cross, an important junction behind the 48th Division line, was heavily shelled in the early hours of 15 June 1918. This set off a nearby ammunition dump. (Author) | 149 |
| Railway bridge situated immediately behind 1/4th OBLI lines on 15 June 1918. (Author) | 150 |
| Asiago No Man's Land. (Author) | 151 |
| Italian trench system remains east of Asiago. (Author) | 151 |
| Entrance to Grenezza Military Cemetery. (Author) | 152 |
| Boscon Cemetery situated immediately behind the British lines. (Author) | 152 |
| Lt Col J M Knox gravesite, Grenezza Military Cemetery. (Author) | 153 |
| Private memorial commemorating Lt Col J M Knox. (Author) | 154 |
| Capt. Edward Brittain, brother of author Vera Britain, gravesite, Grenezza Military Cemetery. (Author) | 155 |

# List of Maps

1 Ploegsteert Wood 1915. 27
2 Poziéres 1916. 62
3 Ypres 1917. 103
4 St Julien 19th and 22nd August 1917. 111
5 48th Division dispositions June 1918. 200
6 Asiago 15-16th June 1918. 205

# Introduction

At 3.00 on the morning of 15 June 1918, the Austro-Hungarian army launched what was be its last major offensive of the First World War. On the eastern flank of the attack, in the foothills of the Italian Dolomites, near the town of Asiago, a small section of the front line was held by two British infantry divisions – the 48th (South Midlands) Division on the left and the 23rd Division on the right.

In the infantry assault that followed a four-hour preparatory barrage, the enemy managed to penetrate the fronts of both divisions. On the right, the incursion was limited and was quickly snuffed out by a determined counter-attack, led by the commanding officer of the 11th Battalion, Sherwood Foresters, Lt Col C E Hudson, for which he was awarded the Victoria Cross. On the left, however, where the enemy had managed to break-in to the British position in several places, the fighting was harder, more costly in terms of manpower, and more prolonged. Nevertheless, in a little over 24 hours, the 48th Division, under its commander, Major General Sir Robert Fanshawe, had contained the enemy penetration, blunted the assault, and forced the attackers back across no-man's-land to their starting point.

Fanshawe, with a much-weakened force, thanks to the effects of the "Spanish Flu" epidemic, that had swept through his troops in the weeks before the attack, fought a text-book defensive battle, using his favoured "elastic" approach. He had contained the enemy penetrations within a pocket, designed for that purpose, and then defeated them by counter-attack. Despite this, a few days later he was on a train bound for home, unceremoniously and unexpectedly sacked by the XIV Corps Commander, Lt General Lord Cavan.

Fanshawe's dismissal, which was a devastating blow for his soldiers, and, no doubt, for the man himself, has never been properly explained. Cavan left no records to justify his decision, and the few historians who have examined the issue have tended to focus on Fanshawe's "generalship" as a potential cause.

In the face of the successful outcome of the fighting on the 48th Division's front, this explanation appears to be thin and unconvincing, and thus worthy of re-examination. That is what this book sets out to do.

In order to properly understand the man – and the division – that fought at Asiago in June, 1918, it is critical to chart the formation's history, from its birth, following the Haldane Reforms in the first decade of the 20th century, to its arrival in Italy, in November, 1917, in the aftermath of the Caporetto debacle that almost knocked the Italians out of the war.

With that in mind, this work begins with the establishment of the division in 1908 and follows its fortunes from mobilisation in August 1914, its introduction to trench warfare, at Ploegsteert Wood, near the Belgian city of Ypres, in the spring of 1915, and its subsequent move to the Somme sector, later that year. It continues with a description of the hard-fought and costly combat around the villages of Ovillers and Poziéres, on the old Roman road that runs from Albert to Bapaume, and the difficult winter months in front of Warlencourt, as the Somme offensive came to a close. From there, it demonstrates how the division made a seamless switch from the static fighting of the trenches to mobile pursuit of the enemy, as the Germans withdrew to the fearsome Hindenburg Line, during the early part of 1917. It goes on to examine the South Midlanders' performance during the Battle of Passchendaele, between August and October of that year, and then describes the move to the Italian front and its initial deployment on the Piave Line, north of Venice, before shifting to the mountains above Vicenza and the Lombardy Plain. After a detailed exposition of the fighting in front of Asiago, the book includes a careful analysis of the division's performance there, together with a detailed reappraisal of earlier attempts to explain Fanshawe's dismissal, and sets out a new hypothesis for Cavan's decision.

The volume employs a wide range of official documentation, mostly army, corps, division, brigade and unit war diaries, and the files of British official historian Brigadier-General Sir James Edmonds, held at the United Kingdom's National Archives at Kew. It has also benefitted from various personal testimonies from the Imperial War Museum's collection, others held by the Churchill Archives Centre, Churchill College, Cambridge, and published accounts, written by men who were there during the events under scrutiny. The author is indebted to all the institutions consulted for their help with this endeavour.

A Territorial Force formation, the 48th (South Midland) Division was never exceptionally successful nor an abject failure. It was, rather, a good, average fighting force. It had proved, through the long, bitter combat of 1916 and 1917, that it was sound and dependable. The men were tenacious and courageous in attack, dogged and determined in defence, the product of effective and skilful leadership at all levels. They could hold their heads high among the bulk of the divisions that formed the British army on the Western Front and in Italy.

Fanshawe was adored by his men, not just for his habit of distributing squares of chocolate to soldiers he met on his regular visits to the trenches, but because they knew and trusted him. He had been their commander from May, 1915 and had led them, with skill and compassion, through the trials of the Somme and Passchendaele. Never a man to shirk his responsibilities, he had driven the men hard when circumstances demanded it, as those who attacked across the Steenbeek and the Stroombeek streams, during the Passchendaele fighting, could testify. But never harder than he had driven himself and his staff to ensure that every operation was planned meticulously, and with the welfare of the men in mind – not to the extent of prejudicing the outcome, but to avoid unnecessary loss. He shared their dangers and privations, frequently turning up in the front line to see the ground and conditions for himself rather than relying on maps, aerial photographs and second-hand accounts.

Robert Fanshawe's personal reputation – together with that of his Division – was trashed by his sacking. It is hoped that this book may go a little way towards righting that wrong, and, in doing so, make a valid and useful contribution to the sadly-limited historiography of the British army's part in the Italian campaign during the First World War.

# 1

# Birth of a Territorial Force Division

## Army Reforms

Following the final defeat of Napoleon Bonaparte at Waterloo in June 1815, the British army re-invented itself to meet the changing demands of the Empire. As *Le Petit Caporal* was despatched to see out his days in exile on the island of St Helena, Britain's perennial fear of a French invasion was superseded by the need to ensure a stable, secure environment in which to facilitate efficient trade and commerce with its overseas territories. This required a different army from the one that had bested the French at Cuidad Rodrigo, Badajoz and Salamanca. Britain now needed a colonial gendarmerie whose main purpose was to manage unruly tribesmen "down some dark defile"[1] on India's North-West Frontier, the Afghan mountains, or the forests of Burma, rather than trading canister shot and volley fire with Bonaparte's Imperial Guard, or "forming square" to repel his Cuirassiers, Dragoons and Lancers on the open plains of Flanders, Portugal and Spain.

Tory Secretary of State for War from 1887-92, Edward Stanhope, in a confidential memorandum, dated December 1888, set out what he saw as the key requirements of the army at that time. These included:

- The effective support of the civil power throughout Great Britain.
- To find the number of men for India which has been fixed by arrangement with the Government of India.
- To find garrisons for all our fortresses and coaling stations at home and abroad…and to maintain these garrisons at all times at the strength fixed for a peace or war footing.
- To be able to mobilise for home defence two Corps of regular troops and one Corps partly composed of regulars and partly of militia, and to organise the auxiliary forces not allotted to Army Corps or garrisons for the defence of London, and for the defensible positions in advance, and for the defence of the mercantile ports.
- Subject to the foregoing considerations, and to other financial obligations, to aim at being able, in the case of necessity, to send abroad two complete Army Corps with a Cavalry Division and Lines of Communication [troops].

---

1   From 'Arithmetic on the Frontier' by Rudyard Kipling.

"But" he added, "it will be distinctly understood that the probability of employment of an Army Corps in the field in any European war is sufficiently improbable to make it the primary duty of the military authorities to organise our forces efficiently for the defence of the country".[2] These were the principles that had shaped the army's thinking up to the start of the Boer war in 1899.

By the closing decade of the 19th century, however, the relative peace that Europe had enjoyed following Napoleon's downfall, looked increasingly fragile. The new, unified Germany, which came into being in 1871, was emerging as a significant power with its own ambitions, including territorial aspirations that were likely to bring it into conflict with longer-established imperial rivals including Britain, France and Russia. Bismarck, the great Prussian statesman, had worked to preserve peace in Europe in order to maintain Prussian influence and to allow his new nation to establish itself. However, when William II succeeded Frederick III in June 1888, after a reign of only 180 days, Bismarck's approach to statesmanship and diplomacy proved incompatible with that of his new emperor. He stepped down in 1890, leaving the young William without a strong, wise, paternalistic hand to help to guide his pursuit of *Weltpolitik*[3] and Germany's "place in the sun" – the very same sun that, it was claimed, "never set on the British Empire".

Geopolitics was changing. A European conflict was beginning to look more likely. But Britain, as an island nation, detached from the European mainland, continued to see herself principally as a maritime power with a strong navy that could protect her overseas interests and secure her trading routes. She was determined to hold on to her small, highly-professional army, skilled in irregular, colonial warfare, and trained and equipped so that it could be deployed quickly over long distances by sea. She was slow to recognise that she might once again be called upon to fight on the European mainland alongside and against nations who had clung on to the concept of the "nation in arms", underpinned by compulsory military service or conscription. As a result, they were able to field massive armies that made the British force seem almost insignificant, even "contemptible".

Fortunately, the Boer War provided the shock necessary to jolt Britain out of her complacency, sparking much-needed debate and, eventually, a programme of modernisation and change. During the Victorian era, Britain, with her diminutive (compared to her European neighbours) but well-trained army, had become accustomed to successfully prosecuting numerous "bush wars". As Spencer Jones has pointed out, the Boer War marked the 226th of 230 imperial conflicts fought during Victoria's reign.[4] Generally, the opposition could not stand up to Britain's superior technology and organisation. That is not to say that the imperial enemies had not been capable of forcing some hard fighting and even the odd defeat. But in the various conflicts from 1857 the British had only twice lost 100 men killed in a single action…until they met the Boers.[5]

Britain thought she could deal with Boer insurrection using her tried and tested methods for curbing unrest in other parts of the empire. She was wrong. Despite the vast differences between the two protagonists, it was the Boers, lightly-armed, highly-mobile farmers who knew how to use the land and their German Mauser rifles and carbines to the best advantage, who soon had the British army reeling. In just over three years of fighting the British Empire lost more than

---

2   Quoted in the report of the *Royal Commission on Boer War*, 1903, p31
3   William II's imperialist foreign policy, designed to transform Germany into a global power.
4   S Jones, *From Boer War to World War*, p.19.
5   S Jones, p.20.

20,000 men before finally bringing the enemy to the negotiating table and the war to a close. In a single week in December 1899 – forever afterwards known to the British as "Black Week" – the Boer commandos inflicted three significant and costly defeats on the British. At Stromberg, on 10 December, a force, led by Lt General William Gatacre, blundered into a Boer position and lost 26 killed, 68 wounded and 696 captured before retreating in disarray. The following day, Lt General the Lord Methuen lost heavily at Magersfontein, near Kimberley, suffering casualties of 210 dead (including 22 officers), 675 wounded and 62 missing. The Highland Brigade alone suffered 747 killed, wounded and missing. On 15 December, at Colenso, General Sir Redvers Buller, Commander in Chief of British Forces in South Africa, launched a clumsy frontal attack on the Boer lines without having properly identified the enemy positions, and sustained over 1100 casualties, including 132 killed, 765 wounded and 228 captured.[6] Included among the dead was Lt Freddy Roberts, only son of British Field Marshal, Lord Roberts. Young Roberts succumbed to wounds received whilst trying to save the guns of 14th and 66th Batteries, Royal Field Artillery, a sacrifice for which he and three others were awarded the Victoria Cross. The Boers were reported to have lost only 8 killed and 30 wounded.

Black Week was a humiliation for Britain and her army, and the conduct of the war was, unsurprisingly, the subject of much press, political and public disquiet at home. Britain responded by ordering a massive reinforcement of the force in South Africa; removing Buller as commander in chief, to be replaced by Lord Roberts; and issuing new tactical guidance, including mandating much greater use of mounted infantry to match the Boers' mobility. Britain had already decided to deploy an expeditionary force consisting of two army corps and a cavalry division (roughly 70,000 men) to support its existing garrison in South Africa. The post-Black Week expansion required more men, but the reserves cupboard was bare. Britain looked to her auxiliary forces which consisted of the Militia, the Yeomanry, and the Rifle Volunteers.

The War Office began to embody[7] the county militias under an Army Order issued on 3 November 1899. 35 battalions were called up in the first tranche, and more followed as the demand for manpower increased. Before long the whole of the militia had been mobilised, and it had also been decided to form detachments of Rifle Volunteers, who would be deployed as formed Service Companies, embedded into the regular regiments to which they were affiliated. For example, the 1st Buckinghamshire Rifle Volunteers were invited to find 60 men for a composite company from Bucks and Oxfordshire, to be attached to the 1st Battalion, Oxfordshire Light Infantry. In the event, 70 men were selected from Bucks, and a total of 42 Oxfordshire Volunteers made up the balance of the 116 other ranks. Two officers, Lieutenants C. A. Barron of Taplow House and Lionel Hawkins from Stony Stratford were also chosen.

The War Office also agreed to form a new Imperial Yeomanry, drawn in the first instance largely from the existing Yeomanry units, but organised and trained to fight as mounted infantry. Again, the men of Buckinghamshire were not slow to come forward. The county's initial contribution to the Imperial Yeomanry came in the form of the 37th (Buckingham) and 38th (High Wycombe) Companies (nominally raised from the local Yeomanry unit, the Royal Bucks Hussars) of the 10th Battalion, Imperial Yeomanry, under the command of Lt Colonel

---

6   *British Battles.com* <https://www.britishbattles.com/great-boer-war/battle-of-colenso/> (accessed 14 December 2022).
7   Embodiment was the term used to describe the act of calling out the militia for full-time service.

the Lord Chesham. Chesham would later become the IY's Inspector General with the rank of Brigadier-General.

In the end, British mass and a range of new tactics, including the rounding up of Boer women, children and elderly into Concentration Camps, where many died of diseases brought about by primitive and vile sanitary conditions, forced the Boers to seek an armistice, and the conflict was brought to a close with the signing of a peace treaty on 31 May 1902.

However, while the shooting and killing might have stopped, the questions did not. People still wanted to know why a war which pitted Britain's apparently elite, well-trained, professional army against a small but determined force of Dutch farmers armed with rifles, a few machine guns and artillery pieces, had cost Britain and her colonies so dearly in blood and treasure. To answer these questions, Tory Prime Minister, Arthur Balfour, established a Royal Commission, headed by the Earl of Elgin. The Elgin Commission, as it became known, was tasked with enquiring into:

> The military preparations, including the supply of men, ammunition and transport by sea and land, in connection with the campaign, and into the military operations up to the occupation of Pretoria.[8]

The Commission's report, presented to both houses of parliament and published in 1903, was comprehensive and forthright. It considered not only the role of the regular army, but also the mobilisation of the auxiliary forces, including the Militia, Volunteers, and the Yeomanry.[9]

The Commission found that in October 1899 the strength of the Militia was deficient by about 600 officers and 24,000 troops. The regular army was also well below establishment and was particularly short of junior officers. The army's immediate solution was to poach the best young officers from the Militia. This then left the Militia with even fewer officers just as it was about to be embodied. The officer shortfall was made good by commissioning soldiers from the ranks, as the Elgin Commission report described it, taking "almost anybody who offered".[10] During the conflict, a total of 68 militia battalions were embodied and although some of these served in Malta and other stations, the vast majority went to South Africa.

Giving evidence to the Commission, Field Marshal Lord Roberts said he found the 'greatest difference' between the militia units, with their subaltern posts often filled by young men who were "quite devoid of previous training", and regular units.[11] As a result, he chiefly used the militia to provide security for his Lines of Communication tasks, rather than in more offensive roles. Even so, he felt "a great anxiety in regard to my communications being held in many cases by partially trained troops such as the militia and hastily-raised yeomanry. The result was that our ill-trained troops often led me into great difficulties – the capture of the Derbyshire Yeomanry at Rhenoster River, and the capture of the Irish Yeomanry at Lindley – showed what a danger it was to depend upon troops who were not thoroughly disciplined and

---

8   *Royal Commission Report of His Majesty's Commissioners Appointed to Inquire into the Military Preparations and Other Matters Connected with the War in South Africa*, p. V
9   A separate commission, headed by Lord Esher, considered the performance of the auxiliary forces during the campaign.
10  *Royal Commission Report on Boer War*, p.61
11  *Royal Commission Report on Boer War*, p.64.

properly trained."[12] However, not all of the auxiliary forces were regarded so negatively. The City of London Imperial Volunteers (later renamed the City Imperial Volunteers)[13], the only Volunteers to serve as a formed unit, attracted high praise from senior officers. Lord Roberts described them as "a particularly useful body…and they did magnificently", while General Sir Ian Hamilton said: "They got better and better every day and at the end they were quite famous".[14] Major General Horace Smith-Dorrien, reflecting on their performance under fire at Diamond Hill in June 1900, told them: "No regiment in the Army of South Africa has done more splendid work."[15]

The use of the part-time Auxiliary Forces – Militia, Yeomanry, and the Rifle Volunteers – received mixed reviews. But the fact that they had existed, and more importantly, that they had been prepared to forsake their liability to serve only at home, and volunteer in large numbers for overseas service, demonstrated that a part-time, volunteer cohort could play a part in future Defence plans, at home and overseas, providing it was properly organised, equipped, trained and well-led with sufficient officers.

The Royal Commission's report provided a blueprint for change, identifying, as it did, the key issues that would need to be addressed in order to ensure Britain had a modern, capable army that was able to protect its interests at home and overseas and provide an expeditionary capability if required. However, with the South African conflict settled, the drivers for change had been considerably weakened. As a result, although there was much debate, little of consequence was done to put right the various shortcomings until the arrival at the War Office in December 1905, of Scottish barrister and committed Liberal Imperialist politician, Richard Burdon Haldane.

Haldane had been appointed as Secretary of State for War in Sir Henry Campbell-Bannerman's first cabinet when the Liberals took power after Arthur Balfour stood down due to the deep unpopularity of his administration. This was in part because of public disquiet about the handling of the Boer War, and also because of his shift away from a policy of free trade. The King invited Campbell-Bannerman to form a new administration ahead of a general election, and Haldane was appointed to the War Office on 13th December, carrying on in that post after the Liberals achieved a landslide election victory the following February.

In his autobiography, Haldane claimed that on taking office he felt there was an "improbable" chance that the Central Powers might invade and occupy France. Such an act, however unlikely, represented a significant threat to the security of the United Kingdom. If it came to a Franco-German conflict, Britain needed a plan to try to ensure that the channel ports were not occupied by the German navy, which was enjoying the benefits of greater financial investment and growing in size and strength. Part of the solution was a strong Royal Navy, armed with the new Dreadnought-class battleships. But, in Haldane's view, the threat also implied a requirement for an Expeditionary Force of sufficient size and mobility to be able quickly to go to the assistance of the French in the event of an attack in the north or north-eastern region of that country.[16] After much debate with his military advisors, it was decided that a force of six fully-

---

12  *Royal Commission Report on the Boer War*, p.64
13  I F W Beckett, *Riflemen Form: A Study of the Rifle Volunteer Movement 1859-1908*, p.212.
14  Royal Commission report on the Boer War, p66.
15  I F W Beckett, p217.
16  R B Haldane, *Richard Burdon Haldane: An Autobiography*, p.187.

equipped divisions and at least one cavalry division would be required for the task. But another key question remained. With a large proportion of the regular army already committed to the Empire, once these expeditionary divisions had deployed, what would be left for home Defence? There was, argued Haldane, a clear requirement for a second-line military force to defend the British Isles against invasion and to provide a framework on which the regular army could be expanded to meet the demands of a large-scale conflict in Europe or elsewhere. Thus, the idea of a Territorial Force was born… or perhaps it would be more accurate to say re-born, since similar proposals had been made by others before Haldane decided to adopt the concept.

This new organisation could have been created by re-rolling the existing militia, volunteers and yeomanry, but such a move would have ignored the short-comings of the auxiliary forces that had been identified in the South African conflict. As Professor Ian Beckett has pointed out, referring to the Volunteers (but the same could be said for the Militia and Yeomanry), the Boer War had proved that "the force was unfit to take the field against Continental troops and reform was necessary".[17] Haldane favoured a different "quite novel" approach.[18] The Volunteers, he noted, had no transport or medical capabilities, whilst the Militia was neither organised nor equipped for such a role. The Yeomanry was "an excellent peace [time] organisation", but still largely run by "country gentlemen".[19] Each of the existing organisations had histories, traditions and influential supporters. The Militias, for example, could trace their roots back to the 16th century, while the Yeomanry and Rifle Volunteers were newer creation, established in the 18th and 19th centuries respectively as responses to fears of invasion by the French or public insurrection. Haldane felt, rightly as it turned out, that the traditionalist supporters of the auxiliary forces would resist change and thus make the sort of reforms he had in mind much more difficult to achieve. If that happened it would cost more parliamentary time, spark more media debate, create political tension, and potentially lose him his slot in the Liberals' busy legislative programme, thus kicking the can of Army Reform a long way down the road. To try to avoid this, he instead opted to weld together the best of the Rifle Volunteers and the Yeomanry to create a Territorial Force of 14 Infantry Divisions with supporting arms, including field artillery, medical, engineer and mounted elements. The Militia, in its traditional form, would disappear, being replaced by a Special Reserve of 74 "semi-professional" battalions, which would be aligned with the pairs of Line (regular) battalions (home and foreign service) that had been created by the earlier Childers Reforms. The role of the Special Reserve would be to provide drafts of men to reinforce the Expeditionary Force in times of conflict, but not to deploy in formed units.

His Territorial and Reserve Forces Bill was introduced in the House of Commons on 25 February 1907 and as predicted, immediately ran into opposition from all sides. The National Service League and its chief cheer-leader, Lord Roberts, favoured conscription and described the new force as being "little better than an armed crowd".[20] The Labour Party was against anything that looked like an expansion of the military. Many of Haldane's Liberal colleagues wanted the army budget reduced and were only won over when Haldane explained that the Territorial Force estimates were expected to be about £2.9m per annum compared with the Auxiliary Forces

---

17   I F W Beckett, p.252.
18   R B Haldane, p.192.
19   R B Haldane, An Autobiography, p.192.
20   I F W Beckett, p.249.

budget for 1906-07 which was £4.4m.[21] The Militia and its prominent supporters were opposed to what they considered to be its absorption into either the Regular Army or the Territorial Force. The powerful Volunteer lobby was strongly against the role of the County Associations, which, they felt, would rob Commanding Officers of much of their authority. However, through a combination of his personal charm – one Colonel remarked after a dinner with Haldane that he "felt like a calf, well licked-over by a boa constrictor, as a preliminary to deglutition"[22] – and some carefully-considered compromises and amendments, he was able to ensure that the Bill passed through all its Commons and Lords stages and achieved Royal Assent in August, 1907, with most of its key provisions intact, and scheduled to take effect on 1st April, 1908.

The new Act contained three key sections. Part 1 created a network of Associations, under the Lord Lieutenant of each county, whose role was to raise and administer the new force. This included recruiting and accommodating the units and ensuring that they had sufficient areas on which to conduct their training, as well as the provision of uniforms and equipment. The Associations would not, however, have command responsibility for the TF units. In an attempt to address some of the weaknesses identified in the Royal Commission report, including the variable military efficiency of the auxiliary forces, the new units would be trained by regular Officers and NCOs, under the direction of the War Office, and the War Office would also exercise overall command.[23] Part 2 gave legal standing to the new Territorial Force and provided for the Volunteer and Yeomanry units to be transferred into it in whole or in part. Part 3 created the Special Reserve, which was essentially a new class of the Army Reserve, with a Crown power to transfer existing Militia units into it. A fourth element contained a number of minor provisions related to the administration of the Act.

Peter Simkins, in his treatise on the creation of Kitchener's New Armies in 1914, says Haldane believed his reforms would result in a much larger force than had previously been available, with a more specific role, which was to provide "the means of home defence on the outbreak of war, both for coast defence strictly, and for repelling possible raids" and as "the sole means of support and expansion of the professional army" in any war that lasted for more than six months.[24] However, although he had been forced to state on the face of the Bill that the force could be compelled to mobilise only for home defence, Haldane was clear during the Commons debates that members of the TF would be free to volunteer for foreign service if required.[25]

At first, recruitment to the new organisation went well. To gain War Office recognition, units had to reach 30% of their establishment. In less than five weeks this was achieved by 174 infantry battalions out of 206, 48 Yeomanry Regiments out of 56, 287 Artillery units out of 369 and 69 Engineer units out of 117. By 1 June 1908, the force numbered 144,620 and after another month it had grown to 183,000. In June 1909, the total had increased again to 268,776 and was 270,000 by October of that year. However, it never reached its establishment of 312,000. In fact, after 1909 it began a slow decline and by September 1913 it had fallen to 245,700 – 1893

---

21  I F W Beckett, p.249.
22  I F W Beckett, p.251.
23  The County Associations still exist today in the form of 13 regional Reserve Forces' and Cadets' Associations but at the time or writing they were about to be reformed into a single Non-Departmental Public Body of the Ministry of Defence, with 13 regional offices.
24  P Simkins, *Kitchener's Army*, p.12
25  P Simkins, p.12.

officers and 64,777 Other Ranks below target. It had had recovered to stand at 268,700 at the outbreak of war in September 1914, although only 18,683 had signed the Imperial Service obligation, agreeing to serve overseas if required.[26]

The South Midland Division, as it was then called, like the other 13 new infantry formations that made up the Territorial Force, came into being on 1 April 1908, with its headquarters at The Old Barracks, Barrack Road, Warwick.[27] Its first General Officer Commanding (GOC) was Major General Sir Herbert Aveling Raitt KCIE, CB. Raitt was 50 years of age when he assumed command of the division. He had been commissioned into the 80th Regiment of Foot[28] in March 1878. He saw action in the Anglo-Zulu war the following year, and commanded the 1st Battalion, the South Staffordshire Regiment in the Second Boer War. Having established the Division, he was posted to India in May 1913 and commanded the Mandalay Brigade before taking over the post of GOC Burma Division in October 1914. He led the British response to the Kachin Rising in January and February 1915, retiring from the Army in November 1918.

On April Fool's Day, 1908, the Division had a name, a commander, an embryonic divisional staff and a headquarters, but it was still a long way from being able to make a practical contribution to the Order of Battle of the new Territorial Force. The route to reaching that objective would be a challenging one.

The division was scaled to consist of 12 infantry battalions, organised into three brigades each consisting of four battalions. These would be supported by three brigades of artillery, two Royal Engineer Field Companies; three Royal Army Medical Corps Field Ambulances and all the ancillary personnel (wheelwrights, farriers, blacksmiths, transport and supply troops, signallers etc) necessary to create a self-contained fighting formation. The recruiting area assigned to the division included the counties of Warwickshire, Worcestershire, Gloucestershire, Oxfordshire, Buckinghamshire, and Berkshire, and the six County Associations created by Haldane's Territorial and Reserve Forces Act (1907) commenced work at once to attract and sign up the 18,000-plus men who would be required to make up the establishment of the formation.

Each county was expected to contribute according to its size. Warwickshire, including Britain's second city, Birmingham, was to provide a complete Infantry Brigade of four battalions; four batteries of field artillery, cap-badged Royal Horse Artillery; a brigade of heavy Artillery (Royal Garrison Artillery); and one mounted and two dismounted Field Ambulances. Gloucestershire was to contribute three infantry battalions, three batteries of field artillery, two Royal Engineer Field Companies and a field ambulance. Worcestershire's share was two infantry battalions and three batteries of field artillery. Berkshire, Oxfordshire and Buckinghamshire were each to raise a single infantry battalion. The supporting elements including the ammunition columns, transport and supply columns of the Army Service Corps, Signalling Companies etc, were to be spread across the six associations. Each Association was also required to raise a regiment of Yeomanry.

Although early signs looked promising, recruiting proved to be an uphill struggle. Many of the Militia, Yeomanry and Volunteers refused to transfer into the TF, some from a deep

---

26  P Simkins, pp, 17-18.
27  The division was re-designated 48th (South Midland) Division in May 1915.
28  The 80th of Foot was the South Staffordshire Volunteers. Under the Childers Reforms it amalgamated with the 38th of Foot (1st Staffordshire Regiment of Foot) to form the South Staffordshire Regiment in 1881.

sense of betrayal at the way their former organisations had been torn up by Haldane's reforms. Bill Mitchinson reckons that only about 30 percent of Birmingham's 2,700 volunteers joined the new organisation and as a result it took 15 months before the four battalions of the Royal Warwickshire Regiment that would make up the division's Warwickshire Brigade, had achieved numbers approaching their full establishment.[29] The recruiting effort was given some additional momentum during 1909 when a media-induced "invasion scare" sparked a renewed interest among the country's young men.

Getting new men in through the doors of the Drill Halls was hard enough. Keeping them in uniform was another problem. Soldiers signed on for an initial period of four years, after which they were encouraged to re-enlist for further service. It was important to persuade as many as possible to continue to serve in order to maintain numbers, gain value from the investment that had been made in their training, and also to ensure a supply of experienced men who could be promoted to NCO rank and thus become the junior leaders of their battalions. The early joiners reached the four-year point in 1912 and 1913 and it was worrying to discover that many were determined not to re-enlist. Part-time volunteers needed to be motivated. Although the Territorials were paid to train, and this would have been an incentive for some, many of the first tranches of part-time soldiers came from the skilled and artisan working classes and would have earned more than the poverty line wages of 20 shillings per week; they certainly earned more than the average 1s 9d a day of the private soldier.[30]

If money was not the main driver, it was essential for Commanding Officers and their company commanders to lay on exciting and compelling training to keep the men interested. This was made more difficult by a lack of training estate and by the TF's unit organisation, which retained the old eight-company battalion structure. For units whose companies were widely dispersed, it was difficult to arrange collective training at battalion level because of the challenges of bringing all eight companies together in a single location. Often this could only be achieved during the annual fortnight training camp to which the Territorials were committed. Although there was an aspiration to run divisional camps, the limited availability of military training areas – the needs of the regulars were prioritised – and the sheer scale of the administrative burden involved meant that organising a divisional exercise was beyond the collective means of the Associations both in staff time and cost. For example, the Division did not maintain its full scale of horses in peacetime and in order to provide the horsepower necessary to deploy the formation on exercise, horses had to be hired from local suppliers. According to the Warwickshire Association, the pre-war cost of horse hire to support the county's territorials for a fortnight camp amounted to £7,000 – assuming the required number of animals could be found.[31] Thus, brigade-level exercises became the norm.

The attitudes of some civilian employers contributed to the "friction" experienced in trying to ensure the force was properly prepared for its role. Some employers actively encouraged their staff to join the Territorials and made sure they got sufficient time off. For example, the Clarendon Press, at that time one of Oxfordshire's largest employers, sponsored a company of 1/4th Oxfordshire and Buckinghamshire Light Infantry, although the County Association took care to manage

---

29  K W Mitchinson, *The 48th (South Midland) Division 1908-1919*, p.24.
30  R D Williams, A Social and Military History of the 1/8th Battalion, The Royal Warwickshire Regiment in the Great War (unpublished MPhil dissertation, University of Birmingham, 1999), passim.
31  K W Mitchinson, p.23.

its relationship with the company by carefully scheduling its annual camps to comply with the employer's wishes.[32] Some local councils agreed to give their Territorials paid leave to train. Other organisations were not so forward-leaning. The Worcestershire Association, for example, found itself having to take up the case of five men of the Second South Midland Brigade Royal Field Artillery who were sacked by their employers because they had attended annual camp.

While the Associations worked hard to build and maintain strong relationships with employers in their areas, this could be undone in an instant by unthinking or uncaring regular officers such as the GOC South Midlands Brigade who, displaying a total lack of understanding of the importance of the civilian employer to a Territorial's ability to serve, decided to reschedule an annual camp at very short notice.[33] It is not hard to imagine how badly this would have been received by employers who had planned to manage the absence of their Territorial staff and now found themselves having to unpick their arrangements.

Meanwhile, the War Office was often critical of the standards being achieved by Territorial units. Levels of fitness and musketry skills were recurring issues highlighted in inspection reports, in which the Territorials were compared unfavourably with their regular counterparts. For example, General Officer Commanding in Chief of Southern Command (to which the South Midland Division was attached), Lt General Sir Charles Douglas – later appointed to the important role as Chief of the Imperial General Staff – considered that the Territorial infantry under his command led such a sedentary life they were incapable of enduring any prolonged periods of hardship. He also believed they were more susceptible to disease than the regulars. Another report described the standard of marksmanship as "dreadful".[34] This may have been true, but it was probably unfair to point the finger at individual soldiers or the County Associations. The soldiers themselves were generally not the problem: their lack of access to firing ranges was largely to blame. There were not enough ranges to meet the needs of both regular and Territorial units and local people objected to shooting practice disturbing their peace on Sundays thus curtailing the part-timers' ability to train. The regulars could shoot on week-days with no such limitations. The minute books of the Associations contain many examples of the difficulties faced in trying to ensure that the South Midland Division units had appropriate shooting facilities. For example, the Oxfordshire Association tried to provide a new range at Noke on the edge of Otmoor, to the north-east of Oxford, but gave up after four years of unsuccessful negotiations over access rights.[35] Warwickshire struggled for many years to obtain permission to build a 1,000 yards range at Kingsbury. Gloucestershire had to rely on the local council rather than the War Office to purchase land for a range near Tewkesbury. In one of its first meetings, on 1st October, 1908, the Buckinghamshire Committee discussed the possibility of establishing a central rifle range at Princes Risborough to replace the existing facility at Little Kimble.[36] In October the following year, the Association agreed to lease land at Wycombe Marsh for a new rifle range, and in July 1910 it authorised the payment of compensation to local farmers whose land abutted the range, "on account of the danger of bullets passing onto their land".[37]

---

32  K W Mitchinson, p.23.
33  K W Mitchinson, p.23.
34  TNA WO 32/9192: Efficiency of Territorial Force compared to Regular Army 1911.
35  *Oxfordshire Territorial Force Association Minutes Book*, n.d.
36  *Buckinghamshire Territorial Force Association Minutes Book*, October 1908.
37  *Buckinghamshire Territorial Force Association Minutes Book*, July 1910.

In some ways, the Territorial Force battalions were forerunners of Kitchener's Pals Battalions. The county-centric nature of the units meant they frequently contained men who worked together in the same factory or office. Their civilian foremen were often their senior NCOs, while their junior managers filled the subaltern posts. Commanding Officers tended to come from the upper middle classes such as architects, lawyers, and factory owners. For example, the CO of the 1/1st Bucks Battalion at the outbreak of war was Lt Col Francis Weathered TD, a member of the Marlow brewing dynasty, and later chairman of the company. Many of the men in the battalion's Marlow company, worked at the brewery in one capacity or another. Weathered was replaced as CO due to illness in January 1915, but went to the front later that year to command 1/6th Royal Warwickshires. The Yeomanry regiments were similar, often drawing their officers from the landed gentry (or their sons), and the rank and file from farm or estate workers, who were capable horsemen, familiar with caring for their mounts.

Despite the birth pains suffered by the Territorial Force as it established itself, by 1914 the South Midland Division was shaping up well for the challenges ahead. As war approached, of the 14 TF divisions in existence, only the neighbouring North Midland Division was closer to its establishment numbers than the South Midlanders. Across the six counties, the infantry brigades – The Warwickshire Brigade, the Gloucestershire and Worcestershire Brigade and the South Midlands Brigade – were within 17 per cent of their officer complement and 10 per cent of their Other Ranks numbers. The six Yeomanry regiments were even better recruited, and the other supporting arms were in equally good condition. The County Associations had taken steps to ensure that their soldiers were properly equipped, although infantry units grumbled that they were still armed with the old CLLE rifle rather than the general issue SMLE carried by Regulars. The gunners continued to train with equally obsolescent 15-pounder field guns and 5-in howitzers, while the eight-company organisation persisted across the infantry battalions.[38]

Although the numbers looked good on paper, however, there was a significant underlying issue: only a small proportion of the troops had signed the Imperial Service Obligation, indicating that they were prepared to serve overseas. In 1/5th and 1/7th Royal Warwickshire Regiment a total of only one officer and 15 Other Ranks had signed for Imperial Service. In the entire Gloucester and Worcestershire Brigade, the total was 14 officers and 333 Other Ranks. None of the other battalions was much better although the Yeomanry regiments of the South Midland Mounted Brigade reported 31 Officers and 199 Other Ranks had signed.[39]

Meanwhile, there had been a number of changes of command. Major General Raitt had been replaced in 1911 by Major General Sir Alexander Whitelaw Thornycroft, a former Royal Scots Fusilier. He served in the role until his retirement in July 1912 when he was replaced by Major General Sir John Keir, who was, in turn, replaced by Major General Sir Edward Graham for only a month from July to August 1914, handing over to Major General Sir Henry Heath. Heath had been commissioned into the South Staffordshire Regiment in 1881 and had served in the Anglo-Egyptian War of 1884-85 including the Nile Expedition to relieve the besieged city of Khartoum, being Mentioned in Despatches at the Battle of Kirbekan.

---

38   P Simkins, p.18.
39   K W Mitchinson, p.29.

2

# War and Mobilisation

---

The dark clouds that heralded the First World War appeared out of a clear blue sky during the long, hot summer of 1914, taking many in Britain by surprise. The assassination of Archduke Franz Ferdinand, heir to the Austro-Hungarian throne, and his wife, Sophie, Duchess of Hohenberg, by Serbian nationalists in Sarajevo on 28th June 1914, acted as a catalyst for the conflict, but was overshadowed in Great Britain by growing fears of an armed insurrection much closer to home.

Prime Minister Asquith's troubled Liberal Government, forced to rely on the votes of Irish Nationalist MPs to keep it in power, had sparked its own crisis by agreeing to Irish demands for a parliament in Dublin, known as Home Rule. This was vehemently opposed by protestants who were in the majority in the northern province of Ulster, fearing a Dublin parliament would be heavily influenced by the Roman Catholic church and thus discriminate against them and threaten their religious liberty. When it appeared that the Liberals were determined to force their Home Rule Bill through parliament, using the Parliament Act to defeat opposition in the Lords, Unionist leader, Sir Edward Carson, and his deputy, James Craig, raised and armed a paramilitary force of northern protestants – the Ulster Volunteer Force – to oppose Home Rule "by any means necessary". The Home Rule Bill was passed in the Commons on 25th May 1914, and Asquith prepared to send troops to Ulster to enforce the new law. However, British Army officers in Ireland refused to act against the Ulster Volunteers, sparking what became known as the Curragh Mutiny, which cost the Secretary of State for War, Col J E B Seeley, his job, and left Ireland on the brink of civil war.

With the British newspapers, public and political interest focusing on the situation across the Irish Sea, the rising tensions in the Balkans and the growing animosity between Russia and France on one side and Germany and Austro-Hungary on the other, did not appear to be a major cause for British concern. Trouble in the Balkans seemed a long way off compared to trouble in Belfast, and many in Britain felt their nation should stay out of the European squabble. However, that view changed in a flash when Germany threatened to invade neutral Belgium in order to attack France. On the evening of 2nd August, Germany delivered an ultimatum to Brussels, stating that its troops must be given free passage through Belgium. Unsurprisingly, the Belgians refused to accept such a demand, pointing out that "Belgium is a country, not a road" and that to agree to the German dictat would be "sacrificing the nation's honour and betraying its engagements to Europe". As a signatory to the London Treaty of 1839, guaranteeing Belgium's independence and neutrality, Britain now found itself right at the centre of the international wrangle. The strongly anti-war Liberals had concluded that they should stay well clear of any conflict in the Balkans. They were similarly prepared to watch from the side-lines if France was attacked by Germany, claiming that they had no treaty obligation to help France (although they were conveniently forgetting that they had a strong moral obligation to do so, having led the French to believe the British Expeditionary Force would come to their aid if Germany attacked). However, even the most reluctant members of Asquith's Cabinet, seeing a rapid and massive swing in the public mood, felt they could not sit by and watch Germany run rough-shod over "plucky little Belgium" in flagrant contravention of a Treaty in which Britain had guaranteed that country's neutrality. As Lloyd George noted, "the threatened invasion of Belgium had set the nation on fire from sea to sea".[1] Britain sent its own ultimatum to Berlin, demanding that Germany should not cross the Belgium frontier, timed to expire at 11pm on 4th August. But even before the deadline was reached, Germany gave its answer by marching into Belgium and declaring war on France. Britain then declared war on Germany.

The War Office and the Admiralty had already taken steps to bring their troops and ships to a state of alert. Plans for such a contingency had been drawn up in advance and were now put into operation. The Territorial Force, tasked principally with defending the UK from invasion, had been required to prepare for mobilisation or "embodiment" as it was referred to in legislation. The County Associations had taken this direction seriously, creating plans covering every conceivable detail, and kept up to date through a process of annual revisions. Some Associations went as far as to maintain a supply of envelopes pre-addressed to Territorial personnel within their areas, to be despatched on receipt of the official mobilisation orders. Units were aware of the locations of their "war stations" and selected officers had conducted reconnaissance visits to ensure that the process of manning these positions would take place smoothly and with military efficiency. Across the country, the British "War Book" was dug out and dusted off. First published in 1912, and amended in 1913 and 1914, the book contained a series of instructions to be followed by government departments and industrial concerns during the declaration of a precautionary period and subsequent mobilisation. It now acted as a step-by-step guide to preparing the nation for conflict.

## Mobilisation

As Everard Wyrall points out in his history of the Gloucestershire Regiment in the First World War, mobilisation in August 1914, came at an awkward time for the South Midland Division, with many battalions already at camp or en-route to their training areas.[2]

The 1/4th and 1/6th Gloucesters, part of the Gloucestershire and Worcestershire Infantry Brigade, had set out for their annual training period on Sunday, 26 July, travelling to Minehead in Devon. Upon arrival and becoming aware of the "grave outlook" they returned to Bristol the following day and all ranks were ordered to go home and await mobilisation.[3]

The whole of the South Midland Brigade, comprising 1/5th Gloucesters, 1/4th Oxfordshire and Buckinghamshire Light Infantry, 1/1st Buckinghamshire Battalion (also part of the OBLI but retaining a title and cap badge that reflected its Rifle Volunteer lineage), and 1/4th Royal

---

1  D Lloyd George, *War Memoirs of David Lloyd George*, Vol. 1, p.40.
2  E Wyrall, *The Gloucestershire Regiment in the War, 1914-1918*, p.59.
3  E Wyrall, p.60

Berkshire Regiment, were encamped on a hill above Marlow, overlooking the River Thames. They stayed for just one night before striking their tents on the morning of 3 August and returning to their home bases. The Bucks Battalion made the short trip back to Kingsbury Square, Aylesbury, and by 6.30pm the following day the unit was concentrated there (except for one of the Wolverton companies whose train had been unaccountably shunted into a siding and abandoned). The formal mobilisation order arrived later that evening and the following day the unit marched through the town to the Great Western Railway station and departed for its war station at Cosham in Hampshire. There they spent three days digging trenches in the downs overlooking Portsmouth before moving on to Swindon on 9th August, where other parts of the division were beginning to arrive.[4]

The Warwickshire Brigade, consisting of 1/5th, 1/6th, 1/7th and 1/8th Royal Warwickshire Regiment, had travelled to Rhyl in North Wales for annual camp on Saturday, 2nd August. But no sooner had they arrived at the seaside than they received orders to return to Birmingham. Their mobilisation orders reached the battalion headquarters in the early hours of Tuesday, 5th August and the rank and file drifted in over the following 72 hours, to drill halls, the Midland Railway Goods Yard and various other locations across the city. As Lt Charles Carrington recounts in his history of the 1/5th Battalion, there then followed "a frenzied but methodical inspection of men, clothing and boots until about 7pm when the battalion entrained for its war station at Portland in Dorset".[5] The Warwickshires had planned for mobilisation. Officers had participated in exercises designed to ensure the process was well-understood. But none of this could prevent the confusion that occurred when the regular garrison, the Royal Welsh Fusiliers, failed to march-out in time for the Territorials to take over.[6] The situation was eventually resolved, however, when the Welsh Fusiliers left for Dorchester. After a few days at Portland, the Warwickshires moved on to Swindon.

After some further training in Wiltshire the whole division moved to Essex. The Bucks Battalion history details their journey, which they undertook "partly by rail but mostly on foot" through Dunstable, Hitchin, Ware, Harlow and Great Dunmow, arriving in the vicinity of Chelmsford on 25th August.[7] The 1/5th Warwickshires went by a slightly different route. Departing from Swindon on the night of the 15th/16th August they stopped at Leighton Buzzard in Bedfordshire until the 21st and then covered 80-odd miles on foot via Dunstable, Hitchin, Epping and Brentwood before reaching Galleywood, about five miles from Chelmsford. The journey took a considerable toll on the men. In Carrington's words it was

> a long, slogging route march in the heat and dust averaging some 16 miles a day, a long stretch for men from factories, in soft condition, and they fell out by the roadside like flies,

---

4   P L Wright, *First Bucks Battalion 1914-1918*, p.2.
5   C E Carrington, *War Record of the I/5th Battalion, Royal Warwickshire Regiment*, pp.3-4.
6   This was the 2nd Royal Welch Fusiliers, which would later include the war poets Siegfried Sassoon and Robert Graves, Capt. Charles Dunn, author of *The War the Infantry Knew* and Frank Richards, *Old Soldiers Never Die*, among its numbers over the course of the war. The battalion eventually moved to Dorchester, making space for the Warwickshires at Portland.
7   PL Wright, p.2.

but march discipline and self-restraint improved daily and the percentage of casualties diminished til (sic) a body of soldiers in cohesive formation finally landed at Galleywood …[8]

The GOC, Major General Heath, expected the Division to be deployed imminently, telling his officers in early September that he hoped they would be sent to France in six weeks.[9] But that was over-optimistic, and may even have been a ruse on the General's part to encourage more of his soldiers to sign the Imperial Service Obligation. The numbers of Territorials who were prepared to volunteer to go overseas were still disappointingly low. Charles Carrington noted, however, that when the 1/5th Warwickshires were asked to volunteer for foreign service on 28th August, the response was "gratifying in the extreme" although he does not reveal the actual numbers.[10] Bill Mitchinson estimates that about 20 per cent of the peacetime division decided, for a variety of family, business or other reasons, not to go overseas with their units.[11] Many of these were cross-posted to the newly-formed second-line South Midland Division, later titled the 61st (2nd South Midland) Division, which was formed on War Office orders at the end of August, intended to replace the first-line division for home defence, and act as a reception and basic training organisation for the new recruits that were starting to appear.

In reality, the South Midland Division was nowhere near ready to go to war in September 1914. The infantry required further training and had yet to receive modern rifles. They were eventually issued with converted CLLE "Long Lees", which had been re-sighted for use with the new Mk VII ammunition. The poor condition of these weapons is the subject of much comment in unit reports, which also bemoan the lack of armourers to deal with the long list of defects. In fact, these were the rifles with which the brigades would eventually deploy to the front. But even if they had received their longed-for SMLEs, there was still a paucity of firing ranges on which to use them, and bad weather was also hindering musketry practice. Infantry soldiers were able to earn extra pay depending on their shooting skills, but a combination of old, damaged rifles with worn barrels, stormy weather and limited opportunities to shoot, was making it almost impossible for the Territorials to achieve the standards necessary to add to their pay. The 1/7th Royal Warwickshires' war diary for the period states that courses of musketry were being carried out, but soldiers were shooting to qualify for higher rates of efficiency pay with bent back-sights and other faults, "all conducive to indifferent shooting".[12] The 1/4th Gloucesters conducted their classification shoots in November 1914, at the newly-constructed range at Woodham Mortimer. The results were not good. The CO reported that the conditions were very difficult. A cold easterly wind was blowing most of the time and the light was generally dull. As a result, the performance "cannot be fairly compared with shooting during the summer months or in mild weather" (which was when the regulars fired their classification shoots).[13]

The gunners had few shells with which to perfect their artillery skills. The divisional transport was seriously short of waggons, and horses with which to pull them, and there was a dearth

---

8   C E Carrington, p.4.
9   C E Carrington, p.4.
10  C E Carrington, p.4.
11  K W Mitchinson, p.36.
12  TNA WO 95/2757: 143rd Infantry Brigade War Diary.
13  TNA WO 95/2757: 143rd Infantry Brigade War Diary.

of veterinarians to maintain the health of those animals that were available. To make matters worse, it appeared to the Territorials that the priority for equipment and training was going to Kitchener's New Armies. The CO of 1/8th Worcesters no doubt spoke for many when he complained that: "It seems unfair that we should not receive the same facilities for training as the New Army."[14] Meanwhile, in early January, 1915, the infantry battalions were instructed to switch to the four-company organisation "for training only" and at the end of the month orders were issued to cease the eight-company system for good in favour of the four-company model already in use by regular units.

There were still many deficiencies in equipment, although most of these were made good over time. By 21st March, the Warwickshire Brigade's war diary noted that stores had been coming in so fast over the past week that the battalions did not have time for anything other than fitting equipment and harness. The 1/5th, 1/6th and 1/8th battalions had been issued with new webbing equipment but there had been no time to fit it properly and few opportunities to train in it beyond a few short marches in the afternoons. Meanwhile, the gaps that had been created when the men who had decided not to sign the Imperial Service Obligation were posted to second-line units, were now being filled by drafts of new personnel. However, the Warwickshire Brigade diarist was uncomplimentary about the state of training of the new arrivals, pointing out that whilst many had several months of service "they have received very little instruction in musketry and are very backward in other forms of training".

Despite the recurring rumours of "shipping out next week" it was late March 1915 before the long-awaited orders to proceed overseas were finally received, sparking much activity and excitement. According to Captain Philip Wright of 1/1st Bucks Battalion, it seemed "almost incredible news, too good to be true". [15]

Officers who had spent six months buying useless items to add to their kit now bought "even more feverishly and imprudently",[16] while the men took the news in their stride, no doubt half-expecting the orders to be countermanded at any moment. But they were wrong. On the afternoon of 30th March 1915, the Bucks Battalion paraded on the barrack square at Chelmsford for the last time before marching to the local railway station. Having spent so long in Essex, the division had become something of a fixture and no doubt many relationships had been formed with local people. It was no surprise, therefore, when the town of Chelmsford turned out *en masse* to wave off "their boys". At 5.30pm the first train carrying elements of the Bucks Battalion left the station, heading for Folkestone and from there to Boulogne.

The first elements of the division to arrive in France were the battalions making up the Warwickshire Brigade, who landed at Le Havre, along with much of the divisional transport. The disembarkation and onward movement were managed fairly efficiently, however, and the Divisional Headquarters opened at St Omer on 31st March. The infantry brigades and supporting elements concentrated in the countryside between Cassel and Hazebrouck.[17] From

---

14  K W Mitchinson, p.33.
15  P L Wright, p.1.
16  P L Wright, p.3.
17  The next generation of Bucks Battalion soldiers were to familiarise themselves with the Hazebrouck area 26 years later, in May/June 1940, when the battalion made a desperate stand in the town as part of the rear-guard, protecting the beaches around Dunkirk as the British Expeditionary Force was evacuated.

there, if the wind was in the right direction, the men could hear the rumble of the guns at the front. Their next move was to Bailleul and then to Armentieres to the south of the Belgian city of Ypres, where they would begin a period of instruction in trench warfare, attached to more experienced divisions.

Ypres was already a household name back in Great Britain after the heavy fighting that had taken place there in October 1914 when the battle-weary British Expeditionary Force managed to halt the Germans from breaking through to the channel ports. Amongst the units engaged at that time was the 1/14th London Regiment, the London Scottish, which had been rushed into the line and earned its place in history by becoming the first Territorial battalion to see active service on the Western Front.

3

# Learning the Ropes

During an epic counter-attack on 31st October 1914, the London Scottish temporarily halted a German attack on the Messines Ridge south of Ypres. It was close to there that the South Midlanders first experienced the firing line in April 1915.

The 48th Division disembarked in France probably as well-trained as any TF formation entering the theatre of war at that time. Although its men would have practiced digging trenches and living in them, they were still novices when it came to the business of position warfare. Under training conditions at home, it was impossible to replicate with any degree of realism, the true nature of living and fighting in the trenches, in some cases just tens of yards from the enemy. GHQ was well aware of this, however, and had developed a process designed to 'ease' the new arrivals into the front line. This involved posting them into a "quiet" sector where they could acclimatise under the guiding hands of more seasoned troops. In the South Midlanders' case this was with the regulars of the 4th and 6th divisions.

The Ploegsteert sector, in the shadow of the Messines Ridge, was low-lying with a high water table. In addition to the wood, which, at that stage of the war, still had many trees standing, the key features were the water courses that criss-crossed the area, such as the Douve, Steenbeek and the Lys. Soldiers did not have to dig down very far before they struck water. This meant that much of the ground was unsuitable for entrenching. As a result, although there were some deep trenches, in many places the defences consisted of sandbagged breastworks built up on the surface, often just 10 or 20 yards long, with gaps between them. For example, the 1/5th Warwickshires in the Douve sector, astride the small river of that name, to the north of Ploegsteert Wood, found themselves in a salient, enfiladed in both directions from the slopes of the Messines Ridge, opposite. Large sections of "trench" had no parados (the side of the trench farthest away from the enemy). The parapet (the front lip of the trench) and the wire in front of it, were constantly broken down by enemy shelling. There were no proper communications trenches here, so movement of stores, rations, casualties and reliefs had to be restricted to the hours of darkness, when they were moved across the open and astride the Messines–Ploegsteert road, still vulnerable to enemy artillery and machine gun fire.[1]

Despite the presence of water near the surface, the substrata beneath the fields were well-suited to mining and both sides waged an industrious subterranean conflict in front of Ploegsteert

---

1   C E Carrington, p.11.

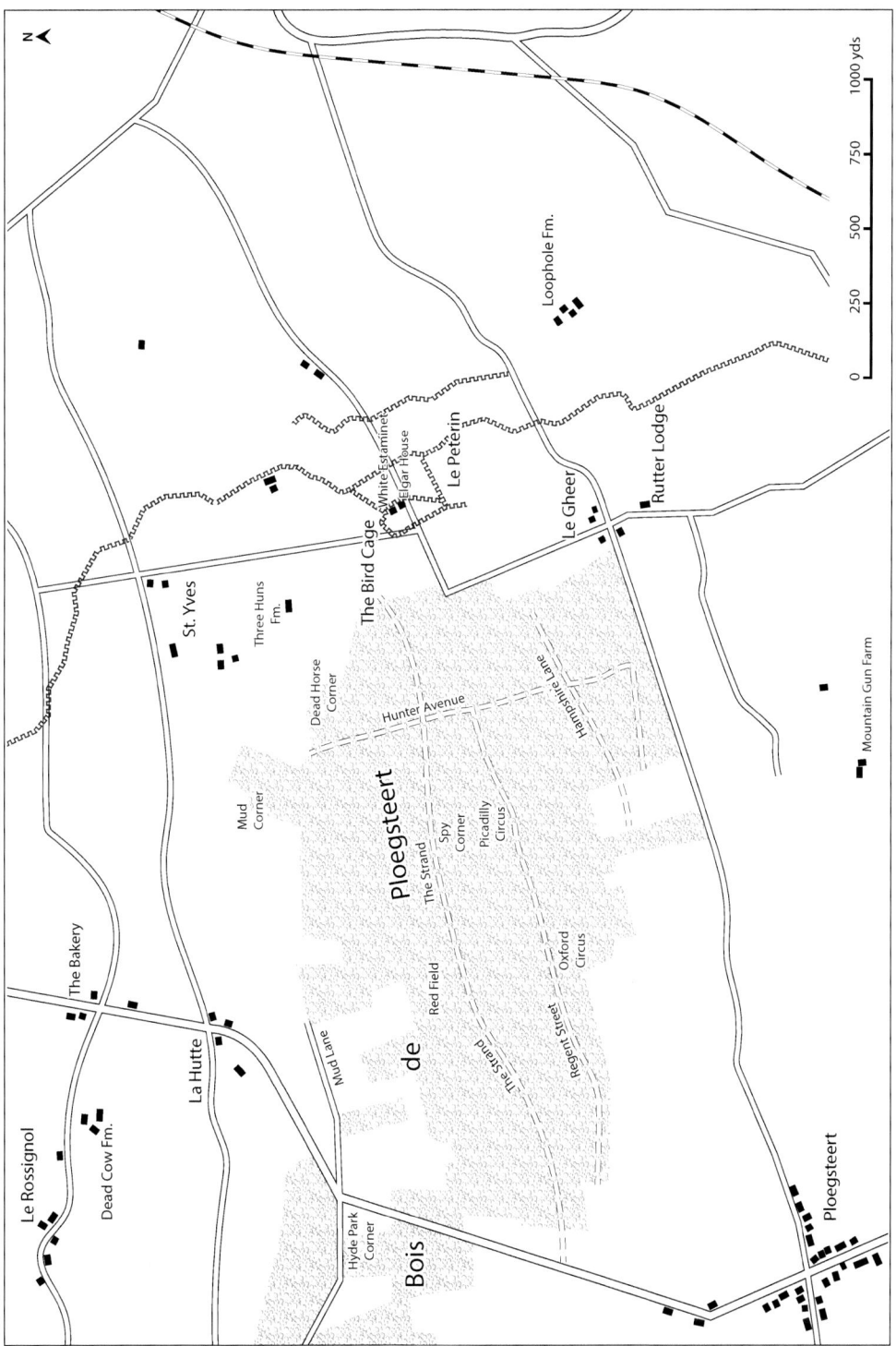

Map 1  Ploegsteert Wood 1915.

Wood, frequently blowing explosive charges under each other's trenches. The evidence of this – the water-filled craters caused by the detonations, many of which were marked on trench maps of the period – can still be seen today. Indeed, some of the mines from later operations are still there. It is believed, for example, that the Petite Douve Farm, on the road between Ploegsteert and Messines, rebuilt after the war, now sits close to where a large and unexploded mine, dating back to the Battle of Messines, lies buried. Having been prepared for detonation at 3.10 on the morning of 7th June 1917, the mineshaft and gallery were lost due to flooding before it could be fired, but the explosives remain in place. Nearby, a similar mine at La Gheer exploded during a thunderstorm in 1955.

On 8th April, the Bucks Battalion found itself attached to units of the 12th Infantry Brigade near Le Bizet, a small hamlet on the north bank of the Lys, just above Armentiéres. A Company was with the 2nd Lancashire Fusiliers, B Company with the 2nd Monmouthshires, C Company with the 2nd Essex Regiment and D Company with the 1st King's Own (Royal Lancashire) Regiment. A and C Companies went into the trenches while B and D Companies received instruction in billets behind the line.[2]

Captain Philip Wright described the Bucks Battalion's introduction to the trenches in his regimental history:

> The march (to the trenches) was carried out in pitch darkness along a road which ran up to and through the British front line. Guides met us five or six hundred yards behind the line and escorted us as far as the trenches. These guides, treating us like the ignorant children that we were, kept the pace as slow as possible, knowing quite truly that we liked that the least. Several of them, not content with this, insisted on telling one how the Boche was in the habit of raking that road with machine gun fire at that hour precisely, and how two men had met their end there the previous evening. We arrived therefore with our nerves highly strung.[3]

The "old sweats" took their entertainment wherever they could find it, and "putting the wind up" newcomers as described above, is a good example of the 'dark' trench humour for which Mr Atkins was – and still is – renowned.

The 8th of April was also the day on which the Bucks Battalion suffered the division's first fatality in action. 2245 Pte William Holland (23) was wounded by shellfire whilst helping to dig a communication trench behind the front and evacuated back to a nearby regimental aid post near Le Bizet Convent, where he died. Pte Holland, the son of Charles, a local councillor, and Ann Jemima Holland, of 13 Chicheley Street, Newport Pagnell, was originally buried in the nearby Le Bizet Convent Cemetery, but after the war this small burial ground was closed, and all the remains were moved to larger concentration cemeteries. Pte Holland was re-buried in the Strand Military Cemetery, which is located off the N365, just to the south-west of Ploegsteert Wood.

On 9th April, while A and C Companies were still in the line, the 4th Division's Royal Engineers exploded a mine under the enemy trenches at Touquet[4], following a short artillery

---

2   TNA WO 95/2763: 1/1st Bucks Battalion War Diary.
3   P L Wright, p.6.
4   Touquet was a hamlet near the town of Frelinghien on the west bank of the Lys.

bombardment. B and D Companies had been ordered into the reserve trenches, as a contingency, in the event that the enemy decided to respond to the provocation. There was no enemy attack but two of the Bucks' men were injured as the Germans opposite replied with rifle, machine gun and artillery fire.

The men of the 1/5th Gloucestershire Regiment were attached to the East Lancashires near Frelinghien for their induction. Visiting his troops in the front line at about 11.30 on the morning of 9th April, the Gloucesters' Commanding Officer, Lt Col John Henry Collett, took the opportunity to observe the enemy positions opposite, using a periscope. Unfortunately, he kept the device above the parapet just long enough for a German sniper to spot it and put a bullet through the upper aperture, shattering the lens and causing slight cuts to Collett's chin.[5] He did, however, avoid the dubious honour of being the first member of the battalion to be officially reported as 'wounded in action". That distinction went jointly to Sgt Lloyd and Pte Lee of C Company, who were wounded in the hand and eye respectively by a sniper at around 10:00 that morning.

The induction process was not a lengthy affair. Each infantryman in the division spent about 24 hours in the front line, just enough time to experience one complete cycle of the daily routine of trench-holding. Once each of the 12 battalions had taken their turn on the fire-step, and after a short rest in the rear, on the night of 12/13th April the South Midland Division began to relieve the 4th Division between the Warnave stream in the south and the Wulverghem–Messines Road in the north, establishing the Divisional Headquarters at Nieppe. This sector encompassed the whole of Ploegsteert Wood and had within it two key enemy strong points – the Birdcage and Petite Douve Farm, both of which would earn notoriety during and after the battle of Messines in 1917.

Arrangements for the relief, which took place over four days, were set out in the South Midland Division's Operation Order No 1. The document describes a phased process, beginning with the Warwickshire Brigade taking over from the 10th Infantry Brigade, in the northern sector between St Yves/Prowse Point and the Wulverghem–Messines Road, with 1/5th and 1/7th Royal Warwickshires going into the line, 1/6th Royal Warwickshires in brigade reserve at Petit Pont, and 1/8th Royal Warwickshires in divisional reserve at Romarin. The 10th Brigade left 1/7th Argyle and Sutherland Highlanders in the line, alongside the South Midlanders, presumably to ensure at least one experienced unit remained in place there until the relief was completed. The South Midland Brigade assumed responsibility for the centre sector to the east of Ploegsteert Wood between Le Gheer and St Yves/Prowse Point, on the night of 15/16 April, with 1/4th Royal Berkshires, relieving the 1st Hampshires and 1/5th Gloucesters taking over from the 1st Rifle Brigade. The 1/5th London Regiment (London Rifle Brigade) remained in place. On the afternoon of 17th April, the Gloucestershire and Worcestershire Brigade occupied the southern sector with the 1/4th Gloucesters and the 1/7th Worcesters entering the line between the Warnave River and Le Gheer. Once the new garrisons were firmly in place, 10th Brigade, and 11th Brigade withdrew the Argyles and the London Rifle Brigade and the men of the South Midland Division were left on their own to grow familiar with the routine of trench life.

---

5   TNA WO 95/2763: 1/5th Gloucestershire War Diary.

The brigade war diaries detail much work being done to improve the trenches, including joining up individual sections of the defences, and the construction of new communications trenches linking the front line with the rear areas. Working parties were sent out at night to ensure the barbed wire in front of the trenches was in good repair, and patrols prowled about between the lines, seeking to dominate no-man's land, and occasionally participating in short, sharp exchanges of fire with the enemy.

Their first proper tour in the trenches was relatively quiet. Although the South Midlanders conducted no deliberate attacks, they nevertheless sustained a number of casualties from enemy shelling and small-arms fire – what some staff officers would later refer to as "trench wastage", a rather callous expression meaning the routine losses associated with defensive operations in trench warfare. There were, however, a few notable incidents that served to keep the men alert or "switched on" in more modern military parlance. For example, at 12.25am on 15th April, just an hour after the South Midland Brigade took over its section of the line, the London Rifle Brigade, holding a stretch of trench between 1/4th Royal Berkshires and 1/5th Gloucesters, reported that Royal Engineers, conducting tunnelling activities in their vicinity, had heard sounds that indicated German mining close by. The Officer Commanding 174th Tunnelling Company, Royal Engineers, was sent for, and arrived at 2.30am. After spending a couple of hours investigating the matter, he decided that German mining was "doubtful" and ordered his sappers to carry on with their work.[6] The Bucks Battalion had a similar experience a week later, when they thought they detected mining sounds apparently coming from under their parapet near St Yves, in the north-east corner of Ploegsteert Wood. A patrol was sent out to listen for further sounds, but nothing was heard.

On 19th April, a three-man listening patrol, from A Company, 1/8th Royal Warwickshire Regiment captured an enemy soldier and brought him back to their lines for questioning. The patrol had gone out just in front of the Warwickshires' front-line trench to listen for enemy movement in no-man's land. They spotted two Germans who appeared to be attempting to get through the British wire. Having failed to penetrate one section, they moved further along and one of them managed to crawl underneath, close to where the patrol was lying in cover. Pte Sheill grabbed the intruder, but the second German opened fire with his pistol, killing Pte Rainsford, who fell on top of the third member of the patrol, Pte Hooper, preventing him from using his rifle. This allowed Rainsford's killer to make good his escape. The surviving members of the patrol escorted the prisoner to their lines, and he was sent back to Brigade Headquarters. Stretcher bearers went out and recovered Pte Rainsford's body before dawn. The prisoner was identified as George Lofolmr of the 5th Bavarian Reserve Infantry Regiment.[7] Pte Wilfred John Rainsford (20), the son of Francis and Ellen Rainsford of 'Dinglecroft', Larches Road, Kidderminster, now lies in La Plus Douve Farm Cemetery not far from where the incident took place.[8]

On 22nd April, the Warwickshire Brigade noted that the neighbouring Staffordshire Brigade[9], holding the line to the north of the Wulverghem–Messines Road, reported the

---

6    TNA WO 95/2760: 145th Brigade War Diary.
7    TNA WO 95/2754: 143rd Brigade War Diary.
8    *CWGC* <https://www.cwgc.org/find-records/find-war-dead/casualty-details/444863/wilfred-john-rainsford/> (accessed 26 January 2022).
9    The Staffordshire Brigade later became 137th (Staffordshire) Infantry Brigade, part of the 46th (North Midland) Division, under the command of Maj Gen Hon E H Montagu-Stuart-Wortley.

presence of "asphyxiating gases" in their trenches, but none were noticed in the Warwickshires' part of the line.[10] The Brigade war diary also mentions heavy firing coming from the direction of Ypres over the following nights. The 22nd was the day the Germans launched what would later become known as the Second Battle of Ypres, when they used chlorine gas to help to penetrate the allied line to the north of the city, between the villages of Langemarck and Gravenstafel, but failed to fully exploit the breakthrough. It has been claimed that the allies suffered around 3000 casualties in the initial gas attack, over 1000 of them fatalities.[11] This was the first recorded use of poison gas on the western front, and at this time allied soldiers had no equipment with which to protect themselves from this weapon of mass destruction. However, by 2nd May, the Gloucestershire and Worcestershire Brigade's diary records the arrival of goggles, mouth and nose pads and bicarbonate of soda (baking soda) as a gas preventative. The baking soda was mixed with water to produce a solution and applied to the pads, helping to neutralise the effects of chlorine. In the absence of the baking soda, the troops were advised to urinate on the pads, as the urea in their urine could also reduce the effects of the gas.

The Battle of Aubers Ridge, part of an Anglo-French offensive in the Artois region, opened on 9th May 1915. Aubers Ridge, a low ridge running to the east of Laventie and Neuve Chapelle, south of Armentiéres, which includes the towns of Fromelles, Aubers and Le Maisnil, had been attacked by the British, without success, during the earlier Battle of Neuve Chapelle (March 1915). However, the British Commander in Chief, Field Marshal Sir John French, and his French counterpart, Joffre, agreed to launch a renewed offensive with the overall objective of capturing the high ground of Notre Dame de Lorette and Vimy Ridge. To support this, British forces to the north, in the Ypres–Armentiéres sector, were ordered to conduct a "demonstration", to prevent the Germans from withdrawing troops to reinforce their line at Aubers, or as the III Corps Orders put it: "attracting the enemy's attention and pinning him to his ground."[12] As part of this, the men of the South Midland Division were ordered to carry out various activities designed to convince the enemy opposite that they were about to be attacked.

The divisional instructions for the "demonstration" were detailed and comprehensive. Units in the line were to send out patrols on the night of 8th/9th May to attempt to cut the enemy wire. Planks were placed behind the British trenches and taken out into no-man's land and dumped where they could be seen, suggesting preparations for an assault. Signallers opened communications between the brigades, using lamps. The Warwickshire Brigade signallers attempted to make contact with III Corps Headquarters at Bailleul. Snipers moved into no-man's land during darkness, and stayed there all day, firing at targets of opportunity and returning after dark. The infantry brigades arranged for their machine guns to come into action, firing on roads in the German rear all along the divisional sector, as well as on communications trenches and support lines, using high explosives to collapse their trenches. The infantry engaged the enemy positions with rifles, trench mortars and rifle grenades and a mine detonated under the German lines at 04.30 on the morning of the 9th. In return, the enemy shelled Ploegsteert Wood heavily throughout the day.[13] The divisional documents do not record if these efforts were successful in holding enemy forces in the line opposite Ploegsteert. However, a report on the operations by

---

10   TNA WO 95/2754: 143rd Brigade War Diary.
11   E Greenhalgh, *The French Army and the First World War*, pp.89-90.
12   TNA WO 95/2745: III Corps Orders, 48th Division General Staff War Diary.
13   TNA WO 95/2757: Gloucestershire and Worcestershire Brigade War Diary, 8-9 May 1915.

Brig Gen McClintock, in temporary command of the division at the time, hinted that a shortage of artillery ammunition, which reduced the weight of the bombardment on the enemy wire, may have given the game away, encouraging the Germans to believe that an attack was unlikely. In McClintock's words: "The shooting of the artillery is reported as good, but owing to the insufficiency of ammunition the damage done to the enemy wire was very slight."[14] In any event, the assault at Aubers Ridge itself was an unmitigated disaster for I Corps, and its commander Lt Gen Sir Douglas Haig. The failure was blamed, by French, on a shortage of artillery shells, sparking the "shells crisis" which ultimately toppled Asquith's Liberal administration and led to the formation of a coalition, with future Prime Minister, David Lloyd George, appointed to run the newly-created Ministry of Munitions.[15]

A single rifle grenade caused the death of Capt. E G Dashwood, 1/4th Oxfordshire and Buckinghamshire Light Infantry, and wounded 2nd Lt J E H Cranmer and two other men on 12th May. The Germans opposite had built an observation tower of sand-bags, strengthened with boards, and a mountain gun had been brought up into the British front line to demolish it. This was successfully achieved at around 03.30 in the morning, and in reply the enemy fired a number of rifle grenades, one of which fell into Capt Dashwood's trench and exploded. Capt Ernest George Dashwood (35), a former Merchant Navy officer, was the second son of Sir George Dashwood, Bt, and Lady Mary, the youngest daughter of the Marquess of Hertford, whose family home was at The Warren, Abingdon. Born in 1880, Capt Dashwood was educated at Wellington College and was a cadet at HMS Worcester before working for the New Zealand Shipping Company and P&O. He retired in 1909 to take up farming on 500 acres in Oxfordshire. He was commissioned into the 1/4th Oxfordshire and Buckinghamshire Light Infantry in December 1911. Writing home from Camp No 16 at Le Havre, on 17th May, as he waited to report to his unit, 2nd Lt Graham Greenwell, who had been held back from deploying with the battalion in March because he was under 19 at the time, said: "I can't tell you how fearfully sorry I am at poor old Dashwood's death. His family must be very much upset. He was such a splendid fellow…".[16] Dashwood now lies in Rifle House Cemetery in Ploegsteert Wood, not far from where he died. Sir George and Lady Mary Dashwood lost two other sons in the conflict. 2nd Lt Lionel Albert Dashwood (27) was serving with 2nd Oxfordshire and Buckinghamshire Light Infantry when he died, four days after Ernest, at the Battle of Festubert, on 16th May 1915. His body was not identified, and he has no known grave. He is commemorated on the Le Touret Memorial. Lt Wilfred James Dashwood (34) died on 2nd August 1917, serving with the 1st Grenadier Guards, during the Third Battle of Ypres, and is buried in Dozinghem Military Cemetery, near Poperinghe, to the west of Ypres.

On the same day that Capt Dashwood died, the South Midland Division was re-designated as the 48th (South Midland) Division, under III Corps Order 142, of that date, and War Office letter No 48/WO/2481 (AG1) of 7th May 1915. This brought the titles of Territorial Force divisions into line with those of the Regular Army and the new Kitchener divisions. At the same time, the Warwickshire Brigade became the 143rd Infantry Brigade; the Gloucestershire and

---

14 TNA WO 95/2745: 48th Division General Staff War Diary, 8 May 1915.
15 M Gilbert, *The First World War: A Complete History*, p.160.
16 G Greenwell, *An Infant in Arms*, p.9.

Worcestershire Brigade became the 144th Infantry Brigade; and the South Midland Brigade became the 145th Infantry Brigade.[17]

On the evening of 25th May, the 143rd Brigade recorded that many men were complaining of sore eyes, not in the front line, but in the rear areas around Petit Pont and Kortepyp. The war diary supposes this may have been the effects of gas from Ypres as the wind was from that direction. 25th May was the day on which the Second Battle of Ypres officially ended.

A few days later, early on the morning of 28th May, a listening post commanded by Cpl William Thomas Bromage, with Ptes Eaton, Hill and Hall, of C Company, 1/7th Royal Warwickshires, was occupying a position in front of the Steenbeck Trenches when a party of Germans attacked at about 1.00am. The post returned fire and drove off the intruders, who left behind the body of an *unteroffizier* (a corporal), killed in the exchange. Pte Hill also died, and Pte Eaton was wounded, although he continued to fire "with great deliberation" despite his injury. According to the battalion war diary, both the German, whose name was Adam Wörner, and Pte Hill, were later buried at La Plus Douve Farm cemetery.[18] 1932 Pte Lewis Henry Hill (19) was the son of Edward and Eliza Hill of Newbold-on-Avon, Rugby. The Commonwealth War Graves Commission database shows that there are a number of German soldiers buried in La Plus Douve Farm cemetery, but none is named Adam Wörner. 1400 Cpl (later Sergeant) William Thomas Bromage received the Distinguished Conduct Medal (DCM) for his part in this action, the award being announced in the London Gazette. The citation states: "His fine example saved a listening post from destruction. He afterwards brought in a wounded man (Pte Eaton) and went out a second time in search of the body of a man who had been shot, both times under heavy fire".[19] Bromage died of pneumonia, aged 25, on 19th November 1918, probably a victim of the Spanish flu epidemic that raged across Europe towards the end of the war, and is buried in Nuneaton Cemetery. He had been discharged from the army due to wounds on 22 May 1916, and married the former Miss Zana Woodward the following year. They lived at Canal Cottage, Atherstone, Warwickshire. 1933 Pte L G Eaton also received the DCM for his part in the fire-fight. Eaton's citation reads: "On the occasion of a listening post being surprised by an enemy officer's patrol, Pte Eaton, though wounded in the head, with great bravery remained at his post and opened rapid fire, which resulted in a [German] non-commissioned officer being killed and the remainder of the patrol, which was estimated at eight strong, being dispersed."[20]

On 1st June 1915, the 1/7th Royal Warwickshire Regiment's diary recorded that Maj Gen Robert Fanshawe CB, DSO, visited the battalion in hutments at Jonesville on taking over command of the 48th Division.[21] Fanshawe assumed command from Maj Gen Heath, who had been diagnosed with angina.[22] Heath took ill in early May, and was initially absent from duty for a couple of days during which command of the division was handed over to Brig Gen W. K. McClintock, 145th Brigade. A few days later, command passed to Brig Gen C M Ross-Johnson (the divisional Commander Royal Artillery) and Heath left for England where he died on 29th July 1915, aged just 54 years. He was buried at Brookwood Cemetery, near Woking. On 29/30

---

17  TNA WO 95/670/5: III Corps War Diary.
18  TNA WO 95/2756: 1/7th Royal Warwickshire War Diary.
19  *London Gazette*, 10 March, 1916, Supplement 29503, p.2653.
20  *London Gazette*, 14 March, 1916, Issue 12914, p.438.
21  TNA WO 95/2756: 1/7th Royal Warwickshire Regiment War Diary.
22  K W Mitchinson, p.51.

May, the division received a telegram stating that Brig Gen Fanshawe had been appointed to command the formation, with the temporary rank of Maj Gen. He arrived at the headquarters, near Nieppe, on the last day of the month, having handed over command of the 6th Infantry Brigade, part of 2nd Division.[23] The War Diary of the 48th Division's General Staff for the period records that on arrival, Fanshawe undertook a busy round of visits to his units in the trenches and in billets over the next few days as he worked hard to get to know his men.

In the meantime, the underground war continued unabated in the 48th Division sector. The tunnellers of the Royal Engineers were busy preparing two mines under the Birdcage feature on 5th June, when they detected sounds of German digging coming from nearby and deduced that their shafts had been discovered.

A staff officer was despatched at once to III Corps Headquarters to seek permission to explode the mines early the following morning, hopefully before the enemy could blow in the tunnels. Authority was received at about 10.30pm that night and orders were issued for the mines to be detonated at 3.00 the next morning.

It was believed that the Germans were holding their front line thinly, adhering to their doctrine of defence-in-depth. In order to cause as much loss as possible, the division was keen to get the Germans to reinforce their front trench before the mines were detonated. The best way to achieve this was to persuade the troops opposite that they were about to be attacked. At very short notice, elaborate plans were made to fool the Germans into thinking an attack was imminent. The 145th Brigade, holding the sector, were told to drive vehicles up and down the road running along the western side of Ploegsteert Wood (the Ploegsteert–Hyde Park Corner Road) between midnight and 2.30am. Troops were to move up and down the tracks inside the wood, making as much noise as possible on the wooden duck-boards. Bayonets and caps were to be allowed to show over the parapet at daylight, suggesting that men were moving into attack positions. The artillery was to open fire on the northeast corner of the Birdcage as soon as the explosion occurred. The guns would then shift fire onto communications trenches and any other targets that might present themselves while the infantry, machine-gunners and trench mortar teams were to be prepared to engage targets of opportunity – Germans trying to leave the scene or those who may have been sent to reinforce the position.

Detonation was delayed several times during the course of the night, but at 10.21am the order was given to explode the mines. At the same time, rifle, machine gun and artillery fire was opened on the German trenches and mountain guns swept the ground behind the crater.

2nd Lt Wolfred Cloutman (25), of 164th Company, Royal Engineers, who was responsible for the mines and their detonation, described the location and the process of preparing the charges:

> From the corner of No 32 trench a gallery runs almost due south to Elger House, on the ruin of which an observation post had been created. The shaft leading to the gallery was 25 feet deep, the length of the gallery 405 feet – it was stopped 15 feet short of its objective owing to sounds of mining being heard ahead. At 333 feet from the shaft, a gallery was run out 700 feet due East under Bennett House.

---

23  TNA WO 95/2745: 48th Division General Staff War Diary.

> The charges used were two of 2,500lbs of gunpower each. The charge was fired electrically with four fuses in series in each charge. Instantaneous fuse was also put in, in case of failure of the electric firing. The powder was placed in waterproof bags with clamps, about 50lbs in each bag. The tamping extended for 55 feet along the gallery in both cases…15 feet of solid tamping (wet sandbags filled with blue clay) then a 5 feet air space, then 15 feet solid, 5 feet air space and finally 15 feet solid. Boards were also set up across the gallery and rammed into position.[24]

According to 2nd Lt Cloutman's report, when he pressed the plunger on the Dynamo Exploder to blow the mines there were two distinct explosions and two columns of smoke appeared. The smoke columns looked to be at least 120 feet high. Debris was scattered over a wide area but only small lumps fell into the British trenches. After the smoke had cleared it could be seen that a large crater had formed, about 30 yards across, and that the earth had fallen as a hill on either side. The total width affected was about 70 yards. The two craters had joined up with only one small mound of debris in between.[25]

2nd Lieutenant Graham Greenwell, now back with 1/4th Oxfordshire and Buckinghamshire Light Infantry, and his platoon, was in the reserve line, about 50 yards behind the front, when the mines erupted:

> There was suddenly the most appalling explosion and the earth quaked alarmingly. This was followed by a positive inferno of noise. The mountain gun which had been brought up into the trenches the night before started about five seconds after with six shells a minute, then our men opened rapid fire, the big howitzer batteries right behind the wood sent over a succession of the largest high explosives, and rifle grenades and trench mortars brought up the chorus to full strength.
>
> Although the Germans must have been taken absolutely surprise, although over 60 yards of their trench had been blown clean into the air, and although they were being bombarded by every conceivable kind of devilish weapon, they began to reply within two minutes, and my God the noise was terrific.[26]

Reporting on the operation to III Corps, Maj Gen Fanshawe explained that it had been intended to coordinate the blowing of the mines with other operations, but when it was discovered that the enemy had got so close, it became a question of whether or not the mines could be packed and fired before the enemy broke into the gallery. Fanshawe also highlighted the work done by 2nd Lt Cloutman, describing it as "arduous and dangerous". The young officer "had been constantly at the mine and I recommend that he be rewarded." 2nd Lt Cloutman was mentioned in despatches for his efforts – one of two such awards he received during his short time at the front.[27]

Promoted to temporary Lieutenant, Wolfred Reeve Cloutman later transferred to 178th Tunnelling Company. He died in the act of rescuing his Serjeant from a mine shaft in the

---

24  TNA WO 95/2745: 48th Division General Staff War Diary.
25  TNA WO 95/2745: 48th Division General Staff War Diary.
26  G Greenwell, pp.22-23.
27  TNA WO 95/2745: 48th Division General Staff War Diary.

Somme sector on 21st August 1915. The Commonwealth War Graves database records that he had carried the Serjeant on his shoulder 45 feet up a ladder from the bottom of a mine. As soon as the Serjeant was lifted off, Lt Cloutman, overcome by foul gases, fell to the bottom of the shaft. The son of Alfred and Mrs C J Cloutman of Old Hall, 17 South Grove, Highgate, London, he is buried in Norfolk Military Cemetery, Becordel–Becourt, near Albert.[28]

The blowing of the Birdcage mines was the last significant act of the division in the Ploegsteert sector. Later in the month, having learned the basics of trench warfare, the division was relieved by the 12th (Eastern) Division and left the Ploegsteert sector, moving south to an area near Bethune, where it went into a period of rest and training. It was also transferred from III Corps to IV Corps on 28th June and then from IV Corps to VII Corps as part of the new Third Army, on 8th July 1915.

---

28   *CWGC* <https://www.cwgc.org/find-records/find-war-dead/casualty-details/39408/wolfred-reeve-cloutman/> (accessed 10 September 2022).

# 4

# Somme Offensive

By mid-1915, the French, certain they were being left to bare a comparatively unfair burden in prosecuting the war, began to agitate for the BEF to take over a greater portion of the front. At the request of the French Commander-in Chief, General Joseph Joffre, it was in early May of that year that Sir John French agreed to extend his line north to Boesinghe on the Ieperlee Canal, north of Ypres. This meant the British took over the Ypres Salient in its entirety. Later that month, Sir Douglas Haig's First Army extended its area of responsibility to the south by five miles from Cuinchy towards Lens. In June, Joffre and French agreed to an autumn offensive, with the British attacking at Loos and the French in Champagne. During August, to free up Petain's Second French Army for the offensive to the south, the newly-formed British Third Army took over a 15-mile front from Curlu, on the north bank of the Somme River, initially to the village of Hebuterne on the high ground above the Ancre Valley.

It was to the Hebuterne sector that the 48th Division was directed in July 1915, and it was in this general area, including the neighbouring village of Fonquevillers, and the billet villages behind, that it would spend the next 12 months, holding the line as the British army prepared to launch the Battle of the Somme.

The South Midlanders' first indication that they were on the move from Ploegsteert arrived in a directive from III Corps in late June 1915. The divisional headquarters immediately issued orders stating that the formation would withdraw from its current position and travel, via Bailleul to Vieux Berquin, which is between Armentieres and Hazebrouck. As each Brigade Group arrived at the new location, it would come under the orders of First Army. This was followed, on 27th June, by a second order which directed the division to move to the area Allouagne – Lozinghem – Burbure, west of Bethune. On arrival there the division would become part of IV Corps (Lt Gen Sir Henry Rawlinson), alongside the fellow-Territorials of 47th (London) Division and the Regular 1st Division. At this point, the plan was for the 48th to take its place in the line in the Bethune sector and on 12th July it was ordered to relieve 47th Division on the night of 13/14th July. However, the following day these orders were revoked and on 15th July the division was transferred from the First Army to the new Third Army.[1]

With effect from 18th July, the South Midlanders became part of VII Corps along with the regular 4th Division. They would be joined by the 37th Division, a New Army formation (K6),

---

1   TNA WO 95/2745: Headquarters 48th Division General Staff War Diary.

at a later date. The move south to the Somme area was completed by rail. The men and much of their equipment entrained at Lillers and Berguette, for the 40-mile journey to Doullens and from there they marched to billets in the Beauquesne–Authie–Louvencourt area.

VII Corps came into being on 14th July 1915 at St. Omer, it's first commander, Lt Gen Sir Thomas D'Oyly Snow (the great-grandfather of television historian, Dan Snow), joining the following day from 27th Division.[2] Snow's Corps was initially detailed to relieve the French 21st Division on a sector that ran from the village of Hamel, just north of the River Ancre, to a point north-east of Hebuterne, about half a mile south of Gommecourt Church.[3] This part of the line was quiet in the late summer of 1915 – although it had been the scene of hard fighting between the French and Germans during the "race to the sea" at the end of 1914. The 48th Division's line ran from Touvent Farm, the ruins of which lay just behind a row of copses named after the four gospels – Matthew, Mark, Luke and John – west of the village of Serre, and on to the northern outskirts of Hebuterne. On 20th July, the infantry brigades began to take over from the French and Major General Fanshawe assumed responsibility for the sector from 0600 on the morning of 24th July.

The French had held the Hamel–Gommecourt sector with nine battalions in the line and initially VII Corps decided to maintain similar force levels, splitting the ground between the 4th Division, with five battalions forward, between Hamel and Touvent Farm, and 48th Division with four battalions from Touvent Farm to the ruined windmill near Pt 136, north of Hebuterne and about half-a-mile south of Gommecourt Church. Orders for the relief of the French troops holding the sector were issued on 20th July, in which Fanshawe directed 145th Brigade to take on the left section with 143rd Brigade on the right, relieving elements of the 93rd French Infantry Regiment. 144th Brigade were in Divisional Reserve. It was agreed that the commanders of the French units being relieved would remain in the line for 24 hours to ensure continuity whilst the British troops settled in to their new surroundings.

The newcomers were impressed by their first experience of the French trenches. Unlike the breastworks at Ploegsteert, which were really not much more than sand-bagged barricades, the positions east of Hebuterne were dug down into the Picardy chalk, at least six feet deep and often more. Captain Philip Wright of the Bucks Battalion, taking over trenches in front of Hebuterne on 24th July, was full of praise for what he found. The parapets were low, and consequently they were much harder for the enemy to see. The risk of being hit by a sniper's bullet was less than in Belgium, because the lines were farther apart – 800-1000 yards in some places. The dugouts seemed, at first sight, to be very luxurious, having been equipped with "a large proportion of the furniture of Hebuterne", including, in some cases, four-poster beds. Unfortunately, these had become home to quantities of vermin and mice and were nearly all dumped within a week.[4] Wright was also delighted to find that his part of the line was still being supported by French artillery batteries, who did not appear to be constrained by any shortage of ammunition.

2   According to the VII Corps War Diary, one of the junior staff officers assigned to the Corps Headquarters on formation was the then Capt. J F C Fuller. Fuller would go on to serve with the Machine Gun Corps Heavy Branch, which would later become the Tank Corps. In the 1920s and 30s, as a Major General, and later, in retirement, Fuller, along with Capt. Basil Liddell-Hart, would become an early proponent of the British approach to mechanised warfare and the use of armour, and a key influence on German Second World War panzer commander, General Heinz Guderian.
3   TNA WO 95/804: VII Corps General Staff War Diary.
4   P L Wright, p.15.

Their gunners were most obliging and took endless trouble to do everything in their power for our front-line infantry. If asked to retaliate when our front trenches were being heavily shelled, they would throw at least three times as many shells back – and then ring up to know if we were entirely satisfied with their work …We revelled, for the first time in our lives, in the sight of the Bosche receiving far more in return than what he had hurled at us.[5]

When they were in the line, the 145th Brigade and the Bucks Battalion headquarters were both located in Hebuterne village. At first, they were able to occupy quarters in shelled buildings above ground, although as time went on and the sector become more active, they were compelled to find subterranean accommodation in cellars and dugouts.

A feature of this period was the constant adjustments to the line as the British worked out how best to manage the real-estate, and also to complete the relief of the French. On the night of 30/31st July, the 48th Division extended to the right to take over a section of trench from 4th Division. Towards the end of August, the Corps Commander called a conference to discuss a further reorganisation. As a result, in preparation for a larger expansion to the north, 4th Division immediately re-occupied a section of the 48th Division's trenches and on 1st September, the South Midlanders relieved the French 56th Division which meant lengthening its front from north of Hebuterne to a point due east of Fonquevillers Church. The divisional line was still held by two brigades, one based at Hebuterne, the other at Ferme de la Haie, south-west of Fonquevillers.[6]

In general, each brigade held its section with two battalions "up", one in reserve where it could easily reach the line if required, and the fourth "resting", probably in one of the billet villages to the rear. The term "resting" requires some explanation. There was little "rest" involved. Battalions back in billets were generally worked just as hard as if they were in the front line – if not harder. If they were not conducting training, they were almost certain to be up all night, providing working parties to repair trenches, digging new trenches, labouring for the Royal Engineers, or carrying supplies, including food, water, ammunition and defence stores (barbed wire, steel screw-pickets etc), up to the front.

At this stage of the war, the battalions in the line would usually have two companies forward, with one in support and the fourth in reserve. However, the exact configuration of brigades, battalions, companies, and platoons was flexible, and the organisation of the troops in the line could, and did, vary, sometimes from day to day, depending on factors such as weather, visibility, the condition of the trenches, or expected friendly or enemy activity. For example, when the 144th Brigade relieved 143rd Brigade near Hebuterne on 7th August, all four the Warwickshire battalions were tasked to take over sections of the front.[7] Inter-division and inter-Brigade boundaries were also shifted as required.

Lt Charles Carrington, who spent more than six months as a platoon commander, holding trenches at Hebuterne and Fonquevillers between January and July 1916, described how his battalion, the 1/5th Royal Warwickshire Regiment, managed their sector.

---

5    P LWright, p.16.
6    TNA, WO 95/2745, 48th Division General Staff War Diary.
7    TNA WO 95/2754: 143rd Brigade War Diary.

Each company had three platoons actually posted in the front trenches and one standing to arms as an 'in-lying picket', under cover but ready to act in any emergency at two or three minutes' notice … By day, the number of sentries was reduced and if your trench was in good order and your rifle clean there was nothing much to do… since the least show of life would bring a quick reaction from the enemy. Men on duty… never took off their boots, or equipment, or unshipped their gas-masks, and kept their rifles at hand, loaded, and with bayonets fixed.[8]

Having established themselves at Hebuterne and Fonquevillers, the division settled into the monotonous yet still physically and mentally draining routine of line-holding in a quiet sector. Battalions generally went into the lines for eight-day tours.[9] The men would rotate between the firing line, support, and reserve positions. Both villages had been strongly-fortified with the construction of a number of "keeps" and an outer defensive line. These positions also had to be manned.

Although the trenches had at first seemed to be considerably better than those at Ploegsteert, it soon became clear that they needed to be strengthened and improved. A lengthy list of works was drawn up and every unit was required to play its part in delivering construction improvements. 144th Brigade's report for the period between 30th July and 7th August provides a picture of the scale of the task, which included:

- Bullet-proofing parapets of front-line trenches (presumably by adding extra layers of sandbags and adding steel firing loop-holes).
- Widening and deepening communications trenches (to facilitate easier movement to and fro and thus more efficient reliefs, re-supply, and evacuation of the wounded).
- Providing more latrines. The better the sanitary arrangements the fewer men would be lost to illness.
- Revetting trench sides and fire-steps to try to prevent them from falling in during wet weather or under shelling (a forlorn hope as time would tell).
- Revetting, thickening and raising traverses.
- Building stores for small-arms ammunition and bombs
- Excavating new dug-outs.
- Improving drainage (by digging deep sump-holes where water could collect and be pumped out instead of flooding the trench).
- Bricking the floors of trenches (using bricks from damaged buildings to improve the bottom of trenches – before the use of A-frames and duckboards became widespread).
- Erecting new wire entanglements and maintaining the existing wire.[10]

Some of the work, such as the construction of new strong points in and between the lines, and building shell-proof battalion headquarters dug-outs, required specialist Royal Engineer support, but mostly it was a case of "self-help" by the individual units, including those supposedly out of the line "at rest".

8   C E Carrington, *Soldier From the Wars Returning*, p. 88.
9   TNA WO 95/2754: 143rd Brigade War Diary.
10  TNA WO 95/2757: 144th Brigade War Diary.

The move south allowed the 48th Division to side-step the First Army's autumn offensive at Loos, unlike their erstwhile colleagues in IV Corps, 47th (London) and 1st Division, who, together the 15th (Scottish) Division found themselves right in thick of the battle. However, on 23rd September, two days before IV Corps "hopped the bags" in front of Loos and Hulluch, the South Midlanders received orders to be prepared to launch a short-notice attack in their sector. These orders are clear evidence of the great hopes that existed for the success of the planned offensives in Artois and Champagne, stating that: "The general situation by the end of the present week may be such as to enable the Third Army to attack the enemy on our front, or to take part in a general advance."[11] Alas, no such advance took place. The Battle of Loos turned into another of the costly failures that characterised British efforts in 1915. The fiasco hastened the departure of General Sir John French as Commander in Chief and ushered in General Sir Douglas Haig as his successor. Allied hopes now turned to 1916 and plans for the next "Big Push" which would be on the Somme.

As Philip Wright recorded, it was a "very quiet war that was waged around Hebuterne when we first arrived…" Although it would not have been condoned by senior British commanders, who were determined to foster an "offensive spirit", there was a certain "live and let live" attitude on both sides, certainly during the autumn and early winter of 1915. If the Germans refrained from shelling Hebuterne the British would hold off on flattening Gommecourt, and if Sailly was left untouched there would be no reprisals on Puisieux or Bucquoy.[12] Unit war diaries for this period contain a lot of entries that begin "A quiet day" or "Situation normal", and deaths and injuries due to enemy action were relatively few. 143rd Brigade's casualty return for the month of August, 1915, reported a total of seven fatalities (three killed outright and four who died of wounds, having been evacuated), and 30 wounded. By way of comparison, the figures for the previous April, in the Ploegsteert sector, were 17 dead, 69 wounded and 1 missing. [13]

But as the balmy summer sunshine gave way to autumn rain and mist, and the mercury began to fall, this relatively benign situation changed: the British sought to raise the stakes and the Germans responded. Artillery duels became more frequent and more intense, and the tempo of patrolling increased. Hebuterne and Fonquevillers attracted increasing numbers of enemy shells and in return the British artillery ensured that Puisieux and Burquoy were no longer comfortable for their German inhabitants. New units and equipment began to arrive throughout the British sector and before the turn of the year, it was becoming evident that something big was brewing on the Allied side of the line. During this time, a steady stream of new arrivals passed through the 48th Division's trenches, receiving instruction in the finer points of trench warfare before moving on to take over their own sections of the front line. In September, infantry units of the 22nd Division learned their trade from the 48th Division in front of Hebuterne while in October it was the turn of the 36th (Ulster) Division.

At the beginning of October 1915, the commanders of 143rd Brigade and 145th Brigade issued instructions that their front-line garrisons should be reduced in numbers.[14] This followed discussions with the divisional commander and reflected recent experience since moving to the Somme area. Each battalion would still hold its part of the line with two companies, but each

---

11  TNA WO 95/2745: 48th Division General Staff War Diary.
12  P L Wright, p.16.
13  TNA WO 95/2754: 143rd Brigade War Diary.
14  TNA WO 95/2757: 144th Brigade War Diary and WO 95/2754: 143rd Brigade War Diary.

company would keep only one platoon in the front line, with a second platoon in the support line, and two in the reserve trenches. The remaining two companies would be dispersed in depth, but close enough so that they could be rushed to the front if the enemy attacked. The advantage of this "thinning of the line", it was claimed, was that in the event of a heavy barrage only two companies in each section of the front line would be affected and each battalion would have two fresh companies with which to defend or counter-attack if required. It was also expected to simplify reliefs.

This change is significant because it is the first evidence of the division's adoption of elements of a new tactical approach known as "defence in depth" or "elastic defence". In time, this approach, copied, in some respects, from the Germans, would become standard British army policy, set out in a tactical pamphlet, SS210 *The Division in Defence* (issued by GHQ in May 1916). However, at this point in the war it was considered novel, and the 48th Division were very early adopters. Not everyone was comfortable with the idea of a thinly-held front line, especially some officers and NCOs who had served through the first winter of the war and had become accustomed to a continuously-manned front. But as Charles Carrington has written, after the summer of 1915, by which time the 48th Division considered itself to be "battle-trained", it never again held a continuous trench-line, manned shoulder-to-shoulder in tightly-packed trenches, where the men were easy prey to enemy artillery fire. Instead, the line was held by a series of posts – three or four per platoon – spread out along the company frontage and arranged to provide mutual support. This means that each post was able to engage targets to its own front, but also to the front of the positions to its immediate right and left. Supports and reserves were trained to move forward quickly as required and to counter-attack to drive the enemy out of any portion of trench he might have occupied.[15]

Fanshawe believed strongly in this approach and was to follow it for the rest of his time in command of the division. Writing to Carrington after the war, he spelled out his understanding of flexible defence:

> … my idea of meeting a very heavy attack was always to have as few men as possible in the brunt of it and the preliminary unpleasant bombardment of the first line in order to have as many men as possible to carry on the fight for the main position and counter-attack to beat the enemy when his first energy was getting exhausted.[16]

But there is evidence that, in these early days, even before he had "thinned" his line, he had been required to defend his defensive arrangements to his superiors. A document in the 48th Division General Staff war diary, dated 13th September 1915 responds to a note from VII Corps headquarters dated three days earlier. It sets out the planned dispositions of his troops in the event of an enemy attack, and the time it will take them to occupy their defensive positions. Fanshawe concludes by stating that his front line was strong, and he did not anticipate that it could be forced by a 'coup-de-main'. "I consider myself strong enough forward to be able to hold on until the situation is cleared up and I can decide in which direction to move my Divisional Reserve."[17] This reassurance apparently satisfied the Corps Commander, since there appears to

---

15   C E Carrington, p.90.
16   G Cassar, p.163.
17   TNA WO 95/2745, 48th Division (GS) War Diary.

be no further correspondence on the issue and Fanshawe felt able to adopt his "elastic defence" dispositions a few weeks later.

## Death of Lt Roland Leighton

Lt Roland Leighton, of 1/7th Worcestershire Regiment, 144th Brigade, died from a wound received on 23rd December 1915. The battalion war diary simply states: "Lt R A Leighton killed while wiring. Sgt Day, Medical Officer [Capt Sheridan] and Capt Adam did excellent work bringing him in during heavy sniping." Leighton did not die during an attack or a raid. He was shot in the stomach by a German machine gun whilst commanding a wiring party – another tragic victim of "trench wastage". He would have remained just another name on a white Portland stone grave marker, had he not been immortalised in the writing of Vera Brittain, and her celebrated memoir *Testament of Youth*. Vera and Roland were engaged to be married and the ceremony was to have taken place when he returned home on leave. Roland had written to say that he would be home on Christmas Day, and she had been given special leave from her role as a Voluntary Aid Detachment nurse and travelled to her parents in Brighton on Christmas Eve. On Boxing Day, Vera was waiting for him to telephone from the railway station to tell her when he would arrive. Instead, she received a call from his family to inform her that he had been killed. The loss was devastating for Vera, made worse by the death of her brother, Capt Edward Brittain, who fell at San Sisto Ridge near the town of Asiago, on 15th June 1918, whilst serving with the Sherwood Foresters.

Vera investigated the circumstances of Roland's death and recorded them in the book. Before taking the wiring party out, Lt Leighton decided to reconnoitre the location himself, and used a path which led to no-man's land through a gap in a hedge, because the communication trench was flooded. The trench had been unpassable for some time and the Germans knew about the alternative path and trained a machine gun on it, firing a few bursts whenever they thought the garrison opposite might be using it. This was, she believed, well-known to the previous occupants of the trenches, but they had not passed it on to the Worcesters during the relief.

> As soon as Roland reached the gap the usual volley was fired. Almost the first shot struck him in the stomach, and he fell on his face …[18]

Recovered from no-man's land under fire, he was sent down the medical evacuation chain to a Field Ambulance (mobile front line medical unit), where he died the next day. Lt Roland Aubrey Leighton (20), was the son of Mr Robert Leighton, Oxford, and Mrs Marie Connor Leighton, both authors of some note, who lived at Lowestoft, Suffolk. He is buried in Louvencourt Military Cemetery, which is situated about 10km behind the front.

18   V Brittain, *Testament of Youth*, pp215/6.

## Patrols and Raids

The domination of no-man's land was always high on the British army's list of priorities at this stage of the war, and a busy schedule of patrolling and raiding was soon in operation across the divisional area. In orders issued as early as 3rd August 1915, Fanshawe directed his battalion commanders to "have the ground thoroughly patrolled" and to prepare schemes for attacking the enemy's positions to their front – trench raids.[19] These activities could be expensive in terms of casualties sustained but were considered vital elements of fostering an 'offensive spirit' among the troops. They helped to restrict the enemy's freedom of movement, provided opportunities to gather intelligence, and impacted on the morale and physical condition of the enemy, requiring them to stay alert throughout the hours of darkness, and playing havoc with their mental well-being by posing a constant threat of injury, death or of being taken prisoner. Standing patrols also provided protection for working parties maintaining the wire in front of the British trenches, and listening patrols went out to give early warning of enemy movement between the lines.

Raiding was deliberately erratic in order to avoid setting patterns that the enemy could recognise and to which they could respond. However, there is evidence that the British raided the same locations more than once. The raids themselves had mixed results, some being spectacularly successful while others failed before the attackers had managed to get into the enemy trenches.

An example of a successful raid occurred on 25/26th August, involving the 1/6th Gloucestershire Regiment, who assaulted German trenches and shelters at the south-east corner of Gommecourt Park, opposite Hebuterne. The enemy position was known to be strongly-fortified and the objectives were to obtain prisoners and to gather detailed information on the trenches and how they were garrisoned. This was a large operation, well-planned and carefully rehearsed, involving five officers and 100 other ranks of C Company, under the overall command of Capt V L Young (OC C Company). The assault had been practiced, by day and in darkness, on a similar stretch of British trench in the rear.

A preliminary bombardment was arranged for the afternoon of the 25th. This was intended to help to cut the enemy's barbed wire defences, damage their trenches and, hopefully, attract working parties into the line that night to effect repairs – thus increasing the number of enemy soldiers who might be captured. Two parties of 25 men, each commanded by an officer, were detailed to enter the enemy trenches whilst the remainder were to be in support at a position known as "Z Hedges", in front of the wood.

As soon as it was dark, a party of one officer – Lt. H. P. Knott – and 20 other ranks, crept out from their lines and headed for the Z Hedges. Their task was to secure the "start line" or "jumping-off point" for the assault, to ensure it was not compromised by a roving enemy patrol. At 11.55pm, the main body, under Capt Young, made their way to the hedges, signallers unrolling telephone wire as they went. Once at the start line, the two assaulting parties, led by 2nd Lt T T Price and 2nd Lt J M C Badgeley, moved forward, crawling very slowly on their belt-buckles in the bright moonlight, to within 70 yards of the German trenches to await the covering artillery barrage. The assault teams reported they were in place at 12.58am. Waiting

---

19   TNA WO 95/2575: 144th Brigade War Diary.

for a passing cloud to cover the moon, Capt Young passed the word to the gunners by field telephone, and they opened fire at 1.03am, targeting the enemy front line, support and reserve lines and local communications trenches. This fire, sometimes known as a "box barrage", was intended to force the enemy sentries to take cover, prevent the movement of reinforcements, and cover any noise caused by the raiders as they went forward – although it was, in itself, a significant indicator that a raid was imminent.

On the left, the party commanded by 2nd Lt Badgeley, cut through two wire entanglements, the second one being very new, with strong, thick wire, about five yards deep. The unavoidable noise alerted the enemy sentries, but 2nd Lt Badgeley and his men got into the trench. Badgeley shot two men and his party bombed the first dug-out they came to, tossing two grenades down the steps. The garrison retired along the trench while others in a parallel trench to the rear, threw bombs at the raiders. 2nd Lt Badgeley was wounded by a bomb which landed at his feet and his party then retired, bringing their injured with them, one of whom was struck and killed by a stray bullet on the way back.

On the right, 2nd Lt Pryce and his party found only low wire which they easily breech and entered the German trenches unseen. The first identified shelter was a telephone office where a German, coming up the steps, was promptly shot by Pryce when he failed to surrender, and three bombs were dropped down the stairway. A blocking party was established along the trench and the NCO in charge pulled up a sump cover which effectively cut off that section of the trench and prevented the German supports from reaching the raiders. Led by Pryce, the main group then proceeded along the position, bombing six further dug-outs as they went and taking three unarmed prisoners, who were passed back along the trench for evacuation. This group managed to get away from their guards and dart into a shelter, where they found weapons and emerged to fire on the raiding party from the rear. They were all killed. Lt Pryce, having lost touch with the left party, began to retire back along the trench where he found a large number of Germans who had used tunnels to by-pass the block. Pryce and his team bombed this group, who were tightly packed into the narrow trench, and then made good their escape, bringing all their wounded, and a single prisoner. They reached the comparative safety of Z Hedges and from there, they were able to move back to their own trenches, covered by Capt Young and his party. Lt D H Hartog led a rifle-grenade team to the left to enfilade the enemy's trench and keep them occupied while the raiders pulled back. Once he was certain the raiders were all safely in the British trenches, Young called down a second artillery barrage to cover his own withdrawal.

Reporting on the outcome of the raid to divisional headquarters, Lt Col A R B Cossard, Commanding Officer, 1/6th Gloucestershire Regiment, assessed that it had been "most successful" and "must have accounted for a large number of Germans, who were caught crowded in big, deep shelters and bombed". From the prisoner's statement, the garrison was a company, about 180-strong, and the trenches were well-constructed and in good condition, almost 10 feet deep and revetted with rabbit wire and stakes. The shelters were very deep, some with spiral staircases, and all appeared to be connected by underground tunnels as well as the usual communications trenches. Traverses were high and broad. It was also identified that the enemy appeared to have developed a way of pulling up a single strand of wire from the trench line, presumably to hold up a raiding party as it withdrew. Such a wire was encountered by the raiders on their way back and they were certain it had not been there on the way in. Cossard attributed the success of the enterprise to "the bravery and keenness of both men and officers and to the careful previous rehearsing and organisation of the parties, full advantage having been taken of the information which has been collected and circulated after former attacks".[20]

But not all actions went as smoothly as this. On 29th January 1916, 143rd Brigade and 144th Brigade planned a joint raid in roughly the same area, to be conducted by 1/5th Royal Warwickshires and 1/6th Gloucestershire Regiment. The Warwickshires called off their part of the attack, deciding that, due to poor visibility – it had been very foggy, and the moon did not rise until quite late – it was doubtful if the raiders would be able to find their way to the breeching point.[21] However, 144th Brigade decided that even if their neighbours did not attack, they could still undertake their part of the plan.[22]

Careful reconnaissance of the German lines had taken place over several nights leading up to the raid. At one point an officer's patrol had remained out all day within 150 yards of the enemy's trenches, to obtain detailed pattern-of-life[23] information and to sketch the enemy's trenches and wire, which were not visible from the British front line. The broad scheme of manoeuvre for the attack was based on the approach that had proved so successful back in August. But any similarities between the two operations ended there. The Gloucesters' war diary simply records: "A raid on enemy trenches at SW corner of the area of Parc de Gommecourt was attempted but, owing to fog, parties had to return to our lines. Four slight casualties."[24] The 144th Brigade war diary added some further 'colour', explaining that: "The Gloucesters completely lost direction when they got to the enemy wire. The obscurity was increased by [smoke from] our own barrage which hung in the fog and blew back on us." In an attempt to put a more positive gloss on it, the diary entry continued: "It is regretted that the principal enterprise (by 1/6th Gloucesters) failed to enter the enemy's trench, but much valuable experience in organising and practising attacks, supported by our own fire, was gained by all ranks, and it is probable that considerable loss was inflicted on the enemy by our artillery fire, bombs and rifle grenades."[25]

Meanwhile, the Germans too staged trench raids, for much the same reasons as the British, and although these were infrequent during the autumn of 1915, the tempo increased after the turn of the year. On 19th February 1916, the enemy attacked trenches defended by the 1/6th Gloucestershire Regiment, at a point about 1000 yards north-east of Touvent Farm and just north of John Copse. For some reason, the Germans decided to make the task more difficult for themselves by mixing poison gas and phosphorus[26] with shrapnel and high explosives in the opening bombardment. The phosphorus did not cause too many problems for the raiders or the defenders but the gas, likely to have been Phosgene, was heavy and persistent and meant the attackers would have had to conduct the break-in and subsequent exploitation wearing gas masks. This was not a major issue: the troops were trained to fight in the masks. However, their

---

20  TNA WO 95/2758: 1/6th Gloucestershire Regiment War Diary
21  TNA WO 95/2754: 143rd Brigade War Diary.
22  TNA WO 95/2754: 143rd Brigade War Diary.
23  Pattern-of-life relates to information and analysis of the behaviours and movements of a target group. This is a modern term, but it can be applied to the intelligence-gathering operation being conducted in front of Gommecourt Park at this time.
24  TNA WO 95/2758, 1/6th Gloucesters War Diary
25  TNA WO 95/2757: 144th Brigade War Diary.
26  Phosphorus burns in air to produce a dense white smoke, which was used to provide cover for attacking /withdrawing troops.

visibility would have been degraded and breathing was more difficult – extra encumbrances for an operation of war that depended for success on speed and agility.

Throughout the day of the 18th the Germans had subjected the right section of the Gloucesters' line to a heavy bombardment including minenwerfers throwing canister bombs (25cm calibre projectiles known as Rum Jars, the equivalent of the British 9.45in Flying Pig), as well as 5.9s, 4.2s and 77mm field guns. The left section was untouched. After dark, enemy machine guns and snipers became active, forcing the Gloucesters' Commanding Officer, Lt Col John Micklem, to bring in a wiring party. Micklem's front was held by six platoons in posts with two platoons in close support, under orders to launch an immediate counterattack if the front was breeched. Two Lewis Guns were positioned to cover the whole of his line.

At 0200, heavy minenwerfer fire opened from the front line at John Copse to the Touvant Farm – La Louviere Road. This fire was continuous, and it was estimated that at least 10 minenwerfers were in action. Despite the heavy shelling, Lt Costin went around the posts checking that all was well. At about 0210, a number of gas shells were fired, forcing the garrison in the centre of the Gloucesters line, who were on the receiving end, to put on their gas hoods. At the same time, a battery of 5.9s dropped a barrage on the various local communications trenches, which was maintained for 40 minutes, preventing the supports and reserves from moving up. This fire was very accurate and many of the trenches were collapsed in several places as a result of direct hits. These shells also cut telephone communications between battalion headquarters and the posts, and this was not restored until shortly after 0500.

At about 0215, a cloud of white, unidentified gas was seen emanating from the German lines – probably released from cylinders – and a party of about 30 enemy soldiers advanced under its cover to an abandoned portion of the British front line. A small number of survivors from the bombardment managed to open fire on the attackers as they crossed No-Man's Land but were too few to prevent them from getting into the trench. Once there, the raiders split into two groups and moved right and left along the line, shooting, and bombing as they went. There were few defenders left in the posts along the trench after the bombardment and those who had survived were no match for the attackers. The Germans were seen attempting to drag off one of the Gloucesters' wounded, pulling him over the parapet, but were unable to get him any further.

At about 0225 the support platoon was ordered up to the front, over open ground, and arrived just as the raiders pulled out. Posts on the right reported that the enemy had attempted to leave the trenches to their front at about 0230 but had been driven back by rapid rifle and Lewis Gun fire. There was a gap in the British wire about 40 yards long, where the wire had completely disappeared, replaced by a mass of shell craters. British casualties totalled 10 other ranks killed, and 10 wounded, three of whom were still at duty. Three men were reported missing, one of whom was almost certainly buried in the communications trench where he had been working. The others had likely been taken prisoner. One officer and 7 other ranks were reported to be suffering from the effects of the gas, the symptoms including tightness in the chest, coughing, breathing difficulties, vomiting, stinging eyes and throat.[27]

---

27   TNA WO 95/2757: 144th Brigade War Diary.

## Battle Plans

The Allies' war strategy for 1916 was settled at a conference in the small northern French town of Chantilly between 6th and 8th December 1915. Representatives from Britain, France, Belgium, Russia and Italy agreed that they would each launch coordinated major offensives, with Britain and France co-operating in a joint effort. The objective of this approach was to engage the Germans on three fronts simultaneously, with the intent of stretching their resources to breaking point. For General Sir John French, representing Britain at the talks, this was to be one of his last acts as Commander-in-Chief of the British Expeditionary Force. Under pressure after the failure of the Battle of Loos, French resigned his position and on 8th December, the Prime Minister, Herbert Asquith, wrote to Haig, offering him the job.[28]

Although not a party to the Chantilly discussions and resulting plan, Haig was broadly content with the proposed strategy, recognising the need to tie the Germans down on his front in order to prevent them from deploying reserves elsewhere. But he did not particularly wish to fight on the Somme, seeing an offensive in Flanders as a better option. In January 1916, at a meeting with his French opposite number and fellow cavalryman, Joseph Joffre, it was agreed that the main British attack would take place in the Ypres area, but with the BEF launching a subsidiary attack on the Somme in the Spring. Joffre was happy with this because it supported his preference for a two-stage campaign, with a wearing-out battle to attrit the Germans and force them to commit their reserves, followed by a second offensive which would deliver the coup de grace.[29] However, this plan did not survive contact with the allies, let alone the Germans. The British political authorities were understandably squeamish about further heavy losses in the wake of the Loos debacle. Russia decided that it could not launch a major attack before the summer, and the Belgians were unwilling to cooperate in a large-scale attack in Flanders. As a result, on 14th February, with British planning for the Flanders offensive already under way, Haig and Joffre agreed to switch their efforts to the Somme at the beginning of July, by which time the Russians would be ready to play their part. Seven days later, the Germans pre-empted the allies and launched their own attack at Verdun, aiming to "bleed France white".

On 4th February 1916, with Britain's available land forces expanding exponentially as Kitchener's new divisions completed their basic training and were declared ready for war, a new Army was formed. The Fourth Army, to be commanded by General Sir Henry Rawlinson, was promptly assigned the responsibility for planning, and delivering the summer campaign on the Somme. By 1st March 1916, Rawlinson had established his headquarters at the chateau in Marieux, south-east of Doullens. For the forthcoming operations, his Army would consist of III Corps (Lt Gen Sir William Pulteney); VIII Corps (Lt Gen Sir Aylmer Hunter-Weston); X Corps (Lt Gen Sir Thomas Morland); XIII Corps (Lt Gen Walter Congreve) and XV Corps (Lt Gen Sir Henry Horne). As part of the re-organisation associated with the creation of Fourth Army, 48th Division was initially transferred from VII Corps to X Corps with effect from 4 March. Three days later the new VIII Corps was formed, also at Marieux, and on 18th March 48th Division was allocated to that formation, together with 4th, 29th and 31st Divisions.

---

28   G Sheffield and J Bourne (eds.), *Douglas Haig: War Diaries and Letters*, 1914-1918, p.172.
29   G. Sheffield, *The Somme*, p.13.

On 20th March, Major General Fanshawe and key staff officers met with their new Corps Commander to discuss aspects of the forthcoming operations, and just five days later, Hunter-Weston issued his initial orders, shaping VIII Corps's contribution to the Battle of the Somme. These stated that "in conjunction with other attacks further south, VIII Corps has been ordered to attack the enemy on the line Q.17.a.8.8 to K.25.d.9.6 (map references)".[30] This corresponds to the area between a point about 800 yards due south of Beaumont Hamel Church and a point on the Serre–Hebuterne Road, about 800 yards north-west of Serre village. To achieve this, the Corps would have at its disposal 29th Division, 31st Division, 48th Division and 4th Division, together with a large force of heavy artillery. At this stage it was thought possible that the Corps would be allocated a fifth division, and the initial scheme of manoeuvre took this into account. The Corps's primary objective was identified as the Beaucourt-Serre Road and the village of Serre, the latter becoming "the nucleus of a defensive flank facing north-east".[31] This means that once the primary objective had been achieved the divisions would go firm on this line, facing north-east, as protection for the left flank of the British attack in the event of a German counter-thrust from that direction.

These orders, which would be constantly refined and adjusted before Z-Day (the day of the attack), included the initial thinking on the tasks for each division, providing the commanders with a basis on which to begin their planning. 29th Division would attack the fortified village of Beaumont Hamel on a 1700 yards front. 4th Division would assault from the northern edge of Beaumont Hamel to a point on the Serre Road due south of Matthew Copse, keeping its left in line with Pendant Copse, deep inside the German lines. 31st Division would attack on a 1000 yards front from Serre Road to Mark Copse. 48th Division, with a single brigade attacking, would head for the enemy line from a point opposite Mark Copse about 800 yards north-west of Serre village. Its task was to capture the first three lines of German trenches and then form a defensive flank facing north-east. The remainder of the division would be in a defensive role but would be expected to carry out demonstrations to give the impression that it was about to attack the enemy within its boundaries. If a fifth division was forthcoming, it would probably be required to push through after the initial thrust and hit the German trenches at the northern end of the ridge between Grandcourt and Puisieux.

At this point, Hunter-Weston directed that all preparations for the attack should be completed by no later than 30th April. To ensure that the divisions became familiar with the ground over which they would assault, he ordered a re-adjustment of the Corps line to put each division into the area from which it would attack. He also pointed out that many parts of the existing line were "beyond reasonable assaulting distance" of the enemy trenches. Measures needed to be taken at once to move the British line to within 200 yards of the Germans, including on the portion of the 48th Division's line where no attack was planned. This was to maintain the pretence implicit in the South Midlanders' proposed demonstrations. The divisional commanders appear to have queried this because on 30th March, Corps Headquarters issued an update stating that "the question of whether it will be advisable to push forward our front-line trenches so as to have a shorter distance over which to assault, is being reconsidered by the Corps Commander. For the present nothing should be done on this matter".[32] The following day the issue was discussed with

---

30  TNA WO 95/820: VIII Corps War Diary.
31  TNA WO 95/820: VIII Corps War Diary.
32  TNA WO 95/820: VIII Corps Administrative Update, VIII Corps War Diary, 30th March 1916.

the Divisional Commanders at Corps Headquarters. The record of this discussion reveals that Hunter-Weston acknowledged the disadvantages of the proposal, which included drawing the enemy's attention to the work and "leading him probably to reinforce his infantry, and what is more important, his artillery on our front". The Divisional commanders were invited to think over the matter and provide their views in writing. Although there appears to be no record of these views having been submitted, the issue was obviously resolved, for the Corps Operational Summary for 7-13th April 1916 records that a new section of trench, closer to the enemy, had been dug and wired by 48th Division's 145th Brigade in the Hebuterne sector on the night of 9th/10th April. A party of 1500 men had been involved in the task, which had been completed between the hours of 9pm and 4am with the loss of two men killed and 16 wounded, including one officer.[33]

By 17th April, it was clear that Hunter-Weston was not going to get a fifth division, and on that date his Chief of Staff (or Brigadier-General General Staff), Brigadier-General the Hon Walter Hore-Ruthven[34], issued updated orders cancelling the plan for a brigade of 48th Division to take part in the attack. Instead, Fanshawe would be required to hold his front with four battalions (all from a single brigade if he wished) and withdraw the rest, including his pioneer battalion, 1/5th Sussex Regiment, to the vicinity of Sailly-au-Bois, where they would form the bulk of the Corps Reserve and be prepared to move to either Beaumont Hamel or Serre as required.[35]

On 15th June, Hunter-Weston completed his plan and issued a final revision. The main elements had not changed significantly, although the Corps objectives had been moved deeper into German territory to include Munich and Puisieux trenches. The update did, however, contain specific directions for Fanshawe as the commander of the Corps Reserve, which would include 144th and 145th brigades, two RE Field Companies, one Pioneer Battalion (5th Royal Sussex), one Motor Machine Gun Battery and six Hotchkiss machine guns of the Lancashire Hussars[36]. This force was to be prepared for two eventualities: to relieve some part of the front line after the objective had been gained; or to "restore the situation in the unlikely event of a serious breakdown by one of the assaulting divisions". In the latter case, however, the reserve "would not be used unless some definite objective could be attained". It would only be used offensively and "will not be dribbled up to reinforce parts of the line that may be hard pressed".[37]

Fanshawe issued his own final orders, setting out the division's part in the attack, on 24th June, just five days before the planned opening of the battle.[38] By now, the mission had been refined even more. So, too, had some of the divisional and unit boundaries. The 48th Division's

---

33　TNA WO95/820, Report on new trench dug last night, VIII Corps War Diary, 10th April 1916.
34　A Scots Guards officer who later became the 2nd Baron Ruthven of Gowrie.
35　TNA WO 95/820, VIII Corps War Diary.
36　A number of yeomanry units were converted into machine gun units during the First World War. However, this did not happen until after the Somme offensive. In this instance, the Corps Commander was utilising the machine gun section of his attached cavalry unit, dismounted, to bolster what was a relatively thin Corps Reserve. The Yeomanry preferred the French Hotchkiss to the Lewis Gun because it was lighter and easier to transport.
37　TNA WO95/820: Notes of Two Conferences Held at Corps Headquarters, VIII Corps War Diary, 21 and 23 June 1916.
38　The Somme offensive was originally timed to begin on 30th June 1916, but the start was delayed by 24 hours due to bad weather.

role as Corps Reserve had not changed, nor had its task of holding its existing front, which was now allocated to 143rd Brigade. However, instead of deploying four battalions for this task as was originally envisaged, the Warwickshire men were directed to do the job with just two – 1/5th and 1/7th. The remaining battalions, 1/6th and 1/8th Royal Warwickshires had already been detached from 143rd Brigade and "loaned" to 11th Brigade to support the 4th Division's attack from north of Beaumont Hamel to the Serre Road. The 48th Division was to be prepared to relieve the 10th and 12th Brigades in the trenches on the Grandcourt–Puisieux Ridge on the second night of operations.

Thus, it was decided that two South Midlands territorial battalions would take part in the opening stages of the battle, while the remainder of the division held the line or sat it out in the rear. But few would have coveted the task given to the Warwickshires. 11th Brigade, consisting of the Old Contemptible of 1st Rifle Brigade, 1st East Lancashires, 1st Somerset Light Infantry and 1st Hampshires – a battalion that had already earned its share of glory at Le Cateau, the Marne, the Aisne and at Second Ypres – along with their "borrowed" territorials, had been ordered to crack one of the toughest nuts on the whole of the 15-miles battle front. When the whistles blew at 0730 on the morning of 1st July, they would be assaulting the fearsome Heidenkopf strong-point, also known as The Quadrilateral, a maze of heavily-defended and mutually-supporting trenches to the west of Serre village, later immortalised as the scene for Wilfred Owen's famous poem 'The Sentry'.[39]

In the meantime, Hunter-Weston was determined to keep the enemy on his front unsure about his intentions. He directed commanders at all levels from brigadiers down to "consider and think out small offensive schemes". This should include the possibility of making small raids on the enemy's trenches, of catching one of the enemy's patrols, or bombing one of his listening posts …" At the same time, as the clock ticked down to the great attack, it was likely that the enemy would step up their intelligence-gathering activities, including trench raids. For that reason, it was vital for his commanders to ensure their local defensive plans were well-formed, and properly-coordinated with flanking units.[40]

The assault on the village of Serre by the 31st Division, would mark the northern boundary of the Somme offensive, the first day of which was focused on capturing the Serre– Gommecourt Ridge and the high ground at Pozières. But to keep the enemy guessing about the actual limit of the attack, it was decided to stage a "feint" or diversionary attack on the Gommecourt Salient. This would be carried out by elements of Allenby's Third Army, specifically Snow's VII Corps. It was designed to help to occupy the German machine-gunners and artillery there and, hopefully, prevent them from turning their fire on the advancing troops of 31st Division as they attacked Serre. The "diversion" would be carried out by the 46th (North Midland) Division and the 56th (1st London) Division, both Territorial formations, who would advance on the northern and southern faces of the salient. At the same time, and dependent on the wind direction, a dense cloud of smoke, possibly including poison gas would be released by the 48th Division from the British trenches between Gommecourt and Serre, to obscure the German view towards Serre

---

39   Owen and his platoon took cover in an old German dug-out in the Heidenkopf later in the battle and were heavily shelled. The poem relates the story of a sentry who was left at the door of the dugout and who was blinded by an exploding shell.
40   TNA WO 95/820: Notes on a Conference held at VIII Corps Headquarters, VIII Corps War Diary, 1st April 1916.

and to maintain the pretence of an attack on the 48th Division front. The Army commander, Rawlinson, was a strong advocate of smoke having seen how it helped the 47th (London) Division to make progress during the Battle of Loos.[41] Obviously, smoke cannot stop bullets or artillery shells, but, if laid correctly, taking proper account of wind direction and strength, it can effectively screen an area from observation, thus reducing the effectiveness of rifle, machine gun and artillery fire, and is undoubtedly an aid, particularly in attack and in withdrawal.

The month leading up to 1st July was characterised by a frenzy of activity along the whole of the 15-mile front as divisions, brigades and battalions made their final preparations. The days between 24th and 29th June had been allocated letter codenames. The 24th was U, the 25th was V, and so on, with Z for Zero being 29th June. However, on the 28th (Y-Day) the attack was postponed for 48 hours due to bad weather. The 29th now became Y1, the 30th Y2, with Z scheduled for 1st July. On 13th June, the 1/6th and 1/8th Royal Warwickshires marched to Beauval to join 11th Brigade for the attack on the Heidenkopf. On 21st June, a party of 820 men carried "Rogers" into the 48th Division trenches. "Rogers" was the code-name given for the gas, a total of 200 cylinders of which were distributed along the divisional line. This gas was intended to be released by sappers of the Special Brigade, Royal Engineers in the days running up to Zero. The next day (22nd June), 143rd Brigade relieved 145th Brigade in the front line, the latter moving back to the rear to join 144th Brigade in Corps Reserve in and around the villages of Couin and Sailly-au-Bois.

General Rawlinson had decided that the attack would be preceded by a five-day bombardment (lengthened to 7 days when Z was postponed until 1st July). This commenced on U Day (24th June), and soon became something of a daily routine for the gunners. Each morning, they fired a concentrated barrage for 80 minutes, using every available gun. For the rest of the day a continuous but less intense fire was maintained, the 18-pounder field guns using shrapnel shells to cut the German wire whilst the mediums and heavies fired high explosives to wreck the trenches and drive the garrisons down into their deep dug-outs. At night half of the artillery pieces were rested, their places being taken by scores of machine guns, which kept up a heavy, indirect harassing fire on the enemy's rear areas.[42]

Despite the artillery bombardment, patrolling and trench raiding continued with increasing frequency throughout the week leading up to Z-Day. Officers led small detachments of men across No-Man's Land to examine the state of the enemy wire while others attempted to enter the German lines in an effort to find out if they had reinforced their positions or made any other changes that could impact on the plan. On the 48th Division front, one such raid was conducted by 1/7th Worcestershire Regiment on the night of 28/29 June.

The objectives for this raid were to assess the condition of the enemy wire, kill as many Germans as possible, discover the strength of the enemy in his first and second lines, and identify the unit holding the section of the front to the west of La Louviere Farm. The plan was straightforward. Under cover of an artillery barrage, the raiders would use Bangalore Torpedoes to cut the wire in front of the trench to be entered. Two assault parties, each consisting of an NCO and eight men, would go forward, bomb dugouts and grab prisoners before making their way back, protected by a small covering force and a second artillery barrage. The operation

---

41   R Prior and T Wilson, *Command on the Western Front*, p.145.
42   M Middlebrook, *The First Day on the Somme*, p.88.

was a complete failure. The raiding party was unfamiliar with the ground and it had not been possible, due to timing constraints, to conduct a reconnaissance beforehand. Guides provided by the 1/5th Royal Warwickshire Regiment, who were supposed to know the ground, were unable to find the route through the British wire. This meant the party had to cut their way through, which delayed them from reaching the jumping off point until after 0200 instead of 0100 as originally planned and agreed with the artillery. Having reached the jumping off point it was decided to abort the raid, because it would have been impossible to complete it before daylight, which was due at about 0300. Reporting on the fiasco, the Commanding Officer of 1/7th Worcestershire Regiment, Lt Col A R Harman noted, ominously for those who would be attacking on 1st July, that despite the preliminary bombardment, which had been falling on the German lines daily since the 24th, the wire was in good order all along this section of front. The enemy were alert and were holding their line strongly with two machine guns covering the planned point of entry.[43]

The following day – Y1 Day (29th June) – although out of the line, 1/4th Oxfordshire and Buckinghamshire Light Infantry were ordered to conduct a raid east of Hebuterne that night. A party of 50 led by Lt T R Fortescue was to enter the German trenches just north of a location known as The Point, south-west of La Louviere Farm, and capture a prisoner. The raiders left their own trenches just after midnight and easily made it through the first section of enemy wire, which had been badly damaged. However, as they moved forward, they found eight rows of concertina wire, just in front of the enemy parapet, which was "quite undamaged". In attempting to get through the obstacle, they were detected and attacked with bombs and rifle fire. Efforts were made to find a way through the wire but the enemy were by now "wide awake" and their trenches were strongly manned. The party was eventually withdrawn, reaching the relative safety of their own lines at 0210.[44]

## Heidenkopf Redoubt

Two companies of 1/8th Royal Warwickshire Regiment, A and B, went into the line opposite the Heidenkopf on the night of 28th/29th June, while the remainder of the battalion, and the whole of 1/6th Royal Warwickshires, remained in billets in and around Mailly-Maillet. The 11th Brigade Operation Order required all the assaulting battalions to be in their assembly positions not later than 0130 on the morning of 1st July, so at around 10.30pm on the 30th six companies of Warwickshire men, and the other 11th Brigade units, left Mailly-Maillet to march to the front. Most of the brigade was in place by 0200. However, the Warwickshires took a slightly different route to the assembly trenches and as a result, they were delayed. The 11th Brigade battle narrative recorded that this was due to congestion in their communication trench. In addition, the front-line trenches that were to have been used by the leading wave of the 1/8th had been badly damaged by shellfire and could not be occupied. The resulting re-organisation caused some confusion, but the Brigade was finally reported complete in its assembly trenches by 0330, as the first streaks of dawn light began to brighten the morning sky.

---

43   TNA WO 95/2745: 48th Division General Staff War Diary
44   TNA WO 95/2764: 1/4th OBLI War Diary.

For many, the period between arriving in the assembly positions and the start of the attack – the seemingly endless wait to launch themselves towards the enemy – would, in some ways, have been just as nerve-wracking as the assault itself.

The Germans were by now well aware that an attack was coming, and their artillery was already searching out the British front positions and rear areas. However, this counter-preparation barrage was not severe, and although some shells fell in and around the assembly trenches, they caused few casualties. The men, experiencing a whole mixture of emotions that spanned from abject, sick-inducing terror to stomach-fluttering excitement, checked their kit, then checked it again. Some pulled out their hand grenades and made sure the ends of the safety pins were properly splayed out to prevent them from working loose accidentally. Here and there a man vomited, sparking off others to follow suit. Some thought about home and loved ones. Some said their prayers….and waited for the signal to advance. The officers peered at their watches as the hands moved slowly towards zero. At 0700, the British barrage increased in intensity, trench mortar batteries, some popping up from Russian Saps dug out into no-man's land, adding to the din. At 0720, to the Warwickshires' right, near Beaumont Hamel, the Hawthorne Redoubt mine erupted, providing the enemy with a significant combat indicator that the attack was imminent. Probably as a result of this, at 0726, the enemy opened a heavy machine-gun fire, sweeping the parapets of the assembly trenches. This fire appeared to be coming chiefly from Beaumont Hamel, Ridge Redoubt and Ten Tree Ally. The German artillery also opened a more concentrated shrapnel bombardment all along the British front. As the last few minutes ticked by, officers drew their pistols, checked to ensure that six .455 rounds were in place in the cylinder, and once they were content, placed their whistles between their lips, and drew in a deep breath. As the watch hands settled on 0730 the shrill note of a thousand whistles echoed along the line. The men stood up and moved forward into the enemy fire.

The 1/8th Royal Warwickshires were assaulting with two companies up and two in support. Each company deployed on a one-platoon front, meaning that the battalion frontage was no more than about 200 yards wide. The two companies on the left suffered heavily from machine-gun fire from that flank. Pte E C Stanley, going forward with the 1/8th, remembered: "On my left I could see large shell bursts as the West Yorks (31st Division) advanced and saw many men falling forward. I thought at first, they were looking for nose-caps (artillery fuses – a favourite souvenir) and it was some time before I realised they were hit."[45]

Brigade and battalion accounts of this action differ, perhaps unsurprisingly given the intensity of the conflict, and the scale of the losses. Describing the initial advance, 2nd Lt Turner wrote: "We went over first, followed by crowds of famous regiments. The 8th was splendid, past imagination…the regulars and the Generals cannot say enough for the dash and spirit of our onrush."[46] According to the Brigade narrative, few of these troops penetrated beyond the enemy front line, although, it stated, members of the leading right-hand company *claimed* to have reached the trench running between Point 49 and Point 05, which was in the fourth line. However, the battalion's own account is clear that although they sustained heavy casualties from enemy machine-gun fire, the attackers passed the first and second lines quickly before they were held up at the third line by a machine-gun post, which they "took by rushes". After that, most

---

45  M Middlebrook, p.127.
46  Imperial War Museum (IWM), Turner Papers.

of the fighting involved bombing their way along the trenches. The battalion account claims their objective – the fourth line between Point 49 and Point 05 – was reached within 35-40 minutes of zero and they immediately began to consolidate under the direction of Capt Martin and 2nd Lt John Turner. By this time, the follow-on battalion – 1/6th Royal Warwickshires – was beginning to arrive, but in small numbers owing to the scale of the losses it had sustained crossing no-man's land. It was not strong enough to push on. As the 1/8th battalion war diarist, acting adjutant, 2nd Lt F H Anstey, noted, the other following battalions appeared to have fared no better. It was decided that the 1/6th Warwickshires would instead help with consolidating the captured positions. This involved securing the flanks by creating bombing blocks, re-orientating the trenches so that the original parapet became the parados, and digging new fire-steps to allow fire to be directed towards the German depth positions.

The enemy, as always, was quick to organise local counter-attacks, and the Warwickshires now faced repeated attempts to throw them back. The men held their own for as long as their supply of hand grenades lasted. "Many times, we were bombed from the position and regained it until bombs ran out," notes the war diary. At that point, they were forced to pull back to the third line from where they used their rifles and Lewis Guns to keep the Germans at bay. Parties of men were ordered to collect as many grenades as they could find – British and German – and when they had built up a healthy supply they attacked again and once more reached their objective. Meanwhile, the German machine-guns and artillery were putting down a fearsome curtain of lead and steel on No-Man's-Land, and this was effectively stemming the movement of reinforcement and supplies up to the attacking troops. The British counter-battery fire was not sufficiently strong to deal with this. There were simply not enough guns to bombard the enemy trenches *and* seek out and destroy their artillery batteries.[47] Without grenades, the Warwickshires could not continue to resist the persistent attention of the German defenders and again they were forced to withdraw, enemy machine-gunners and snipers taking a heavy toll as they went. Arriving back in the third line, they were able to hold on there until they were relieved and made their way to the rear. The journey back across no-man's land was as dreadful as the initial attack. 2nd Lt Turner described it thus: "Oh that awful journey. The dead and the dying, lying, crawling along the ground…my God!"[48] From there they eventually moved back to Mailly-Maillet, arriving at about 11.00pm. The battalion's casualty list was compiled the following morning after a unit roll-call. They had lost eight officers and 57 other ranks killed in action, including the Commanding Officer, Lt Col Edgar Innes. 12 officers and 255 other ranks were reported wounded, one officer was listed as wounded and missing, and another (2nd Lt F R Brettell) was wounded and a prisoner. 251 other ranks were missing.[49] Writing to the father of 2nd Lt Brettell, 2nd Lt Anstey said: "…our regiment was roughly handled but thank God we did our duty and have made a name in the British Army which will never be forgotten."[50]

The 1/6th Royal Warwickshires left their assembly trenches 10 minutes behind the 1/8th and walked straight into the teeth of the blizzard of German fire. They had lost 80 men before they even crossed their own front lines and quickly became mixed up with the preceding unit. They got as far as the German third line and could see that the other 11th Brigade units to

---

47  R Prior and T Wilson, pp.171-72.
48  IWM, Turner Papers.
49  TNA WO 95/2756: 1/8th Royal Warwickshire Regiment War Diary
50  IWM, Brettell Papers.

their right had managed to go no further. To their left, they were able to observe that some elements of the 31st Division had managed to reach Serre. The 12th Brigade following behind, were unable to make any further progress. The battalion's single unwounded officer, 2nd Lt J G Cooper, managed to return to the Brigade's advanced headquarters with a situation report, but no further forward movement was possible, and eventually this battalion too was forced to pull back. Their casualties amounted to 120 listed as killed or missing and 316 wounded. The dead included seven officers with three others listed as missing, believed killed. Among the wounded they had accounted for was their Commanding Officer, Lt Col W H Franklin.[51]

To the north-west of the Heidenkopf, during the night of 30th June/1st July, the remainder of the Warwickshire Brigade were in the trenches between John Copse and the Puisieux Road, the 1/7th on the right and the 1/5th on the left. Their job was to hold that section of the line and create a smoke screen to hide the troops attacking to their right. At 0720 they duly discharged their smoke candles and P Bombs[52] from the front-line trenches. Although not attacking, these two battalions successfully managed to attract the attention of a portion of the enemy's artillery, which bombarded their trenches at intervals throughout the day. Casualties were light. The 1/5th reported 1 other rank killed, 1 missing, three officers and 21 other ranks wounded. The 1/7th had a similar experience. This battalion formed a carrying party of 65 other ranks to move ammunition for the 4-in Stokes mortars which were to advance when the planned defensive flank was consolidated. But since no defensive flank was created, they did not leave the British trenches. There were 19 casualties, including four fatalities in the carrying party, but among the troops holding the trenches there were only three casualties during the whole of the day. Conversely, no-man's land to the right of the 1/7th was "strewn with bodies [of the men of 31st Division] after the attack". Many wounded were trying to crawl back, being sniped at by the Germans opposite (reported by Lt E W Fowler). The two Warwickshire battalions remained in the trenches overnight and the next day reported that there were still wounded in no-man's land making efforts to reach the safety of the British line.[53]

At 1630 on 1st July, Hunter-Weston telephoned Fanshawe to discuss the situation. At this time, part of 31st Division was believed to be in Serre and part of the 4th Division in the front-line German trenches at the Heidenkopf. The remainder of VIII Corps was back where it had started at 0730 that morning. The Corps Commander proposed a new attack by 48th Division, southwards from John Copse. Fanshawe would have been well-aware of the fate of 31st Division's earlier attack, and the low likelihood of success of a further assault over the same ground, in much less favourable circumstances, with the defenders alerted and no longer occupied by flanking attacks. He set off at once to Corps Headquarters for a face-to-face discussion with his boss, returning at 2000 after which the action was postponed and then cancelled.[54]

However, in its place VIII Corps ordered Fanshawe to plan and deliver a separate attack, timed to commence at dawn on the morning of 3rd July. This was to be part of a new Fourth Army push, with VIII Corps tasked to secure the German intermediate line between Beaucourt

---

51   TNA WO 95/2755: 1/6th Royal Warwickshire Regiment War Diary
52   Phosphorus Bombs. The phosphorus burned on contact with the air and gave off a dense cloud of smoke. These were designed to create a smoke screen to 'shield' troops from enemy fire, but they could cause serious burns if the phosphorus made contact with bare skin.
53   TNA WO 95/2756: 1/7th Royal Warwickshire Regiment War Diary.
54   TNA WO 95/2745: 48th Division General Staff War Diary.

Redoubt and Serre. The 48th Division was to advance from the line now being held by 29th Division on the Corps's right boundary, from the Ancre River to the southern edge of Hawthorne Ridge, east of Auchonvillers and west of Beaumont Hamel. 143rd Brigade was still recovering from its mauling on the opening day of the battle and would not be in a fit state to fight again until it had been rested and its losses made good. Its place was filled by the 88th Brigade from 29th Division, with three of its four battalions still largely intact bringing Fanshawe's force up to something approaching full strength for the coming action. At 0800 on 2nd July, Fanshawe called in the commanders of his two fresh infantry brigades, 144th and 145th, and after a discussion, dictated orders for the operation. They were to seize and hold the high ground north of the Ancre as a defensive southern flank, with 145th Brigade on the right from the river, 88th Brigade in the centre and 144th Brigade on the left, with its left boundary on the northern edge of Y Ravine. An artillery bombardment would pound the German positions to be attacked, beginning that afternoon, and increasing in intensity prior to and during the advance. Smoke screens would obscure the enemy's view from both flanks (if the wind was favourable). Zero was set for 0315, the guns lifting from the enemy front line at 0320 and from the second line at 0325.

At 1900, 145th Brigade left its bivouacs south of Mailly-Maillet and marched to assembly trenches in the 29th Division's line, north of the river, with 144th Brigade setting off an hour later. The latter's officers were probably aware that they were being asked to lead their men in an advance over the same ground on which the Newfoundland Regiment of 88th Brigade had been cut to pieces by German machine-gun fire two days earlier. It must have come as something of a relief then, when they received a flash message from their divisional headquarters, cancelling the operation and ordering both brigades to return to their billets. They arrived back at Mailly-Maillet at around 0430, footsore and fatigued, but no doubt thankful for their little piece of good fortune. There were rumours that they would be required to attack that night or early the next morning, but these proved groundless. Rawlinson had been urged by Haig, to hold in his current position in the centre and north and to concentrate instead on the sector south of the Ancre, between Longueval and Bazentin Le Grand.[55] As a result, on 4th July, 144th Brigade relieved 143rd Brigade in the trenches north of John Copse, while 145th Brigade took over the line being held by 93rd and 94th Brigades from John Copse to the Serre Road. At 11pm that night Fanshawe assumed responsibility for the whole of his own line as well as the section that had been previously held by the 31st Division.

Although the men would not have realised it – nor cared very much at the time – the 48th Division, together with the whole of VIII Corps and X Corps, had just transferred from Rawlinson's Fourth Army to General Sir Hubert Gough's Reserve Army (later to be named the Fifth Army)[56], and while they would continue in their present positions for several days, they would soon be on the move to another part of the Somme battlefield, where they would make intimate acquaintances with the villages of Ovillers–La Boisselle and Pozières.

---

55  R Prior and T Wilson, p.186.
56  Haig was already referring to it as the "Vth Army" in his diary entry for 2nd July, but it was not until 30th October 1916 that it was formally designated Fifth Army. See National Library of Scotland, Acc. 3155/97 and TNA WO 95/518: BEF GHQ War Diary.

## Ovillers–La Boisselle

The tiny village of Ovillers, really not much more than a hamlet in 1916, sits on the side of a low hill, near the end of a spur that runs south-west from Courcelette. It is just to the north of the old Roman road – now the D929 – that runs needle-straight from Albert to Baupaume. Ovillers and the neighbouring La Boisselle were on the German front line on 1st July 1916, and had been turned into fortified positions, the cellars of the shell-battered houses providing top-cover for machine gun nests, the slightly-elevated position affording wide fields of fire over the British lines. North of Ovillers, the land continues to rise to the crest of the spur before toppling away into a valley that runs from Authuille, on the banks of the River Ancre, to Mouquet Farm. This was known to the British as Nab Valley. Opposite Authuille on the tip of the Thiepval spur, lay the formidable defences that constituted the Leipzig Salient and beyond Mouquet Farm was Thiepval village. North-east, the ground rises gently towards the village of Pozières, another heavily-fortified position, initially just in front of the German second position, its location providing excellent 360-degree observation for miles in all directions.

On 1st July 1916, Ovillers and La Boisselle had been allocated by Rawlinson as objectives for Lt General Sir William Pulteney's III Corps. The attacks, by 8th Division (Ovillers) and 34th Division (La Boiselle) were preceded by the blowing of huge mines – Y Sap and Lochnagar,[57] which, unlike the charge at Hawthorne Ridge, were both detonated just two minutes before zero at 0728. Despite the damage, disruption and dislocation of the German defences caused by the explosions, these attacks were repulsed, with both divisions sustaining very heavy losses. 34th Division's casualties were the highest of any British division on that bloodiest of days.[58]

Haig was deterred neither by the casualty numbers nor the lack of early success and was determined to push on, noting in his diary that "on a sixteen-mile front of attack varying fortunes must be expected".[59] In any case, with the French still under considerable pressure at Verdun, it was vital to keep on attacking astride the Somme if there was to be any chance of forcing the Germans to shift their focus – and their reserves – to the north. Throwing in the towel and closing down the offensive after one day would have been considered by France, Russia and Italy to be a significant default against the terms of the Chantilly agreement.[60]

12th (Eastern) Division received orders on 2nd July to attack and capture Ovillers, while 19th (Western) Division was to take La Boisselle. These actions would be coordinated with a renewed X Corps assault at Thiepval. The 12th Division advance was to be made with two brigades, starting at 0315 on the 3rd, following an hour of intensive artillery bombardment. The divisional war diary complains that there was very little time available to make the necessary arrangements and to reconnoitre the ground before zero. To make matters worse, at 0300 the next morning, III Corps headquarters telephoned to say that the X Corps attack to the north had been postponed but that the 12th and 19th divisions' advances must continue as planned. They had mixed fortunes. In the north, the attacking brigades managed to penetrate

---

57  Named after the British trenches from which they were excavated. The Lochnagar Crater remains, a much-visited feature of the Somme battlefield. The Y Sap Crater was filled in by the landowner in the 1970s.
58  G Sheffield, p 55.
59  G Sheffield and J Bourne, p.196.
60  G Sheffield, p.75.

the German lines at Ovillers but soon ran short of bombs and were forced to pull back to their starting position. They had sustained significant casualties, losing 97 officers and 2277 other ranks (including 12 officers and 143 other ranks killed). To the south, however, 19th Division managed to clear La Boisselle after some tough fighting and to consolidate their hard-won gains.

Later that day (4th July), the task of securing Ovillers–La Boisselle was given to the Reserve Army. Operation Order Number 5, of that date, stated that Gough's priority in the immediate future was the capture of the village, noting that as a result of the operations to date "the enemy's strength had been gradually reduced and his reserves drawn into battle and worn out".[61] Now was the time "to continue operations relentlessly and allow the enemy no respite".[62] The job of taking the village was promptly handed to Morland and X Corps (to which 12th Division had been transferred). On 5th July, Reserve Army issued new orders instructing Morland to relieve III Corps at La Boisselle and to prepare a new attack on Ovillers, with zero set for 0800 on the 7th. This was to be a joint operation, involving two brigades of 12th Division and 74th Brigade of 25th Division, under the command of 12th Division's GOC, Maj General Arthur Scott.[63] Some ground was gained, at significant cost, before a now-exhausted 12th Division handed over to 25th and 32nd Divisions on 9 July, to continue the advance. Further slow but definite progress was made against determined opposition and heavy artillery and machine gun fire, before, on 13th July, with 25th Division badly depleted, 143rd Brigade was detached from 48th Division in front of Serre and bussed across to support further attacks.

The South Midlanders' first taste of their new sector came on 14th July, and it was not one to be savoured. In coordination with a Fourth Army attack against the German second line, two battalions of 143rd Brigade were ordered to support 25th Division to complete the capture of Ovillers and extend to the north-east. With 1/5th Royal Warwickshires held in reserve in cellars and dugouts at La Boisselle, 1/7th Royal Warwickshires was directed to push patrols across the Albert–Pozières Road to the east of the village and move directly to capture a section of German line that would later be known as Sickle Trench. Once there, they would be joined by other elements of the battalion moving up over the open. Having consolidated the position, they were then to bomb down an old communication trench towards the village and establish a blocking position while two brigades of 25th Division (7th and 75th) assaulted from the south, and 14 Brigade of 32nd Division from the west, hopefully catching the enemy between the three forces and leaving them with little choice but to surrender or die.

It was a good plan on paper, but it failed almost as soon as it was launched. At 0400 the Warwickshires' patrols set out towards Sickle Trench as ordered, but moving in daylight, they were quickly spotted by the defenders, and sustained heavy casualties before withdrawing back to their starting point to the north of La Boisselle. The remainder of the battalion attempted to move forward over the open ground but suffered a similar fate. The leading platoon advanced about 70 yards before coming under heavy machine gun fire, which stopped them in their

---

61 TNA WO 95/518: Reserve Army War Diary.
62 TNA WO 95/518: Reserve Army War Diary.
63 Maj General Arthur Binny Scott, a Second Anglo-Boer War veteran, later served in India. He died when a VI rocket landed on his house, Red Lodge (now Red Leys), Chestnut Lane, Chesham Bois, Buckinghamshire. Ironically, Maj Gen Scott and his wife had moved from their previous home in West London to escape the Blitz.

tracks. The second and third platoons never got beyond the parapet of their jumping off trench, losing about a third of their number to the enemy machine guns in just a few minutes. Seeing that movement over open ground was a death sentence, it was decided to move the men up through the 3rd Worcesters (7th Brigade, 25th Division), who had advanced on the right of the Warwickshires and had managed to get into the southern end of Sickle Trench. On the map, this appeared to be a deep, well-traversed fire-trench, but, in reality, it was very shallow – in some parts no more than two feet deep – and it was enfiladed by machine guns firing from north of Ovillers. Further heavy casualties were sustained by the Warwickshires before the Brigade Major, Maj Percy Whalley, who was on the spot, conferred with the Commanding Officer of the Worcesters and agreed that the Warwickshires should be withdrawn. They had lost four officers and 45 other ranks killed and three officers and 165 other ranks wounded, including the battalion's Commanding Officer, Lt Col J M Knox.[64]

The following day, the remainder of 48th Division moved across from the Serre area and relieved the 32nd Division on the left of the 25th Division (143rd Brigade remained attached to 25th Division). On 16th July, The Warwickshire Brigade cooperated with 74th and 75th Brigades in a further attack on Ovillers. This time all three brigades were advancing in line from southeast to northwest with 1/5th Royal Warwickshires on the right, 75th Brigade in the centre and 74th Brigade on the left. Zero was set for 0100 but it appears that the Warwickshires were late getting to their start line. The 143rd Brigade War Diary records that they reported reaching the assembly area at 0100 and they were ordered not to attack unless they could do so before 0215. They obviously went ahead, however, because at 0350 they reported that they were in the German trench on the eastern outskirts of the village and consolidating, although they had enemy troops to their front and on both flanks. 74th Brigade failed to make progress, probably owing to the late showing of the Warwickshires, who, nevertheless, held on to their position throughout the rest of the day as 74th and 75th Brigades made repeated attempts to bomb their way through to them from the south and west. At about 0630 the following morning, with 74th Brigade making progress, Germans began to appear from dugouts between the two British forces and surrendered, obviously recognising that further resistance was futile as their withdrawal route had been cut off by the Warwickshires. Two officers and 124 other ranks were taken prisoner along with three machine guns. The attack had cost the Warwickshires three officers, and 35 other ranks killed, and four officers and 63 other ranks wounded. The remainder of 143rd Brigade moved up and relieved 74th Brigade, and later that day 143rd Brigade returned to 48th Division command. The Germans had put up a stout defence of the village, which, by that point had held out for 16 days, and exacted a heavy price on the attackers in terms of the numbers killed, wounded and missing and ordnance expended. But the relentless British assaults had driven the garrison to the edge of exhaustion. Cut off and running out of ammunition, food and water, they had little option but to capitulate. On 17th July the 144th Brigade moved forward to continue the advance through the village and by the afternoon Ovillers was finally in British possession, the last of the defenders putting up their hands at about 1700.[65]

If the men of 48th Division thought the fall of Ovillers signalled a break from the fighting, however, they were in for a disappointment. No sooner had the village been made secure than

---

64 TNA WO 95/2754: 143rd Brigade War Diary.
65 TNA WO 95/2754: 143rd Brigade War Diary

Gough and his staff at Reserve Army headquarters began to look to their next objective, a little further along the Albert–Bapaume Road.

## Pozières

Pozières is situated on high ground astride the Albert–Bapaume road. In geographical terms its location is really no more than the crest of a low ridge, but in an area that is characterised by rolling chalk downland, its relative height provides commanding views of the surrounding territory, particularly of Thiepval, which was perhaps the key to unlocking this sector of the Somme front. The modern-day visitor can test this by standing on the ruins of the Pozières Windmill, just off the Roman Road and taking in the vista in all directions. It was this all-round observation that gave Pozières its significance for British and the Germans alike and why Rawlinson and Haig had identified it as a day-one objective. With Pozières in their hands, the allies could potentially take Thiepval from the rear. As the days went by, this would become an increasingly attractive solution, particularly in the wake of the disastrous failure of the more direct, frontal approach attempted on 1st July, and the losses incurred there by the 36th (Ulster) Division and the 32nd Division.

The village, with its nearby windmill, Gibraltar Blockhouse, and the neighbouring Mouquet Farm ("Moo Cow Farm" or "Mucky Farm" to the soldiers), has, rightly, become synonymous with the ANZACs, to which the credit for capturing the village is justifiably ascribed. But it was not only Australians who bled and died in the fields and trenches around Pozières during the Battle of the Somme. Much South Midland blood was also spilled in the bitter fighting to capture this place and its name should hold the same significance for the 48th Division and the villages, towns and cities of Buckinghamshire, Berkshire, Oxfordshire, Gloucestershire, Worcestershire, and Warwickshire, as it does for Queensland, Victoria and New South Wales.

General William Birdwood's I ANZAC Corps, consisting of the 1st, 2nd, and 4th Australian Divisions, was placed under Gough's orders on 18th July, and on the same day, the 1st Australian Division was split out of the Corps and placed directly under Reserve Army command with a view to conducting an attack on Pozières.[66] The Australians were new to the Western Front. They had fought well against the Turks at Gallipoli the previous year, but they had no experience of the trench warfare that was being waged in France and Belgium… and the Germans were not the Turks. When Haig learned of Gough's plan to throw the Australians at Pozières, he warned him to make sure they were properly prepared. Writing about the discussion in his diary that evening, Haig observed: "I told him [Gough] to go into all the details carefully as the Australians had not been engaged [in France] before and possibly overlooked the difficulties of this kind of fighting."[67] On 20th July, the 1st Australian Division took over a section of the allied line immediately south of Pozières, putting them between the 48th Division and X Corps on their left and III Corps on their right.

With Ovillers in British hands, the 48th Division's 144th and 145th brigades spent the next few days consolidating their gains, reconnoitring the ground ahead, and conducting shaping

---

66 TNA WO 95/518: Reserve Army War Diary.
67 G Sheffield and J Bourne, p.208.

62 A Brilliant Little Victory

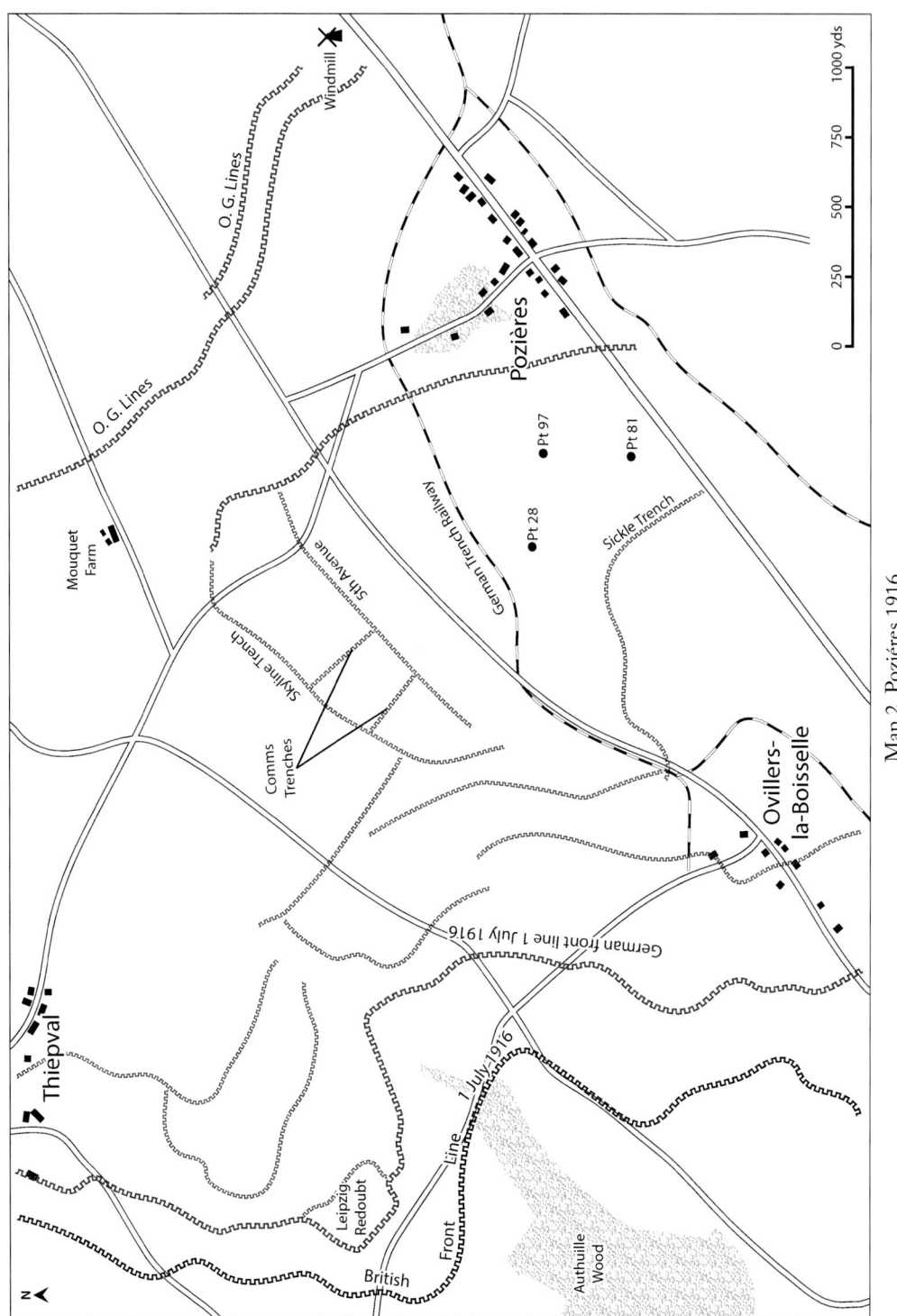

Map 2 Pozières 1916.

operations in preparation for the next big advance. This involved a series of small, limited attacks, pushing north-east from the outskirts of Ovillers, initially to gain the ridge north of the village and secure Mash Valley from enemy observation – at least at ground level. One such action was undertaken by the Bucks Battalion on the night of 17/18th July.

The 145th Brigade orders for the operation required the battalion to conduct a "reconnaissance in force" to assess enemy dispositions at key points to the north of Sickle Trench ahead of a planned attack the following night. The primary aim of the mission was to obtain information, but the orders went on to say that if any of the points were found to be unoccupied, or occupied so lightly that they could be taken "without serious fighting", they were to be captured and held, with reinforcements being called up from the rear. The Bucks Battalion's commanding officer, Lt Colonel Lewis L C Reynolds, allocated the task to A and D Companies, under the command of Capt Edward V D Birchall, Officer Commanding D Company.

During the evening of the 17th, the raiders moved up from behind Ovillers and took up positions in Sickle Trench, ready to move forward at zero, which was set for 0130. At about 0100 on the 18th, a platoon of A Company, led by 2/Lt Brian C Rigden, left the assembly trench and crawled out across no-man's land towards the enemy line, heading for Point 97, which was located about 500 yards west of Pozières. The party managed to get into the position at about 0200 and immediately set about consolidating it for defence, erecting barricades to block the adjoining trenches. The enemy made several attempts to drive them out and these were beaten off, each time repulsed by rifle and Lewis Gun fire and grenades. However, the failure of the other patrols to make similar progress had left Rigden and his men isolated in enemy territory. In a difficult position, the youthful Rigden (he was just 20 years old) took the bold but entirely sensible decision to withdraw his platoon and they made their way back to Sickle Trench in reasonably good order.

Rigden was awarded an immediate Military Cross for his part in this action. His fellow platoon commanders were not so fortunate. 2/Lt Charles Hall, also from A Company, led his platoon towards a point about 400 yards north-west of Rigden's objective, near the light railway line that ran across the sector, roughly from north-east to south-west. This platoon was held up by machine gun fire before it reached its target and Hall was ordered to withdraw, which he did, sustaining a serious head wound as he helped to bring in casualties. 2/Lt Robert C Norwood's platoon, from D Company, had a similar experience as it headed to a point about 150 yards west of Hall's objective. Norwood was hit by machine gun fire soon after leaving Sickle Trench, and command of the patrol passed on the platoon sergeant, who managed to lead the men forward, but was then ordered to withdraw. Norwood had been seen to fall but it was a very dark night, and his men were unable to find him as they made their way back. He was posted as missing, presumed killed, and this was how his loss was recorded in the battalion history, published in July 1920.[68] However, his story does not end there. That same year, 1920, members of a Canadian burial party helping to clear the battlefield around Pozières, was working just in front of the northern end of Sickle Trench when they found the decomposed remains of a British officer. The bones and remnants of uniform were identified as those of 2/Lt Robert Cecil Norwood, and he was reinterred in the nearby Pozières British Cemetery where he now lies in Plot 1, Row C, Grave 39 – just a few hundred yards from where he fell that July night in 1916.[69]

---

68  PL Wright, p.26.
69  *CWGC* <www.cwgc.org.> (accessed 12th March 2023).

These operations did not result in the permanent capture of any German trench, but they were, nonetheless, regarded as a success, achieving the principal aim of identifying enemy dispositions in the area, for which the Bucks Battalion received the congratulations of the Army Commander (Gough).[70] The information gained would be invaluable to Army, Corps and Divisional staff who were by then conducting detailed planning for the capture of Pozières village.

However, before that could happen, there was more "shaping" to be done to create the best possible conditions for the Australian advance. This included further efforts to clear the enemy from the trenches immediately to the west of the village to prevent them from interfering with the ANZACs when they made their assault from the south, across the Albert–Bapaume Road. The enemy had been on this ground for two years and they had used that time wisely, constructing strong, layered defences, heavily wired, with multiple machine guns positioned between each line of trenches and also in the rear, often on higher ground where they had good fields of fire over the territory being defended. Although Pozières village had been pounded into rubble by artillery fire, the cellars of many of the houses remained intact. These had been fortified, with good overhead protection, and linked up by subterranean passageways, creating a very strong defensive position.[71]

Progress to the north was steady but it was a slow, grinding, fatigue-inducing, costly, often hand-to-hand fight in which the results were measured in yards won and lost. The German "potato-masher" stick grenade, with a wooden handle which allowed it to be hurled farther than the British Mills Bomb, gave the defenders a distinct advantage in the numerous skirmishes that developed, but the South Midlanders were undeterred. The attackers would bomb their way along a section of trench, driving the garrison out. When they could go no farther, they established a "bomb block" and called up the Royal Engineers and pioneers to build a strong, defensive position that could withstand the inevitable enemy counter-attacks. Once the new position was secure, they would repeat the process, each time pushing the enemy a little further back until defence became untenable. At that point, the Germans might pull back to the next defensive line, or, if the way back was blocked, capitulate. But, as was their custom, the Germans yielded ground very grudgingly and they made the attackers pay dearly in blood and treasure for every yard that was won.

On 18th July, new orders were issued by the division for a coordinated attack north from Ovillers, 144th Brigade on the left and 145th Brigade on the right, commencing at 0130 the following morning. On the left, this was launched as directed but made little progress due to heavy cross-fire from enemy machine gun teams engaging at short range. By 0300 the attackers were back at their start point.[72] On the right, the 1/4th Oxfords had a similar outcome, the attacking troops losing direction in the face of very strong enemy resistance. A second attack was organised but was countermanded by divisional headquarters as it could not be conducted before daylight. Meanwhile, 1/8th Worcesters, who had been detailed to provide a working party to dig a new communications trench astride the Albert–Pozières road, were subjected to a heavy gas and HE barrage, suffering 58 casualties due to gas and several more as a result of the HE.[73] Later that night, 1/5th Gloucesters were ordered to bomb up an enemy trench to capture

---

70  TNA WO 95/2745: 48th Division General Staff War Diary.
71  AWM 1/42/18 1st Australian Division General Staff War Diary.
72  TNA WO 95/2757: 144th Brigade War Diary.
73  TNA WO 95/2745: 48th Division General Staff War Diary.

point 79, a trench junction about 1000 yards west of Pozières. The attack was supposed to be supported by Stokes Mortars, but it proved impossible to bring up sufficient mortar ammunition for the task in time and the Gloucesters made the assault unsupported, gaining some ground but failing to secure the position. They were pushed back and established a bombing block about 40 yards short of their objective, where they consolidated.[74]

On the 20th the division spent the day licking its wounds and resting ahead of the next move. That night the 1/6th Gloucesters were able to move the left flank of 144th Brigade forward slightly, before being driven back again by a counter-attack. The right of the brigade also tried to advance with the assistance of Stokes mortars and machine guns, but this was halted by heavy enemy machine gun fire.

With just over 24 hours to go before Gough unleashed the Australians on Pozières, the 48th Division made a final attempt to push its line to the north. Orders were issued for another carefully-choreographed, deliberate attack on the same objectives by the same brigades, again with 144th on the left and 145th on the right. The assault was to be carried out behind a short, intense bombardment. The infantry would enter the enemy trenches almost in the barrage, which was timed to lift off the objectives at zero plus two minutes. The divisional machine guns were detailed to give intimate and area support. Some guns would provide short-range cover, raking enemy flanking positions to the east, and the objective itself, until the assaulting troops were almost upon it. Others would engage the enemy's rear areas and depth positions in a bid to supress hostile fire and prevent reinforcements or counter-attackers from moving up over the open. Smoke was to be used to screen the attacking troops from observation from the east, north and west. 2-inch Trench Mortars, sometimes known as "toffee apples" would target enemy positions on the left. Importantly, there were specific orders to avoid over-loading the attackers with unnecessary equipment. On 1st July, many assaulting troops were weighed down with picks and shovels and other defence stores, restricting their movement across no-man's land. Now they were directed "to go as light as possible, taking plenty of bombs and ammunition…"[75]

Zero was set for 0245 on the 21st.[76] 145th Brigade, on the right, nearest Pozières, allocated the job to the 1/5th Gloucesters and the 1/1st Bucks Battalion. The attacking units moved into their assembly areas before midnight, with the Bucks Battalion taking over the southern end of Sickle Trench from the 1/4th Berkshires. At around 0230 on a clear, moonlit morning, both battalions moved out into no-man's land and formed up, each on a two-company front, along a tape, about 175 yards from the German lines. The tape had been laid earlier by Royal Engineers. Reporting on the action to divisional headquarters afterwards, the Bucks Battalion CO, Lt Col Lewis Reynolds noted that "everything went like clockwork up to the assault".[77] But from then on it was a disaster. With the attacking troops in their jumping off positions, the enemy suddenly began to launch numerous white flares. These were followed a few minutes later by red

---

74  TNA WO 95/2763: 1/5th Gloucestershire Regiment War Diary.
75  TNA WO 95/2745: 48 Division General Staff War Diary.
76  The 145th Brigade War Diary and 1/1st Bucks War diary record that zero was 0245. However, the Gloucestershire Regimental history claims it was 2330. This is probably based on the war diary account, which appears to be wrong. The Brigade orders are clear that zero was to be 0245 and the 1/5th Gloucesters CO states in a written report on the action for divisional headquarters that the leading companies deployed for the attack at 0230. See TNA WO 95/2760: 145th Brigade War Diary and WO 95/2745: 48th Division War Diary.
77  TNA WO 95/2745: 48th Division General Staff War Diary.

flares, which were the signal for the enemy machine guns to open fire. Reynolds continued: "The enemy opened terrific machine gun and rifle fire 10 minutes before the barrage commenced, which [the barrage] had absolutely no effect on the enemy, who kept up their fire throughout."[78] Capt Philip Wright, of 1/1st Bucks observed:

> So long as the hands of the watch did not point to 2.45am it was possible to lie flat, though even so some few were hit. The moment to go forward, however, arrived, and still the German machine guns chattered unceasingly. At 2.45am our guns opened with a roar and shells flew over our heads by the thousands, busting their shrapnel in a line of flashes along the trench opposite us. It was the signal to advance.[79]

By this point, however, few men were able to move forward. As men rose, they were cut down by the enemy machine guns, although some managed to struggled on. Reynolds recorded that as his men approached the trench they were met with "a very thick barrage of bombs". The attackers got as far as the parapet. One or two brave souls managed to jump down into the trench but too few to stand any chance of taking the position against a plentiful and determined foe. Eventually, the withering machine gun fire forced the Bucks men back. Concluding his report, Reynolds attributed his battalion's failure "largely to the absolute ineffectiveness of our barrage". In addition, with the moon at their backs, the attackers were clearly silhouetted as soon as they started to advance, making easy targets for machine gunners and riflemen alike.

Meanwhile, on the left of the 145th Brigade line, the 1/5th Gloucesters, attacking with three companies forward and the fourth in support, like the Bucks, managed to get into their jumping-off position unseen by 0230. On their left, however, the Worcesters, who were attacking with 144th Brigade, were spotted and enemy fire was opened all along their front. Unlike the Bucks Battalion's experience, the British preparatory barrage here succeeded in checking the enemy fire, allowing the companies to rush forward as the barrage fell, but as soon as it lifted the enemy resumed heavy machine gun and rifle fire, taking a heavy toll on the leading platoons. The Gloucesters were also forced back without achieving their objectives.

Submitting his commanding officers' reports of the fighting to division, the 145th Brigade commander, Brigadier-General H R Done, in a covering note, praised the efforts of both battalions. The Bucks, he said, seemed to have carried out their attack with great determination and to have very nearly succeeded. The Gloucesters' attack appeared to have "hung fire", owing to the men being seen and fired upon before the assault commenced. Done concluded by suggesting that in order to gain success by night assaults on strongly-held posts, the barrage must be very heavy and very accurate. He believed that in this instance the barrage, lasting only two minutes had not been sufficient.[80]

Both battalions suffered heavy losses. The 1/5th Gloucesters reported three officers missing, presumed killed. These included Lt William Fream, 2/Lt Cyril Vincent Noel Puckridge and 2/Lt J Farrimond. All three have no known grave and are commemorated on the Thiepval Memorial. Capt H C B Sessions, Officer Commanding C Company and 2/Lt P Badham were wounded in action, Among the other ranks, five were killed in action, 79 wounded and 45

---

78 TNA WO 95/2745: 48th Division General Staff War Diary.
79 P L Wright, pp.28-29.
80 TNA WO 95/2760: 145th Brigade War Diary.

reported as missing. The Bucks Battalion had four officers killed and three wounded. The dead included one of the unit's most-popular and long-serving company commanders, Capt Lionel William Crouch of B Company. Lionel Crouch (29) was a son of William Crouch, a Clerk of the Peace to Buckinghamshire County Council and Helen Marian Crouch. The family home was at Friarscroft in Aylesbury. Educated at Marlborough College from 1900 to 1904, he qualified as a solicitor in 1909 and worked for the Aylesbury legal firm, Horwood and James. His brother, Capt Guy Crouch, later commanded B Company before transferring to the 1/5th Gloucesters in 1918. Lionel Crouch was originally buried by his unit close to where he fell. He was later reinterred in the Pozières Military Cemetery (grave 1.D.17). His original battlefield grave marker (a wooden cross bearing identification details), and his medal group, are in the Buckinghamshire Military Museum Trust's collection. The other officer fatalities were 2/Lt Charles Gordon Abrey (23) and 2/Lt Charles William Trimmer (19), who are both buried in Pozières Military Cemetery (1.C.20 and 1.C.9), and 2/Lt John Percy Chapman (34) who is named on the Thiepval Memorial. The wounded included 2/Lt Brian Rigden, who had just been awarded the Military Cross for his actions on 18th July, 2/Lt H C E Mason, and 2/Lt H V Shepherd. Capt G G Jackson, OC C Company, was originally reported as missing presumed dead, but was later discovered to have been wounded and taken prisoner. Other Ranks casualties were 7 killed, 97 wounded and 42 missing.

Recording the action in his battalion history, Capt Philip Wright noted that the failure to take its assigned objectives was "a great blow" to the unit, as it was their first serious attack. "It was as disappointed and sadder men that we made our way back to the bivouacs [near Albert]: nearly everyone had lost a real pal, temporarily or for always."[81]

The battalion was exhausted after its exertions. The men needed a hot meal and rest, and the Commanding Officer needed to reorganise his now depleted force, which was very short of officers and NCOs. Luckily, four officers had been Left Out of Battle (LOB) for the attack, and they were able to fill some of the gaps. Unluckily, there would be little time to rest or re-organise. At 1500 on 22nd July, new orders were received, calling the battalion forward again and warning them to be prepared to support the planned attack on Pozières the following morning. At 2200 the still-weary Buckinghamshire men buckled on their kit, picked up their weapons, and trudged back up the road to Mash Valley, between La Boisselle and Ovillers.

The Reserve Army's orders for the attack on Pozières on 22nd and 23rd July make it clear that this was a subsidiary action to a much larger attack, which was the Fourth Army's assault on the German switch line that ran past the north-eastern end of Pozières and then on through the northern side of High Wood. The 1st Australian Division was to conduct a three-stage attack on Pozières itself while the 48th Division would seek to push its line north and east. The right flank would attempt to join up with the Australians on the western edge of the village.[82] Once again, Fanshawe ordered 144th and 145th Brigades to do the heavy lifting. This meant renewing their attacks on either side of the light railway that ran from Ovillers, past the northern outskirts of Pozières, and then on to Martinpuich. 144th Brigade, to the west of the railway, would first secure point 90 and point 23 before attacking point 40 from the west and north. 145th Brigade were to take point 79 from the west and north and point 40 from the east and north. 143rd

---

81 P L Wright, p.30.
82 TNA WO 95/518: Reserve Army War Diary.

Brigade were to occupy part of the front held by 145th Brigade, providing a firm base against potential enemy counter-attacks.

Mindful that a short, intense artillery bombardment had failed to silence the enemy machine guns in the previous attack, Fanshawe opted for a four-hour barrage this time, with zero set for 0030 to comply with the Australians initial assault on the German defences to the south-west of the village. On the left, 144th Brigade attacked with a single battalion, 1/6th Gloucesters. They ran into heavy machine gun fire and a German 5.9in barrage including HE, poison and lachrymatory gas, which caused heavy casualties. The battalion could not get forward and eventually called off their advance, the survivors withdrawing back to their starting point. On the right, 145th Brigade assaulted with two battalions forward, 1/4th Oxfords on the right and 1/5th Gloucesters. The Oxfords met with mixed fortunes. On the right, A Company reached their objectives quickly, taking Point 97, Point 81 and Point 28 by about 0200. D Company, going forward on the left, was met by a stiff barrage of bombs when they were 30 yards from the objective, and lost a number of men. A party led by a sergeant managed to enter the enemy trench between Points 28 and 81 but was bombed out again, although they re-organised themselves and later took part in A Company's successful assault on Point 28. The Gloucesters, however, were stopped by heavy machine gun and artillery fire. The attacking companies, A and C, found the enemy trenches strongly held and they were unable to make progress, despite calling up reinforcements from the support company (B).

At about 0500, having taken stock of the situation and considered his options, Fanshawe ordered the Bucks Battalion back into the fight. They were to launch a new assault on the Gloucesters' original objectives, behind a second, heavy artillery barrage. This advance was timed for 0630. The Bucks had to struggle forward from their stand-by positions behind Ovillers and at Brigade headquarters there was some doubt as to whether the battalion would be in its jumping-off position in time. However, this pessimism was unfounded, and the attack went in as planned. The assaulting companies, D on the right and B on the left, were to approach their objectives by advancing along two parallel communications trenches. When just short of the enemy line, they were to get out of the trenches, extend towards each other to join up, and then rush the enemy positions.

B Company, led by Capt Oscar Viney, ran into the British barrage which was falling well short of the objective. This caused them some casualties and forced them to pull back. The resulting confusion meant they were unable to take part in the assault as it had been planned. However, one platoon managed to work their way up the communications trench and into their objective. On the right, D Company, commanded by Capt Edward Birchall, fared better. They managed to pass through an enemy barrage of 5.9s, and, keeping right up to the British bombardment, reached the enemy trench before the guns lifted and while the occupants were still in their dugouts. This was confirmed by a German officer who admitted that his men had been taken by surprise, waiting for the barrage to lift.[83] Seeing that D Company was on its objective, Capt N S Reid brought the support company, A, straight up the communication trench, and together with D Company, began to consolidate the position before the enemy were able to react. They then fought off numerous German bombing attacks. During the afternoon, a bombing section reached Point 40 and advanced about 90 yards along the German trench before

---

83   P L Wright, p.33.

being driven back by rifle grenades and a heavy artillery barrage. The Bucks Battalion held their gains until relieved by 1/5th Gloucesters at noon on 24th July and went back to bivouacs in Albert. Again, the battalion's casualties were severe. Capt Birchall had been badly wounded in the leg during the break-in. He was evacuated back to a casualty clearing station in the rear, and eventually to a base hospital at Etaples where he died of wounds on 10th August. He was 32 years old, the son of Mr John and Emily Birchall of Bowden Hall, Gloucester. 8 Other Ranks were killed in action. Capt Oscar Viney was wounded, together with Lt E N C Wollerton and 70 Other Ranks. 8 men were reported missing. The 1/5th Gloucesters counted 13 dead, including platoon commander, 2/Lt W B Lycett (Northamptonshire Regiment, attached). Four Company Commanders were among the 117 wounded. 23 Other Ranks were posted missing. 1/4th Oxfords' casualties totalled 240. Two company commanders, Capt B B B Brooks and Capt J E Blake, and 40 Other Ranks had been killed. Eight officers were wounded, including one Company Commander and seven platoon commanders, together with 164 Other Ranks. Five men were reported missing believed killed, and three were missing believed wounded.

Left largely unmolested by depth fire from their left flank, where the enemy were kept fully occupied by the 48th Division attack, the 1st Australian Division made good progress as it assaulted the village from the south-east. By 0400 the area south of the Bapaume Road had been captured with the exception of some ruined houses on the extreme north-east. This had been achieved in three bounds, each covered by a heavy artillery bombardment. By 0900 the Australian line had been advanced across the road and by 2100 they had secured about half of the village in the direction of the cemetery. But it would take another two days of hard, yard-by-yard fighting before the village was finally cleared.[84] On 25th July 143rd Brigade finally closed the gap between 48th Division and the 1st Australian Division, advancing north and east to gain contact with the Australians just north of the village.

The following days were spent consolidating the gains and continuing the step-by-step push north with the ultimate aim of taking Mouquet Farm and potentially cutting off Thiepval. The Australians, meanwhile, were also to extend to their east, to seize the high ground around the Pozières Windmill and achieve observation over Courcelette and Grandcourt. On 28th July, a by now exhausted and greatly-depleted 48th Division was relieved by the 12th Division and moved to the rear for a much needed and very welcome period of rest and rehabilitation in villages mostly to the west of Doullen.

The fighting described above to capture the villages of Ovillers and Pozières, was formative for the 48th Division. This was the time when the South Midlanders went from the relatively straight-forward, static, defensive line-holding and patrolling, as they had been trained for during their time in Flanders, to conducting high-intensity, offensive operations. But the Division's contribution to the opening weeks of the Somme battle, also shows how Fanshawe and his staff had quickly learned the lessons of 1st July and were putting these into effect within days. There would be no more walking across no-man's land with rifles at the high port in the face of enemy machine gun fire and shrapnel. Short but intense artillery bombardments – they were constantly experimenting with the length of the barrage from a couple of minutes to several hours – were used to drive the defenders down into their dug-outs where they could not engage the advancing troops. The attackers, now unencumbered by large amounts of equipment,

---

84  AWM 1/42/18 Part 2: 1st Australian Division War Diary.

were more mobile and agile, allowing them to move quickly over No Man's Land, to rush the front line at speed. This, together with advancing right on the edge of the friendly artillery fire, would hopefully put them on to the objective before the garrison could get out of the dug-outs and into firing positions, as they had done with such deadly and devastating effect on the first day. Indeed, it was now widely believed that if an advancing unit was not taking casualties from its own barrage, it was not keeping close enough to the falling shells. Setting zero hour for the early morning allowed the attackers to take advantage of the darkness to move out into no-man's land unseen, establishing jump-off points within 175 yards of the trenches to be assaulted. But it was important not to set patterns, so the start times often varied considerably, and it was not unusual for infantry advances to begin during daylight, sometimes in the late afternoon. Clearly, these new tactics did not work every time, and they were still a long way from the coordinated, all-arms battle that the British used so effectively during 1918. However, they demonstrate that the 48th Division was a learning organisation. It was not "fixed" by pre or early-war tactics. Fanshawe and his command team demonstrated the mental agility, flexibility – and the moral courage – to learn from experience and to adjust their approach accordingly, all within a very short period of time. The II Corps War Diary contains a detailed "lessons-learned" paper, written by the 36th (Ulster) Division, setting out its experiences on 1/2 July, an assessment of what worked and what did not, and suggestions for improvements in the British approach. The very first of these notes that: "The opportunity for the infantry is the moment at which the artillery lifts. Their success depends chiefly on keeping very close to the barrage, and jumping in the moment that it lifts."[85] Of course, it was not just the allies who were learning during this period: the Germans too were constantly evaluating their own performance as well as that of their enemies and they soon recognised that British success in the assault was often due to their willingness to accept casualties in order to reach the enemy position before the shell fire lifted. As a result, as the battle progressed there is evidence that some German units began to keep troops in their front line during the bombardment, despite the cost in casualties, in order to engage the attackers before they reached the parapet.

## Skyline Trench and Beyond

While the 48th Division began its much-needed break from the fighting, and with Pozières village securely in allied hands, Gough now turned his Reserve Army north, at right-angles to the Bapaume Road, towards Mouquet Farm and the Leipzig Salient. His hope, initially, was that instead of repeating Rawlinson's hideously costly frontal attacks of 1st July, he could roll up these positions from the southern flank, and then punch his way into Thiepval from the rear, using II Corps[86] and the ANZACs as his battering ram. Unfortunately, by opting to nibble at the German line, he was ignoring the lessons of 14th July. On that day, two corps of Rawlinson's Fourth Army, XV and XIII, attacking together, side by side on a broad front along the Bazentin Ridge, secured 6000 yards of the German second line. This was achieved mainly through tactical surprise and by forcing the enemy to defend across a wide area, thus diluting

---

85  TNA WO 95/638: Brief Notes on the Operations of 36th Division on 1st and 2nd July 1916, II Corps War Diary.
86  48th Division had been transferred to II Corps.

the effectiveness of his defensive fire. By choosing to advance in a series of minor actions on a narrow front Gough was undoubtedly achieving concentration of force, a key principle of war. However, by constantly attacking in the same small area of real-estate, he was failing to generate true operational tempo. He might have been getting inside the enemy's decision-action cycle in terms of his day-to-day activities, but his approach was never going to overwhelm the enemy and lead to a breakthrough which might have resulted in the early capture of Thiepval. Instead, he appears to have contented himself with a wholly attritional approach and required his divisional commanders to do likewise. In doing so, he allowed the enemy to focus his machine guns and artillery on the same narrow front, creating the conditions for another long, slow, costly slogging match, advancing yard by yard along the trenches rather than over them, while the Germans exacted a further heavy toll, and the blood of yet more Tommies, Fritzes and Diggers soaked the fields of Picardy. The ANZACs alone sustained 23,000 casualties here in the space of six weeks, equating to the scale of losses they had suffered in eight months during the Gallipoli campaign.[87]

The 48th Division's rest period did not last long. On 7th August, orders were received to return to the front. They were to relieve 12th Division a little to the north of where they had been fighting during the Pozières battle. Two days later the men began the long trek back from whence they had come. In the meantime, on 10th August they transferred to II Corps, coming under the command of Lt General Sir Claud Jacob.

On 13th August 144th Brigade relieved 37th Brigade in trenches to the north of Ovillers, while 145th Brigade took over from 35th Brigade in Fifth and Sixth Avenues. The latter, also known as Skyline Trench, was now part of the British front line in this sector. As its name suggests, it ran along the crest of a ridge on the skyline to the north-east of Ovillers, in the direction of Mouquet Farm, connected to Fifth Avenue by two communications trenches. The 2nd Australian Division was on the right and the 49th Division on the left.

The 48th Division had been ordered to conduct local operations that night to tidy up the situation at the south-western end of Skyline Trench, where the enemy remained in occupation and thus posed a threat to the South Midlanders' left flank. But before that could happen, after a day-long artillery bombardment of Skyline Trench, the enemy attacked at 2200 from the north-west. Their initial thrust against the garrison (1/4th Oxfords) was repulsed. However, a second attempt was successful, the initial entry being made at a point where a machine gun team had been wiped out earlier. Having broken in, the attackers were able to gain possession of a long section from just short of Point 81 in the north-east, the junction with 2nd Australian Division, where a small party of the Oxford managed to hold out, to Point 90 at the south-western end. The 1/4th Royal Berkshires (145th Brigade) counter-attacked with three companies at 0500, advancing from Fifth Avenue "with the greatest bravery, most gallantly led by their officers".[88] But heavy machine-gun fire from the left prevented them from reaching Skyline Trench, and they retired, having lost 32 killed, including 4 officers (Capt Attride, 2/Lt Beasley, 2/Lt Bartram and 2/Lt P G W O'Hara, 3rd East Surrey Regiment, attached), and 84 wounded including 3 officers.[89] 31 were reported missing. Capt Raymond George Attride (26) was the son of Charles and Emma Attride of "Aves", Wellington College, Berkshire. 2/Lt Albert Willliam Beasley

---

87   G Sheffield, p.101.
88   TNA WO 95/2762: 1/4th Royal Berkshire Regiment War Diary.
89   TNA WO95/2762: 1/4th Royal Berkshire Regiment War Diary.

had been a holder of the Military Medal, which suggests that he had been commissioned from the ranks. 2/Lt Patrick G W O'Hara, the son of Major Patrick and Mrs Elizabeth O'Hara, came from Mornington, Crookwood in Co Westmeath, Ireland. All three are commemorated on the Thiepval Memorial. 2/Lt Alan Bartram (24) was originally buried on the banks of the Ancre, behind Thiepval Wood (map ref 57d.Q.30.c.4.3) but at the end of the war his remains were exhumed and he was reinterred in Lonsdale Cemetery on the slopes above the village of Authuille, on the old front line of 1st July, 1916.[90]

With the Germans now in possession of the trench, and busily consolidating the position, the Bucks Battalion, in support, in old gun pits near the Usna Redoubt, west of Ovillers, was ordered to eject them. They moved up during the afternoon of the 14th, through a stiff artillery barrage, taking over from the 1/4th Oxfords in Fifth Avenue. Describing the move, Capt Philip Wright wrote: "…it was one of the most uncomfortable proceedings ever taken part in. The ground all round was going up like a bank of earth due to the enemy's 5.9s and progress was distinctly difficult".[91] But eventually they reached their jumping off position and prepared to assault along an 800-yard front.

The task was allocated to C Company, under Capt Philip Hall, and the plan was to split into two parties and bomb along the communications trenches that connected Fifth Avenue with Skyline Trench. At about 2200 two bombing sections and a rifle platoon, commanded by 2/Lt D Fallon, worked their way along the eastern trench and reached Skyline without opposition. They then extended to their right and eventually made contact with the 2nd Australian Division. 2/Lt J F Arnott with a platoon from D Company, followed Fallon's party and worked to the left. In the meantime, two bombing sections from A Company had advanced up the left communications trench, again without meeting enemy opposition, and worked their way right, joining up with Arnott's D Company men. A bombing block was built at Point 88. By 0500 on the 15th the whole of Skyline Trench with the exception of a small section at the south-west end, was firmly back in 48th Division's possession, with the Bucks Battalion's C and D companies providing the garrison, B Company in support in Fifth Avenue, and A in reserve at Ovillers.[92]

The temporary loss of the trench was clearly of some concern to the Corps Commander, Lt Gen Jacob. A tersely-worded letter, penned by his Brigadier General, General Staff (the Corps Chief of Staff and Jacob's de-facto second-in-command), Brigadier-General Philip Howell[93], demanded "a full report upon the operations of the night of the 13/14th August." This was, he explained, "not merely with the idea of apportioning blame but largely so that the lessons may be taken advantage of for future guidance." The letter then continued to set out a long list of questions to which Jacob required answers, including why there were only two platoons in the trench by night.[94] There is no record of Fanshawe's response to these queries in either the divisional or corps war diaries, although a large number of documents appear to have been removed from the

---

90   *CWGC* <www.cwgc.org.> (accessed 24th March 2022).
91   P L Wright, pp 37-38.
92   TNA WO 95/2763: 1/1st Bucks Battalion War Diary.
93   Brig-Gen Philip Howell was a highly-regarded "rising star" who had been predicted to reach the highest levels in the army. However, this promise was never achieved. He died, aged just 38, during a bombardment near Authuille on 7th October 1916, having just conducted a personal reconnaissance of the ground in front of Thiepval.
94   TNA WO 95/638: II Corps War Diary.

latter at some point. It is, however, reasonable to assume that Fanshawe had thinned his front line in keeping with the principles of his favoured "flexible defence" approach. By doing so, he undoubtedly prevented large numbers of his men from being wounded or killed in the day-long artillery bombardment that proceeded the enemy attack. Although the trench was in German hands for some hours, Fanshawe had ensured that he had troops nearby to conduct a local counter-attack, and when that failed, to deliver a prepared counter-stroke which successfully ejected the enemy and reinstated the status quo ante. But the fact that Jacob had felt it necessary to query the division's defensive posture is evidence that there was some concern at Corps, perhaps a view that Fanshawe's arrangements for holding the line in darkness were not quite in keeping with the Army's extant policy, as set out in the General Staff's *Notes for Infantry Officers on Trench Warfare* of March 1916 which stated:

> By day… the front line should be lightly held in order to minimise loss from shell fire and the enemy's snipers… By night, the front line must be held in sufficient strength to repulse raids by the enemy and to prevent his reconnoitring patrols from penetrating the front line; and also, because in a line thinly held by night the men are apt to become 'jumpy'.[95]

By August 1916, Fanshawe's division had been holding its front lines in accordance with the principles of "flexible defence" for over 10 months. The men would have been well accustomed to operating that way. They may not have liked it; they may not have been very comfortable with it; but it was the 48th Division's way and it had proven results.

In responding to the Corps Commander, Fanshawe would have been justified in pointing out that the German attack on Skyline Trench was neither a raid nor a reconnaissance patrol. It was a well-prepared, well-resourced, deliberate attack at multiple points along a front of nearly 1000 yards, by a clearly determined enemy, who, undeterred by early failure, pursued their assault with vigour until it was successful. This was not merely an attempt to harass the British or to gain intelligence. It was launched with the intention of re-capturing and securing this tactically-important trench in order to drive back the British from their position of advantage overlooking Thiepval and the Leipzig Salient. A more densely-manned front line might have prevented the penetration… but it might not. And if it had, what would the price have been? And would that bill, paid in human flesh and blood, have been greater than the cost of re-taking the position by counter-attack? At a range of more than 100 years, we can never know the answers to these questions. But neither could Jacob nor Fanshawe, looking at the situation after only a few hours. The best they could do was to apply their military judgement and experience and reach their own considered conclusions, about which, sadly, no evidence has survived. Whatever the outcome of Jacob's inquiry, however, Fanshawe continued to lead the South Midland Division, and to practice his doctrine of "flexible defence".

With Skyline Trench now back in British hands, the enemy subjected it to perhaps the heaviest artillery bombardment yet experienced by anyone in the Division. Their infantry having been ejected, the German gunners opened fire at about 1130, initially on the right of Fifth Avenue. At mid-day they began the systematic destruction of Skyline Trench, starting on the right and working their way slowly west. Philip Wright recalled:

---

95  General Staff, *Notes for Infantry Officers on Trench Warfare* (1916).

It seemed as if all the power of destruction in Germany had suddenly got to work on this trench, and that the enemy were determined that, since they were not able to hold it themselves, no other men should either. Every size of shell was flung with unerring accuracy, so that one great volume of smoke rose from the ridge and covered the trench in a dense black pall. This terrific bombardment continued for nine consecutive hours, systematically destroying everything.[96]

By 1500, the battalion commander, Lt Col Lewis Reynolds, decided to pull his men out of Skyline Trench and hold the ends of the communications trenches. At about 2000, with the shellfire continuing unabated, B Company was ordered to establish a new front line in a series of posts 100 yards in rear of the trench. The whole of D Company, and two platoons of C, were pulled back to Fifth Avenue while the remaining two platoons of C were sent back to Third Avenue. The ordeal continued for another hour, after which the enemy fire began to slacken. Casualties among the front-line garrison were heavy. Indeed, there were many, watching from the rear, who wondered how anyone had survived the onslaught. Those that did were absolutely exhausted, physically and mentally. Few men did not suffer a wound of some description. By this point, Skyline Trench was completely uninhabitable, and it was decided to evacuate it entirely and establish a new line of posts in shell-holes to its front.

The Bucks Battalion was nearing breaking point and badly needed to be relieved and allowed to rest. But despite their worn-out state, and with their nerve now sorely tested, the men were ordered to remain in position in order to make one final effort. At midnight on the 15th, in conjunction the 1/5th Gloucesters, A Company, with C and D in support, launched a bombing attack against the portion of trench on the extreme left which was still in enemy hands. The Bucks men pressed the assault with great determination, but, in the end, they were beaten by their own exhaustion. The battered remnants of C and D Companies were simply unable to keep the attackers supplied with sufficient bombs to complete the task. At 1100 that morning (16th), the Bucks Battalion was finally relieved by 1/4th Oxfords and the survivors, bruised, bloodied and battered, wearily dragged themselves back through Ovillers to billets between Albert and Bouzincourt. Despite the intensity of the German bombardment, and the hard fighting that had taken place during their tour of duty, the Bucks Battalion's fatalities were relatively low at 15, all Other Ranks. But a further 163 men had been wounded, including four officers, and 23 were missing.[97] These now needed to be replaced before the unit could again be considered an effective fighting force.

The division did not conduct operations on the night of 16-17th August, but during the 17th the division ordered 143rd Brigade to continue the drive north-west towards the Leipzig Salient while the Australians continued to work forward in the direction of Mouquet Farm. The brigade orders for this were issued at 1130 on the morning of the 18th. These gave each battalion three sets of objectives and stipulated that the units were to advance in waves, with 1/5th Royal Warwickshires on the left and 1/6th Royal Warwickshires on the right. The 1/7th battalion would conduct a subsidiary attack on the extreme left, bombing north along the old German front line facing Authuille Wood. This was designed to protect the left flank of the

---

96   P L Wright, pp.38-39.
97   TNA WO 95/2763: Bucks Battalion War Diary and P L Wright, p.39.

main advance. Meanwhile, 145th Brigade (1/4th Royal Berkshires), on the right, would cooperate by bombing south-west along the bottom end of Skyline Trench. Supported by a heavy artillery barrage, the first waves were to capture and secure the initial objectives, with the following waves advancing through them to the subsequent targets.

The infantry attacked at 1700. On the left, 1/5th Royal Warwickshires were immediately successful, and both of their objectives were taken. The battalion war diary records that this was achieved "without any serious resistance". Lt Charles Carrington, in his battalion history, recounts that:

> A Company formed the first wave and followed so close on the barrage that they reached the first German trench without a shot being fired against them. B Company and two platoons of C Company then passed through and went on to the second objective. The attack was carried out with the precision of a field day. 250 Germans were trapped in their deep dug-outs and forced to surrender without striking a blow. A whole company, complete with its officers and two machine guns, was taken complete in one huge dug-out in the second objective. Many more of the enemy were killed in the trenches.[98]

On the face of it, the war diary account, and that of Carrington, suggest that the gains had been achieved with relative ease. However, the casualty list tells a different tale. Two officers and 14 Other Ranks died in this short advance while three officers and 99 Other Ranks were added to the long list of wounded.

On the right, the 1/6th Royal Warwickshires were initially held up by an enemy strongpoint, where the garrison put up a stiff resistance before finally capitulating. Six German officers and 245 Other Ranks were sent back to the Prisoner of War cage, and the battalion eventually linked up with 1/4th Royal Berkshires who had successfully pushed their way down Skyline Trench. Again, these gains were achieved at a considerable cost in dead and wounded. The 1/6th Battalion had lost six officers and 23 Other Ranks killed and 93 wounded, including three officers. 10 men were reported missing.

Meanwhile, on the left, the Brigade war diarist noted bluntly that "the 1/7th Royal Warwickshires were unable to reach their objective".[99] However, this is not the whole story, and the diary entry fails to do justice to this battalion's valiant efforts to secure their goals. The 1/7th initially sent forward two bombing teams from C Company, led by Lt W E Murray and 2/Lt A G Pirie. The two officers were wounded almost immediately, and their bombers retired without reaching the objective, a German barricade. However, the men were re-organised by Company Commander, Capt Arthur Godfrey-Payton, and the attack was renewed at 1820.[100] This time they managed to enter the enemy position, but were driven out by the inevitable German counter-attack. A third assault was organised but postponed by Brigade Headquarters, who, in a demonstration of good sense, ordered that it should wait until darkness. At 0200 on the 19th, a new party, under Lt G H Crow of B Company, tried a different approach. Instead

---

98   CE Carrington, *War Record of 1/5th Royal Warwickshires*, p.33.
99   TNA WO 95/2754: 143rd Brigade War Diary
100  Capt. Arthur Godfrey-Payton (27) was wounded by shellfire on 27th August and died on 29th August. He is buried at Puchevillers British Cemetery (1.D.53). He was the son of Mr and Mrs H G Godfrey-Paton of Bridge House, Myton, Warwick.

of bombing along the trench they climbed out of cover and assaulted the position "over the top" but were again beaten back. Finally, at about 0500, two groups of bombers, under Lt V C R Caley, managed to capture the position and push on north-west until they ran into a strong force of German defenders, and were again forced to halt and consolidate their gains.[101] The 48th Division line now ran uninterrupted from the extreme right of Skyline Trench, where it joined with the 2nd Australian Division, to the old German front line north of Ovillers, overlooking the Ancre Valley towards Authuille Wood. The conditions were set for an assault into the fearsome Leipzig Salient and thus to threaten Thiepval from the south.

The 32nd Division had gained a footing on the tip of the salient on 1st July, including the heavily-defended Leipzig Redout strongpoint, known to the Germans as the *Granatloch* (grenade hole). This small area had been held against repeated German counter-attacks. However, if the British were to press on towards Thiepval they now needed to snuff out the whole of the salient, including Hindenburg Trench and the Wonder Work strongpoint (*Wundt Werk*).

The 144th Brigade launched two battalions of the Gloucestershire Regiment against the salient on 21st August, supported by 25th Division on their left. 1/4th Gloucesters were to advance against the southern face from trenches near a position known as The Nab, and to push on to the support trenches to the rear. At the same time, 1/6th Gloucesters were to attack from the right, entering the German line directly north of Nab cross-roads and bombing their way to the left to join up with their 4th Battalion west of a bank on the left of the road that ran along the valley bottom towards Thiepval. The 1st Wiltshires (25th Division), who already held the south-west corner of the Leipzig Redoubt, were to bomb to their right to link up with the 1/4th Gloucesters in the old German front line.

1/4th Gloucesters went forward on a two company front with C on the left and B on the right. The attackers had left their assembly areas expecting to reach the front line and organise themselves well before zero, which was set for 1800. However, they found the communications trenches leading to the front line had been very badly shelled and this delayed their progress. Nevertheless, they reported themselves in position at 1715 and at 1750, B Company began to move out to their jumping off point, crawling forward about 100 yards under the cover of the rising ground to their front. At 1800 C Company also moved forward. Both were now arranged each in two waves at 50-yard intervals. The artillery barrage increased in intensity for five minutes and at 1805 it lifted onto the second objective. This was the signal for the attack to proceed. The battalion war diary recorded that "the barrage was so excellent that the leading wave was able to get right up to the enemy parapet and waited there a few minutes for the lift, at which they rushed the trench". By keeping right on the edge of a very accurate bombardment, the attackers were able to enter the trench before the garrison could leave their dugouts: nearly all the defenders were taken as prisoners. Only in the centre did the attackers meet any serious opposition, and this was soon dealt with, Pte Bizley sniping at enemy officers as they tried to withdraw to their support line. The following wave leap-frogged through the first and headed for the next line, which was again captured with very little resistance.[102]

On the left, the 1st Wiltshires also met with success and were quickly able to make contact with the 1/4th Gloucesters, while on the right, 1/6 Gloucesters successfully bombed their way

---

101 TNA WO 95/2756: 1/7th Royal Warwickshire Regiment War Diary
102 TNA WO 95/2758: 1/4th Gloucestershire Regiment War Diary

down the front-line trench to meet up with the 1/4th as planned. As soon as the positions were reported to be in British hands, A Company was sent up in support and consolidation was commenced, just as the enemy gunners began intermittent shelling, the prelude to a series of counter-attacks. All of these were repulsed, however, thanks to the liberal application of bombs, Lewis Guns and the defensive barrage. Over the next day, 144th Brigade continued to press forward to bring the right of their line into alignment with the left, providing a launchpad for the next phase of the operation. This was to be against Hindenburg Trench, which was to be rolled up from east to west, commencing at 1500 on 23rd August.

To support this attack, 143rd Brigade was ordered to establish a line of machine gun positions on the north-western slopes of the Skyline Trench spur. Their task was to enfilade German trenches in Thiepval village to supress fire from these positions, and also to engage any other targets of opportunity that might show themselves. The attack itself was to be carried out by 145th Brigade's 1/1st Bucks Battalion, launching from the line just cleared by 144th Brigade, against the eastern end of Hindenburg Trench, with 1/4th Oxfords on their right and 3rd Worcesters (25th Division) on their left. The preliminary barrage was fired by II Corps' Heavy Artillery batteries, and from 1500 to 1505 the division's field guns took over, dropping a standing barrage on the German front line itself. The attacking companies, advancing in two waves, gained some ground but were stopped short of the objective. The battalion war diary suggests the failure was the result of a heavy barrage of enemy field artillery and machine guns.[103] However, the 145th Brigade diary ascribes the lack of progress to the fact that some of the German garrison had remained in their trenches during the bombardment instead of seeking shelter, and were able to disrupt the attackers as they waited for the artillery fire to lift.[104] If this is true, it demonstrates that, here at least, the Germans had quickly identified the effectiveness of the new British tactic of advancing right up against the preparatory bombardment, and were taking fairly drastic steps to overcome it. Two Bucks Battalion officers, 2/Lt E H G Bates, and 2/Lt W R Heath, and 24 Other Ranks died in this action while two officers and 61 Other Ranks were wounded. 14 Other Ranks were reported missing. 2/Lt Bates is buried in the Ovillers Military Cemetery, not far from where he fell. 2/Lt Walter Roland Heath (37) son of Mrs Jane Elizabeth Heath, and her late husband, Richard, of "Handford", Salisbury Road, Herne Bay in Kent, has no known grave and is commemorated on the Thiepval Memorial.

Four days later, on 27th August, coordinated with a thrust by 35th Division, north-east from the Leipzig Redoubt towards Thiepval village, 48th Division repeated the attack, this time with two brigades – 143rd and 145th. The original 48th Division Operation Order called for a two-phased assault, led by 145th Brigade with 143rd following on to exploit early gains. However, this was changed at short notice and both brigades were ordered to attack simultaneously, with 143rd Brigade on the right and 145th Brigade on the left.

The objectives had been subjected to a heavy artillery bombardment since the previous attempt, and during the day the assaulting companies had moved up into new trenches that had been dug over the previous two nights to facilitate the attack. At zero, 1900, an intense artillery bombardment opened on the German front line, signalling the time for the attackers to leave their trenches and move out towards their objectives. On the left, where 145th Brigade had only

103 TNA WO 95/2763: 1/1st Bucks Battalion War Diary.
104 TNA WO 95/2760: 145th Brigade War Diary.

a short distance to go, the bombardment lifted after three minutes, while on the 143rd Brigade front, where the advancing troops had to cross over 300 yards of no-man's land, it continued for a further minute. The gunners did a good job, not only in keeping the defenders' heads down, but in suppressing enemy artillery and machine gun positions in depth: there were few casualties from enemy fire during the initial advance. On the left, 1/4th Royal Berkshires and 1/5th Gloucesters quickly reached and captured their objectives, although a party of Germans made a stubborn defence of one post before being over-run. On this side of the attack, it was estimated that over 200 of the enemy were killed, many falling to heavy and accurate Lewis Gun fire.[105] The right-hand Brigade did not have such good fortune. Here, the attack had been entrusted to two companies of 1/8th Royal Warwickshires, C on the right and D on the left. Both companies lost direction, probably due to the condition of the ground which had been completely obliterated by the shelling, rendering the target trenches unrecognisable. The battalion war diary describes the objective as being "only a very indistinct mark" which the attacking companies "found impossible to discern" in the midst of the bombardment.[106] C managed to get into an enemy trench and took a few prisoners, but the men found themselves on their own in a mini-salient. Attacked from both flanks, with casualties rising, and having run out of bombs, they fell back to the jumping off point. Only one officer from this company returned and it took him five hours to make his way back. D Company, losing its commander, Capt Robert Denison, and a platoon commander, 2/Lt Conwell Barton early on in the advance, completely overshot its objective. With few officers left to steady the men, they began to double forward and found themselves in the midst of their own barrage, from which they took a number of casualties. They withdrew to their starting point and built a bombing block. No further forward movement was possible and the Warwickshires were ordered out of the line later that morning. Stopping to rest on the way to the rear, near Ovillers, the roll was called, and the full extent of the battalion's losses became clear. Three officers, including Capt Denison, Lt Day and 2/Lt Barton were reported killed along with 7 Other Ranks. 150 were wounded, including Officer Commanding C Company, Capt S H Coxon; the battalion Medical Officer, Lt Courtney; 2/Lt Holmes; and 2/Lt Snowdon; 37 were reported missing, including 2/Lt Toogood.[107]

Capt Robert Charles Denison was 26 years old, the son of Robert Henry and Emily Denison, of Avino, Fowey, Cornwall. His body was found during the battlefield clearance after the war, some distance ahead of his objective that day, possibly buried initially by the Germans.[108] He now rests in Mill Road Cemetery, Thiepval (VIII.B.9). Lt Geoffrey Reynolds Day (28), 5th Bedfordshire Regiment, attached 1/8th Royal Warwickshires, was the son of Rev Archibald Day, The Vicarage, Malvern Link, Malvern, and husband of Mrs Jane Day. 2/Lt Conwell Paris Barton (23), 6th East Surrey Regiment, attached 1/8th Royal Warwickshires, came from Stockwell in London. Lt Day and 2/Lt Barton have no known graves and are remembered on the Thiepval Memorial.

---

105  TNA WO 95/2745, Report of Action on 27th August 1916, 48th Division General Staff War Diary.
106  TNA WO 95/2756, 1/8th Royal Warwickshire Regiment War Diary.
107  TNA WO 95/2756, 1/8th Royal Warwickshire Regiment War Diary.
108  Map Reference 57d.R.32.a.2.3, CWGC Concentration of Graves Burial Return for Mill Road Cemetery. See *CWGC* <https://www.cwgc.org/find-records/find-war-dead/casualty-details/544096/robert-charles-denison/#&gid=2&pid=1> (accessed 9th April, 2022).

The attack on 27th August marked the end of the 48th Division's part in the fight for Thiepval. The village and the neighbouring Schwaben Redoubt would not fall until the end of September when Gough launched the Reserve Army (about to be re-named Fifth Army) in a new offensive that would become known as the Battle of the Thiepval Ridge. Opened on 26th September, over the space of two days the 1st and 2nd Canadian divisions (Byng) pushed the Fifth Army line well to the north of Courcelette while 11th (Northern) Division captured Mouquet Farm and Major General Ivor Maxse's 18th (Eastern) Division finally took Thiepval and the Schwaben Redoubt.

In early September, the South Midlanders had moved to the rear for a much needed and well-deserved period of rest, although the 144th Brigade was required to participate in a "feint" in support of an attack by 39th Division (V Corps) and 49th Division (II Corps) astride the River Ancre on 3rd September. Being out of the line the 48th Division also missed the Battle of Flers-Courcelette, which opened on 15th September and was notable for the first use of tanks. While this piece of military history was being made, the South Midlanders were enjoying relative peace, comfort, and local hospitality in the Doullens – Beauval area, well behind the lines.

## Le Sars – Warlencourt

Having moved into the V Corps[109] area on 28th August, on 19th September, the division transferred to XIII Corps and on 28th September new orders were received, moving it under the command of VII Corps. The next day, it was directed by VII Corps to proceed to the front and take over trenches from 33rd Division in the familiar surroundings of Hebuterne. Fanshawe assumed command of this sector on 1st October, putting 143rd Brigade into the line, and establishing divisional headquarters at Henu. After just three weeks, the division was relieved once more and moved back to the Doullens area and then to Baizieux where, on 25th October, it became part of III Corps (Pulteney), rejoining Rawlinson's Fourth Army. On 31st October new orders were received to move to the Albert area and by the end of the following day, 143rd Brigade was in Mametz Wood, 144th Brigade was in Albert town, 145th Brigade was established at Millencourt and divisional headquarters was at Lozenge Wood, near Fricourt. Three days later the division relieved 15th Division in very wet trenches in the Martinpuich–Le Sars sector. The appalling conditions there prompted one officer to describe the new location as "the most miserable one the battalion ever occupied".[110] Apart from the poor weather, the British line here was under constant enemy observation. This made movement very difficult, particularly during daylight hours, hampering resupply and reliefs. The trenches were full of water and had started to cave in at many points. The ground was pitted with water-filled shell-holes and every track was deep in glutinous mud. Life here was bad enough for those units holding the trenches, where illness and trench foot soon added to the usual battlefield hazards of bullets, bayonets, bombs, shrapnel and gas. For supply parties, carrying up food and ammunition from the rear, the experience could be even worse, perhaps as close to purgatory as most men could imagine. The task of manhandling heavy loads for nearly a mile over the devastated, flooded

---

109  Commanded by Lt Gen E A Fanshawe, brother of Maj Gen R Fanshawe.
110  P L Wright, p.47.

landscape, in the darkness, with few landmarks to aid navigation, and all the time running the gauntlet of well-directed enemy shelling, was not one that many would have wished to repeat. But for those who survived their time in the wasteland between Le Sars and Warlencourt, it was a taste of what was to come in the autumn of the following year in the killing fields to the east of Ypres. Lloyd George might have coined the term "Campaign in the Mud"[111] with the Battle of Passchendaele in mind, but it is a description that applies equally well to the final months on the Somme.

In the meantime, despite the awful ground conditions, and the protests of some of his junior commanders[112], Haig was not ready to close down the Somme offensive. This was largely due to what Gary Sheffield has called "the straight-jacket of coalition warfare".[113] The French on the British right, remained keen to continue to attack on a broad front, and demanded that the British, who they considered to be their junior partner, should press on. Haig felt he had no option but to comply. Gough and Rawlinson thus continued their slow, costly, advance in the general direction of Bapaume, alongside General Fayolle's Sixth French Army, in a series of actions that the post-war Battles Nomenclature Committee would call the battles of Transloy Ridge, the Ancre Heights and the Ancre.

The men of the 48th Division would play only a small part in these final stages of the Somme offensive, and this would be confined to holding the line rather than having to "hop the bags" and advance across the flooded, shell-torn desolate wilderness that characterised the battlefield in the autumn and winter of 1916. However, they would have been aware – and no doubt thankful also – that fate had dealt them a lucky escape, a planned attack having been called off at the last moment.

Seeking influence at the forthcoming Chantilly Conference (15th November 1916), where the allies would decide their war-fighting strategy for 1917, Haig was anxious to appease the French – Foch had accused him of easing off on the BEF's efforts during the Somme offensive – and to achieve one last advance before the winter weather finally put an end to the 1916 campaign. In pursuit of this, Rawlinson planned another attack on the Transloy Ridge, in which Gough's Fifth Army, on the left, would cooperate. III Corps' part in this would be to throw the 50th Division at the Butte de Warlencourt and parts of Grid Line trench that remained in the enemy's possession, while 15th Division would attack the German first and support lines to the south-west of Warlencourt village, an area known as Little Wood. The III Corps orders were clear, however, that this latter element of the attack would only go ahead in conjunction with the planned Fifth Army assault. If the latter did not attack, neither would 15th Division.[114] The whole operation was delayed by bad weather and as a result, 15th Division was relieved by 48th Division on 1/2nd November, the latter then assuming responsibility for delivering the planned attack. However, on 3rd November, the Fifth Army received orders from GHQ authorising Gough to postpone his operations indefinitely, owing to the bad weather.[115] The following day, III Corps called off the 48th Division's associated attack, although at that stage it was intended to be reinstated once the weather improved. There was to be no such "get-out-of-jail-free" card

---

111  D Lloyd George, *War Memoirs of David Lloyd George*, Vol. 2, p.1313.
112  R Prior and T Wilson, pp256-57.
113  G Sheffield, p 141.
114  TNA WO 95/674: III Corps War Diary
115  TNA WO95/518: Fifth Army War Diary

for 50th Division, however. It was to carry on as planned, and on 5th November, it attacked the Butte de Warlencourt, achieving early success. By the afternoon, however, the Germans had counter-attacked and re-occupied the Butte. The Australians, attacking on the 50th Division's right, had more success, achieving nearly all their objectives.

With the weather showing no signs of improving sufficiently to allow further significant operations, and with Haig largely content with the outcome of the Chantilly Conference, the Battle of the Somme was brought to a close on 18th November 1916. It had resulted in an advance of some seven miles, at an horrific cost in terms of losses on all sides. The actual casualty numbers are disputed. The Official History suggests the British lost 419,654 killed, wounded, missing and prisoner and a total of 680,000 for the Germans. Historians tend to agree with Edmund's figure for British losses, but his assessment of the German total is considered by many to be inflated. Others have put the German number at between 465,000[116] and 600,000.[117]

---

116 H Herwig, Holger, *The First World War*, p.204.
117 R Holmes, *The Western Front*, p.139.

5

# From Peronne to Passchendaele

With large-scale fighting now at an end on the Somme sector, the 48th Division, together with the other formations that made up III Corps. (1st Division and 50th Division) reverted to the routine of line-holding and all that entailed, including patrolling; raiding; providing men for work details to help maintain infrastructure which was suffering from the cold, wet weather; and periods out of the trenches. Meantime at BEF GHQ, Haig and his staff were developing plans which had been previously agreed upon at Chantilly.

Initially, Haig and his French counterpart, Joffre, had agreed on the continuation of operations on the Somme once campaigning weather returned in the Spring. However, Joffre was removed from his post in December 1916 and replaced by General Robert Nivelle, regarded by many Frenchmen as the saviour of Verdun. Nivelle had an entirely different plan for the year ahead. An artilleryman, Nivelle, who penned the famous slogan *ils ne passeront pas* (they shall not pass), believed he had found a war-winning formula after his success in re-conquering the Douament fortress, elevated above the Meuse, on 24th October 1916. Writing to Haig on 21st December 1916, he set out his plan and demands for BEF support. The British, he said, would attack between Bapaume and Vimy to "fix" the enemy in that sector while to the south the French gunners would blast a massive gap in the German defences on the Chemin de Dames. A large attacking force of French poilu would then storm through the breech, achieving the much sought-after breakthrough, and, hopefully, forcing the Germans to withdraw or seek peace. To do this, Nivelle needed to create a French *masse de manoeuvre* of three armies – at least 27 divisions. And to facilitate this, the British, would be required to take responsibility not only for their existing section of the line but for large part of the French front between the Somme and the Oise, from Bouchavesnes to as far south as the Amiens-Roye Road. This extension of the British line would have to be completed by 15th January 1917 in order to ensure that the proposed offensive could be delivered in accordance with Nivelle's timetable.[1] Having earlier outlined the plan to British Prime Minister, Lloyd George, during the return journey from an inter-Allied conference in Rome, Nivelle had already secured senior British political support for the operation before he put his proposals in writing.[2] Haig was unhappy that his original plan for 1917 was being over-written, and frustrated that the British element would be subsidiary to

---

1    Nivelle-Haig correspondence, 21 December 1916 quoted in Lloyd George, Vol. 1, pp 881-883.
2    R Neillands, *The Great War Generals*, p.317

the French. However, he felt he had no option but to agree with the broad thrust of the French proposals, although he demanded – and was granted – some important amendments regarding exactly where he would deliver his attack.

With the overall plan settled, the British now began to make the necessary arrangements for their part in the offensive. Rawlinson's Fourth Army would be required to replace the French between Bouchavesnes and the Amiens-Roye Road, leaving him very thinly spread and unable to mount any significant offensive action. The attack on the left, in the Arras sector, would fall mainly to Allenby's Third Army, and the Canadian divisions of First Army (Horne), with a small contribution by Gough's Fifth Army. Rawlinson's part would be restricted to firing a heavy artillery bombardment on his section of the front in an attempt to keep the Germans guessing about where the main blow would fall. Rawlinson described it as "a Cinderella role".[3] He was not wrong.

In pursuance of this plan, on 16th January, 1917, Fourth Army issued orders to III Corps to relieve XVIII French Corps in the line from the River Somme to Genermont, on the Amiens-Roye road, and on 21st Januaury, III Corps directed 48th Division to take over from the French 152nd Division between Barleux and Biaches, the latter being on the western bank of the Somme canal, opposite Peronne.[4] By 28th January, Fanshawe had established his divisional headquarters at Mericourt-sur-Somme and his infantry brigades were in Cerisy, Mericourt and Hamel.[5] Three days later, 143rd Brigade moved up to the Cappy area and relieved a regiment of the 152nd French Division in the Biaches sector on the morning of 2nd February. 144th Brigade completed their relief in the southern sector between Barleux and the junction with 143rd Brigade that afternoon and Fanshawe assumed command from the 152nd French Division at 1000 the following morning (3rd February). III Corps completed its take-over from XVIII French Corps on the night of 14/15th February.[6]

Throughout the Relief-in-Place process described above, the weather had remained very cold and the ground well-frozen and hard, which meant the roads and tracks, the communications trenches and front-line positions stayed in reasonably good condition, despite the increased traffic. On 17th February, however, a slow thaw began, and the snow that had prevailed – on and off – for the past few weeks, turned to rain. As a result, the roads quickly became a muddy quagmire and the trenches flooded and began to cave in. By 20th February, the 48th Division was reporting that its trenches were "very wet" and by the following day, all its main communications trenches were impassable.[7]

Writing in his diary on 11th March 2/Lt Edwin Campion Vaughan (20), a recently-arrived platoon commander with D Company, 1/8th Royal Warwickshires, holding a section of trench near Biaches, described the conditions as he toured his platoon's position in the front line:

> The rain has set in now, and all snow has long since disappeared. The trench sides are falling in and the mud is up to our waists. It is impossible to walk through it and the only way to progress is to bury our arms in the sloppy mud of the trench sides and drag ourselves along.[8]

3    R Prior and T Wilson, *Command on the Western Front*, p.265.
4    TNA WO 95/674: III Corps War Diary.
5    TNA WO 95/2745: 48th Division General Staff War Diary.
6    TNA WO 95/674: III Corps War Diary
7    TNA WO 95/674: III Corps War Diary
8    E C Vaughan, *Some Desperate Glory*, p.39.

Small wonder, then, with these dismal ground conditions prevailing, that some proposed minor attacks, which had been planned to improve the division's position and in particular, its observation of the surrounding area, could not take place during this period.[9] For both sides, activity on the 48th Division front was restricted to patrolling no-man's land, mostly in darkness, and to conducting a few small-scale trench raids, while, to the north and south, the British and French armies prepared to launch the Nivelle offensive. Once again, however, the enemy was about to pre-empt the Allies' plans, just as he had done with his attack at Verdun the previous Spring.

On a miserably cold autumn day at the end of October 1916, a Royal Flying Corps pilot was patrolling well to the rear of the German lines north of Queant. Peering through a break in the thick cloud cover, he spotted what appeared to be a section of new trench being dug by the enemy, a long way behind its current front. On 9th November, with visibility much improved, eight FE2b aircraft of 11 Squadron RFC took off on a reconnaissance mission to gather further intelligence on the sighting. Returning unscathed to their home airfield, they reported a new and continuous defensive line, stretching from west of Bourlon Wood, passing Queant and Bullecourt before crossing the Sensee River and then running south of Heninel to join the German third line near Arras.[10] To the Germans this was the northern part of the infamous *Seigfreidstellung*. The British named it the Hindenburg Line, after the German Commander-in-Chief. The new position, which ran from just north-east of Arras to the River Aisne near Reims, in some places nearly 20 miles behind the existing front, had been built by Belgian and Russian labourers, under the direction of German army engineers. It was over 8 miles deep in places with numerous MEBUs,[11] deep dugouts and machine-gun emplacements, fronted by thick belts of barbed wire. With the new position well away from the day-to-day fighting on the front, the Germans had been able to choose the course of the line free from Allied interference. This had allowed them to take their time and select the most advantageous ground on which to establish the defences. As a result, the Hindenburg Line was a masterpiece of military engineering and "a truly formidable defensive system".[12]

According to Haig's third despatch, dated 19th June 1917, between November 1916 and March 1917, there had been a number of indications that the enemy was preparing to withdraw. This, he suggested, was in order to escape from the salient between Arras and Le Transloy, which "had become increasingly difficult and dangerous to hold" as the British advance on the Ancre drove ever more deeply into his defences.[13] In reality, with the huge losses sustained during the Somme offensive, the Germans were also hoping to reduce the length of the line, so it could be held by fewer men, allowing them to move some of their hard-pressed divisions into reserve. In moving to the Hindenburg Line, the Germans straightened the front, removing many of the kinks and twists that had existed since it was established in late 1914. This reduced the trace by 25 miles, releasing 10 divisions from ground-holding duties to prepare for future offensive operations.

The British Armies between Arras and the Somme had been warned to be on the look-out for signs that the enemy was on the move. On the morning of 1st March 48th Division reported to

9 TNA WO9 5/2745: 48th Division General Staff War Diary.
10 H A Jones, *War in the Air*, Vol II, p.318.
11 MEBU: *Mannschafts Eisen Beton Unterstande* (lit. crew iron concrete shelter).
12 R Prior and T Wilson, p.265.
13 Haig's Third Despatch, *London Gazette*, 19th June 1917.

III Corps HQ that the village of Mons-en-Chaussee, behind the enemy lines, appeared to be on fire. However, patrols sent out the following day found that the enemy was holding his line as usual and there was no sign of an evacuation. On 6th March, the neighbouring 50th Division spotted a fire in the direction of Guizancourt, and three days later, 59th Division (which had replaced 50th Division in the III Corps Order of Battle) noted another fire, this time at Brie. On 13th March the 1st Division informed III Corps that German artillery was registering its own front line, another significant combat indicator that a withdrawal was imminent. However, on 15th March patrols from all three divisions in the line found that the German front was still being held as usual. At 0500 on 17th March, the 48th Division's 145th Brigade conducted a raid on German trenches at La Maisonette. Finding few enemy troops, the brigade commander pushed patrols on towards Biaches and Eterpigny. Both areas were deserted. Similarly, 1st Division troops entering enemy trenches to their front found them empty.

The German withdrawal to the Hindenburg Line, codenamed Operation Alberich, had begun. And it heralded a period of mobile warfare unseen on the western front since the closing months of 1914. Alberich was, of course, the King of the Elves of German mythology, who was defeated by Seigfried, and also (and perhaps more appropriately, given the devastation left behind during the withdrawal) the evil dwarf of Wagner's Ring Cycle.

Recognising an opportunity to catch the enemy before he had time to become established in his new line, Fourth Army gave chase. Initially, Rawlinson was concerned that the withdrawal might be a German trap.[14] With that in mind, he proposed to move forward cautiously in a series of carefully-prepared bounds, securing his line after each advance against a possible enemy counter-attack. At the same time, he was conscious that be needed to get his heavy and field artillery into shelling range of the Hindenburg Line in time for the start of the Battle of Arras – now scheduled for 9th April – in order to ensure Fourth Army could play its cameo part in Haig's deception plan for the attack to the north at Arras.

At 1100 on the morning of 17th March 48th Division reported that one of its patrols had occupied Halle, a hamlet north-west of Peronne, and was continuing to advance towards the town. By mid-day a general advance had been made along the whole of the III Corps front, to a line running from the Somme at Biaches, west of La Maisonette, Barleux, Villers Carbonnel and Mazancourt, to the south-east corner of Sphinx Wood. From here, patrols were pushed forward during the afternoon, and these reported that Eterpigny, Villers Carbonnel, Misery and Mazancourt were no longer held by the enemy.

As they advanced, the division found that the Germans had taken the term "scorched earth" to a new level of beastliness. A sign left behind on the ruined town hall in Peronne's Grand Place, in letters a foot high, read *Nicht Ärgern, nur Wundern* (don't be angry, only wonder),[15] perhaps seeking understanding for the wanton vandalism and destruction the German army had left in its wake. Buildings had been blown up or burned down, whole villages put to the torch; wells had been poisoned or demolished; fruit trees had been hacked down; and farm animals killed and left to rot. Roads had been cratered or blocked by felled trees and key crossroads had been mined. Bridges had been blown and the banks of rivers breached to flood the land behind. In addition, the retreating enemy had left a liberal sprinkling of booby-traps to

---

14   R Prior and T Wilson, p.265,
15   E C Vaughan, p.60.

catch out the unwary. Cellars that might be used as shelters or for battalion or brigade headquarters had been rigged with explosives attached to timer devices and set to explode days after their German occupants had left. On 16th April, an explosion ripped through a cellar in Villers Faucon, occupied by 144th Brigade machine gunners. Five men died. The next day a mine exploded in a barn in Tincourt, wounding two and killing eight.[16] Improvised Explosive Devices consisting of six stick grenades tied together, were buried in the roadside, attached to a trip wire which was fastened to a tree. When an advancing waggon or motor vehicle hit the trip wire it initiated a friction striker which, in turn, detonated the bomb. A 1/5th Gloucesters' war diary note was scornful of these devices, explaining that "being merely explosives (ie no shrapnel components) they had a small radius of action" (killing zone). Consequently, little damage was done when they exploded.[17]

The advance continued on the 18th, and it was quickly becoming clear that there were few enemy soldiers immediately east of the Somme. 48th Division patrols passed through St Radagonde, Mt St Quentin, Quinconce and Peronne, finding them all evacuated. The same situation was discovered the next day at Doingt, Le Mesnil, Brie and St Christ, although at Estrees a bicycle patrol ran into German troops, and evicted them after a short, sharp exchange of fire.

The Bucks Battalion, marching into a still-burning Peronne on 20th March, over a pontoon bridge that had only just been completed by the Royal Engineers, was confronted with "the most awful of pictures":

> An earthquake could not have produced a more appalling effect or a scene of grater chaos. House fronts in many cases had been blown completely out and had fallen right across the street so that one looked from the street straight into the rooms of the houses. Those rooms were bare of all furniture, every stick of which had been either carried away by the enemy or sent to Berlin as souvenirs. Everywhere lay huge masses of rubble…The only two buildings which remained more or less intact were the Town Hall and the Castle, and these, we guessed, must be mined.[18]

2/Lt Edwin Campion Vaughan, 1/8th Royal Warwickshires, exploring Peronne early that same morning, found the Grand Place in a state of "cruel and dreary devastation":

> All the houses on my left were in ruins, whilst those on the right, though still standing, were badly battered, all doors and windows being smashed in. Opposite me the whole side was enveloped in tremendous walls of fire.[19]

The enemy appeared to be retiring at some speed, leaving small parties of troops behind to harry the pursuers. Here, at last, was a task for which the Corps' mounted troops – whose employment had been limited during static trench warfare – were ideally suited. They were able to use their superior mobility to maintain a reconnaissance screen ahead of the main force, keeping in

---

16   TNA WO 95/2746: 48th Division (GS) War Diary.
17   TNA WO 95/2763: 1/5th Gloucestershire Regiment War Diary.
18   P L Wright, pp.54-55.
19   E C Vaughan, p59

touch with the retiring Germans, and reporting back on their progress. However, lightly-armed cavalry was very vulnerable against machine guns and dug-in infantry and required artillery and infantry support to allow it to function effectively. To provide this, on 21st March 48th Division formed a mobile column under the command of the divisional Commander Royal Artillery, Brigadier-General Ward. This was a self-contained, all-arms formation, consisting of two infantry battalions (initially 1/5th Gloucesters and 1/4th Oxfords), two batteries of field artillery, and a machine gun section. To simplify command and control arrangements, the Corps Mounted Troops were also placed under Ward's command.

The column's initial mission was to conduct reconnaissance and to gain touch with the enemy.[20] Rawlinson was in the process of moving up the 5th Cavalry Division (formerly the 2nd Indian Cavalry Division) to take on this role, but the 48th Division's mobile column, now formally named Ward's Column, would meet the need in the short-term, moving into Bouvincourt while the Corps mounted troops occupied the line Poeuilly – Flechin – Bernes – Marquaix on 21st March. By the following day, Ward had established his headquarters at Catelet, while Vendelles and Roisel were discovered to be strongly-held by the enemy. Two days later (24th March), the 5th Cavalry Division, which was functioning as an independent formation, reporting directly to Fourth Army, took over the advanced line.

## Capture of Roisel and St Emilie

The capture and consolidation of the villages of Roisel and Ste Emilie was typical of the many skirmishes that took place during this period. Roisel in particular provides an example of the sort of fighting undertaken by the mobile column[21] during the pursuit to the Hindenburg Line, and also how the fighting had changed compared with the infantry's recent experience in the trenches in front of Warlencourt.

Roisel sits on rising ground on the southern bank of the Cologne River, a tributary of the Somme. It is surrounded by low hills and valleys and in 1917 it was a junction for two railway lines, one running between Peronne and Epehy and the second a small branch line linking Roisel with nearby Montigny. To its west lie the villages of Marquaix, which is to the north of the river, and Hamelet on the opposite bank. The Hindenburg Line defences were some 7000-8000 yards to the east. Roisel's significance for III Corps was that it sat on a potential avenue of approach to the Germans' new position, and its occupation by the enemy had created a block on the Corps' line of advance.

On 24th March, a patrol of 1/4th Oxfords pushing east from Hamelet, entered Roisel and, finding the village unoccupied, had quickly established an advanced post there. A squadron of 18th (King George's Own) Lancers, part of the 3rd (Ambala) Cavalry Brigade (15th Cavalry Division), which was acting as the reconnaissance screen for III Corps, was supposed to take over the outpost later that day. However, on moving up along the river

---

20  TNA WO 95/675: III Corps General Staff War Diary.
21  On 26th March, Brigadier General Ward handed over command of the mobile column to Lt Col Dobbin and returned to his duties as CRA 48th Division. The force then became Dobbin's Column or Dobbin's Force, before being disbanded on 1st April 1917 the component units returning to their original brigades.

towards the village the horse soldiers came under enemy fire and decided to pull back to Marquaix. The Oxfords' post held on until 0500 on the 25th when the enemy re-entered the village in force and drove the defenders back to Hamelet. Patrols sent up to establish the strength of the German force reported that Roisel appeared to be strongly held and it was decided that a deliberate attack would be required to bring it back under British occupation and open the way to continue the advance in that sector. The Oxfords' A and B Companies were tasked to carry out the operation.

At around 1000 on the 26th a battery of 18-pounder field guns and a section of 4.5in howitzers opened a bombardment of the village. Covered by the shelling, two platoons each of A and B Companies moved forward. The A Company platoons – Nos 1 and 4, commanded by 2/Lt G E Pearson and 2/Lt C H Bowman respectively – advanced by sections along the Hamelet-Roisel road on the south bank of the river. Despite the barrage, which lasted for 30 minutes, they found themselves held up by rifle and machine gun fire as they approached the railway branch line in front of the objective. Unable to deploy into attack formation due to the boggy ground, they lined the railway embankment and waited. Meanwhile, Nos 5 and 6 platoons of B Company left Marquaix on high ground to the north of the river and again, came under enemy fire, forcing them to advance in two extended lines. On cresting a ridge, the platoons, under 2/Lt A Allen, found themselves looking down on the village. These troops were quickly able to gain fire superiority over the garrison, forcing the defenders into cover. With the enemy suppressed, a small patrol under Sjt Wiggins was able to enter the village from the north and engaged and silenced the machine gun that had been holding up A Company. With the enemy apparently pulling out, Sjt Wiggins and his team were joined by the remainder of B Company and together they moved quickly through the streets, finding them completely deserted with the exception of a single private of 113rd Infantry Regiment, who was taken prisoner. No longer pinned down by machine gun fire, A Company, advanced over the branch line and entered Roisel from the west. The Oxfords' attack was supported by two armoured cars of 15th Cavalry Division, who entered from the track on the north and engaged the enemy with their machine guns. Seeing the enemy retiring, the Officer Commanding B Company, Capt Graham Greenwell, acting with admirable youthful impetuosity, borrowed a Hotchkiss gun from one of the armoured cars and sent it forward to the high ground to the north from where it fired on the retreating Germans.[22] Writing to his mother on March 28th, Greenwell depicted a slightly different version of the action, which he described as "the greatest fun and a howling success."[23] However, the battalion war diary puts a more sober spin on it, noting that during the fight the 1/4th Oxfords suffered four dead and 14 wounded. Unusually, the diarist took the time to record the names of the casualties, all junior ranks. The fatalities were:

200505 L/Cpl Harold Percy Wake (21), the son of Walter and Martha Wake, 303 Cowley Road, Oxford; 203284, Pte A E Colmer, B Company, both of B Company and both buried at Tincourt New British Cemetery. Pte William James Fowler (29), son of William and Sophia Fowler and husband of Olive Elisabeth Fowler, Quainton Road, Waddesdon, Aylesbury, Buckinghamshire; 202256 Pte H Summer (29), son of Mrs Caroline Summers, 6 Council

---

22   TNA WO 95/2764, War Diary: 1/4th Oxfordshire and Buckinghamshire Light Infantry (OBLI).
23   G Greenwell, pp.168-70.

House, Tadmarton, Banbury, Oxon, both of A Company, and both buried in Roisel Communal Cemetery Extension.[24, 25]

By 28th March, the Fourth Army had established its main line of resistance, running through or near Beauvois, Poeiully, Bernes, Marquaix, Longavesnes, Lieramont and Nurlu. 48th Division was ordered to occupy the Marquaix-Longavesnes sector by 2200 that evening and establish an outpost line further east at Villers Faucon and Saulcourt as a jumping-off line for the next phase of operations. Rawlinson's plan was to push his front to Maissemy – Hargicourt–Epehy–Gouzeaucourt by 7th April, giving observation over the Hindenburg Line and putting him within field artillery range of the new German position. As the next step towards that objective, 48th Division received orders on 29th March to seize the line L1 central (1200 yards W of Templeux le Guerard)–St Emilie–Epehy, whilst 59th Division would seize the line Vendelles–Jeancourt and the high ground in L8 (directly south of Templeux le Guerard). In preparation for this, 144th Brigade took over the whole of the divisional line from 143rd and 145th Brigades later that day, and the following day 1/4th Gloucesters (144th Brigade) were ordered to conduct a preliminary operation to secure the village of Ste Emilie.

Like Roisel, Ste Emilie is situated on a hillside above the valley carrying the Peronne – Epehy railway line, lying between the larger villages of Villers Faucon and Ronssoy. Before a formal attack was launched, 1/4th Gloucesters were ordered to send out a reconnaissance party to discover the enemy dispositions there. A patrol, led by 2/Lt L E Wakefield, found the enemy in the village in some strength. After being reinforced by 2/Lt C F Holland and a Lewis Gun team, the Gloucesters tried to move closer but were spotted by the defenders, who promptly called down an artillery strike, forcing Wakefield and his men to retire. A second patrol fared no better and it was clear that a deliberate attack by a larger force was required to drive out the enemy.

At 1600 on 30th March A and D Companies of 1/4th Gloucesters assaulted the village while two platoons of C Company occupied a ridge above Pleasant House, from where they could enfilade trenches running south. D Company, attacking from the north-west, made good progress before running into a German counter-attack, which they repulsed with rifles and Lewis Guns. Meanwhile, approaching from the north-west, A Company found themselves held up by heavy machine gun fire. However, a Lewis Gun post was established in a corner of the Sugar Refinery, from where the German machine gunners were enfiladed, allowing A Company to move forward. Describing this action, the Gloucesters regimental history noted that the enemy machine gunners had held their positions until the last, allowing perhaps 2-300 of their comrades to escape towards Epehy, "their gallant stand revealed by their dead bodies which lay about the gun positions".[26] The Gloucesters too had paid a heavy price for their victory. 2nd Lt A McClelland and six other ranks were killed in action. Both of the attacking company commanders, Capt F L Hall, and Lt A J Gardiner, were wounded, along with 2/Lts Holland and Wakefield and 47 other ranks.[27] 2/Lt Albert McClelland (22) was the son of John and Jane

---

24 TNA WO 95/2764: 1/4th OBLI War Diary.
25 *CWGC* <https://www.cwgc.org/find-records/find-war-dead/> (accessed 12 December 2023).
26 E Wyrall, *The Gloucestershire Regiment in the War, 1914-1918*, p.189.
27 E Wyrall, p.189. The battalion war diary (TNA WO 95/2758) contains no casualty details. The 144th Brigade War Diary (TNA WO 95/2757) includes a casualty estimate of 5 officers and 75 other ranks but provides no further details.

McClelland of 136 St Catherine's Terrace, South Circular Road, Dublin. He died of wounds on 2nd April and is buried at Bray-sur-Somme Military Cemetery.

## Epehy

With Ste Emilie now firmly in the division's hands, defensive posts well-established, and with the III Corps sector pushed forward to the line Vendelles – Jeancourt – Hesbecourt – Ste Emilie–Saulcourt, about 7000 yards west of the Hindenburg Line, Fanshawe's attention turned to Epehy and a hamlet immediately to its north, called Peiziere. Having verbally briefed the commanders of 143rd and 144th Brigades earlier in the day on 30th March, he issued formal orders for the attack at 2130 that evening. 143rd Brigade was to assault Peizier while 144th Brigade would take Epehy, with zero fixed for 0500 the following morning. However, this was pushed back and the attack took place on 1st April.[28]

The delay allowed time to conduct a thorough reconnaissance of the objective. When the commander of 144th Brigade, Brigadier-General H R Done, issued his own orders on the 31th, he placed particular emphasis on this element of the operation. At 1700 that evening, the divisional artillery would put down a barrage on the village as if preparing for an attack. The gunfire would be the signal for the attacking battalions, 1/6th Gloucesters and 1/7th Worcesters, to each send out two patrols, in platoon strength, to establish a reconnaissance screen about 1000 yards to the south and west of the target village. Once there they were to dig themselves in for the night and report back to their battalion headquarters on the situation to their front. This line would be the starting point for the follow-on assault on the village itself the next morning.[29]

The 144th Brigade war diary provides a detailed account of their part in the attack. At 1500 on 31st March as the division's guns opened up on Epehy, two platoons from C Company, under the command of 2/Lt Campbell, left Saulcourt Wood and moved towards their objective whilst the company commander, Capt Butcher, probably accompanied by an infantry section for protection, and a few signallers, established a position in dead ground about 1400 yards due east of Saulcourt. From there he was able to establish field telephone communication with his battalion headquarters (the signallers had laid a line between the two points). When Campbell and his patrols crossed the ridge at Capron Copse, they came under observation from the German garrison at Epehy and were shelled. Campbell and his men pushed on, but the artillery fire became intense. Losing four men killed and six wounded, the young officer wisely withdrew his patrols back behind the ridge. Butcher reported the situation to battalion headquarters and arranged for another attempt when the light faded. By 2000 the patrols had successfully pushed forward and were digging in as planned.[30]

At midnight the Worcesters' Commanding Officer, Lt Col F M Tomkinson, issued updated orders for the attack. His battalion would advance on the right of the Villers Faucon – Epehy Road (1/6 Gloucesters would be on the left), with the leading company in position between the railway and the road, ready to go at 0600. The three companies would go forward in waves with

---

28 TNA WO 95/2757: 144th Brigade War Diary.
29 TNA WO 95/2745: 48th Division General Staff War Diary.
30 TNA, WO95/2747/5, 144th Brigade War Diary.

B leading, followed by A and D, each on a two-platoon front. There would be no friendly artillery fire unless called for, either by the OC B Company or via SOS rockets.

The attack went in as planned at 0600. The enemy garrison was evidently taken by surprise: there was no hostile fire until the attackers were within 50 yards of the edge of the village, and by then it was too late. The garrison at the southern end resisted strongly for a time, assisted by fire from Malassie Farm, but this was supressed by the division's artillery and by 0715 Epehy had been cleared, the attackers taking up positions beyond the village boundary. This reflected recent experience. Throughout the pursuit the Germans had tended to wait until they were sure their troops were clear of a village and then bombard it heavily, hoping to catch the attackers without cover. By digging in outside the village the Worcesters avoided significant casualties from the inevitable enemy artillery barrage. 1/7th Worcesters' total casualties from this attack were 1 officer (2/Lt Fellows) and 9 other ranks killed, 40 other ranks wounded. Lt Arthur Simpson Fellows (22) was the son of Mr J A and Mrs S A Fellows, 67 Heath Street, Stourbridge, Worcestershire. He is buried in Epehy Wood Farm Cemetery, alongside a number of his regimental comrades who fell on the same day.

## Ronssoy, Lempire and Basse Boulogne

The initial pursuit of the enemy towards the Hindenburg Line had tested the 48th Division. The whole formation was, without doubt, operating in a new and unfamiliar environment. The mobile nature of the fighting since 17th March, was a significant departure from the static, trench-based, siege warfare for which they had been trained, and with which the men had become so accustomed from their time at Hebuterne, Ovillers, Poziéres and Warlencourt. The ground over which they were fighting was also quite different, the steep hills and valleys contrasting with the gently-rolling downland they had left behind to the west, above the Ancre. Mobile warfare created different pressures, and not just on the men at the sharp end. Supplying units in the trenches had its own challenges, but at least the line was static for long periods and a supply system, once established, was relatively straightforward to maintain. With units constantly on the move, however, the task faced by the Q Staff[31] to ensure that men were kept adequately supplied, would have been much more difficult. But the whole division had risen to the new challenge, testimony both to strong and effective leadership at all levels, and a well-trained and capable divisional staff, under an adept and competent GOC. It is noticeable, too, from the divisional, brigade and unit war diaries and personal accounts, that the troops' morale throughout this period, does not seem to have been a particular issue, despite the cold, wet weather, poor, sometimes non-existent billeting arrangements, and the daily losses.

Following the capture of Epehy and Peiziere, on 3rd April, the Commander-in-Chief, Field Marshal Sir Douglas Haig, wrote to Fanshawe congratulating the division on its recent success. The following day, Haig visited Fanshawe and his staff at Tincourt, after which a further letter was received, stating: "The Commander-in-Chief wishes the Divisional Commander to tell the General Officers Commanding the artillery and infantry of the Division, and the Commanders

---

31  Quartermaster Staff: were part of divisional, brigade and battalion headquarters. They were responsible for supplying everything required to keep formations/units fighting.

of the other units of the Division, that he was well-satisfied with the way they and their units had carried out their tasks, both fighting and working, since the advance began."[32] No doubt the compliment was well-deserved and much-appreciated. But there was little time to bask in the praise from on high. The advance had to continue, and the next objective was the capture of neighbouring villages, Ronssoy, Lempire and Basse Boulogne, all located on the crest of a long, high ridge with good observation over the surrounding countryside. Fanshawe allocated this task to 145th Brigade.

A Warning Order for the attack was distributed by the Brigade Headquarters on the late morning of 3rd April, setting out initial plans for a coordinated, three-battalion operation.[33] In preparation, 1/4th Oxfords, moved up into the outpost line, while 1/4th Royal Berkshires and 1/5th Gloucesters held at Villers Faucon, along with 1/1st Bucks Battalion, which was to be in Brigade Reserve. Before confirmatory orders were issued, however, the Brigade Commander called for a thorough reconnaissance of Ronssoy by 1/4th Oxfords. At 0330 the following morning, a patrol from D Company made its way forward from the outpost line. The patrol commander clearly got his timings wrong. The men were still out on the ground at daybreak, when, denied the cover of darkness, they were spotted as they made a rush for their lines and heavily bombarded, forcing them to take cover in shell holes.[34] Two men were killed, and the remainder were unable to get back to their company positions until after mid-day. However, the losses had not been in vain. The Oxfords had proved that the enemy held the village in strength, that the garrison was alert, and that it had artillery support on call. This was confirmed at 1900 that evening, when new patrols also drew fire and suffered five further casualties. Having received the reconnaissance reports, Brigade Headquarters issued updated orders. The Royal Berkshires would assault the village early the next morning from the south and south-east; the 1/5th Gloucesters would attack from the north-west, including a subsidiary attack on Maye Copse; and the 1/4th Oxfords would hit the village from the south-west.[35]

The Royal Berkshires left Villers Faucon at 0220 on the morning of 5th April, and moved, via Pleasant House and Templeux Wood, to their forming-up point, which was at the head of a valley, about 1600 yards west of their objective. A secondary objective, Basse Boulogne, was 1100 yards further east. The approach march was difficult. Visibility was poor – down to about 100 yards – due to a heavy mist. The tracks were in bad condition after the day's snow-fall. Landmarks were difficult to see and identify, making cross-country navigation challenging, and the fact that the ground was entirely unfamiliar to the troops added to the problems. However, they reached their start-line in time and at 0430 they organised themselves into their assault formation, each company in six lines on a 200 yard frontage and started towards the objective. B Company on the right, was initially held up by wire, rifle fire from trenches behind the wire, and machine gun fire from a position known as the Slag Heap. Wire cutters were sent forward to make a gap and a Lewis Gun team was pushed through to cover the flank, while a second engaged and supressed the riflemen in the trenches. A platoon was despatched to outflank the machine gun and this, too, was duly silenced.

32  TNA WO 95/2746: 48th Division General Staff War Diary.
33  TNA WO 95/2760: 145th Brigade War Diary.
34  TNA WO 95/2764, 1/4th OBLI War Diary.
35  TNA WO 95/2760: 145th Brigade War Diary.

The British artillery barrage was called down at 0545 and at 0605 B Company was able to move forward, making contact with D Company on the left. It then turned right and dug-in to secure the right flank. A Company in the centre, came under enemy fire after advancing about 300 yards. This came from the front and from the right. They were briefly held up by wire but managed to find gaps and continued to move forward towards the first objective. Lt Pring and his platoon carried on past the cemetery and turned right to take up position in a bank of a sunken road to the south-east of Ronssoy. The company commander and one platoon joined up with 1/5th Gloucesters between Ronssoy Wood and Lempire at about 0545. D Company, on the left, moved forward at zero and the first wave soon overwhelmed an enemy post on the south-western outskirts of the village. The company then came under heavy machine gun fire from a strong point behind the post, which was immediately attacked. This position was held very strongly, however, and was only subdued when the following waves closed up and added their fire-power. Two enemy machine guns were captured, their crews, the battalion war diary noted, were "killed to a man". Having dealt with the main point of resistance, the company continued to advance to the village and linked up with the Oxfords at about 0500. By this stage the enemy troops were retiring in large numbers by road and across open fields in the direction of Hargicourt. Lewis Gunners accounted for some of these but the attackers were prevented from following by the British barrage. As the bombardment lengthened, they were eventually able to complete their advance and dig in.[36]

The 1/5th Gloucesters' primary objective was to attack down the Epehy-Ronssoy Road and go firm on a line stretching for 250 yards north and south of the road between Ronssoy and Lempire. A subsidiary assault by two platoons, commanded by Lt Cornish, was to capture Maye Copse and establish a strong post from which to protect the left flank, supported by two Vickers gun teams. By the time the leading company started to move to the forming-up position, which was along the railway embankment south-east of Epehy, the earlier snow had stopped and the poor visibility that had plagued the Berkshires' approach march had improved markedly. As a result, their final approach was spotted by a keen-eyed enemy observer, who called down artillery fire. Luckily the first rounds did not fall until the rear company had cleared the enemy gunners' mean point of impact and there were few casualties. The element of surprise had been lost. Nevertheless, the battalion went forward as ordered, finding the north-west corner of Lempire strongly garrisoned by riflemen in pits and machine guns. With their blood up, however, the Gloucesters easily outmatched the German defenders and by 0600 this part of the operation was over, and the objective was firmly in British hands. At Maye Copse, the enemy decided not to make a fight of it and withdrew almost as soon as Lt Cornish and his men appeared. The Gloucesters' casualties totalled 15 killed and 40 wounded, two of whom subsequently died as a result of their wounds.[37]

The 1/4th Oxfords, who had been holding the outpost line, moved forward, and formed up on the northern side of the valley running towards Ronssoy on a north-south line. The frontage of their main assault was no more than 150 yards. To the north, two platoons of D Company were tasked to maintain touch with the 1/5th Gloucesters while two platoons of C Company had a similar role to the south, where they were to stay in contact with the Berkshires. The remaining

---

36  TNA WO 95/2762: 1/4th Royal Berkshire Regiment War Diary.
37  TNA, WO 95/2763: 1/5th Gloucestershire Regiment War Diary

platoons of C and D were held in battalion reserve at Ste Emilie. With no preparatory artillery barrage to signal the attack, A and B companies were able to advance to within a few yards of the village before being fired upon. Rushing forward they seized the enemy positions, killing many of the garrison, while their Lewis Gun teams supressed the German machine guns that were firing from depth. By 0538, B Company commander, Capt Greenwell, was able to report that he had reached the village and, by 0555, that he had worked through to the eastern side, inflicting heavy casualties on the garrison. Five minutes later, 2/Lt A W Proctor, commanding A Company, reported that he was also through to the eastern outskirts, but could not progress further owing to the friendly artillery barrage. As a result, a German gun battery that had been well forward in close support to the occupying infantry, had managed to limber-up and pull out before he could reach them.[38]

Acting Captain Graham Greenwell, commanding B Company, wrote a detailed account of the Oxfords' part in this operation in a letter home, dated 6th April 1917. Greenwell described it as: "Quite a bloodthirsty affair but with remarkably few casualties on our side. We are all as pleased as Punch – it's the best and biggest show we have had since we came to France". And he added:

> The old Bosche were caught absolutely napping. They fought their machine guns to the end – or rather till all their men were killed. Then, for the first time, our fellows got a chance with the bayonet. It was simply glorious …[39]

On learning of the successful capture of the hill-top villages, Haig sent the following message via Fourth Army: "Please convey my further congratulations to the 48th Division on its recent successes." To this, Rawlinson added: "In forwarding the Commander-in-Chief's message, I desire to congratulate the 48th Division most heartily on the brilliant successes they have achieved since the advance began. I offer all ranks my warmest thanks."[40]

As young Graham Greenwell was penning his letter home, General Fanshawe and his staff were preparing some rather more sinister correspondence, concerning the division's programme for the coming days. Three main objectives were set: to make the division's main line of resistance as strong as possible to cover the deployment of the heavy artillery and to enable the front-line garrison to be reduced; to ensure the road through Ste Emilie was fit for heavy motor transport, presumably to make it easier to supply the line, and to improve other local roads so they could be used by field guns and horse-drawn transport; and to push the existing outpost line further forward. On 8th April, the division was ordered to extend its line to the right to take over the ground currently held by the 39th Division. The following day it was directed to move its outpost line even further east, and on 10th April 144th Brigade was tasked to take up positions on the high ground to the north-east, east and south-east of Ronssoy, including Sart Farm, about 1000 yards east of Lempire.

In the III Corps sector, the enemy's approach during the first four weeks of the retirement had been to trade ground for time in a series of well-organised rearguard actions designed to

---

38 TNA WO 95/2764: 1/4th OBLI War Diary. The diary does not record the casualties from this action.
39 G Greenwell, pp.173-74.
40 TNA WO 95/2746: 48th Division (GS) War Diary.

give their main force time to become established in its new line. To do this, they had sought to occupy and hold individual villages just long enough to force their pursuers to develop deliberate attacks against them, during which they inflicted as many casualties as possible before pulling out, moving back to the next village, and repeating the process all over again. This was hard, wearing combat for both sides. It slowed up the pursuit and consumed men, ammunition and rations. This was a particular issue for the British, who, as the pursuers, were constantly moving ahead of their logistics support and heavy artillery. For the Germans, falling back on their supply lines and their own gun batteries, it would have been slightly less onerous. But the differences were probably only marginal.

By the middle of April, however, as a series of minor actions pushed the enemy closer to the Hindenburg Line, the British began to notice that the German defence was stiffening. III Corps reported that the enemy was now offering "considerably more resistance" than in the first stages of the advance, and had, on many recent occasions, launched strong counter attacks against the positions that had been captured.[41] It was becoming clear that the Germans in the III Corps sector had given up about as much ground as they dared and were now determined to maintain an infantry screen, consisting of a series of outposts, in front of the Hindenburg Line. This would act as a buffer against the British and help to disrupt and blunt any attempt to break through. The short period of mobile fighting was coming to an end, and a new phase of static siege warfare was about to begin. But now the German fortress was stronger than ever and, the defenders hoped, even more difficult to penetrate.

## Battle for the Farms

If the Germans were resolved to stand fast in front of the Hindenburg Line, Rawlinson was equally resolute in his wish to dominate this same vital ground. By now the enemy had established themselves in a line of well-defended posts. In the 48th Division sector these ran south-north from Guillemont Farm to Tombois Farm, then Petit Priel Farm, Catelet Copse and on to the village of Villers Guislain. On the morning of 16th April, Fanshawe directed a division-level attack to evict the enemy and take over these positions which would then become the British outpost line. On the right (south) 145th Brigade would assault Guillemont Farm, Tombois Farm, and the German trench 600 yards north of Tombois Farm, with a secondary objective a low ridge, 600 yards further east. On the left, 143 Brigade would capture Petit Priel Farm and Catelet Copse, advancing as far north as the spur between Pigeon and Tarvelle Ravines and 500 yards south of Petit Priel Farm.[42]

In military operations, a multitude of factors can influence success or failure, and a good plan must take these into account, recognising that some may be within the control of the troops and their commanders, while many others are not. In this case, it was one of the latter – the weather – that was to have a significant impact on the outcome. Throughout the day a Spring storm had been whipping itself into a frenzy across the divisional front. Rain and snow fell continuously,

---

41  TNA WO 95/675: III Corps War Diary, Summary of operations for April 1917.
42  TNA WO 95/2748: 48th Division (GS) War Diary.

and the freezing wind penetrated the solders' greatcoats and even the Mk VI "waterproof" groundsheets that some would have wrapped around themselves as they waited for the "off".

The night was very dark, with visibility, by one account, down to less than 10 yards. The ground was sodden, the men were soaked and freezing. In fact, as one battalion war diary put it, the conditions were "about as bad as they could possibly be".[43]

On the right of the 143rd Brigade attack, 1/5th Royal Warwicks, was to assault Catelet Copse, lying in low ground in Catalet Valley, and then, in sequence, Petit Priel Farm, above the valley, on a spur to the south-east. B and C Companies were to go forward initially, with D Company in support and A Company holding the battalion's sector of the outpost line. Advancing at 2230, in pitch blackness, without a preparatory artillery barrage, Acting Capt Charles Carrington thought it was a considerable success that the platoon and section commanders managed to reach the enemy lines at the correct point. During the approach, a platoon of the left battalion blundered into C Company and shots were exchanged before they identified each other.[44]

On reaching the objective, they found the copse itself had been heavily-fortified with a thick belt of wire, and was held in strength by the enemy, who stood their ground. Unable to make progress, the Warwicks pulled back a short distance, dug themselves in to the west of a track running from Petit Priel Farm to Villers Guislain, and waited for daylight. On their left, the 1/6th Battalion, also unable to make progress, did the same. Patrols sent out at dawn found that the enemy had slipped away under the cover of darkness and the now-vacant positions were quickly occupied and consolidated.[45] The 1/5th battalion's casualties amounted to 18 Other Ranks killed and two officers and 40 Other Ranks wounded.[46] The 1/6th had lost two officers and 10 Other Ranks killed and 32 Other Ranks wounded. Two men were reported missing.[47]

On the right of the division's line, 145th Brigade's objectives were Guillemont Farm, which was allocated to 1/4th Royal Berkshires, and Tombois Farm, which was the target for 1/1st Bucks. Zero for these attacks was set for 2330 -1.5 hours later than for the 143rd Brigade assault.

The Berkshires moved off from their billets near Templeux le Guerard to their jumping-off point to the east of Sart Farm, heading into the teeth of the wind, snow and rain. The approach march was over two miles long for each of the attacking companies (C and D) so by the time they reached their start lines the men were already quite fatigued. Just as they were forming up, enemy troops were spotted advancing on the right and Capt James, OC D Company, immediately ordered a platoon to move out in that direction to provide flank protection. They were seen, however, and the Germans retired over a ridge before they could be engaged. As the attacking companies moved off, they were heavily shelled by German 77mm and 5.9s, causing significant casualties. In the circumstances, the company commanders decided that they could not continue and ordered a withdrawal to trenches just behind their start-lines. At 0130 Brigade ordered that they were not to attempt another advance. Reporting on this action later, the battalion second-in-command, Major J N Aldworth wrote: "No blame is attached to the officers and men of the two attacking companies for their not succeeding. The efforts to advance after the march and

---

43  TNA WO 95/2762: 1/4th Royal Berkshire Regiment War Diary.
44  C. Carrington, *War Record of 1/5 Battalion, Royal Warwickshire Regiment*, pp.48-49.
45  C Carrington, pp 144-45.
46  TNA WO 95/2755/1: 1/5th Royal Warwickshire Regiment War Diary.
47  TNA WO 95/2755/2: 1/6th Royal Warwickshire Regiment War Diary.

the heavy shellfire at the point of deployment were worthy of all praise and even though they did not succeed, the companies retained the reputation they had previously gained."[48]

Meantime, on the left of the 145th Brigade attack 1/1st Bucks had some success, but only after a very uncertain start. C and D Companies ran into thick wire and heavy rifle and machine gun fire and were unable to get forward. All of D Company's officers had become casualties, and at about 0030 Capt Hales decided to withdraw both companies to Sart Farm and reorganise them for a second attack. However, B company, attracting rather less enemy attention, managed to get into a trench to the south of Tombois Farm and by 0200, after tough hand-to-hand fighting in which the bomb and bayonet played key roles, had gained possession of the farm and the surrounding area, and began to consolidate. At this point, three platoons of A Company, 1/5th Gloucesters, who were in support of 1/1st Bucks, were sent forward, arriving to find B Company in possession of the farm, but with some of the enemy holding out in the orchard immediately to the south. Despite the Gloucesters' additional combat power, some further hard fighting was required before the orchard was finally cleared at 0400. C and D Companies, now re-organised, were sent up to help with consolidation. Around 30 enemy dead in and around the farm complex, and nine prisoners, stood testimony to the stiff German defence and the resolute determination of the attackers, as did the Bucks Battalion's own casualties, which amounted to 18 killed and 47 wounded. Among the wounded was OC D Company, Capt Reginald George Gregson-Ellis and his four platoon commanders. Gregson-Ellis was recovered from the battlefield and evacuated to a field ambulance in the rear where he died of his injuries on 17th April.[49] He was buried at Peronne Communal Cemetery Extension. He was the son of the late Charles Gregson-Ellis, a barrister, and husband of Lucy. Their family home was at High Wycombe.

Two days later, the 1/4th Oxfords made another unsuccessful attempt to capture Guillemont Farm. The task was then switched to 144th Brigade. An attack by 1/8th Worcesters and 1/6th Gloucesters, on the farm and a feature known as The Knoll, about 1500 yards to the north, early on the morning of 24th April, managed to get onto the objectives but strong German counter-attacks immediately re-took much of the ground. Brigade Commander, Brigadier-General H R Done, decided more combat power was required and that evening he issued orders for a fourth attempt, this time with three battalions. His own 1/4th Gloucesters and 1/7th Worcesters would assault The Knoll and the Farm respectively, while 1/4th Royal Berkshires, borrowed from 145th Brigade, would attack a copse about 1500 yards to the south. Done also made another change, which may have had a significant influence on the eventual outcome. During the pursuit to the Hindenburg Line, it had become common practice to dispense with a preparatory bombardment in order to give the attackers the advantage of surprise. This had worked successfully for the division's brigades on a number of recent occasions. However, by now the enemy was well aware that Guillemont Farm was a key objective; there was little advantage to be gained from trying to advance undetected. He therefore decided to reintroduce the preparatory bombardment. As a result, this attack began with a short but intense barraging of the enemy positions, commencing at 2300 – 10 minutes before the infantry assault went in.[50]

It was a very dark night with not even a star to illuminate the gloom. With little time to reconnoitre the route in, the company commanders, unfamiliar with the ground, had some difficulty

---

48  TNA WO 95/2762: 1/4th Royal Berkshire Regiment War Diary.
49  TNA WO95/2763/2, 1/1st Buckinghamshire Battalion War Diary and P L Wright, pp.59-62.
50  TNA WO 95/2757 144th Brigade War Diary.

in getting their men into position but despite this, the troops were in their jumping-off points on schedule and without incident. The gunners opened fire at 2300 as planned and this was immediately answered by the enemy's 77mm and 10.5cm batteries. Fortunately, this fire caused few casualties. However, on the right, C Company lost men to British guns, and this disrupted their advance, although some elements managed to move forward towards their objective. D Company, on the left, unmolested by the friendly fire, were able to get forward in good order. A party under Sgt Darby formed a post on the eastern side of the farm while 2/Lt Little engaged a group of enemy and killed them at short range with his rifle before being wounded by an exploding stick grenade. The remnants of the left platoons of B company pushed forward and dug in to the north and north-west of the farm buildings under Lt Melhuish and 2/Lt Bartlett. On B Company's right, the platoons were held up 3-400 yards short of the objective but were re-organised by the company commander, Capt Prescott, and then pressed on, coming into line with their comrades and forming another post. There were now two lines of posts established, covering the farm to the east and on both flanks.[51] These were quickly consolidated for defence. And not a moment too soon.

At 0600, the enemy launched a concerted counter-attack, later estimated to have involved three companies. Under cover of an effective British SoS barrage, the first line of posts made a deliberate withdrawal to the second line. There the companies held firm, their Lewis Guns and snipers combining with accurate artillery fire to break up the German assault. A party of enemy infantrymen who tried to enter the farm complex was obliterated by Lewis Guns and rifles from Capt Prescott's post to the east. A total of 20 bodies were counted there later that morning. Sniper, L/Cpl Williams, claimed eight of these himself. A second, less enthusiastic, counter-attack took place at about 0645, again failing to re-take the position. The remainder of the day was relatively quiet, and the battalion was relieved by 1/4th Royal Berkshires on the evening of 25th April, with Guillemont Farm firmly in British hands. Worcesters' casualties during this period amounted to two officers and 12 other ranks killed, 94 wounded and 29 missing.[52]

## Flanders Beckons

The Guillemont Farm fighting marked the 48th Division's last significant act during their pursuit of the enemy to the Hindenburg Line. With the failure of the Nivelle attack on the Chemin des Dames ridge, the British Commander in Chief immediately shifted his attention north towards Flanders. He had earlier agreed with Nivelle that clearing the Belgian coast should be part of the plan for 1917 and when Nivelle was replaced by General Petain, he was quick to seek – and receive – a renewed French commitment to supporting operations in the Ypres sector, even though he knew that following the unrest among the French army after the Aisne debacle, the support was unlikely to amount to a significant contribution.

Haig had, for some time, favoured the Belgian front for his next 'big push' but this was given added impetus in February 1917, when the German navy re-introduced a policy of unrestricted submarine warfare, hoping to starve Britain out of the war. As a result, U-Boats, including those sailing from the Belgian ports of Zeebrugge and Ostend, had been taking an increasingly

---

51   TNA WO 95/2759: 1/7th Worcestershire Regiment War Diary.
52   TNA WO 95/2759: 1/7th Worcestershire Regiment War Diary.

heavy toll on Britain's merchant fleet. Losses had shot up from 300,000 – 350,000 tons per month during the winter of 1916/17 to 520,000 tons in March 1917 and 860,000 tons the following month.[53] Britain's war effort was heavily reliant on foodstuffs, munitions and raw materials, carried across the Atlantic from Canada and the US. It was clear to Haig and his naval colleague, Admiral Sir John Jellicoe, the First Sea Lord, that if the U-Boat threat was not tackled, if Germany was able to sink merchant ships faster than Britain could build new ones, there was a danger that the Allies would be defeated for want of food, fuel, munitions, and other commodities vital to prosecuting the conflict.[54]

With that in mind, and while the Battle of Arras was still in progress, Haig began to re-organise his forces with a view to launching a new offensive designed to punch through the German lines to the east of Ypres, seize and hold the important railway junction at Roulers (now called Roesalare), disrupting Germany's ability to supply that section of the front, and then push on to clear the Belgian coast and shut down the U Boat bases there.

This re-organisation heralded a period of uncertainty for the 48th Division. On 28th April, Fourth Army issued instructions to III Corps that the division should be withdrawn from the line as soon as possible and undertake a period of training.[55] This was probably recognition that the South Midlanders had been heavily engaged throughout the pursuit to the Hindenburg Line and now needed rest and rehabilitation if they were to be of further utility. By 3rd May, the division had been relieved by 42nd Division, and had moved back towards Peronne while Major General Fanshawe departed for England on leave, handing over temporary command to Brigadier-General D M Watt, GOC 145th Brigade.[56] On 9th May, Fourth Army ordered a restructuring of its corps and, as part of this, directed that 48th and 20th Divisions, were not to be used in the line and "were to be given every opportunity for training".[57] On 11th May, however, this was overturned and GHQ directed the transfer of 48th and 20th Divisions to IV Corps, and moved IV Corps to Gough's Fifth Army.[58] As they left the Fourth Army, Rawlinson wrote to Fanshawe on 22nd May to pay him and his division the following compliment:

> I cannot allow the 48th Division to leave the Fourth Army after seven months [of] strenuous service without expressing to all ranks my appreciation and warm thanks for the valuable services they have rendered. After a winter of unexampled severity in indifferent trenches the change to open warfare in March and April found them in a high state of efficiency. The skilful leadership and dash displayed in the capture of Peronne, St Emilie, Epehy, Basse Boulogne and Tombois and Guillemont Farms are deserving of the highest praise and show that the standard of efficiency that has been reached, more especially in the close combination of Artillery and Infantry, is an exceedingly high one. I congratulate all ranks on the successes that they have attained, and I shall look forward to some future date when I trust I may have the good fortune to find the Division once more under my Command.[59]

---

53  R Holmes, p.159.
54  R Neillands, p.386.
55  TNA WO 95/432: Fourth Army War Diary.
56  Fanshawe returned from leave and assumed command on 17th May 1917.
57  TNA WO 95/433: Fourth Army War Diary.
58  TNA WO 95/43: Fourth Army War Diary.
59  TNA WO 95/2746: 48th Division General Staff War Diary.

It is unlikely that Rawlinson actually penned this note himself: it was probably drafted by a staff officer, perhaps his Chief of Staff, Major General Sir Archie Montgomery[60], or someone more junior. However, the Army Commander signed it personally and he would not have done so if he had not agreed with the sentiments it expressed. It was not unusual for army and corps commanders to write to divisions being transferred out of their commands, but in this case, it is worth noting Rawlinson's assessment of the South Midlanders' "exceedingly high" standard of efficiency, and his praise for their "skilful leadership and dash". These, together with the list of the division's successes during the advance to the Hindenburg Line, are strong evidence of a well-trained and highly-motivated formation, supported by effective, able staff officers, delivering operational plans in which the troops had confidence. The creation of such an organisation did not happen by chance. It was, to a large extent, the product of the abilities, style and leadership of the General Officer Commanding, Major General Robert Fanshawe.

At this stage, the Fifth Army was still in the line in the Bullecourt area in front of the Hindenburg Line, but Haig's intent was for Gough and his command to move north to take on the leading role in the forthcoming offensive in the Ypres sector. The South Midlanders were heading back to Flanders and another major battle… but not just yet.

On 12th May, the division moved to the Combles–Rocquigny–Le Transloy area, south of Bapaume, and came under temporary command of the 1st ANZAC Corps, relieving 11th Division in reserve before taking over the ANZAC Corps' right sector on 15th May. The ANZACs were themselves relieved by IV Corps on 26th May and 48th Division reverted to IV Corps command. There now followed a period of line-holding, during which the division had a busy patrolling and raiding programme, before being replaced by 3rd Division and moving to the Gomiecourt–Achiet-Le-Petit–Bihucourt area. A further move followed to Adinfer – Pommier–Basseux, between Arras and Bapaume, where, between 1 and 19th July, the men enjoyed another period of rest and training before the division began to entrain for the Ypres sector on 20th July. Within just three days – by 0800 on 23rd July – it was complete in its new location, just north of Poperinghe, testimony to the abilities of divisional, brigade and battalion movements staffs, and the increasing efficiency of the British Army's transport and logistics system, by now well-practiced in the business of moving large quantities of men and equipment over significant distances.[61]

## Pilkem Ridge

On arrival in Flanders, the 48th Division came under command of Lieutenant General Sir Ivor Maxse's XVIII Corps, just as the planning for the opening phase of the Third Battle of Ypres was being completed. Haigh's scheme of manoeuvre for the offensive envisaged a series of bounds, wearing out and grinding down the enemy whilst moving relentlessly towards Roulers and then the coast.[62] Gough's Fifth Army would deliver the opening blow, attacking on a 10-miles front in the centre while the French First Army in the north and General Herbert Plumer's Second Army in the south would assault simultaneously to secure the flanks of the

---

60   Later Field Marshal Sir Archibald Armar Montgomery-Massingberd.
61   TNA WO 95/2746, 48th Division War Diary.
62   G Sheffield, *The Chief*, p.227.

principal advance. The key objective for this opening thrust was to take the German first and second trench systems along the entire army front with II and XIV Corps pushing on to capture the enemy's third line from Polygon Wood to the St Julien–Passchendaele Road in preparation for the next phase.[63]

XVIII Corps role in what would become known as the Battle of Pilkem Ridge, was to go forward in the centre of the Fifth Army's line, sandwiched between XIX Corps on its right and XIV Corps on the left, to secure crossings over the Steenbeek stream and seize ground on its eastern bank to provide a suitable jumping-off point for future operations. This included capturing the village of St Julien on the right, and its road bridge over the river. Having crossed the Steenbeek, Maxse's right flank was to push on towards the Langemarck – Gheluvelt Line, on a front extending between Winnipeg and Springfield farms, conforming to the advance of the left flank of XIX Corps. This task was allocated to 39th Division (right) and 51st (Highland) Division, with 48th Division and 11th Division in Corps Reserve.[64]

Maxse believed in the power of detailed planning and tactical training. He would no doubt have subscribed to the modern British Army's "7Ps" maxim – prior preparation and planning prevents piss-poor performance – although perhaps not in those exact words. Ahead of this attack he made sure his divisions were as well-prepared as possible. He arranged for them to train over practice trenches "similar in every respect" to those they would have to negotiate in the battle. Copying Plumer's approach before the Battle of Messines, he had a scale model constructed, covering an area of roughly two acres, demonstrating the exact lie of the land to be assaulted. He also established a "Battle Course" at the Corps School for the company commanders of those units tasked with the initial assaults, and personally lectured the attendees on the general plan of attack.[65]

This prior preparation and planning paid off, at least at first. Attacking early on the morning of 31st July, behind a heavy, rolling barrage, the leading waves of 39th and 51st Divisions easily took the first and second objectives (Blue and Black Lines) before pressing on to the third objective, (the Green Line), including St Julien, which was captured by 116th Brigade, despite firmer German resistance. The Green Line marked the limit of exploitation for the 51st Division, but the 39th had one more step to take and its reserve brigade, 118th, moved up to attack the German positions in the Langemarck-Gheluvelt Line (the Green Dotted Line) from positions between Winnipeg and Springfield, commencing at 0800. 118th Brigade succeeded in reaching its objective and began to consolidate, but the enemy then launched a series of strong counter-strokes which, despite a spirited defence, eventually forced the divisional line back over the Steenbeek, where it stood at the end of the day's fighting.

XVIII Corps had achieved much of what had been asked of it during the opening assault. The Germans opposite were shocked by the ferocity of the opening blow, and Haig was desperate to keep them on the ropes by resuming the offensive as quickly as possible. Unfortunately, this was not to be. The rain, which began to fall heavily during the afternoon of 31st July, continued unabated over the following days, turning the low-lying Flanders ground into a quagmire. The British watched the pouring rain and cursed their luck. The initial advance had outrun the range of the heavy guns in their original positions to the west of the Yperlee Canal. They now needed

---

63  TNA WO 95/951/4: XVIII War Diary.
64  TNA WO 95/951/4: XVIII Corps War Diary.
65  TNA WO 95/951/4: XVIII Corps War Diary.

to be brought forward to engage their next set of targets, but the rain and the terrible ground conditions made this very difficult. At the same time, roads and tracks between Ypres and the front, damaged by artillery fire, had to be repaired, and in some cases completely reconstructed. A new light railway system also had to be built to ensure that sufficient artillery ammunition could be carried to the new gun positions. Once the heavy artillery was in position, and a sufficient supply of ammunition provided, a further period of time was required to reduce the enemy's trench system, concrete bunkers and strongpoints before another assault could take place.[66] As a consequence, the Fifth Army was not in a position to resume offensive action until the middle of August, giving the Germans time to recover, reorganise and reinforce. This delay would cost the 48th Division and their flanking formation, the 11th Division, dearly in the next phase of the battle. Rather than facing a dislocated, weakened, and demoralised enemy in makeshift defences, the attacking troops would be going up against opponents who had recovered, at least to some degree, from the previous fighting, in well-prepared positions, strengthened with wire and ferro-concrete shelters. In effect, the attackers would be starting the battle all over again, almost from scratch. As Capt Philip Wright put it, the delay had presented the enemy with "a priceless opportunity of reorganising, bringing up reinforcements, and making new positions preparatory to our next onslaught".[67]

In August 1917, as today, the Steenbeek was not a significant obstacle. It was not a wide river, nor was it particularly deep or fast flowing. It could easily be waded. A contemporary map recorded that the river was 10ft wide and its banks were 5ft high.[68] But that was before bombardments had churned up the drainage stream banks, adding to the quagmire by allowing water to escape from the original course, and turning the surrounding area into a small lake. Wading was no longer a sensible option, and the 48th Division's orders for the attack show that 21 temporary foot bridges (probably no more than a few planks lashed together) were constructed in the divisional area to ensure the troops could cross the river as quickly as possible.[69] However, the ground on the approach to the Steenbeek, and on the far bank, in front of the German outpost line, although above the level of the river, was also heavily cratered by shellfire. The incessant rain which had characterised the opening stages of the offensive, had created a veritable swamp through which the assaulting troops would have to pass, slowing them down and making them easier targets for German machine guns, snipers, and artillery fire.

In this phase of the Third Ypres offensive (Battle of Langemarck, 16-18th August 1917) the Fifth Army would be attacking on an 11-mile front that extended from Santier Farm, 1.5 miles north-west of Langemarck, to Stirling Castle, south of the Ypres-Menin Road. Maxse issued his orders for the attack on 7th August. In big-picture terms, this was to be almost a replica of the 31st July assault, but starting a few hundred yards further east. Under a heavy, creeping artillery barrage, XVIII Corps would go forward in the centre of the Fifth Army line, between XIV Corps (left) and XIX Corps. The 48th Division would attack on the right, 11th Division on the left. The South Midlanders' main objective was the Langemarck – Gheluvelt Line, known to the Germans as the Wilhelm Stellung, the third line of enemy defences, which ran through the division's battle front from north-west to south-east. This was to be achieved in two distinct

---

66   TNA WO 95/951/5: XVIII Corps War Diary.
67   P L Wright, p.71.
68   See Map Sheet 28NW, 1:20,000, Edition 6A, July 1917, trenches corrected to 30th June 1917.
69   TNA WO 95/2746/2: Divisional Order No 210, 10th August 1917, 48th Division War Diary,

From Peronne to Passchendaele 103

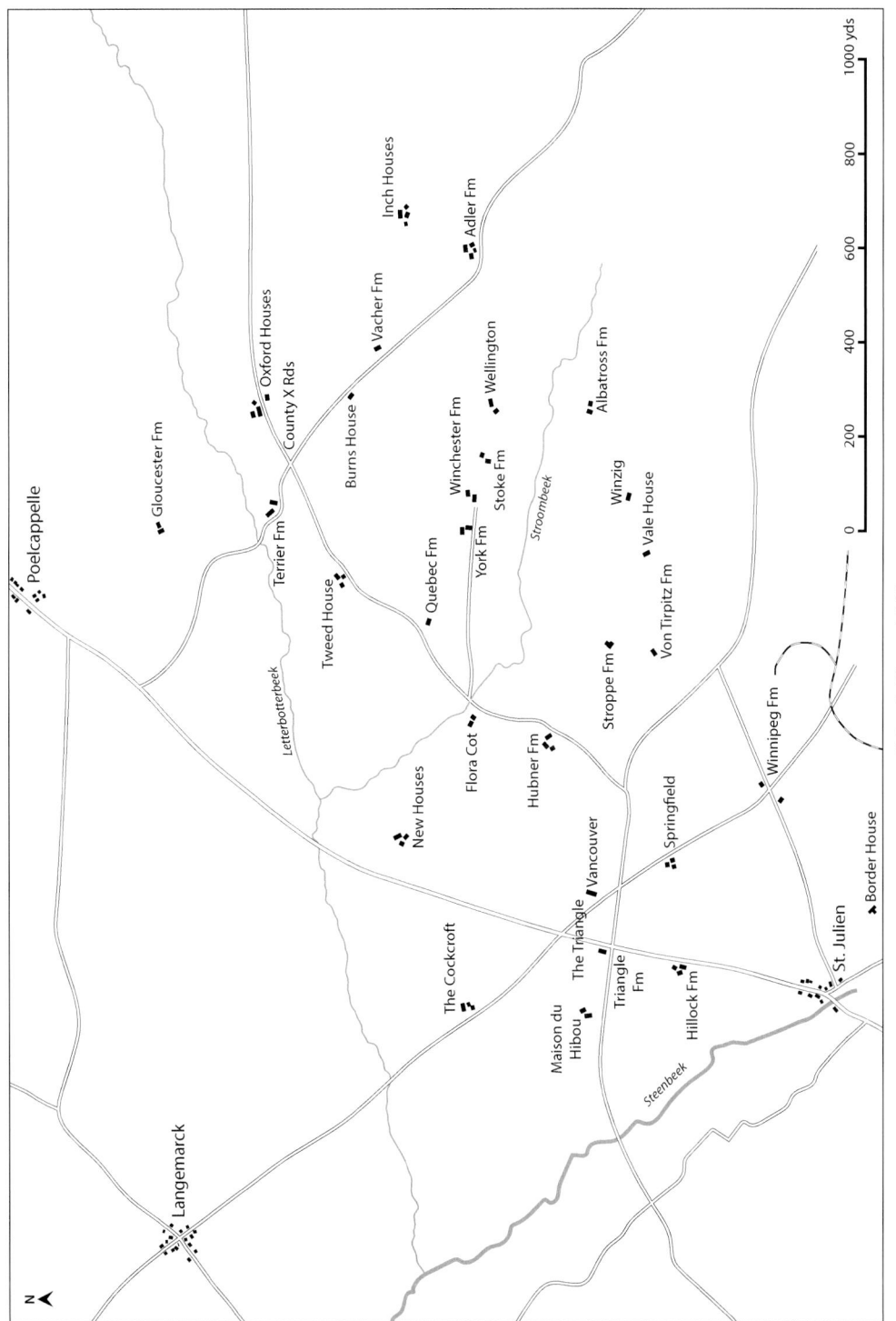

Map 3 Ypres 1917.

bounds, with eight tanks of 20th Company, G Battalion, Tank Corps, allocated to provide the infantry with intimate fire support. On reaching the primary objective the 48th Division was to establish an outpost line running through Von Tirpitz Farm, Stroppe Farm, Hubner Farm and Flora Cot and to construct strongpoints behind this, beginning at a point 500 yards due east of St Julien and including Winnipeg, Springfield, Maison du Hibou, and Hillock Farm.

Once again, as part of the detailed preparation for the advance, Maxse ordered a model to be created, depicting the area east of the Steenbeek. This was located in a field, near the 48th Division headquarters, to the north of the Poperinghe–Vlamertinghe Road, about mid-way between the two towns. All officers taking part in the attack, together with as many NCOs and men as possible, were ordered to view the model to ensure they were well-acquainted with the ground over which they would be attacking.[70]

Fanshawe and his staff produced their plan for achieving the Corps Commander's intent, and this was issued as divisional orders on 10th August, setting out instructions for a Brigade-level attack by 145th Brigade with 143rd and 144th brigades in divisional reserve. The first objective was identified as the line Winnipeg – Spot Farm – Springfield – Langemarck Road –Vancouver (known as the Green Line). The second was to be the Langemarck-Gheluvelt Line within boundaries. The assaulting battalions would be 1/5th Gloucesters on the right, 1/1st Bucks Battalion in centre and 1/4th Oxfords on the left. Each battalion would attack in four waves on a two-company front and each company would be organised on a two-platoon front. The 1/4th Royal Berkshires were in Brigade reserve and would be arranged in artillery formation (each platoon in a diamond with sections in files) behind the assaulting units. According to Wyrall's wartime history of the Gloucestershire Regiment, the assembly points for the two leading waves was on the east (ie enemy) bank of the Steenbeek, but this requires some explanation.[71] Although the original Brigade orders, dated 10th August,[72] did indeed stipulate that the attack was to be launched from the east of the river, this was amended on 15th August. Amendment No 4 to 145th Brigade Order No 241 stated: "The 4 waves of the Assaulting Battalions will deploy W [west] of the R. Steenbeek, except on the extreme Right which will be East of the river."[73]

Fine weather had returned, bringing with it improved visibility and good observation, but the ground underfoot remained very soft, and the mud deep. This, coupled with multiple water-filled shell craters meant that there was no possibility of using tanks to support the infantry attack in the 48th Division's sector, and these were withdrawn in a supplementary order, issued on 14th August.[74] This was a considerable set-back as the assaulting troops would be left to deal with multiple concrete machine gun posts and fortified buildings on their own, after the creeping barrage had passed over the German positions, using only rifles, Lewis Guns, grenades … and guts.

Zero was set for 0445. During the night of 15/16th August, the troops began to move up to their assembly positions. For some, this was a long, hard, energy-sapping slog. The Bucks

---

70  TNA WO 95/951/5: XVIII Corps War Diary.
71  E Wyrall, p.222.
72  TNA WO 95/2761/4: Order No 241, 10th August 1917, 145th Brigade War Diary,
73  TNA WO 95/2761/4: Amendment No 4 to Order No 241, 15th August 1917, 145th Brigade War Diary.
74  TNA WO 95/951/5: XVIII Corps Order GS 66/23, 14th August 1917, XVIII Corps War Diary.

Battalion left its billets at Dambre Camp on the morning of 15th August and marched to the Canal Bank where the men waited for darkness before making the final move to their forming-up points. This was, to quote Capt. Philip Wright, "a most trying march", much of it being over ground pocked with water-filled shell-holes, in pitch darkness, and under enemy shellfire. The German gunners, clearly aware that something was brewing, opened a counter-preparation barrage at 2045 on the evening of the 15th and maintained it throughout the night. A trench-board track had been laid to guide the troops, but this was of little help and in some places, it had been completely destroyed by shells. Wright continued: "With nothing else to aid us in keeping direction it was no real wonder that three platoons of C Company lost their way and failed to reach the start-line in time for the initial assault."[75] According to the Brigade battle narrative, this delay was actually caused by a Lewis Gun limber becoming bogged down.[76] Whatever the reason, this was not a major issue because these platoons were part of the follow-on waves and were not required for the first objectives. Forming-up trenches were not dug, due to the sodden condition of the ground. Instead, the men took cover in shell holes as they waited for the signal to move forward. Just before zero they began to cross the river. Promptly, at 0445, in the pre-dawn darkness, the opening barrage came down, 200 yards east of the stream, and the leading waves moved off towards the enemy line which was being illuminated by the explosions of hundreds of shells.

In the centre, the Bucks Battalion had a very rough time from the start. Ground conditions were poor, and in the darkness the men struggled to keep up with the creeping barrage. As a result, the protective bombardment had lifted off the German forward positions before the attackers reached them, and the defenders immediately opened a heavy machine gun fire from numerous concrete emplacements and fortified ruins of farmhouses where the garrisons had survived the shelling. This was quickly supplemented by rifle fire from German infantry in trenches to the sides and in front of the concrete machine gun shelters, and from old gun-pits that had been re-organised as defensive positions. This wall of fire took a heavy toll on the attackers. Almost immediately the leading wave of the right company (B) was cut down, losing two of its three officers. The second wave closed up and engaged the enemy with rifle and Lewis Gun fire while parties of men tried to work around the flanks. The defenders resisted strongly and showed no signs of capitulating until the third wave arrived and closed on them in a rush. This was followed by a short bout of hand-to-hand fighting before the enemy in one position finally threw in the towel. On seeing this, the other garrisons, probably deciding that honour had been served, soon followed suit. On the left of the battalion's attack, A Company met with less resistance initially, but after advancing about 150 yards east of the stream the first wave came under very heavy cross-fire from machine guns in depth positions, claiming many casualties. As a result, this wave reached the gun pit line with only about 16 men still in fighting condition. The second wave moved up to support, but the left platoon was stopped in its tracks by fire from the left gun pit and a trench immediately to the north-east as well as from Maison du Hibou and Triangle Farm. Meanwhile, the right platoon appears to have pushed through the gun pits, passing southeast of Hillock Farm, collecting the remaining men from the first wave as they went which took their number to about 25. They reached Springfield and the road to the left at about 0645, losing some

---

75  P L Wright, p.57.
76  TNA WO 95/2761/4: 145th Brigade War Diary.

men en-route, especially near the line of gun pits due east of Hillock Farm. Six men were spotted at Springfield at about 0900, and shortly after this, four were seen being led away as prisoners. On the right of the battalion's attack, after the initial success, it was impossible to make further progress. The assaulting troops were faced by a large area of standing water and the surrounding ground was "nothing short of a morass". To make matters worse, on the far side of the water was a concrete blockhouse and a gun pit, housing machine gunners and snipers. Every attempt at movement resulted in casualties. 2/Lt G A Johnston, the battalion Intelligence Officer, was badly wounded in this sector whilst attempting to make contact with a party of D Company. By 0700, with the exception of the men who had got to Springfield, the battalion had reached the limit of its advance for that day. Small groups of men with rifles and Lewis Guns were dug in and holding positions to the north-east of St Julien and to the south of Hillock Farm, astride the St Julien-Poelcapelle Road. About 0800 the enemy were spotted coming over the ridge north of Springfield and dropping into a trench southeast of the nearby cross-roads. An hour later two or three lines of enemy troops came over the ridge and moved down towards Triangle Farm. There was also an attempt made to reinforce the gun pit on the battalion's right. However, by this point a Vickers medium machine gun had been established on the roof of a captured concrete shelter and two further guns arrived and were quickly brought into action, while all non-essential men were taken from battalion headquarters to reinforce the line south of Hillock Farm.[77] A platoon of the reserve battalion, 1/4th Royal Berkshires, was sent up to establish flank protection south-west of the farm. The German attack was halted within 20 minutes and many of the enemy were seen retiring back from whence they had come. By mid-day, losses from snipers and machine gun fire forced a withdrawal on the left to the south of Hillock Farm. As the war diary noted, however, "this proved to be but a slight improvement as enemy fire from Hillock Farm and Maison du Hibou never stopped sweeping the Triangle–St Julien Road and the ground to either side of it". A further counter-attack at 1930 was also halted by rifle and machine gun fire, but at 2130 an enemy advance from Triangle Farm succeeded in driving in some posts before things quietened down for the remainder of the night.[78]

During this attack, the First Bucks Battalion had managed to struggle forward for about 2-300 yards from their start point. For this small advance, the casualty list included one company commander (Capt G V Neave, OC C Company) and 43 Other Ranks dead, eight officers and 188 Other Ranks wounded, including Capt G R F Knight (22), OC A Company, who was recovered off the battlefield but died from his injuries the following day at a Casualty Clearing Station at Dozinghem to the north of Poperinghe. A further 49 men were reported missing. The battalion was relieved by 1/8th Worcesters (144th Brigade) on the night of 17/18th August and moved back to Dambre Camp via Reigersberg Camp. Gerald Vansittart Neave, whose parents lived at Ealing, in west London, had been educated at Bedford School and HMS Conway before joining the merchant navy. He had been working as a tea and rubber planter in Ceylon (now Sri Lanka) and returned to the UK at the outbreak of war. He was commissioned into the Oxfordshire and Buckinghamshire Light Infantry in February 1915. Capt. Neave has no known grave and is commemorated on the Tyne Cot Memorial.[79]

---

77  TNA WO 95/2763: Bucks Battalion War Diary.
78  TNA WO 95/2763: Bucks Battalion War Diary.
79  *Lives of the First World War* <https://livesofthefirstworldwar.iwm.org.uk/story/97359> (accessed 30th May 2022).

On the left of the Brigade attack the 1/4th Oxfordshire and Buckinghamshire Light Infantry had a similar experience. All companies were reported in position by 0400. This was done via telephone, using the code phrase "socks received at Transport Lines".[80] The Oxfords started well and faced only light rifle fire during the initial move forward. But 200 yards east of the Steenbeek was a low ridge, and once the attackers crested this feature, they came under effective machine gun fire from Maison du Hibou and from their right flank (possibly Hillock Farm). The rear waves came up and efforts were made to push forward, but the sheer weight of enemy fire brought the advance to a halt about 100 yards in front of Maison du Hibou and Triangle Farm. The battalion war diarist recorded, with an understandable hint of bitterness: "Protected by strong concrete shelters the enemy maintained their fire while our barrage passed over them."[81] Most of the company officers became casualties in attempts to get forward and the Oxfords could do little but dig in where they were and attempt to hold what ground they had gained. Meanwhile, battalion headquarters at Alberta Farm, west of the Steenbeek, came under heavy artillery fire, severing all communications for several hours. 1/7th Worcesters from 144th Brigade, in reserve, was sent forward and made two attempts to capture Maison du Hibou in an effort to neutralise the machine gun threat from that location. The first effort was driven back. In the second a foothold was gained in the enemy position, but this was short-lived, the attackers being driven out by a bombing attack before they had a chance to exploit the opportunity. The survivors sat tight in their line of shell-holes, sustaining further losses from snipers until they were relieved by the 1/7th Worcesters after midnight on the 18th. The Oxfords too had paid a heavy price for such a small advance. Five officers and 60 Other Ranks were killed; five officers and 100 Other Ranks were wounded; and 4 men were reported missing. Among the dead were Capt Andrew Scott Wotherspoon, Lt Hamilton Jefferson, Lt Felix Ernest Jones MC, 2/Lt Claude Herbert Bowman, and 2/Lt Andrew Frank Salmon. None of these officers' bodies was recovered after the advance, no doubt due to the condition of the ground, and the further heavy fighting that took place there. All are commemorated on the Tyne Cot memorial.

On the right, the 1/5th Gloucesters gained their first objectives – Border House and gun pits to the north and south of the St Julien–Winnipeg Road with some tactical efficiency. Unfortunately, early success was to be no indicator of the ultimate outcome. Here, again, the end result was a small advance at a very heavy cost. The Gloucesters were stopped by withering machine gun fire coming from Janet Farm, and other positions further back, causing many casualties. In addition, the Germans had installed a machine gun team in the remains of a house on the northern outskirts of St Julien, which was enfilading them from the left. This had to be knocked out if any further advance was to be made. The position was attacked with rifle grenades and by a Lewis Gun team and was eventually silenced. However, by the time this had been achieved the barrage had left the attacking troops well in its wake. With no artillery support, the surviving Gloucesters were left with little option but to dig in where they stood, beating off a German counter-attack with rifle and Lewis Gun fire. During the night troops from 1/8th Royal Warwickshires moved forward under cover of darkness and established a new line of posts about 100 yards in advance of the Gloucesters, who were relieved during the following evening. Casualties totalled 217 killed, wounded, and missing.

---

80  TNA WO 95/2746/2: Order No 209 (Assembly Instructions), 10th August 1917, 48th Division General Staff War Diary.
81  TNA WO 95/2764/1: 1/4th OBLI War Diary.

In the face of stiff, determined enemy opposition – and appalling ground conditions – the 48th Division failed to get anywhere near the main objective – the Langemarck–Gheluvelt Line. This was not, however, due to any lack of determination on the part of the attacking troops. Indeed, as Brigadier-General Donald Watt, GOC 145th Brigade, pointed out in his post-operational narrative, "all ranks appear to have behaved with great gallantry".[82] He was particularly glowing in his praise of the Bucks Battalion which, he said, had "specially distinguished itself" in the fighting. He singled out the part played by the Commanding Officer, Lt Col L L C Reynolds DSO, who moved forward at a critical moment and took personal command of three officer-less companies, rapidly reorganising them to fight off the enemy's main counter-attack.[83] Fanshawe praised the Brigade for its efforts. In a note to Watt, dated 19th August, he wrote: "I appreciate very much the stubborn and determined fighting spirit shown by you, and your officers and men, in the battle of the 16th. Although the fortunes of war, in the form of concrete shelters and an unexpectedly strong preliminary position, prevented us from gaining more than a portion of the objectives we want, we made a very valuable improvement to our position for future progress."[84]

Analysing the reasons for the failure, XVIII Corps pointed squarely to the absence of tanks to provide intimate fire support to the infantry as they tackled the numerous pillboxes, fortified cellars, and the machine gun teams therein.[85] With some impunity, these teams, protected by several feet of reinforced concrete, had sprayed death and destruction at the attacking troops, as they advanced, largely without cover, once the British protective artillery barrage had rolled off into the distance. Interestingly, though, Watt reported that these same gunners, who created such havoc among the assaulting platoons, chose not to fire on British stretcher parties moving about in the open along the St Julien-Winnipeg Road – proof that even in the muddy, bloody hell of Third Ypres, chivalry had not entirely died.[86]

The bunkers, and the machine gunners they protected – almost impervious to artillery fire – were undoubtedly the main problem for the attacking foot soldiers. As the XVIII Corps scribe pointed out: "The creeping barrage had practically no effect…and it would have required a direct hit from a shell of the largest calibre to make any impression on them." Tanks would, he believed, have made a significant difference. "Their cooperation in reducing the many strong points encountered would most probably have resulted in the final objectives being reached on both divisional fronts."[87] The veracity of that statement would be tested in the coming days.

The XVIII Corps attack had gained a toe-hold on the east bank of the Steenbeek. However, the main objective – the Langemarck-Gheluvelt Line – remained stubbornly in enemy hands. This now needed to be taken before the offensive could continue towards the Passchendaele – Staden Ridge and on to Roulers and the coast. But with only a couple of hundred yards of ground between the British line and the Steenbeek, and a number of German strongpoints still blocking the way, Gough believed he had to improve his current position before he could make another attempt on the German third line. This involved pushing forward to knock out the enemy strongpoints and create more space on the east bank of the river in which to assemble

---

82   TNA WO 95/2761/4: 145th Brigade War Diary.
83   TNA WO 95/2761/4: 145th Brigade War Diary.
84   P L Wright, p.79.
85   TNA WO 95/951/5: XVIII Corps War Diary.
86   TNA WO 95/276/1: 145th Brigade War Diary.
87   TNA WO 95/951/5: XVIII Corps War Diary.

his forces for the next stage of the offensive. This series of "minor operations" as they are called in the Corps War Diary – shaping operations as they would be known today – began on 19th August and again involved 48th and 11th divisions.

With the ground conditions improving, and noting the need to suppress the concrete shelters, tanks were once more factored into the battle plan.[88] In the 48th Division sector eight tanks, each allocated to specific locations, were to advance from St Julien at zero (0445) to clear Hillock Farm and the gunpits to its east, as well as Triangle Farm, Maison du Hibou and the crossroads at the apex of The Triangle. Two tanks were to carry on along the Langemarck Road to support an 11th Division attack on a position known as The Cockcroft. Just two companies of infantry would accompany the tanks and their job was to occupy and consolidate the positions cleared by the armour. B Company, 1/5th Royal Warwicks (143rd Brigade), were to go for Hillock Farm and the gunpits, and B company 1/8th Worcesters (144th Brigade), were targeted at Triangle Farm, Maison du Hibou, and the crossroads. A dense smoke and shrapnel barrage was to be fired on all the high ground from which the St Julien–Poelcapelle Road could be observed while high explosive shells were used to suppress the Langemarck – Gheluvelt Line.[89]

The tanks arrived in their assembly area near California Trench, north of Wieltje, on the night of 17/18th August and remained there throughout the 18th before leaving for their start line at St Julien that evening. Eleven tanks managed to make it into St Julien by 0430, the twelfth having broken down on the way. They lined up in a column on the St Julien–Poelcapelle Road, led by the two tanks heading for the Cockcroft, and as the opening barrage came down, they moved off, hidden behind a very effective smoke screen. Blinded by the smoke, the German artillery fired wildly and with little effect. Four vehicles broke down or became ditched as they lumbered forward, but the remainder, moving reasonably well on the roadway, carried on towards their objectives, the infantry following in their wake. At 0600 a single tank arrived at Hillock Farm and found it and the adjacent gun pits empty. A platoon of B Company, 1/5th Royal Warwicks, immediately occupied the positions. At 0615 one male and one female tank approached Maison du Hibou but could get no closer than 80 yards due to the condition of the ground. The male tank opened up with its 6-pounder gun, firing 50 rounds into the strongpoint and after 10 minutes 20-30 Germans were seen bolting from the buildings. The female tank engaged them with her machine guns, killing eight or nine while others managed to get away. However, some of the garrison remained at their posts, determined to make a fight of it. They got their wish. A platoon of B Company, 1/8th Worcesters rushed the buildings, capturing 10 prisoners and a machine gun. A few minutes later a tank arrived at Triangle Farm. Here the enemy also decided to make a stand and another platoon of Worcesters took the position at bayonet-point. None of the garrison survived.

Two tanks reached the crossroads at the apex of The Triangle, north-east of Maison du Hibou and found the garrison there had fled. The crossroads due west of Keerslare was also unoccupied and the Worcesters took possession of both positions. Further north, a female tank got to within

---

88 A total of 12 MK IV tanks were allocated to XVIII Corps for this operation. They were from the Tank Corps' G Battalion and the tanks names all began with the letter "G" 8 were to take part in the attack while four were held in reserve.
89 TNA WO 95/2746/2: Order No 212 dated 18th August 1917, 48th Division General Staff War Diary.

50 yards of The Cockcroft where it became ditched, but the enemy garrison had already pulled out and the position was occupied by troops from the 11th Division.[90]

In stark contrast to the previous assault which had been a day of hard fighting and high casualties for little reward, this attack had secured all of its objectives within just two hours. Charles Carrington credited the infantry with this success, pointing out that tanks could do little in the glutinous mud.[91] The riflemen and Lewis Gunners certainly played their part. However, as predicted by XVIII Corps, there can be no doubt that it was the tanks that made the difference on this occasion, providing a good, early example of all-arms (artillery, infantry, armour) cooperation. The ground, still muddy, had certainly reduced the utility of the tracked vehicles, but even with their restricted mobility, which prevented them from straying from the roads, they had been game-changers, getting around behind the strongpoints and attacking from the rear. The tanks' 6-pounder guns proved to be a potent antidote to the concrete and steel blockhouses, and the sheer shock effect of these lumbering monsters had been enough to encourage some enemy troops to run. But there was another factor at play in this advance, which also helps to explain the success: limited and manageable objectives. This time, the planners did not ask too much of the fighting troops. The tanks and infantry were able to operate within the limits of their capability, proof, if it were needed, of the benefits of the "bite-and-hold" approach utilised so effectively (although on a larger scale) by General Herbert Plumer and his Second Army, later in the Passchendaele battle. Remarkably, according to the XVIII Corps report, the 48th Division's casualties in the operation amounted to just 12, and these were all sustained by the 1/8th Worcesters.[92]

The next "bite", scheduled for 22nd August, was a Corps attack to secure the Green Line of the original plan – Winnipeg – Spot Farm – Springfield – Vancouver – joining up with XIX Corps at the road junction south-east of Winnipeg and with 11th Division near Keerselare. Again, this was to be a short, sharp advance with tanks supported by infantry. 12 tanks were allocated for the task, split into two groups. In the north six vehicles would launch from the cross-roads near Triangle Farm to deal with Vancouver and Springfield (two of these were detailed to head for Bulow Farm to support 11th Division). To the south the remainder would start from Jew Hill and advance on Winnipeg, Spot Farm, and a fortified cemetery, located just off the road, midway between these two positions (two tanks were directed to work down to Schuler Farm to support the 61st Division (XIX Corps) attack in that sector. 143rd Brigade would support the northern attack while 144th Brigade would seize and hold the southern positions). A dense smoke barrage would be fired to obscure the advance until zero plus 20 minutes.

After the success of the earlier assault, in which the tanks had demonstrated their worth in providing close fire support for the infantry, and with a new set of limited objectives, the 48th Division's planners were no doubt confident of a similar outcome. If so, their confidence was misplaced. Although the flanking formations (61st Division on the right and 11th Division on the left) achieved their objectives, the South Midlanders were only able to make a small advance after the tanks failed to arrive on time.[93]

The trouble began almost as soon as the attack got under way at 0445. In the southern sector, the leading tank took a direct hit from an artillery shell as it moved along the St Julien

---

90 TNA WO 95/951/5: Report on Operations on 19th August 1917, XVIII Corps War Diary.
91 C E Carrington, p.54.
92 TNA WO 95/951/5: XVIII Corps War Diary.
93 TNA WO 95/951/5: XVIII Corps War Diary.

From Peronne to Passchendaele 111

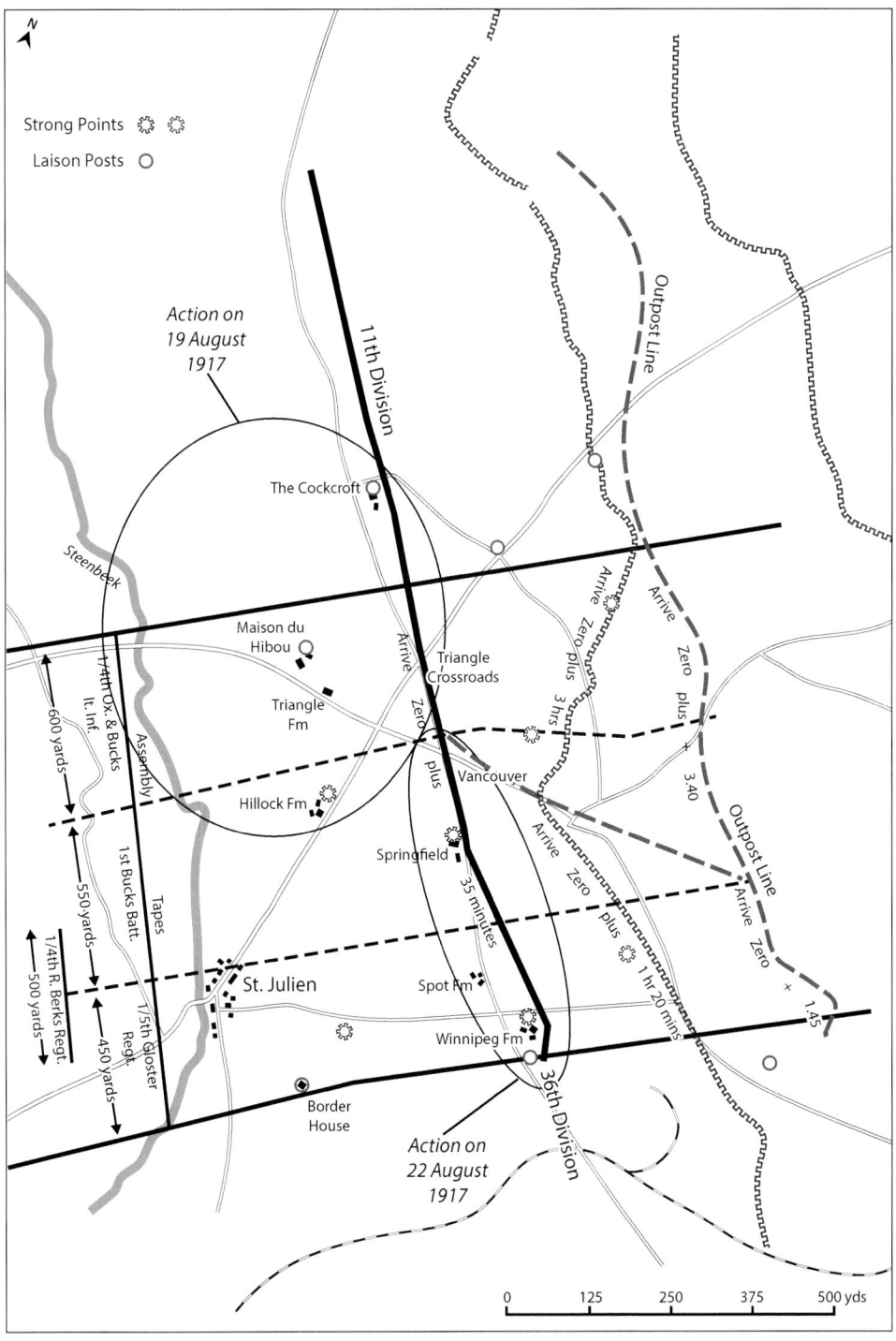

Map 4 St Julien 19th and 22nd August 1917.

– Winnipeg Road, which knocked it out, blocking the way forward.[94] The following tanks were unable to leave the road because of the condition of the ground on either side. So although the infantry, 1/5th and 1/7th Royal Warwicks (143rd Brigade), following closely behind the creeping barrage, arrived in front of their objectives on time and in good order, the tanks, vital to deal with the concrete strongpoints, did not, most of them becoming "ditched".[95] Jury Farm, an intermediate objective, was taken and the enemy were driven out of gunpits to the south of the farm (both positions were lost in subsequent counter-attacks).[96] However, under orders not to assault the main objectives without tanks, the Warwickshires dug in and the creeping barrage rolled on towards the Langemarck-Gheluvelt Line. Winnipeg, Springfield and Spot Farm remained in German hands. During this action, the 1/5th Royal Warwickshires' Commanding Officer, Lt Col Charles Retallack, was seriously wounded.

Meanwhile, to the north, where 1/6th Gloucesters were making for Vancouver, the tanks also ran into difficulties in getting forward. The Gloucesters reported themselves in position for the assault by 0650 but their armour was late. The barrage lifted off the objective before the tank support arrived and, unable to manoeuvre off-road, the two tanks allocated to this assault could not silence the strongpoint and its machine guns.[97] The Gloucesters had no option but to dig in where they stood, about 100 yards west of the Winnipeg – Langemarck Road.

Probably aware that Haig was becoming frustrated by Fifth Army's lack of significant progress,[98] Gough immediately issued orders for 48th and 11th divisions to resume their attacks on 27th August, after a short period of preparation.[99] In an attempt to surprise the enemy, it was decided to dispense with the by now fairly standard dawn attack, and instead set zero for early afternoon (1355). In 48th Division's sector, all three infantry brigades would be engaged. 143rd Brigade (right) and 144th Brigade (left) were to seize the Winnipeg – Springfield line before moving on to take the remainder of the Langemarck – Gheluvelt line and establish themselves in new positions immediately to the east of the old German defences. In the second phase, commencing at zero plus five hours (1855), 145th Brigade was to pass through the leading brigades and head for the line Von Tirpitz Farm–Stroppe Farm– Genoa Farm–Hubner Farm. Having captured these positions, it was to consolidate against an enemy counter-attack, establishing strongpoints at each of the farms.[100]

Although the ground conditions were no better than on 22nd August, a section of tanks (four tanks) was allocated to the division.[101] However, having learned from the previous attack, the infantry were ordered not to wait for armoured support before assaulting their objectives. The tanks, meanwhile, were directed to focus their efforts on assisting 145th Brigade to take the final objectives (a single tank was allocated to each of the four farm positions). If the leading infantry brigades found that they needed tank support to deal with an enemy blockhouse, they were to signal for help (by sending a runner) and the nearest tank would respond "if able". [102]

---

94  TNA WO 95/2746/2: 48th Division War Diary.
95  TNA WO 95/2756/1: 1/7th Royal Warwickshire Regiment War Diary
96  TNA WO 95/2746/2: 48th Division War Diary.
97  TNA WO 95/2757/5: 144th Brigade War Diary.
98  G Sheffield, p.235.
99  TNA WO 95/951/5: XVIII War Diary.
100 TNA WO 95/2746/2: 48th Division (GS) War Diary.
101 D Battalion, 1st Brigade, Tank Corps.
102 TNA WO 95/2746/2: 48th Division (GS) War Diary.

The attackers moved up to assembly positions on the west bank of the Steenbeek during the night of 26/27th August. The tanks, likewise, used the cover of darkness to move into St Julien where they remained undiscovered, under camouflage nets, until the creeping barrage signalled the start of the operation. At that point they advanced in pairs along the Poelcapelle Road to Triangle Farm, where they were to lie-up until required.

For the infantrymen of 143rd and 144th Brigades, huddled in the shallow, water-filled assembly trenches, the wait for the attack must have been nearly as agonising as the act of going "over the top". Any movement risked giving away their position and bringing down enemy artillery fire, so the men had to sit still in muddy water for more than 10 hours, as the clock ticked down the minutes to zero. When that moment arrived, many of the troops, their muscles stiff from the long wait, struggled to get going. As the 144th Brigade war diary recorded: "Great difficulty was experienced in getting the men out of the assembly trenches before the barrage lifted." They had become quite literally "stuck in the mud".[103]

Even when the men had been extricated from the clawing, clinging, slippery Flanders sludge, the attackers immediately found that the "going" was almost impossible, and as rain began to fall it became even worse. The creeping barrage had been planned to dwell on the first objective for 12 minutes and then lift 100 yards every 8 minutes. This pause was designed to give the infantrymen time to get close to the objectives while the enemy machine gunners and riflemen were forced to remain in cover, unable to fire. But the muddy, waterlogged ground slowed the attackers even more than expected and the guns lifted off the first objective before the assaulting troops arrived. The enemy had at first seemed inclined to surrender, but, as the XVIII Corps battle narrative reveals, once they saw that the attacking troops were practically immobile, the defenders took full advantage of what had now become an unequal contest. Every available machine gun and rifle was trained on the South Midlanders as they struggled in the mire, and German snipers, taking up forward positions in shell holes, were able to pick off easy targets "at their leisure".[104] Meanwhile, the assaulting troops found that the mud which was reducing their movement, was also getting into the working parts of their rifles and Lewis Guns, rendering them practically useless and preventing the troops from returning fire. With the artillery barrage now far behind them, the Germans in the front breastworks were able to stand unhindered on the parapets to get a better view.

In the face of such awful conditions, the 48th Division achieved a minor miracle. Despite tough and determined German resistance, Springfield, and Vancouver – both objectives for the initial attack on 31st July – were finally captured. Springfield, in particular, put up a spirited defence and delayed the advance for some hours before falling to a joint effort by troops of 1/8th Royal Warwicks (143rd Brigade) and 1/8 Worcesters (144th Brigade) at around 1830 that evening. 1/7th Worcesters took Vancouver a short time later. At that point the divisional line ran just east of Vancouver and Springfield and from there it continued about 100 yards west of the Winnipeg-Springfield Road to the boundary with XIX Corps. This marked the limit of the Division's advance for the day. The leading brigades having failed to reach the Langemarck – Gheluvelt Line, 145th Brigade was not in a position to launch its planned attack against the Von Tirpitz Farm–Stroppe Farm–Hubner Farm Line. Instead, it relieved the two assaulting

103 TNA WO 95/2757/5: 144th Brigade War Diary.
104 TNA WO 95/951/5: XVIII Corps War Diary

brigades, the survivors making their weary way back to Reigersburg and Dambre camps, where they arrived quite exhausted.[105] The tanks had helped where they could, but they were no match for the ground conditions. All four vehicles became "ditched", one several times, and although some managed to extricate themselves using their un-ditching gear and carry on for a while, in the end all were either stuck fast or disabled and had to be abandoned.[106]

Casualties for the two leading brigades were as follows:

|  | Killed | Wounded | Missing |
|---|---|---|---|
| **143rd Brigade** |  |  |  |
| 1/6th R Warwicks | 28 | 123 | 14 |
| 1/8th R Warwicks | 35 | 83 | 54 |
| **144th Brigade** |  |  |  |
| 1/7th Worcesters | 22 | 72 | 7 |
| 1/8th Worcesters | 42 (+1 DoW) | 63 | 3 |
| **Totals** | **128** | **341** | **78** |

The action on 27th August marked the end of 48th Division's part in the opening phase of the Passchendaele battle. It also marked the end of Haig's patience with Gough's policy of successive, small-scale attacks for little gain and at high cost in men and materiel. Primary responsibility for the battle now switched to General Herbert Plumer and his Second Army, with Fifth Army relegated to a supporting role.

The South Midlanders were relieved by 58th Division on 28th August and moved back to camps to the west of Ypres where they could rest, recuperate, refit and train ahead of a return to the fight that autumn. Nothing they had previously experienced, at Ploegsteert, the Somme, or the Hindenburg Line, could have prepared them for the conditions in which they were obliged to fight in the Steenbeek valley. As Charles Carrington later noted, August 1917 was the worst month his battalion had experienced so far. The unit had lost over 300 men, including the Commanding Officer and seven other officers, for the capture of "a few paltry farms and gun pits".[107] The only consolation, and it was a small one, was that no other unit had achieved much more. Philip Wright would, no doubt, have been speaking for many when he wrote: "In our joy to be rid of the Ypres area, we began at once to entertain hopes of never seeing it again …"[108] Edwin Campion Vaughan, who had taken part in the capture of Springfield, and trudged back to Reigersberg Camp with the remains of his company, "soaked in mud and blood from head to foot" remarked, "Feeling sick and lonely, I returned to my tent to write out my casualty report; but instead I sat on the floor and drank whisky after whisky as I gazed into a black and empty future."[109]

---

105 TNA WO 95/2746/2: 48th Division War Diary; WO 95/2757/5: 144th Brigade War Diary and WO 95/2754/5: 143rd Brigade War Diary.
106 TNA WO 95/951/4: Narrative of Operations, 27th August 1917, XVIII Corps War Diary.
107 C E Carrington, pp.55-56.
108 P L Wright, p.83.
109 E C Vaughan, p.232.

# 6

# Road to Caporetto

To understand why Italy went to war in April 1915; how it ended up on the side of the Allies; the military and political failings that led to the Caporetto disaster and the subsequent British and French intervention, it will be useful to begin with a summary of how modern Italy came into being, and the road that led to the defeat of the Italian armies at Caporetto.

Before unification, Italy consisted of a number of independent states and statelets. The birth of the nation as we know it today started with the pain of invasion by Napoleon in 1796. Bonaparte immediately set about re-shaping the old Italian states into three elements – the Northern Italian Republic, later the Kingdom of Italy; the Kingdom of Naples; and areas that were annexed to imperial France, including Piedmont, Tuscany, and Rome. With Napoleon's downfall in 1814, the Congress of Vienna (1814-15) redistributed his conquered territories. Most of the old states were re-constituted, becoming the Kingdom of Piedmont-Sardinia; the Grand Duchy of Tuscany; the Duchy of Parma; the Papal States; and the Kingdom of the Two Sicilies.

The old social orders might have been back in charge, but the years of Napoleonic rule had left their mark. Some of the political ideas that had brought about the French revolution had been imported with the forces of occupation. And although the peninsula continued as a loose conglomeration of states during this period, the heart of a new political theory was beginning to beat, pumping the blood of nationalism and the oxygen of unification.

Secret societies were formed with the goals of promoting nationalism and unity. Among these was Young Italy, founded in 1831 by Guiseppe Mazzini, who expounded the importance of achieving Italian unification through the desires and actions of the Italian people – a movement that became known as the *Risorgimento* or resurgence. Revolutionary unrest in 1848 acted as a catalyst for nationalist sentiment. Uprisings in several cities, led by professionals such as doctors, lawyers and students, were quickly put down as the old regimes took steps to hold on to their power. But Mazzini's ideas did not go away: more people rallied to the cause, continuing to demand a new, united Italy, under a new, accountable Government and state.

The final chapter of the *Risorgimento* began in 1859 when the Kingdom of Piedmont-Sardinia, under King Victor Emmanuel II, and his Prime Minister, Count Camillo di Cavour, secured a new alliance with France, leading to the Franco-Austrian War of that year. The Austrians were defeated by a joint force of French and Piedmontese–Sardinians at the battles of Magenta and

Solferino (1859),[1] and this resulted in the northern province of Lombardy being handed over to Victor Emmanuel II. The northern states held plebiscites in 1859 and 1860, voting to join Piedmont-Sardinia, bringing unification a step closer. In the south, Giuseppi Garibaldi formed an army and invaded Sicily before conquering Naples, overthrowing the old Bourbon regime and handing the southern states to Victor Emmanuel. In 1861 a national parliament was formed and announced the creation of the Kingdom of Italy, with Victor Emmanuel as its monarch. But two important territories – Rome and Venetia – remained outside the new nation. The *Risorgimento* could not be considered to be complete until this situation was rectified.

In 1866 Italy and Prussia formed an alliance against Austria and the resulting conflict (the Austro-Prussian War) saw Venetia being ceded to Italy. In 1870, with their old ally, France, still responsible for guarding the Papal states, but distracted by the Franco-Prussian War (1870-71), the Italian army entered Rome led by Gen Raffaele Cadorna. Rome and the Papal States were incorporated into Italy and in 1871 the capital was moved from Florence to Rome, thus completing the *Risorgimento*. Even then, however, some Italian nationalists – the *Irridenta* [2]– believed that their work was not finished and continued to yearn for other ethnically-Italian regions such as the Trentino, Istria, Trieste and the Dalmatian coast to be included within the borders of the new state. This would be a factor in determining Italian decisions in the coming *Guerra Mondiale*.

Having acquired nation status, Italy found herself having to service a nation-sized debt, and thus needing to improve her economic performance. To do this she sought new markets for the output of her agricultural and industrial production. This included an obsession with gaining territory overseas, particularly in Africa, where she seized Eritrea in the east and Tripolitania (part of Libya) in the north. Expansion in Africa brought with it the risk of coming into conflict with other colonial powers including France and Great Britain. To protect herself from external aggression, particularly from France, who clearly had a history of intervention on the Italian peninsula, Italy sought a defensive alliance that might help to shield her from future aggression. She achieved this in 1882 when she joined what would become known as the Triple Alliance, which tied her to Germany and the Austro-Hungarian Empire.

Necessity makes for strange bedfellows. The Danube Monarchy was regarded by most Italians as a hated enemy and the Austrians felt the same about the Italians. But both nations were prepared to overlook their mutual history in the pursuit of mutual support. It was, nonetheless, a controversial alliance in Italy, to the extent that successive governments in Rome denied the existence of a pact until 1915.[3]

Membership of the alliance guaranteed Italy that if she were attacked by France the other signatories would come to her aid, while she agreed to do likewise in the event that Germany or Austria were to be attacked by France or Russia. The pact also improved security along the border with Austria, fostered better relations with Germany, and brought with it the international respectability that came with membership of a defensive arrangement with two of the major geo-political players in the northern hemisphere at that time. However, the treaty

---

1   The Battle of Solferino was the last time European armies took the field directly commanded by monarchs. The Emperor, Franz-Joseph, commanded the Austrians; Napoleon III led the French and King Victor Emmanuel II was in charge of the Piedmontese-Sardinians.
2   Irredenta – unredeemed.
3   M Thompson, *The White War*, p.12.

document, as amended in 1912, contained one very significant clause that would have critical implications for the pact in 1915. Article 7 stated that:

> Austria-Hungary and Italy… engage to use their influence to forestall any territorial modification which might be injurious to one or the other of the Powers signatory to the present Treaty. However, if, in the course of events, the maintenance of the status quo in the regions of the Balkans or of the Ottoman coasts and islands in the Adriatic and in the Aegean Sea should become impossible, and if, whether in consequence of the action of a third Power or otherwise, Austria-Hungary or Italy should find themselves under the necessity of modifying it by a temporary or permanent occupation on their part, this occupation shall take place only after a previous agreement between the two Powers, based upon the principle of a reciprocal compensation for every advantage, territorial or other, which each of them might obtain beyond the present status quo, and giving satisfaction to the interests and well-founded claims of the two Parties.[4]

For Italy, this meant any Austrian moves in the Balkans could, in principle, be leveraged to deliver Trentino and/or Trieste as compensation.

As the war clouds gathered in the late summer of 1914, Italy sat firmly on the fence, choosing to declare herself neutral on 3rd August, despite her treaty obligations to Germany and Austria. To excuse her apparent treachery, she pointed out that Austria had decided to take action against Serbia without consulting Italy – a clear violation, she claimed, of Article 7 of the Triple Alliance Treaty, which had been renewed two years before. In reality, however, Italy was buying time. In 1914, she was quite unprepared for war, having failed to take the necessary measures to recover from a difficult campaign in Tripolitania in 1912. The Italians needed to regenerate the army and to decide which way to jump.

Although they had never really counted on Italian help as far as their war plans were concerned, the German hierarchy still felt it was important to prevent the Italians from throwing in their 'lot' with the other side. Britain, France, and Russia, meanwhile, concluded that having Italy on their side would have three important benefits. It would help to occupy the Austrians, thus easing the pressure on Russia in the east; protect France's southern border from attack by an Austrian or combined German-Austrian force; and prevent Austrian reinforcement of the western front.

Both sides tried to entice Italy to join them (although Germany would have been quite happy if Italy had simply remained neutral). Germany put pressure on Austria to agree to hand over Trentino and Trieste. Austria, unsurprisingly, refused. The allies were more generous. The Treaty of London was signed, in secret, on 26th April 1915. Italy, unashamedly pursuing a policy of *Sacro Egoismo* (Sacred Selfishness), undertook to employ all her resources to prosecute the war in common with France, Great Britain and Russia and in return, she would obtain, in the Treaty of Peace, the Trentino, Cisalpine Tirol, Trieste, all Istria, Dalmatia, Valona (now Valore in Albania), and the islands of the Dodecanese.[5] Eyebrows were raised in Downing

---

4 *Text of Triple Alliance Treaty as amended, 5th December 1912* <https://wwi.lib.byu.edu/index.php/Amended_Version_of_The_Triple_Alliance> (accessed 23rd November 2021).
5 *World War I On-line Document Archive* <https://wwi.lib.byu.edu/index.php/The_Treaty_of_London_(1915)> (accessed 21st November 2021).

Street when the terms of the Treaty were set out. Cabinet members described the price of Italian support as "considerable" and even "excessive".[6] Russia initially objected. However, in the end the deal was done. As Mark Thompson rightly put it, ultimately the Allies wanted Italy *in* the war more than Germany and Austria wanted them *out* of it.[7]

On 3rd May, the Italian Ambassador in Vienna was instructed to hand the Austrian government a note, formally denouncing the Treaty of the Triple Alliance. On 23rd May, the same Ambassador presented the Italian declaration of war to Austria-Hungary. Germany immediately broke off diplomatic relations with Italy but stopped short of declaring war. Likewise, Italy did not declare war on Germany until 28th August 1916, the day following Rumania's declaration on Austria-Hungary.

As the Italian Foreign Minister, Baron Sidney Sonnino, negotiated with Vienna, Berlin, London, Paris and Moscow, the Commando Supremo,[8] General Luigi Cadorna, son of the conqueror of Rome, set about preparing his army for war. He had a significant task on his hands. The imperial adventure in northern Libya in 1912 had used up more troops and material than the army could spare, and by August 1914, it was the weakest of any aspiring great power of the time. Despite decades of high military spending, averaging a quarter of the nation's total budget from 1900 – 1914, it had failed to overcome two key problems: the professionalism of the army, and a shortage of critical equipment. The army was constrained by administration and red tape. It had too many support units such as field hospitals, veterinarians, and engineers for its needs. Procurement and supply problems were everywhere. About half of the troops could not read or write; the officer class was severely under-recruited, down by 15,000 men according to some accounts. With only 27 regular divisions, its standing army was about half the size of that of Germany or France and only 13 reserve divisions could be mobilised for war. Cadorna was given the go-ahead for a modernisation programme in October 1914, and he set to work at once. But when the nation eventually took up arms, in May 1915, although the army had sufficient manpower, uniforms, vehicles, rifles and bullets, it still lagged behind in the things that would really matter in the coming fight – machine guns and heavy artillery pieces.

To comprehend the conduct of the war along the Italo–Austrian border, it is first important to comprehend the ground on which the fighting would take place. The common frontier between the two nations had been fixed after the Austro-Prussian War of 1866. Those responsible for drawing the line on the map did Italy no favours. As a result, wherever Italy might choose to fight along the 375 miles of border, with the exception of a small strip along the Mediterranean coastal corridor leading to Trieste, her army would be faced with having to attack uphill against one natural fortress after another, with the Austrians looking down from the high peaks. In addition, with a salient thrusting south, deep into Italian territory on either bank of the Adige River, there was a permanent risk that an Austrian army could break out here and quickly reach the Plain of Lombardy, cutting off and annihilating Italian forces to the east – something the Austrians attempted in 1916 and again in 1918. In the east, a spur of the main Alpine chain running south-east, known as the Julian Alps, extended south as far as Tolmino before broadening out into a series of limestone hills and plateaux. On the Austrian side of the border flowed

---

6  J E Edmonds, *Military Operations Italy*, p.6.
7  M Thompson, p.37.
8  *Commando Supremo* meant both the Supreme Commander himself (in this case General Luigi Cadorna) and the Italian Supreme Headquarters or High Command.

the Isonzo River, not a significant military obstacle in itself, but running through a deep rocky valley where crossing points would have to be selected with care. East of the river sat dry limestone uplands, sloping westwards, criss-crossed with a series of ridges and valleys, including the Bainsizza and Carso plateaux, names that would feature frequently in the fighting to come.

On 21st August 1914, Cadorna issued a memorandum in which he set out his approach to fighting the Austro-Hungarian Empire. He did not wish to fight the old enemy everywhere, and he was particularly reluctant to take them on where they were heavily fortified, such as along the northern border, and in particular, in the South Tyrol salient, which jutted out southwards on either side of the Adige Valley, supported by a railway system going back via Bolzano to Innsbruck and then deep into the heart of the Dual Monarchy. Knowing that he lacked the heavy siege artillery necessary to defeat them in their mountain strongholds, his strategy would be to neutralise them there by a series of limited incursions, designed to keep them off-balance. Meanwhile, his main effort would be in the east, where he would attack in a giant pincer movement over the Isonzo river. Having broken through there, his left arm would drive for Ljubljana and Zagreb and capture the high passes leading to inner Austria whilst his right would surge over the Carso towards Trieste, capture that great port city on the Adriatic, and then swing inland, the arms of the pincers converging again on the Slovenian Plains, to head for Vienna.

During the period of Italian neutrality, the Austrians, who were focused on defeating the Russians in the east, had left their borders with Italy weakly protected, guarded mostly by local militias of boys and old men. Over time, these were gradually reinforced by Landsturm (reserve units) until they totalled about 120 battalions' worth. By February 1915, these battalions had been partly re-organised into divisions. The Isonzo front (also known as the Julian front) was held by two divisions, the Trentino by two divisions, and the Carnic sector by 14 1/2 battalions, or a division plus. Further reinforcements followed after the unexpected success of the Gorlice-Tarnow offensive in May 1915. By the time Italy finally declared war, on 23rd May, the Isonzo front, so critical to Cadorna's strategic vision, was defended by seven divisions – still not enough, but better than nothing, according to some Austrian officers.

Italian mobilisation, planned to take 23 days, ended up taking twice as long, and Cadorna's army was not fully deployed until mid-July. This gave the Austrians more time to prepare their defences and draft in further troops. When hostilities finally commenced, Cadorna had amassed 400,000 men on the plains of Venetia and Friuli. But for some reason, these troops included only two of the army's 17 regular corps – not more than 80,000 bayonets.

On the lower Isonzo, the Third Army was ordered to cross the river, establish bridgeheads and capture Monfalcone while Gorizia was to be isolated by the capture of the flanking hills. The Second Army, further north, was to occupy the Caporetto Basin and the Krn–Mrzli Ridge. In the west, the Fourth Army was to drive into the eastern face of the Trentino Salient, capturing Cortina, Tolbach and Bruneck whilst the First Army stood on the defensive against the western side of the salient. These were bold strokes on paper, and if they had been executed sooner, and with flair and dash, the outcome on the Italian front might have been quite different.

However, the execution did not live up to the rhetoric. Instead of demonstrating Latin elan and lightning speed, the Italians were ponderous and timid. They did not dash; they felt their way forward. For example, at Monfalcone, the cavalry, designed for shock action, was ordered to charge ahead and seize the bridges above the town on the morning of 24th June. Fearing he was about to run into tough resistance, the cavalry commander hesitated. He wanted to keep in touch with his supporting infantry. But the infantry lagged behind, unable to keep up with his horse soldiers. As a result, the cavalry's advance was held up, giving the Austrians time to drop the bridges, leaving the attackers facing a difficult, opposed bridging operation and, at a stroke, killing the attacking momentum that might have helped to deliver an early Italian victory. Instead, the fight turned into another version of trench warfare, a costly slogging match. In this first Battle of the Isonzo, which lasted from 23rd June to 7th July, an opening clash that had been aimed at securing favourable positions on the Carso and Gorizia, from which to mount the next phase of operations, Cadorna lost 14,947 men, including 1,916 killed. The Austrian casualties totalled 9,958. The line had hardly moved. After a pause to bring up more heavy artillery Cadorna tried again with the Second Battle of the Isonzo opening on 18th July and closing on 3rd August. Again, no significant progress was made for the loss of 41,866 Italian casualties (6,287 dead).

Over the following 26 months, from August 1915 to October 1917, Cadorna launched his men at the Austrian positions east of the Isonzo a further nine times. The third battle took place between 18th October and 4th November, the objective again being Gorizia. More artillery was brought in to pound the Austrian positions, but the result was the same – a small gain for significant casualties, 67,008 this time with nearly 11,000 dead on the Italian side alone. After a week's pause to re-organise, the fourth battle was launched on 10th November, this time continuing until 2nd December with no better results and still more dead, wounded and missing. Between declaring war in May, and the end of 1915, Italy had suffered around 250,000 casualties for little territorial gain. She had managed to draw up to a dozen additional Austrian divisions to the Isonzo line, but this had made no appreciable difference to the Central Powers' push against the Russians or the Serbs.

On 6th December 1915 Cadorna was represented at the Inter-Allied Conference at Chantilly b his deputy, General Carlo Porro. It was agreed by all present that in 1916 Britain, France, Italy and Russia should attack simultaneously – or as near simultaneously as they could manage – delivering their 'maximum effort' on all fronts, on a date "as soon as possible after the end of March".[9]

Porro returned to the Italian Supreme Headquarters at Udine and began planning for the Fifth Battle of the Isonzo, which actually commenced early, on 11th March, as a response to the German attack at Verdun (21st February). This time, the weather played its part, with snow falling on the high ground, and rain and fog in the valleys, making for very unfavourable conditions. The Second and Third Armies assaulted the Austrian lines on the Carso and at Plava but made no headway and the offensive was called off after four days.

The Italian official history concluded that the army "could not advance victoriously on the Carso or elsewhere until it had been able to increase its resources in heavy artillery", a case that was being made by Porro at Chantilly on 12 March, even as the latest fighting continued to rage. Cadorna took up the subject at a meeting in Paris on 27th March, explaining that although Italy had increased her war production, she had "not yet manufactured the quantity of artillery which corresponded to her requirements". With France in the midst of the Verdun nightmare and Britain preparing for the Battle of the Somme, Cadorna's timing was not good. His plea for heavy artillery fell on deaf ears, although a request for machine guns met with a more positive response.

9   J E Edmonds, p.15.

Meanwhile, having sat on the defensive for months, soaking up Italian offensive pressure, the Austrians now decided to test the enemy's mettle, not along the Isonzo, but in the Trentino. Austrian Chief of Staff, Conrad von Hotzendorf, who was determined to make Italy pay for their treachery in siding with the allies, began to build up his forces in the South Tyrol, with a view to launching an attack in April. Bad weather made this impossible, however, and the offensive, which Conrad named the *Strafexpedition* (Punishment Expedition) was delayed until 15th May. With all the Italian efforts up to this point being focused on the Isonzo front, the Trentino defences were lightly held by the small Italian First Army, which only consisted of four divisions. When signs of the Austrian build-up became apparent, Cadorna, although sceptical about a serious enemy attack in the Trentino, ordered two divisions to reinforce the First Army, with two more standing by in GHQ reserve, prepared to move to the Trentino if required.

Behind a heavy opening bombardment, the Austrians attacked on 15th May, on a 21-miles front, east of the Adige, and in the first five days they pushed forward between three and five miles, in some places breaking through the Italian third line. But they had not managed to generate sufficient tempo and weight to force a general breakthrough and as the days passed, the Austrian advance slowed to a halt. By 10th June they had advanced about 12 miles in the Asiago area, and about 9 miles on the right near Monte Pasubio. They had not succeeded in their key objective, which was to break out into the plains. On 4th June, Russian General, Brusilov, heard the Italian calls for help and launched an offensive in the east between the Carpathian Mountains and the Pripet marshes, forcing the Austrians into a hasty retreat along a 50-miles front, and obliging Conrad to bring his Trentino attack to a halt.

The Trentino operations cost the Italian army 35,000 dead, 45,000 prisoners and 106,000 sick and wounded. From the start of the year until 1st July 1916, total casualties sustained by Cadorna's forces amounted to 524,760. However, with wounded, missing and sick men rejoining, the actual loss was put at 203,298. With over 800,000 men being called to the colours over the same period, Cadorna's force was stronger than ever. It needed to be, because he was already planning the sixth Battle of the Isonzo, sometimes known as the Battle of Gorizia.

Apparently undaunted and unperturbed by the scale of his losses so far, Cadorna was determined to continue battering the Austrians on his eastern front. Even before the fifth battle had properly ended, he had issued orders to resume the offensive against the town of Gorizia. Preparations had been halted whilst he dealt with the Austrian incursion in the Trentino, but as soon as he was satisfied that the northern threat was being contained, he began to re-organise his forces to undertake a more limited attack with the objective of securing the right bank of the river, opposite Gorizia on the left, as a start line for the next phase of operations.

The Austrians had withdrawn about 70,000 men from the Isonzo front to support the offensive in the Trentino. Cadorna now judged that if he was able to build up his forces in front of Gorizia quicker than the Austrians were able to reinforce their line, he stood a good chance of breaking through. With a combination of secrecy and speed, Cadorna managed to achieve local superiority, launching the assault on Gorizia on 6th August, after a nine-hour bombardment. In two days, the Italians had crossed the river, captured Gorizia, and reached the Austrian second position at the foot of the hills, east of the town. Pausing to bring forward his artillery, the second phase commenced on the 10th, the right of the Third Army securing a foothold on the Carso before the Austrians managed to stiffen their line. Cadorna called a halt to the offensive on 17th August, having failed to push the Austrians out of the Tolmino bridgehead as planned.

The Italians had gained a strip of land 15 miles long and three miles deep. The price they paid for it was 51,232 casualties, compared to Austrian losses of 41,837.

The next three attacks, named, post-war, by the Battles Nomenclature Committee as the Seventh, Eighth and Nineth Battles of the Isonzo, were, in fact, three phases of the same battle, each lasting just a few days, with pauses to re-group, commencing on 14th September. The intent for these actions was to increase the size of the Gorizia bridgehead. The Third Army was to press over the Carso to about six miles beyond the Carso Valley while the Second Army was ordered to secure Selva di Ternova. After an eight-day artillery bombardment, the Third Army advanced on a six-mile front, gaining some ground initially, but a combination of dogged Austrian defence and bad weather slowed the advance, and it was finally suspended on 17th September. The offensive was renewed on 10th October, after a 20-hour bombardment, when the left corps of the Second Army cooperated with the Third Army to attack San Marco. Some further ground was gained on the Carso before the fighting was again suspended on the 12th. The final phase, launched on 1st November, saw two corps of the Second Army attack east of Gorizia while two corps of the Third Army went forward on the Carso. Yet again, little was achieved, and Cadorna brought the offensive to a close on the 4th, blaming heavy losses, exhaustion and bad weather. Once more the Italians had paid a heavy butcher's bill and received little in return. Casualties totalled about 9,000 killed, 43,000 wounded and 23,500 missing.

Secretary of State for War David Lloyd George replaced Herbert Asquith as British Prime Minister in December 1916. The following month, at British prompting, the allies met in Rome to consider their campaign plan for that year. Lloyd George, always keen to find a way of shifting the fighting away from the western front, had drawn up a memorandum proposing a major offensive against the Austrians in Italy. In his diary, General Sir Henry Wilson, who accompanied Lloyd George to Rome for the discussions, described the memorandum as "an amazing document, written without Sir William Robertson's knowledge or approval".[10] In Lloyd George's opinion, Italy's military failures thus far were attributable to a lack of heavy artillery. Consequently, he proposed that they should be reinforced with British and French guns and ammunition in return for an undertaking to deliver a significant operation during the course of the year. The French opposed the idea. They were already committed to the Nivelle offensive on the Aisne, in which they expected to be supported by a British push at Arras and would need all the guns they could muster. They could provide some heavy guns to Italy for a few months, providing they were returned by April. Cadorna, already worried that the Germans and Austrians were going to launch their own offensive in Italy, using troops freed up by the collapse of Rumania, pointed out that a short-term loan of guns was pointless since it would be impossible to consider attacking in Italy until April at the earliest.

The conference failed to achieve an agreement on the matter, but Sir William Robertson and France's General Maxime Weygand, visited Italy at the end of March for further discussions. As a result, Britain agreed to despatch 10 newly-raised 6-in Howitzer batteries (a total of 40 guns) to Italy as soon as possible. France provided a dozen further batteries. The British guns, organised into two groups, were directed to the Carso, and on 12 April, as the Battle of Arras got under way in France, Cadorna gave orders for a tenth attack on the Isonzo.

---

10  J E Edmonds, p.25.

The scheme of manoeuvre was straightforward. General Capello's Second Army would attack at Gorizia, securing the hills to the east of the town and the Monte Kuk ridge on the Bainsizza Plateau. As Austrian reinforcements were drawn to the fighting in the Gorizia area, The Duke of Aosta's Third Army would launch what was intended to be the decisive blow on the Carso. To the north, Capello's army advanced on 12th May, capturing the Monte Kuk ridge as planned, and then held it for a week against repeated and heavy counterstrokes. However, at Gorizia the assault ended in failure almost immediately. The Third Army attacked as planned but because the Gorizia operation had already been halted, they faced stiff opposition and advanced only a few thousand yards before being stopped by the defenders. Much of this ground was re-taken by Austrian counter-attacks, which began on 28th May and continued on 4th June, before the battle was brought to a close, both sides exhausted. In three weeks of heavy fighting the Austrians and Italians suffered dreadful losses. The Italians recorded 36,000 killed, 96,000 wounded and 25,000 taken prisoner. On the Austrian side the numbers were lower but nonetheless hard to bear: 7,300 dead, 45,000 wounded and 23,400 taken prisoner. Cadorna was livid at the number of Italians who had surrendered, blaming revolutionary and pacifist propaganda. The Pope, in an Encyclical issued on 15th August, appealed for peace.

The Third Battle of Ypres having opened on 31st July, Cadorna decided to resume operations on the Isonzo. This time, instead of issuing specific orders to his army commanders he provided a more general directive. This approach was designed to give Capello and the Duke of Aosta greater freedom to prosecute the battle as they saw fit, rather than following a detailed plan, drawn up in Udine, that took no account of what was happening on the ground or how the enemy responded. However, both armies would still be required to achieve objectives as set by the Commando Supremo. The Third Army was to capture the Carso and then Trieste while the Second Army was to seize the Bainsizza Plateau and then Selva di Ternova. A diversionary attack would be launched against the Austrian bridgehead at Tolmino.

After a day-long bombardment, the 11th Battle of the Isonzo commenced on the night of 18/19th August. Capello's Second Army conducted an opposed river crossing and pushed forward on an eight-mile front. The Tolmino diversion was an utter failure, and the Third Army made some ground but lost most it in subsequent enemy counter-attacks. On the 22nd Cadorna decided to stop the Third Army thrust and divert resources to the Second Army front, which then made further ground as the Austrians began a slow, fighting withdrawal across the Bainsizza Plateau. Capello's army tried to pursue, but the 'going' was hard on the shell-pocked surface of the plateau with few serviceable roads and little water to quench the thirst of the attackers. Unable to bring forward artillery to support further operations, Cadorna decided to pause the offensive on the 29th, although some further fighting continued around Monte San Gabriele and north and east of Gorizia. It was expected that general offensive operations would resume towards the end of September. Yet again, the Italian losses were eye-watering: 40,000 dead, 108,000 wounded and 18,000 taken prisoner. The Austrians lost 10,000 dead, more than 45,000 wounded and about 30,000 missing (the Italians claimed they had taken about 29,000 prisoners).

On this occasion, the fighting was observed by, British Lt Col C N Buzzard, Commanding the XCIV Heavy Artillery Group, who reported to his superiors on what he saw. His narrative helps to explain the Italians' lack of success. The main characteristics of the Italian approach to the offensive were:

> Almost entire lack of information supplied to the Heavy Artillery. We were never told which way the infantry would attack [and] hours named [in the operation order] were never adhered to. Fire was lifted far too soon: infantry had no support in passing over four or five hundred yards of open and difficult ground. We could have kept on firing until the infantry was 200 yards from objectives. Austrian prisoners say that during our bombardment all their men were in caverns, and they hardly lost any: the trenches were quite wrecked: no shells can touch their caverns. The remarkable thing is that with such utter lack of co-operation between artillery and infantry the Italian infantry ever take any of their objectives. The artillery preparation is good, a large number of the infantry are quite heroic; but to advance behind a proper creeping barrage is unheard of.[11]

It is clear from the above that the Italians had learned little from their own experiences in the war to date, and similarly, not much from the painful experiences of their allies at Loos, the Somme, Arras and Cambrai, particularly in relation to fire and movement on the battlefield. It must have been obvious from the earliest attacks on the Isonzo that success on the 20th century, industrially-enabled battlefield required the careful coordination of artillery and infantry in order to overcome the effects of a well-entrenched enemy, supported by machine guns, rifles and its own artillery. And yet, the Italians seem to have been incapable of understanding or acting upon this inescapable fact. The infantry soldiers were brave, and the gunners could shoot. But it is obvious from Lt Col Buzzard's account, that no-one was doing the staff work to ensure the effective coordination of the two arms. It was indeed remarkable that the Italian infantry ever managed to take an objective. Ludendorff once described being allied to the Austro-Hungarian empire as being "shackled to a corpse". For the British and French, watching the Italians throwing themselves fruitlessly at the Austrian lines, making the same mistakes over and over again, it would have been difficult not to share some of the same frustrations. The Italian soldiers were as brave as lions, but Cadorna's tactics owed more to Solferino than to the Somme. As a result, the bones of many valiant men from Lombardy, Veneto, Tuscany, Sardinia, Piedmont, Umbria, Lazio, Puglia, Calabria littered the barren rocks of the Carso and the Bainsizza Plateau, bleached white by the hot summer sun, their blood soaking into the limestone for eternity. And yet there was little to show for the losses, little with which to ease the pain and heartache of the Italian people – the mothers and fathers, wives, and sweethearts of those who had died. And the bloodshed was not yet done.

Despite the repeated failure of Cadorna's armies to make significant inroads into enemy territory, the incessant battering of the Austrian lines did, nonetheless, take its toll on the defenders. They had suffered unsustainable losses which prompted the Austrian Emperor, Karl to write to the Kaiser thus:

> The experience we have acquired in the eleventh battle has led me to believe that we should fare far worse in a twelfth. My commanders and brave troops have decided that such an unfortunate situation might be anticipated by an offensive. We have not the necessary means as regards troops.[12]

---

11   Quoted in J E Edmonds, p.36.
12   J Keegan, p.372.

Karl went on to ask the Germans to replace Austrian troops on the eastern front so that the Isonzo front could be reinforced. The Kaiser passed the request on to Ludendorff, who replied with a counter-proposal: it would be better, he thought, to use German troops directly against the Italians. An initial proposal for an offensive from the Tyrol was rejected in favour of a plan to commit seven German divisions, formed, with six Austrian divisions, into a new Fourteenth Army, and launch a direct counter-offensive on the Isonzo. Ludendorff despatched a mountain warfare expert, Lt Gen Krafft von Dellmensingen, to the Italian front to conduct a detailed reconnaissance and come up with a plan. At this point, the German intent was not to conduct a decisive operation, but to advance far enough, and do sufficient damage, to prevent the Italians from launching further offensives before the following spring or summer. That would give the Austrians some much-needed breathing space in which to recover, and, hopefully, persuade them to stay in the fight.

The small town called Caporetto by the Italians (Karfreit in German and Kobarid in Slovene) had a strategic significance that far outweighed its size. Sitting on the banks of the Isonzo, in a stretch of open valley between the looming, high walls of the Julian Alps, it guarded one of the few breaks in the Alpine barrier between Austria and Italy, a pass through the mountains that led down to the plains of Friuli. When Napoleon fought the Austrians in the same area a century before, he too recognised the importance of the town, warning his local commander that if the enemy broke through there, they would be unstoppable until they reached the Piave River.[13] Not much had changed in 100 years.

Cadorna's lack of success in pushing his line eastwards, beyond the Isonzo, and his policy of keeping most of his troops and machine guns in the front line, meant he had very little depth to his position, and his reserves, being held mostly on the west bank, were too far away, behind a river barrier, to be quickly deployed in an emergency. In the event of a serious Austrian offensive, he was vulnerable to being cut off on the east bank. At the same time, the Italians' failure to capture the Tolmino bridgehead had gifted to the Austrians a ready-made jumping-off point right on the river should they wish to take the offensive. Looking at the ground in August 1917, von Dellmensingen recognised the possibilities offered by a breakthrough at Caporetto and the Italians' vulnerabilities further south. He submitted an outline proposal designed to exploit both.

General von Dellmensingen's plan put Caporetto right at the heart of an Austro-German attack. From the Plezzo Basin (Flitsch in German, Bovec in Slovene), beneath the towering sheer face of Monte Rombon, assaulting troops were to advance towards Saga (Zaga), capture Monte Stol and continue along the river towards Caporetto before turning west. From Tolmino they would burst out of the bridgehead, assault the Monte Jeza massif, capturing the Kolovrat Ridge and Monte Matajur before joining up with the northern arm and heading down Val Natizone to capture the city of Cividale on the Friuli plain. Once the Austro-German troops were on the plain, the position of the Duke of Aosta's Third Army would be compromised. His northern flank would be open, and he would be forced to withdraw, or risk being cut off.

The Austro-German attack was planned for mid-October, leaving only about six weeks to complete the necessary preparations. Road and rail transport in the area began to increase as

---

13  M Thompson, p.296.

men and supplies poured in. October rains caused problems on the roads, but they also helped to hide some of the movements from Italian observers, while the German Air Force arrived, quickly gained aerial supremacy, and prevented Italian aircraft from flying over the area. Austrian prisoners spoke of an impending attack, but this was discounted by Italian intelligence officers who could not believe the enemy would consider a significant offensive so late in the year.

On 18th September, Cardorna ordered his armies to move to a defensive posture. In the south, the Duke of Aosta complied. In the north, General Capello did not, preferring to keep his troops organised for attack. Convinced that there would be no offensive before 1918, Cadorna went on holiday to Venice, returning on 19th October. By then, the Commando Supremo was aware that an attack on the upper Isonzo was likely, but Cadorna was convinced this would be no more than a feint. It there was to be an attack it was much more likely to be on the Carso, he told his staff.

At 0200 on 24th October, the German and Austrian artillery opened fire along the whole of the front between Monte Rombon and Gorizia, smashing Italian batteries, observation posts and communications. German veterans of the Somme and Verdun said they had seen nothing to compare with the weight of fire that was brought down against the Italian lines. This was not a softening-up barrage. The purpose was to completely obliterate the Italian defences. In the north, where Capello had decided to remain poised for attack, the Italian batteries had not been moved back into more secure positions and were easy targets for the Austrian and German gunners. At Plezza, the opening artillery fire was followed by a gas attack on the infantry positions along the valley floor (just to the east of the modern airfield that lies there today). Over 2,000 gas shells were fired electrically from tubes similar to the British Livens Projectors, delivering a dense, yellowish cloud, a mixture of phosgene and diphenylchloroarsine. The issue Italian gas masks could withstand chlorine, but not this. Over 700 men of the Fruili Brigade died at their posts before, at 0730, the Austrian infantry advanced, almost unopposed, into the mist and fog that blanketed the valley below Monte Rombon. By mid-afternoon, the Italian forces on Rombon itself were ordered to fall back before they were surrounded. By dawn on the 25th, the attackers reached Saga, but again there was little fighting. The town had been evacuated by the Italians who had pulled back in the night, planning to block the pass of Uccea, from positions on Monte Stol to the south.

Progress had been just as dramatic at Tolmino. Although the Italian defences were stronger here than at Plezzo, two Austrian and one German division burst out of the bridgehead, across the river and up the steep hills to the west, untroubled by the guns of the Italian XXVII Corps, which held the ground. Here, the artillery commander telephoned his Corps Commander, Lt Gen Pietro Badoglio, asking for permission to open fire. Badoglio refused on the grounds that there was a shortage of shells. The Italian guns remained silent. Without artillery support, the infantry of the Italian 19th Division, holding the line in front of Tolmino was over-run in a few hours by the German 12th Silesian Division, who then captured the important Monte Jeza feature, giving them access to the Kolovrat Ridge. On the right flank of the force attacking out of Tolmino was the German Alpinkorps, a specialist mountain unit, made up of Bavarian regiments and the Wurttemberg Mountain Battalion. Amongst them was a 25-year-old company commander named Erwin Rommel.

Austro-German forces advanced north along the river valley, reaching Caporetto by 1600, and by evening they had joined up with Krauss's 1st Austro-Hungarian Corps at Saga – behind the Italian second line. The bridge at Caporetto was blown early on in the fighting, effectively cutting off the Italian 43rd and 46th Divisions, who had little option but to capitulate. Although there were individual acts of valour by Italian units here and there, organised defence began to fail. By the afternoon of the 24th Italian troops started to stream down in disorder from the high ground along the river. Military police detachments tried to halt them. They stopped soldiers who still had rifles and sent them back to the fighting but allowed unarmed troops from the support branches to carry on withdrawing. When the infantry soldiers saw this, they threw away their weapons to avoid being returned to the front. The rot had set in.

By the evening of the 25th, the new Austro-German Fourteenth Army had occupied the high ground along the west bank of the Isonzo – the peaks of Kolovrat, Matajur, Stol – smashing through all three lines of Italian defences, poised to pour out into the plains, where some would head for the Tagliamento while others swung south, threatening, as planned, to cut off the Duke of Aosta's Third Army on the Carso. Cadorna had prepared orders for the 2nd and 3rd Armies to pull back to the Tagliamento, and these were issued early on the evening of 26/27th October. By then, the Italian 2nd Army had ceased to exist as an organisation. The men, mostly weapon-less, and seemingly under the command of no-one, were in head-long, uncontrolled retreat. Around Gorizia and on the Carso, however, the 3rd Army, until the withdrawal order was received, was continuing to stand. But with its northern flank in tatters, the instructions to fall back was simply confirmation of the inevitable.

## From the Isonzo to the Tagliamento and Piave

The Third Army included among its number two groups of British 6-in howitzers of the Royal Garrison Artillery. The northern group, XCIV Heavy Artillery Group, commanded by Lt Col Charles Norman Buzzard, consisted of the 302nd, 307th, 315th, 316th and 317th Siege Batteries, who were engaging targets on the Carso. The 302nd Battery was located on the banks of the Vippacco River, a tributary of the Isonzo, near the village of Pec (now Peci), just south of Gorizia. Among its officers was Lt Hugh Dalton, who was destined to become a Labour Chancellor of the Exchequer and a founder of the Special Operations Executive in the Second World War. Dalton wrote a record of his service in the Italian campaign, entitled *With British Guns in Italy* first published in 1919, in which he describes the long, slow and eventful withdrawal to the Tagliamento and beyond.

On 27th October, Dalton's battery received the "staggering news" that the Third Army had begun to pull back. But unlike their comrades further north, who had panicked and retreated in an uncontrolled stampede, the Third Army planned and conducted a deliberate, fighting withdrawal behind well-led and determined rearguards.

As night came, the Italians began to blow up ammunition dumps, causing "great flashes of light, brighter even than an Italian noonday". Ordered to leave a single gun behind, the men of the 302nd Battery hauled three of their guns out by motorised tractors and these set off west. The last gun, No 2, continued to fire. The Italian battery next door heaved what was left of its ammunition into the Vippacco and pulled out at around 1830. The British gunners received orders to destroy any ammunition that could not be fired, and leaving a healthy supply for their single gun, followed the Italians' lead and threw their ammunition into the river also. When No 2 gun had finally used up its allocation of shells, it too was hauled out of its firing pit and onto the road to join the throng of troops making their way to the rear. It was now about 2100.

Dalton and his men moved along the banks of the Vippacco to its confluence with the Isonzo at Peteano where they crossed the main river and headed for Gradisca:

> As we passed the railway embankment at Rubbia, we saw and spoke to some Italian machine-gunners … whose orders were to hold up the enemy till the last possible moment. They were quite quiet and calm, those boys, knowing perfectly well that by the time the enemy came, the Isonzo bridges would have been blown up behind them.[14]

Leaving the Italian machine-gunners to their fate, the British artillerymen made their way via Versa to Palmanova. Towns and villages along the way were in flames, set alight by the retreating army who were systematically destroying anything that could be of use to the pursuing enemy. After Palmanova, the roads became ever more congested as civilians as well as soldiers joined the trek westwards. Reaching San Giorgio di Nogara, they were directed to head for Latisana, on the banks of the Tagliamento, but by this stage, the tractor unit that was hauling two of 302nd Battery's guns and another belonging to a different unit, was beginning to fail under the strain, breaking down three or four times in an hour. Just when all seemed lost, they managed to get some assistance from an Italian artillery unit, who hitched the guns to one of its own tractors and lurched off at a snail's pace towards the river.

Fate was not on their side. Having just got going again, on the morning of 30th October, they ran into a solid mass of traffic at a complete standstill. By this stage, the men were exhausted and hungry. There had been little opportunity to rest, and food was scarce, the supply system having broken down early on in the withdrawal. Officers were forced to ration the small amounts of emergency bully beef and biscuits they had managed to pack for the journey, but it was hardly sufficient to sustain the party. Dalton headed off on foot to try to find a way through. Having reached the Tagliamento, he discovered that the route had been deliberately blocked, in order to allow traffic coming from the north to get through. He had no option but to return to his guns and wait. Before he reached them, he met four of his men coming towards him carrying a stretcher on which lay the body of the battery's Staff Sergeant Artificer, killed in a freak accident after falling under the wheels of one of the guns. This was almost certainly 318431 Staff Sgt Sydney Charles Rees (33). Born in Highbury in North London, Rees was the husband of Mary Ann Rees, whose home was at 28 Harrogate Road, Caversham, Reading. Waving down a lorry from another battery, Dalton detailed two men to accompany the body to Portogruaro, where it was buried in the grounds of the local hospital. The grave was lost in subsequent fighting in the area, and S/Sgt Rees is commemorated on the Giavera Memorial to the Missing.

The road subsequently cleared, and the guns were able to continue to Latisana, where they crossed the Tagliamento just before the old stone bridge was blown. From there, they found their way to Treviso and then to Arquata Scrivia, north of Genoa, for a well-earned rest and re-fitting.

---

14  H Dalton, p.107.

## Rapallo and Reinforcement

By 1st November, the bulk of what was left of the Italian armies was established on the west bank of the Tagliamento. British Chief of the Imperial General Staff, General Sir William Robertson, and his French opposite number, Gen Ferdinand Foch, arrived on a fact-finding visit and reported that the armies were being reorganised and reconstituted. However, on the night of 2nd/3rd November, the Austrian 55th Division managed to cross the river in the north via a damaged railway bridge at Cornino, while the German 12th Division crossed at Pinzano. This effectively broke the Tagliamento line where it entered the mountains, and on 4th November, triggered a further retreat to the Piave. This was conducted behind a determined rear-guard in which the Italian cavalry played a heroic but costly part. By 10th November, the main bodies of the Italian armies were on the Piave position, where Cadorna decide to make a stand. Although he did not know it, Cadorna's time in command was coming to its end – part of the price demanded by France and Britain for coming to Italy's aid.

In the same way that Germany was keen to keep Austria in the war, the allies were equally determined that Italy should not capitulate as a result of the Caporetto disaster. On 26th October Lloyd George, on learning of the situation, directed Robertson to send two British divisions from France to Italy right away, as a preliminary measure. This was forwarded to Sir Douglas Haig, at General Headquarters in France, along with instructions to select two "good divisions" and a "good man" to command them. Haig followed his orders to the letter, choosing Lt Gen the Earl of Cavan, commanding XIV Corps, part of the Fifth Army, and 23rd and 41st divisions, both from X Corps, which had recently been engaged in the Battle of the Menin Road Ridge, part of the Third Battle of Ypres (Passchendaele). Robertson, meanwhile, left for Italy to assess the situation in person.

As early as 30th October, the British and French Prime Ministers had met in London to discuss further assistance for their Italian ally. At the same time, they also discussed the possibility of establishing a Supreme War Council to oversee the future conduct of the wider conflict from the Allies' perspective. It was agreed that they should meet in Italy to scope out an assistance programme and to settle the War Council proposal The Ligurian coastal city of Rapallo, about 15 miles east of the port city of Genoa, was chosen as the venue and the opening session of what would become the Rapallo Conference was scheduled for 5th November, as the Italians began the withdrawal to the Piave.

On the train journey through northern Italy, Lloyd George and the other senior members of the UK delegation, which included War Cabinet member, the South African, General Jan Smuts, and General Sir Henry Wilson, were able to gain a first-hand insight into the scale of the Caporetto debacle. Writing in his war memoirs, Lloyd George recorded that:

> At every wayside station we witnessed dejected fragments of the shattered Italian divisions, many without rifles. This gave us some idea of the extent of the defeat and of the demoralisation that had followed defeat. But we were reassured by accounts we received of the Duke of Aosta's army and of the forces under the command of General Diaz. [15]

---

15   D Lloyd George, *War Memoirs*, Vol. 2, pp.1396-97

The Italian delegation, led by the Prime Minister, Sr Vittorio Orlando, who was flanked by his Foreign Minister, Baron Sidney Sonnino, War Minister, General Vittorio Luigi Alfieri and Deputy Chief of the General Staff, Gen Porro, representing Cadorna, painted a wildly exaggerated picture of the situation on the ground which, they claimed, required a significant allied response. They suggested that 15 British and French divisions should be despatched immediately. General Porro said that nine German divisions had participated in the Caporetto attack, and that 12-15 more had subsequently left the western front for Italy. Foch and Robertson disagreed, the latter pointing to the latest British intelligence estimate, which had only six German divisions on the Italian front (there were actually seven). Lloyd George was deeply unimpressed by Gen Porro, noting that he "made the poorest impression on every mind…"[16] Porro seemed to have no grasp of what had happened or why, and his performance during the discussions reinforced the view that the fault lay not with the fighting soldiers but with the higher echelons of command. It was obvious, Lloyd George wrote later, that the first step to be taken, in order to restore confidence, was to make a complete change in the Supreme Command.[17] Briefing the War Cabinet on 13th November 1917, on the outcome of the Rapallo discussions, he observed:

> The Headquarters Staff had been quite unable to grip hold of the situation and to keep in touch with and control the movements of the Italian forces. The dispositions were bad, the Staffs generally inefficient, and no communication had been maintained. Both our own and the French Military Advisors had represented that General Cadorna was quite unfitted to retain the supreme command of the Italian forces.[18]

The French and British delegations, meeting informally before the conference got under way, had already agreed that any reinforcement would be dependent on the removal of Cadorna and a reorganisation of the Italian High Command. This was discussed with Orlando and Sonnino who agreed that change was "inevitable". When this was presented to the King of Italy on 8th November, at a separate meeting at Peschiera, at the southern end of Lake Garda, the King revealed that it had already been decided to replace Cadorna with General Armando Diaz with effect from the following day. General Giardino, the former Minister of War, and General Badoglio, commander of IV Corps (despite being partly to blame for the defensive failure at the Tolmino bridgehead), were appointed as joint Deputy Supreme Commanders. Given Diaz's relative anonymity, there were those who felt the Duke of Aosta would have been the obvious choice to replace Cadorna. However, as Edmonds has pointed out, there were "dynastic" reasons why he could not be appointed to that position. He was a cousin of King Victor Emmanuel, and it was considered improper to give him the top post because, in theory, the King was the Commander-in-Chief.[19] In any case, the loss of the Duke, a charismatic, effective and highly-regarded Army Commander, would have potentially done more harm than good. Diaz, although relatively unknown, even in Italy, had proved to be a very effective Corps Commander. But more importantly, he also possessed a good understanding of the all-important political dimension, thanks to an earlier appointment as secretary to General Pollio, a

16 D Lloyd George, Vol. 2, p.1396.
17 D Lloyd George, Vol. 2, p.1397.
18 TNA CAB 23/4/46: War Cabinet Minutes, 13th November 1917.
19 J E Edmonds, p.81.

previous Chief of the General Staff. As time would prove, the decision to keep the Duke as an Army Commander and raise Diaz to be Commando Supremo, was exactly correct, making the best use of two different but complimentary sets of talents. To sweeten the pill of his dismissal, Cadorna was given the role of Italian Permanent Military Representative at the Supreme War Council, which, it had been decided, would sit at Versailles.

Haig, meanwhile, was concerned that the provision of additional support for Italy would curtail his plans for the Passchendaele offensive, which was making slow, unspectacular progress in the Flanders mud. He lost no time in attempting to head off any further reduction in his forces. On 31st October he wrote to Robertson to set out his views on "the probable effect of such a decision on the campaign on the Western front". It was his intention to continue the offensive on the Flanders front for several more weeks, pointing out that from the position already reached, Passchendaele and the high ground around it, would be in the possession of the Allies by the middle of November, if not sooner. The British Field Marshal also observed:

> If it should be necessary to abandon any further advance before the ridge has been captured, a proportion of our line for the winter on the west of the ridge will be low-lying, waterlogged, and overlooked; difficult to hold against a determined attack. The loss of troops already detailed to proceed to Italy will not compel me to abandon my plans for the Flanders front, although it will throw a much greater strain on my resources and involve heavier demands and greater hardships on the troops … A decision to send larger forces to Italy, however, will reduce the forces in France below what is required for the continuance of the offensive, and I trust the effects of this will be very thoroughly considered before such a decision is formed…the abandonment of the attack now would certainly be hailed in Germany as a victory, and exploited by our enemies as a British failure.[20]

Haig's plea fell on deaf ears. Although Robertson was, as usual, supportive of his position, Lloyd George had already signalled his determination to send further divisions to Italy. Recognising the political realities of the situation, Robertson and Foch told the Rapallo Conference, correctly, as it turned out, that with the Passchendaele fighting continuing, it was very unlikely that Germany would be inclined to send additional troops to the Italian front. In these circumstances, they recommended, a joint force of eight allied divisions would be sufficient to shore up the Italians until they were able to re-organise themselves.[21] The Italians' problem was not a shortage of manpower – they had plenty of troops – but ensuring that the armies were re-equipped, re-trained and re-invigorated after their Caporetto experience.

Allied reinforcement of Italy in the event of a significant attack by the Central Powers had been discussed at the Rome conference in January 1917. Although there was no immediate agreement to augment the Italian forces, the British did despatch a delegation, led by Brigadier-General J H V Crowe, with instructions to work with the Commando Supremo to plan for the possible transfer of a force of about six British divisions and supporting services (approximately 120,000 men and 26,000 animals) by rail to Italy. This resulted in the creation of an Anglo-Italian Convention, co-signed by Crowe and General Porro, which made provision for the

---

20 TNA CAB 23/4/46: War Cabinet Minutes, 13th November 1917.
21 This was later increased to 12 divisions divided evenly between France and Great Britain.

transport, concentration and forward deployment of a British contingent. This included billeting facilities, a base area at Arquata, and port facilities at Genoa. It also included arrangements for the creation of advanced depots, hospitals, postal and telegraph services, maps, interpreters, and liaison arrangements – in fact, everything that would be required to ensure the smooth reception, staging, onward movement, and integration of a a significant British expeditionary force.

A railway route from France to Italy already existed to supply the Egypt and Salonika fronts. This was known as the Taranto or Overland route, and it ran from Cherbourg to Modane via the Mont Cenis tunnel and then down through Italy to Taranto. This was the route that had been used to transport the British heavy artillery batteries to Italy earlier in the year, but it did not have sufficient capacity to supply an army. A second, longer route via Etaples, the Rhone Valley and Ventimiglia was also identified for use. In the event, the preparatory work, conducted by Crowe and his team, ensured that the movement of the British divisions from France to Italy was completed smoothly, although not always without delays and some confusion.

As a result of the Rapallo decisions, on 8th November, Haig selected 7th Division from X Corps (Second Army) and 48th (South Midland) Division of XVIII Corps (Fifth Army) as the second cohort to be transferred along with various army, corps and lines of communication units and 14th Wing, Royal Flying Corps, consisting of four squadrons of aircraft, and a Brigade headquarters under Brigadier-General T I Webb-Bowen. A second Corps Headquarters, XI Corps under Lt General Sir Richard Haking was warned off to head for Italy on 15th November, and later in the month, two further divisions, 5th and 21st were also ordered south.

Given the size of the force now being despatched, Lt Gen the Earl of Cavan was considered to be too junior to be in overall command. It was decided that General Sir Herbert Plumer, the exceptionally-talented commander of the Second Army, and the architect of the successful assault on the Messines Ridge in June 1917, who had taken over responsibility for much of the fighting around Passchendaele, should be appointed to oversee the British Expeditionary Force in Italy. Plumer, accompanied by his Chief of Staff, the hugely-capable and ever-loyal Major General Charles "Tim" Harrington, was ordered to meet Lloyd George in Paris, the latter on his way back from Rapallo. In his war memoirs, Lloyd George claimed that Plumer "did not conceal his satisfaction at the prospect of exchanging the Flemish swamp, where he had been fighting a characteristically stubborn battle, for the more genial surroundings of his new command". According to Harrington, who wrote a biography of his boss after the war, however, Plumer was devastated at having to leave his Second Army. In a letter to his wife, on 7th November, Plumer wrote: "I have been ordered to go to Italy and assume command of the British Force there. I am very sick about it and do not want to go in the least." The following day he observed: "I simply loathe leaving the Second Army and feel very depressed."[22]

---

22   C Harrington, *Plumer of Messines*, p.134.

Warwick Barracks. (Author)

The 1/1st Buckinghamshire Battalion enjoying Christmas day dinner, Chelmsford December 1914. (BMMT)

1/1st Bucks Battalion 1914: A rifle platoon of 1/1st Buckinghamshire Battalion marches past Aylesbury courthouse, August 1914. (BMMT)

Men of the 1/1st Buckinghamshire Battalion in a breastwork trench at Ploegsteert Wood, April 1915. (BMMT)

Final resting place of Pte William Holland, 48th Division's first fatality. Killed near Ploegsteert Wood on 8th April 1915, his remains were originally buried in a small wartime cemetery near Le Bizet Convent. They were subsequently re-interred at Strand Military Cemetery by Ploegsteert village. (Author)

Lt W Cloutman grave. He died whilst attempting to rescue his sergeant during the Somme offensive. Cloutman was responsible for detonating the mines at the Bird Cage during the 48th Division's time at Ploegsteert Wood. (Author)

Lt R Leighton gravesite. Engaged to be married to Vera Brittain, author of the celebrated memoir Testament of Youth, he died of wounds at Louvencourt on 23rd December 1915. (Author)

General view from Poziéres towards Albert depicting the ground over which 48th Division fought during July and August 1916. (Author)

The medal group belonging to Capt Lionel Crouch of 1/1st Buckinghamshire Battalion. The medals include (L to R) the 1914-15 Star, War Medal, Victory Medal and George V Coronation Medal. (Author)

Capt. L Crouch gravesite. He was killed near Poziéres on 21st July 1916. (Author)

Lt R G Norwood gravesite at Poziéres Military Cemetery. His remains were uncovered during post-war battlefield clearance. (Author)

Maj Gen R Fanshawe c. 1907. (Open Source)

Lt Gen the Earl of Cavan. (Open Source)

1/1st Bucks Bn Lewis Gunners, Italy 1918. (BMMT)

1/1st Bucks and 1/4th OBLI battalion officers sight-seeing in Venice 1918. (BMMT)

Austrian trench remnants on Mt Zebio. (Author)

Remains of British trench systems. (Author)

Maj E A M Bindloss gravesite Magnaboschi Military Cemetery. (Author)

British ferro-concrete dressing station situated between Grenezza and Pria del Acqua. (Author)

British lines from Mt Zebio. (Author)

Carriola base site. (Author)

Clo, short for Casello, a small structure situated astride the light railway running from Asiago to Cesuna. (Author)

Ghelphac Stream which ran opposite the British lines. (Author)

British machine gun post situated above the light railway that extended from Asiago to Cesuna. This portion of the line was held by 1/4th OBLI on the morning of 15 June 1918. (Author)

British dugout, Pria del Acqua. (Author)

Pelly Cross site. (Author)

Grenezza base site. (Author)

Handley Cross, an important junction behind the 48th Division line, was heavily shelled in the early hours of 15 June 1918. This set off a nearby ammunition dump. (Author)

Railway bridge situated immediately behind 1/4th OBLI lines on 15 June 1918. (Author)

Asiago No Man's Land. (Author)

Italian trench system remains east of Asiago. (Author)

Entrance to Grenezza Military Cemetery. (Author)

Boscon Cemetery situated immediately behind the British lines. (Author)

Lt Col J M Knox gravesite, Grenezza Military Cemetery. (Author)

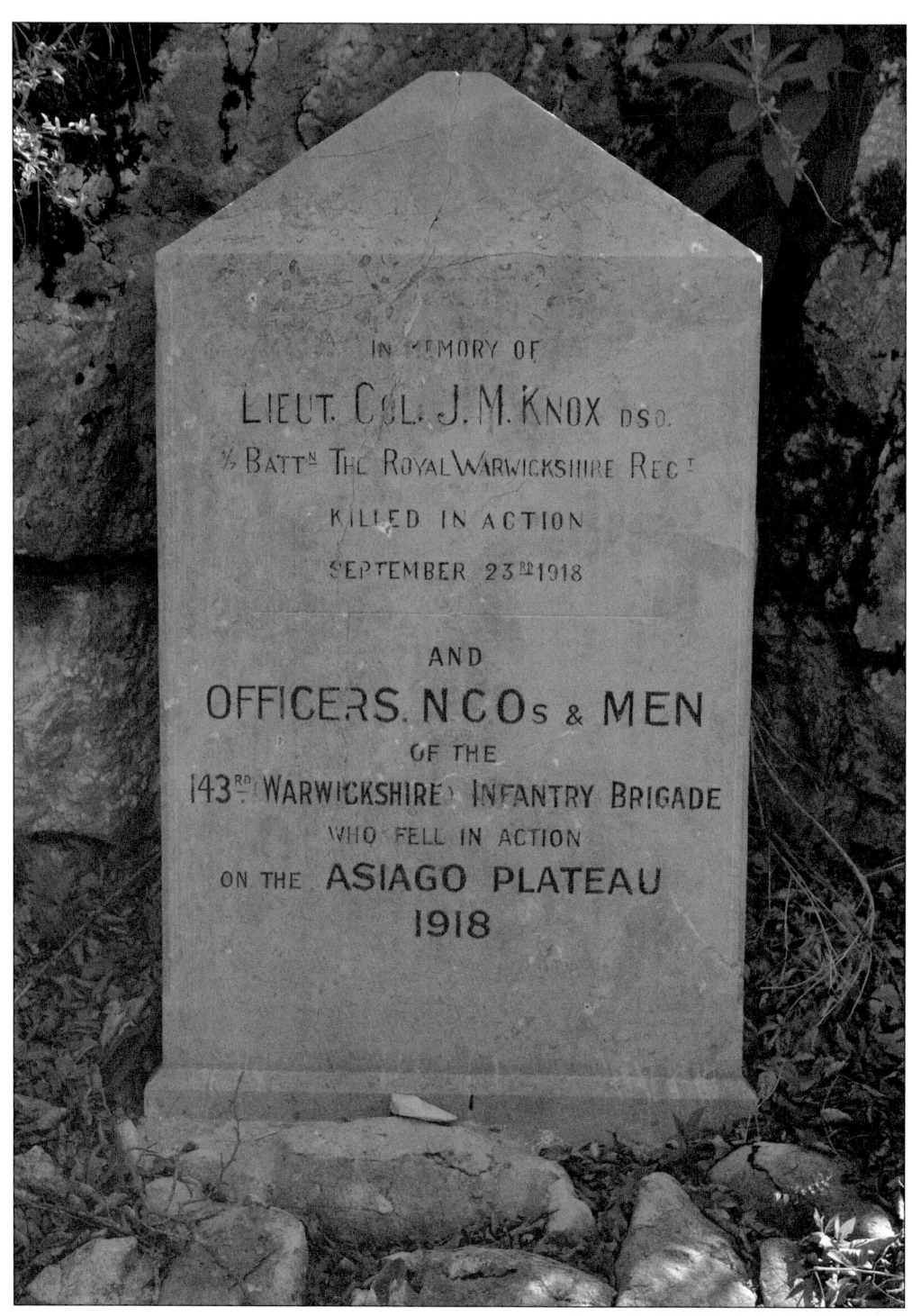

Private memorial commemorating Lt Col J M Knox. (Author)

Capt. Edward Brittain, brother of author Vera Britain, gravesite, Grenezza Military Cemetery. (Author)

7

# From Flanders Mud To Italian Sun

The 48th Division's last act in the great military drama that was the Third Battle of Ypres, was to take part in the campaign sub-battle that would later be designated as the Battle of Broodseinde (4 October 1917). Charles Carrington described this assault with some justification as "all-in wrestling in the mud".[1]

This was the last of three well-planned and executed 'bite and hold' attacks launched by General Plumer during the Passchendaele campaign. The overall objective was the capture of the ruined villages of Zonnebeke, Gravenstafel and Poelkapelle and the Broodseinde Ridge which was the last significant geographical barrier before Passchendaele itself. The ridge was an important piece of real-estate, providing the enemy with good observation over the city of Ypres. Taking it from them would be a major step towards securing Passchendaele.

Plumer's plan called for 12 British, Australian and New Zealand divisions from Second Army's IX, X, I ANZAC and II ANZAC Corps and Fifth Army's XIV and XVIII Corps, the latter including 48th Division, to move forward behind a heavy artillery bombardment.

Orders for the 48th Division's part in the attack arrived on 2nd October and required an advance on a three-battalion front, which would be undertaken by the 143rd Brigade, under Brigadier-General George Sladen. The 1/5th, 1/6th and 1/7th Royal Warwicks would be the attacking battalions while 1/8th Royal Warwicks would be in Brigade reserve. Two battalions of 145th Brigade – 1/5th Gloucesters and 1/4th Oxfordshire and Buckinghamshire Light Infantry – were allocated as a forward Divisional reserve.

The South Midlanders' objective was to capture a series of German strongpoints to the North-East of St Julien – only a few hundred yards east of where they had fought so desperately during the August battles. The first line of objectives included Tweed House, York, Winchester and Albatross Farms. The second targets were to be County Crossroads, Vacher Farm and Burns House. The 143rd Brigade plan was for the attacking battalions to push ahead in close touch with the barrage, which would creep forward, lifting 50 yards every two or three minutes. In addition, a box barrage would be put down around the key targets which included the strongpoints themselves, and some ferro-concrete bunkers close by. This was designed to prevent the enemy from reinforcing or resupplying the positions, and to fix the garrisons and stop them from

---

1   C E Carrington, *Soldiers from the Wars Returning*, p.191.

withdrawing. Once the assaulting troops had secured these positions, machine guns, trench mortars, engineers and pioneers would move up to help with consolidating the ground gained.

The assault waves moved into their jumping-off positions during the night of 3rd/4th October, and at 0600 on the 4th, "under an excellent barrage which could not have been improved"[2], the Warwickshire battalions advanced.

The 1/7th R Warwicks, on the left, made good progress and quickly reached their objectives – Tweed House and Terrier Farm and a small cemetery – where they consolidated, making contact with 9th Lancashire Fusiliers on their left. It was in the fighting around Terrier Farm that Coventry man, Pte Arthur Hutt won the Victoria Cross. According to the citation for the award, with all his officers and NCOs dead or wounded, Pte Hutt took command and led forward his platoon. He was held up by a strongpoint on the right but ran forward alone, shot the officer and three men in the post, and caused 40 or 50 others to surrender. Realising that the platoon had pushed too far ahead, he withdrew his party, personally covering the withdrawal. He carried back a wounded comrade before organising and consolidating the new position. Learning that some wounded had been left out in the open and were likely to become prisoners, he set off to rescue them, bringing back four men under heavy fire. Hutt then held his post until relieved on the night of 7th/8th October. He survived the war and served again in Coventry Home Guard in the Second World War. He died in 1964.[3]

1/6th R Warwicks, in the centre, also made good early progress, over-running enemy posts west of the Stroombeek before being driven to the right by heavy fire coming from York Farm. A Company took the higher ground to the west of Winchester and pushed on towards York Farm, where D Company was already attacking. C Company was waiting for the barrage on Wellington to lift before it too moved onto its objective. This battalion was also supposed to capture Vacher Farm and Burns House, but was unable to do so, largely due to the disorganised state of the companies after their initial assaults.

For a closer look at the fighting, the account by the Commanding Officer of 1/5th R Warwicks, Lt Col W C C Gell MC, paints a vivid picture of the battle from a unit perspective, and is typical of the experiences of the other attacking battalions.[4]

Having moved up to their jumping-off positions under cover of darkness, at zero hour (0600) the battalion went forward in a square formation, with A Company (right) and B Company (left) forming the leading wave, followed by C (right) and D (left). To their left was 1/6th R Warwicks and on the right, men of the 1st Auckland Battalion, a unit of the New Zealand Division, the left flank of the II ANZAC Corps.

On the right, A Company made good early progress. No. 1 platoon, under 2/Lt W Shadbolt, reached Vale House with only a few casualties and began to consolidate on the flanks. No. 2 platoon passed through Shadbolt's men and captured Winzig after a short but violent fight, taking 20 prisoners. This platoon then went firm on its objective, digging in and preparing to repel any counter-attack. 3 and 4 platoons leapfrogged past but were held up when New Zealanders of the 1st Auckland Battalion lost direction and began to push the Warwickshires

2   K W Mitchinson, p.181.
3   *Private Hutt VC Obituary* <http://www.earlsdon.org.uk/history/arthurhutt.html> (accessed 17 December 2021).
4   TNA WO 95/2755: Commanding Officer's battle narrative, 4-7 October 1917, 1/5th Royal Warwickshire Regiment War Diary.

to the left. Despite this, 3 platoon, commanded by 2/Lt A F Foreman, carried on, reaching the high ground in front of Wellington and Stoke Farms and consolidated, joining with men of 1/6th R Warwicks on the left and the New Zealanders on the right. By this stage, Foreman had about 10 men remaining. No. 4 platoon, having suffered heavy casualties from machine gun fire, reached a position just north-east of Winzig and dug in. At about 0650, the enemy put down a heavy artillery bombardment on Vale House, almost wiping out 2/Lt Shadbolt's platoon, wounding the platoon commander and killing or wounding all of the A Company forward HQ personnel who had just moved there.

Following behind A Company, C Company had moved up at zero plus 20 minutes (0620) and some men of the leading platoons became embroiled in the fighting that was still going on at Winzig before finding themselves being pushed to the left by the New Zealanders. 2/Lt F W Hale, with No. 9 platoon, closed up behind 3 platoon near Stoke Farm, and began to build a defensive position. 10 and 11 platoons became lost and stopped just north of Vale House, where they were discovered by the Commanding Officer at around 0915 and pointed in the correct direction. They apparently lost their way again, however, and ended up consolidating behind some New Zealanders near Albatross Farm.

B Company, assaulting on the right, took some casualties from fire from an enemy post north of Vale House, where five of the new German light machine guns and a number of snipers were located. This position was eventually cleared but at some cost in men, the company being reduced to about 30 effectives. The company commander and a party of 10 worked north of the Stroombeek to a position between Wellington and Winchester. Later in the day, this company was ordered to withdraw into a supporting position around Albatross Farm.

In command of B Company, Lt (Acting Capt) Charles Carrington, included an account of this action, in which he was awarded the Military Cross, in his book, "Soldier From The Wars Returning".

Carrington recalled that even before they left the start-line, in front of St Julien village, the company had suffered at least eight casualties, including a platoon commander, from enemy shelling. However, they shook themselves out into assault formation and moved forward, with two platoons up front, about 200 yards apart, and two following. Company HQ, consisting of Carrington, his Company Sergeant Major, and some orderlies, were in the middle of the two waves, accompanied by a section of signallers, who were unrolling a large drum of telephone wire as they went.

Carrington was a veteran of the Battle of the Somme. He had seen hard fighting at Pozieres and Le Sars and had been under some heavy bombardments. However, the opening artillery barrage at Broodseinde was far beyond anything he had witnessed up to that point. "It was," he wrote, "of such weight and intensity as to belittle anything we had seen on the Somme."[5] In addition to the artillery fire, a number of key enemy positions received attention from Livens Projectors, firing gas canisters from a range of nearly a mile behind the line. There was a standing barrage on his objective – Winchester Farm, a ferro-concrete bunker, about 1000 yards to his front – while the main bombardment of shrapnel moved ahead as planned. Between this and the objective, yet more shells were falling to discourage enemy movement forward or to the rear.

5    C E Carrington, p.192.

Just opposite the ground was "a lunar landscape of shell-craters, one touching another, filled with water or with sludgy clay that could almost wrench the boots off your feet".[6]

> To keep direction or to maintain the formations we had practiced in battle-drill were equally impossible as the sections straggled round the rims of shell-holes. A party of sappers was detailed to follow the attack with signboards to be posted up on captured objectives. We questioned more than one of their identifications and were much amused when a sapper marched out into No Man's Land and nailed up his notice on a tree-stump, well inside the German front.[7]

The Company HQ party's advance came to an abrupt halt when they ran into a group of four or five Germans in a shell-hole. The enemy proceeded to engage them with rifle fire at short range, hitting three of the Warwickshires before they could react, and pinning down the others. But the support platoon spotted their predicament, and a Lewis Gun was quickly turned on the enemy position, silencing the fire and allowing the advance to continue, until:

> Just then, twenty or thirty Boches (sic) rose out of the ground and came running at us. Counter-attack! We all opened fire until we saw their hands above their heads …"[8]

By now it was daylight and looking out from the cover of a shell hole, during a moment's pause, Carrington could see the battle spread out before him. The barrage was 300 yards in front, a continuous line of explosions, pausing on the first objective. On his right the New Zealanders were advancing, one of their platoons veering towards him through the mud. To his front, the ground fell away to the Stroombeek stream, which, with its banks destroyed by shellfire, had spread out into a small, shallow lake, where someone had placed a few planks as a crossing point. In the distance he could see a couple of tanks clanking towards the village of Poelkapelle, and up ahead was the spire of Passchendaele church "rising not from the mud, but from green trees, an amenity it would not enjoy much longer."[9]

Remarkably, as he moved forward, Carrington ran into a school friend, commanding a platoon of the New Zealanders. Greeting each other by their old school nick-names, they shook hands and went on their separate ways. B Company eventually found itself at the Winchester blockhouse, where the survivors briefly joined forces with a platoon of the 1/6th R Warwicks. C and D companies then passed through the position and on to the next objective while Carrington moved his small party back to the Stroombeek and re-organised his troops. There was not much of the company left. Both of the forward platoon commanders had gone, all four platoon sergeants were missing, as were 11 out of 12 section commanders. He managed to pull together 27 men out of the 109 who had started and began to consolidate the position against an expected enemy counter-attack, making use of all four of the company's Lewis Guns, which, surprisingly, were still manned and functioning. Stretcher-bearers, searching for wounded,

---

6  C E Carrington, p.192
7  C E Carrington, p.193.
8  C E Carrington, p.194.
9  C E Carrington, p.194.

found two B Company sections who had dug themselves in nearby and were awaiting further orders, bringing the company's strength up to 44.

Spread out in the cover of various shell-holes, the survivors then had to sit in the rain and mud for a further three days. Unusually, the enemy did not counter-attack here, but their artillery systematically shelled the whole area, night and day, putting a heavy strain on the nerves of the survivors. But despite this 'trial by shellfire', the Warwickshires held firm until they were relieved by 1/4th Oxfords, 1/4th R Berks, and the Bucks Battalion of 145th Brigade on the evening of 7th October, and made their way back via Irish Farm, to Poperinghe and well-deserved rest.

The Warwickshire Brigade had taken and held many of its initial objectives, but the second-line positions, including Vacher Farm and Burns House, were still in the hands of the enemy. In his post-battle narrative, the Brigade commander, Sladen, blamed the failure on a shortage of men. The left battalion (1/7th R Warwicks) had the easier task and sufficient men to achieve it, not having been involved in heavy fighting at the start of the advance. This was not the case for the right and centre battalions (1/5th and 1/6th R Warwicks), who had to fight hard to take their initial targets, sustaining a large number of casualties. In the circumstances, he "did not consider there were sufficient men for the taking of both sets of objectives on the whole front".[10] In retrospect, he thought he should have ordered a company from the brigade reserve battalion, 1/8th R Warwicks, to move forward of Winchester:

> If this had been done and the [company] been skilfully led and in close touch with the situation in front, it might have gone forward at the right moment to take Burns and Vacher. The second-in-command of the 6/R Warwicks says that he certainly could have taken it at one time if he had had more men.[11]

The 143rd Brigade might have done better, but their failure to take all their objectives should not be allowed to obscure the success they did achieve. 450 prisoners had been rounded up. The advance had extended for 1200 yards against well-defended positions. 1/5th R Warwicks, alone, had taken 150 prisoners, an anti-tank gun and a number of machine guns, four of which were sent back as trophies. This was undoubtedly a worthy contribution to the Passchendaele campaign, although it came at a heavy price. Of the 500-plus men of 1/5th R Warwicks who had attacked on the morning of 4th October, only about 230 were still in the fight by that evening. Over the course of the four-day battle, this single battalion had lost 4 officers and 81 other ranks killed and 6 officers and 171 other ranks wounded.[12] Brigade losses in this action totalled 764 killed and wounded.[13]

The 143rd Brigade had moved the British line a step towards Passchendaele. Now it was 144th Brigade's turn to try to take a further stride in that direction. On 7th October, orders were received for a continuation of the attack, which was planned to commence at 0520 on the morning of 9th October. By this stage, conditions on the ground were truly appalling. The assaulting troops were exhausted even before they arrived at their jumping-off points due to the

---

10   TNA WO 95/2754: 143rd Brigade War Diary.
11   TNA WO 95/2754: 143rd Brigade War Diary.
12   C E Carrington, p.196.
13   TNA WO 95/2756: 1/5th, 1/6th, 1/7th, 1/8th Royal Warwickshire Regiment war diaries.

rain which had once again turned the ground into a muddy swamp. Trying to move across the landscape was energy-sapping in the extreme. The thick, grey, glutinous Flanders mud gathered on boots and clung to putties, making every step a struggle. Any movement could only be achieved with great difficulty, the men moving with an awkward, high-stepping gait caused by having to lift their feet up clear of the mud at every pace. Small wonder that the move up to the line, dragging not only themselves, but all the equipment necessary for the attack, was so utterly exhausting.

As they moved up, the men strained their eyes in the darkness to look over a barren, shell-pocked landscape in which buildings had been pulverised to mush and roads and tracks had disappeared. Maps were almost useless because many of the features they depicted no longer existed on the ground. Without recognisable landmarks it was difficult to navigate, and some platoon commanders resorted to trying to march their men forward using compass bearings, with mixed results. Although some of the attacking units, particularly in the centre and on the right, managed to get into position with time to spare, on the left, where the ground was at its worst, 1/4th Gloucesters had a terrible time. Their guides failed to turn up. The Commanding Officer, Lt Col J H Crosskey, decided to follow a different route, but one with which he was somewhat familiar, and reached Tweed House at 0145. However, he then discovered that three of the following companies, and the rearmost platoon of the leading company, had lost touch. Runners were sent back to look for them while C Company, in the lead, was directed down to the jumping-off point, marked with white tapes. Until 0430, just 35 minutes before zero, only three platoons of C Company were in position. Luckily, at that point, A and B Companies and two platoons of D arrived and were just taking up their attack positions when the opening barrage came down. These stragglers had been on the move for over 14 hours by that point.[14]

The Gloucesters came under heavy machine gun and rifle fire right from the start, which slowed their advance behind the creeping barrage. They lost the barrage after the first lift and from then on, they were easy targets for the enemy machine gunners and riflemen. Most of the fire directed at them was coming from Oxford Houses, Berks House and the north bank of the Lekkerboterbeek. The advance slowed to a halt about 100 yards east of County Crossroads, although a small party, led by a sergeant, managed to get into an enclosure close to Oxford Houses, establishing themselves in a fortified shell hole. The battalion advancing on their left appeared to have made no progress, leaving the Gloucesters' left flank open. To deal with this, C Company was ordered to form a protective line in that area, facing north, with three posts of riflemen and a single Lewis Gun team.[15]

In the centre, the 1/6th Gloucesters were also subjected to heavy machine gun fire as they started to move forward. Clearly the opening barrage had not managed to silence the enemy machine gun teams, protected by concrete shelters or MEBUs. Despite the hail of fire being poured down on the attackers, the cemetery, to the left of Burns House, was soon cleared together with two concrete shelters in the area, bringing a haul of four machine guns and 20 prisoners. The right Company was held up by the occupants of a trench, but they managed to force an entry and then bomb their way along it, taking 10 prisoners and four machine guns.

---

14   TNA WO 95/2758: 1/4th Gloucestershire Regiment War Diary.
15   TNA WO 95/2758: 1/4th Gloucestershire Regiment War Diary.

This battalion was then counter-attacked, the enemy coming forward in two waves, each broken up by friendly artillery, rifle and machine gun fire.

By now the first wave of attackers had fought itself to a standstill. Numbers were significantly reduced and there were too few men left to take on the remaining objectives. The second wave was ordered forward, and, on the left, four more machine guns and some prisoners were taken in a strongpoint. Meanwhile, on the right the advance was carried on beyond Vacher Farm which, according to the battle narrative, "could not be recognised on the ground",[16] presumably because it had been blasted to out of existence by the weight of the artillery barrage.

On the right, the 1/7th Worcesters' progress was halted by heavy enemy fire after 300 yards. However, while the men took shelter in shell holes, their protective barrage could not be stopped and it continued to roll forward at the assigned rate, leaving the Worcesters far behind and without their supporting artillery. Despite this, the Commanding Officer, Lt Col F. M. Tomkinson, managed to re-organise his companies and launch a renewed attempt to take his main objective, Adler Farm. In his narrative, Tomkinson describes the action:

> About 0600 A Company (the right support company) was ordered to push on through B Company and renew the attack. A Company officers were all casualties and OC B Company, Capt T C F Harris, personally organised and led the attack, making progress to within 50 yards of the enemy line.[17]

By this point the sky had lightened, the attacking riflemen and Lewis Gunners were able to identify and engage targets, and, in Tomkinson's own words, "the killing of Germans commenced".[18]

This covering fire helped the advancing troops to enter the German breastwork in front of Adler Farm, where they found large numbers of enemy dead, and numerous machine guns with their deceased crews beside them. Tomkinson noted that many of the machine gunners appeared to have been shot in the head.[19] About 7.30am, under heavy rifle and Lewis Gun fire, the will of the garrison began to break. Men started to surrender in large numbers. As soon as this position was taken, Tomkinson pushed patrols out along his front, including towards Adler Farm itself, which was reported captured at 11.16am.

The Brigade Commander now committed a company of his reserve, 1/8th Worcesters to support 1/7th Worcesters and Tomkinson re-organised his troops, putting B Company on the right with C in support and the 1/8th Worcesters company (confusingly, another B Company) on the left. The remnants of A and D Companies became the battalion reserve. B Company, 1/8th Worcesters was then ordered to attack Inch House, commencing at 5.00pm, but ran into a British barrage being fired to protect 1/6th Gloucesters, in the centre. The Worcesters could make no progress and this attack was eventually called off.

At about the same time, two further companies of 1/8th Worcesters, A and D, were ordered to push through the survivors of 1/4th Gloucesters and attack Oxford Houses, but this too was unsuccessful, largely due to the withering machine gun fire coming from enemy depth positions to the north of the Lekkerboterbeek.

16 TNA WO 95/2758: 1/6th Gloucestershire Regiment War Diary.
17 TNA WO 95/2759: Lt Col F M Tomkinson Report, 1/7th Worcesters War Diary.
18 TNA WO 95/2759: Lt Col F M Tomkinson Report, 1/7th Worcesters War Diary.
19 TNA WO 95/2759: Lt Col F M Tomkinson Report, 1/7th Worcesters War Diary.

After dark, the brigade commander began to readjust his force. One company of 1/8th Worcesters (C) was tasked to reinforce 1/4th Gloucesters and 1/7th Worcesters. 1/4th R Berkshires and the Bucks Battalion, both of 145th Brigade, were moved up and placed under 144th Brigade orders to provide extra manpower in the event of an enemy counter-attack. None developed and that night and the following day passed quietly before 144th Brigade was relieved on the night of 10th/11th October. The brigade had achieved a number of its objectives and captured 160 prisoners, 21 machine guns and 2 Trench Mortars. Its casualties were 167 killed and 469 wounded.

## From Ypres to Vimy Ridge

The Third Ypres battle continued until 10th November, by which date the Allies had secured the village of Passchendaele and the ridge on which it sat. However, the 48th Division did not see that hard-won victory. After a few days of rest, the division was ordered to head south to relieve the 2nd Canadian Division, part of V Corps, at Vimy Ridge, north of the French city of Arras. Thus, in the space of 36 hours, the South Midlanders exchanged the perpetual mud and shelling and the desolation of the Ypres sector for a quieter part of the line, where things had calmed down significantly since the Arras offensive had concluded the previous May. As Capt Philip Wright noted in the history of the Bucks Battalion, when, on 1st November,1917, the unit went into the line in front of Vimy, it became clear that "we had taken over some very good and reasonably quiet trenches".[20]

It is fair to say that the conditions at Vimy were a significant improvement on their previous location, but line-holding in a quiet sector still had its challenges. It was certainly not a holiday, even if it felt like one after their time in front of Passchendaele. The Royal Engineer Field Companies were put to work building huts, laying tramways, burying cables, strengthening trench parapets, all the on-going tasks required to sustain a division in the line in trench warfare. The men took to the work with enthusiasm, believing they were helping to ensure they had a comfortable winter. But it was not long before the rumour mill began to grind into full production. Home leave was stopped at the beginning of November, an indicator that something was afoot. One report suggested the division was to attack Lens before Christmas. Another had it that they were being sent to German East Africa, while a third was certain that Russia was their next location. On 20th November, the Battle of Cambrai was launched, sparking suggestions that they might be headed there. However, as Capt Wright noted, the smart money, watching newspaper reports of the events that were unfolding along the Isonzo River, where the Italian army appeared to have suffered a significant reversal, "was inclined to consider this as our probable destination".[21] The smart money was correct.

The Canadian Corps, having left Vimy for the Ypres Sector and taken part in the final push up onto the Passchendaele – Staden Ridge, now needed to go to a quiet sector to regenerate after their exertions. It made sense to send them back to the familiar territory of Vimy, releasing, among others, the 48th Division for the long trip south to the plains of Lombardy.

---

20   P L Wright, p.88.
21   P L Wright, p.89.

## Long Journey South to the Sun

23rd and 41st divisions were already on their way to Italy when, on 15 November, the 48th Division's GSO1, Lt Col G. W. Howard, AA&QMG, Lt Col G. H. Barnett, and a small group of support staff (in total, seven officers and nine other ranks), formed an advance party, tasked with making all the necessary arrangements for the arrival of the division.

Barnett and his team spent a night in Paris before catching the Modane Express on the evening of 17th November, arriving at Mantua, via Turin and Milan, on the evening of 19th November. Before leaving they had managed to find one soldier, a gunner, who could speak Italian, to act as an interpreter.

Mantua, or Mantova as it was then called, appeared to be "a regular pandemonium". The railway station and streets were packed with Italian soldiers, but the party managed to find their way to British General Headquarters, where General Sir Herbert Plumer and his staff were located. There they received instructions to establish a divisional headquarters at Cologna Veneto, about 50km north-east of Mantua. On the way there they met elements of 23rd Division. Barnett recalled:

> The well-ordered march discipline, spick and span transport, well-conditioned animals, and, above all, the cheerful and confident faces of the men, were already acting as a powerful antidote to the wave of depression spreading over the civilian population …[22]

Arriving at Cologna Veneto, they set about preparing billeting in the area, learning that the first units of the division were scheduled to arrive on 25th November. The GHQ transport staff informed them that the division would detrain at Isola della Scalla, Bovolone and Cerea. But, as Barnett put it, with barely-disguised frustration, 'nothing happened as expected".[23] The detrainment and concentration of the division was saved from chaos mostly by luck rather than judgement.

No divisional units arrived on the 25th. The following day, some artillery personnel and guns turned up at Isola. Units then began to arrive, one after another, but in no particular order. In some cases, half a battalion would arrive at a station in one town while the other half might turn up at a different station, maybe 50km away. The 1/5th Gloucesters managed to concentrate by accident. Having detrained at two stations, many kilometres apart, they marched into the town of Noventa Vicentina, from two separate directions, at roughly the same time.[24]

The Italian railway system was creaking under the strain and the movement of troops from France to Italy was not the carefully-choreographed transport plan that the British Army would have wished for. But, with a lot of hard work, and a sense of humour – severely tested at times – Barnett and his small team managed to get the division concentrated by brigades in time for the arrival of Major General Fanshawe, and the remainder of his staff, on 29th November.

For the men of the Bucks Battalion, the journey turned out to be "one of the most magnificent holidays the battalion ever had". The move was completed in two trains, one following the other, at a 12-hour interval. The first contingent, including the Commanding Officer, Adjutant,

---

22  G Barnett, *With the 48th Division in Italy*, p.5.
23  G Barnett, p.9.
24  G Barnett, p.12.

Transport Officer, half of battalion headquarters and A and C Companies, marched out of Tinques at 2100 on 23rd November, clambering into a train at Savy, which departed at around midnight. The second group, made up of the Second-in-Command, the Assistant Adjutant, Medical Officer, Intelligence Officer and B and D Companies boarded their train at Savy at 0900 the following morning. The route, which took six days to complete, took them through Arras, Achiet-le-Grand, Albert, Amiens, Dijon, Pierrelatte, Bologna and then to their concentration area.[25]

According to Capt Wright, conditions on his train were "unusually commodious". Instead of the usual crush, the men had enough space to be comfortable, while the officers were three to a compartment. If one of them slept on the floor they could all get a comfortable night's sleep. The train also included a number of flat cars that were not required for the battalion's vehicles so the men were able to use these as viewing platforms as the weather grew warmer on the way south. The sights of the Rhone Valley and the Riviera, untouched by conflict, must have been a tonic for the men after what they had just endured in northern France and Flanders.[26]

By the afternoon of the 27th they crossed the Italian border, where the men detrained at Ventimiglia for a short, sharp march through the town and along the sea front before rejoining their transport for the next part of the journey.[27] Once in Italy, the signs of the Caporetto disaster were everywhere. At Bologna among the refugees crowding the station, the Bucks men saw strings of Italian deserters, chained together. From there they moved north and east. Crossing the river Po, the first train arrived at its destination, Bevilaqua, at 1900 on 29th November. The second arrived at Este at 0800 the following morning. From their detraining stations, both elements of the battalion marched to Agugliaro, where they joined up. For the next four days they marched through Bosco di Nanto, Villafranca and Marsango, arriving at Villa del Conte on 8th December.

The men of the Bucks Battalion had expected to be rushed into the line to stem the Austro-German advance, but by the time they arrived, the Italians had established themselves behind the Piave, the front had stabilised, and the need for early action to help shore up the line had begun to subside. However, unknown to the rank and file, their senior commanders and politicians had, for some time, been locked in discussions about exactly where the British (and French) reinforcements should be located and what they should do.

The original plan, as set out by the General Staff at the War Office in Whitehall, was to concentrate the British divisions well back from the fighting. This was to ensure that the troops could complete their journeys, re-organise themselves, and deploy as required, without the pressure of an advancing enemy. Cavan's written orders from London, dated 28th October, noted that although the final location had not yet been agreed, it had been provisionally fixed in the neighbourhood of Verona. However, Cavan was instructed to satisfy himself, before agreeing to any area of concentration proposed by the Commando Supremo, that the area would be adequately secured and that concentration could be completed without interference from the enemy.[28] Upon his arrival in Italy, Cavan found himself being heavily lobbied by General Cadorna to locate the British contingent much closer to the fighting. Cadorna was not confident

---

25  P L Wright, p.91.
26  P L Wright, p.92.
27  P L Wright, p.92-93.
28  TNA WO 97/67: CIGS to Lt Gen Cavan correspondence, 28 October 1917.

that his forces could hold the enemy on the Piave and he wanted the French and British reinforcements to be based where they could provide "close active support" if required.[29] Cavan agreed, subject to War Office and ministerial approval, which was forthcoming, to concentrate in the area of Mantua, on the west bank of the Mincio River, and this is where 23rd and 41st divisions detrained on 11th and 16th November respectively. If Cavan thought the matter was settled, however, he was to be disappointed.

On 8th November, he received a telegram from Chief of the Imperial General Staff, General Sir William Robertson, informing him that the Italians were anxious for British and French troops to concentrate even further forward. Generals Foch and Sir Henry Wilson had been despatched to report on the military situation and, in particular, to examine the question of where the reinforcements should be located. The telegram added that the Prime Minister, Lloyd George, "desires you to act on General Wilson's instructions in this matter", but if Cavan disagreed with Wilson he was to make his views known and the responsibility would then rest on Wilson and the Prime Minister.[30] Cavan met with Wilson on the evening of the 9th November, and the following day wrote to Robertson, reporting that the situation on the Piave was not as secure as he had anticipated, and that he was in complete agreement with Wilson that it was advisable to alter the concentration of the 23rd Division. If the situation on the Piave improved, 41st Division might concentrate in the Verona area as originally planned. He was, however, strongly averse to a concentration east of the Mincio if it did not appear that the Piave line could be held long enough for the two British divisions to complete their arrivals unmolested.[31]

General Armando Diaz took over from the sacked Cadorna on 9th November, and on the morning of 11th November, hosted a lengthy discussion with Foch and Wilson, the latter in his short-lived capacity as the British Permanent Military Representative at the Supreme War Council in Versailles. During this meeting, Diaz read out a telegram from Orlando, the new Italian Prime Minister, urging that Allied troops should be moved further forward, and stating that the impression was gaining ground that the Allies were "hanging back".[32] After a long, and at times heated, discussion, Foch agreed that four French divisions should be brought forward to the Vicenza area. The following day, Cavan received a letter from Wilson notifying him of the decision that while the French force advanced to a position with its right on Vicenza, the British XIV Corps should join up on the right of the French, behind the Bacchiglione River, with its own right at Montegalda, well to the east of the Mincio.[33] Despite his earlier views, Cavan ordered preparations to be made for 23rd and 41st Divisions to march to the new line, where they would be joined by the 48th Division.

Whilst taking part in these various discussions, Cavan knew he was about to be replaced as Commander in Chief, although he would retain command of XIV Corps. Cavan had already been told by Robertson that General Sir Herbert Plumer would be arriving to take over command of the British contingent. On 10th November, Cavan wrote to Robertson to say he expected Plumer to arrive on the 11th or 12th and arrangements had been made for him and his staff to be based in Mantua. He was sure that Plumer would agree that under the circumstances

---

29  J E Edmonds, p.89.
30  TNA WO 79/67: CIGS to Cavan correspondence, 8th November 1917.
31  TNA WO 79/67: CIGS to Cavan correspondence, 10th November 1917.
32  J E Edmonds, p.92.
33  J E Edmonds, p.92.

"it would be most unwise to concentrate any further forward than we are doing. The roads are already choked with refugees between Padua and the Po."[34]

In Paris, Plumer met with Lloyd George and the French Prime Minister, M. Painleve, at the Hotel Meurice. Sir Maurice Hankey, the Secretary to the War Cabinet, was also present. Plumer's senior staff officer, Major General Charles Harrington,[35] noted that they found Lloyd George "only too anxious to take as many troops from the Western Front…" as Plumer wished.[36]

In his written orders from Robertson, dated 9th November, Plumer was given clear instructions in relation to his new command. His main objective was to assist the Italians in defending their country against invasion, and to give them time and opportunity to reorganise their armies and generally to restore them to an efficient condition. In pursuance of this, he was to conform to the wishes of the Italian Commander-in-Chief with respect to the dispositions and employment of British troops. However, he was to regard himself as an independent commander, responsible to the UK Government for ensuring that his troops were not placed in a compromising position. No part of his force should be detached except as a temporary measure, and then only with his agreement. If, at any time, he was requested by the Italians to carry out operations which he believed would unduly endanger the safety of his troops, he was to make the requisite representations to the Commando Supremo, and, if necessary, refer to CIGS for the instructions of the War Cabinet. Plumer was to report directly to CIGS regarding operational matters, and as soon as possible after arriving in Italy, he was to produce a report on the situation there, with particular reference to any reinforcements he might require.[37] Plumer subsequently requested that two further infantry divisions should be added to his Order of Battle, joining the four already assigned to the theatre, and that a cavalry brigade should follow.

The 5th and 21st divisions, both from X Corps, were warned off to head to Italy, and the former departed as ordered on 27th November. However, the situation at the Battle of Cambrai, where the Germans had launched a general counter-offensive in a bid to regain ground lost in the British attack of 20th November, caused a re-think. In a War Cabinet discussion on 3rd December, General Jan Smuts said that in view of the circumstances at Cambrai, it would be a serious mistake to send further reinforcements to Italy. He believed the Germans had lost their chance to break through on the Piave and it was improbable that they would now try to make significant efforts at Cambrai and in Italy simultaneously. "It would," he said, "be a great mistake on our part to concentrate our troops in a position where they would not be urgently needed." He advocated cancelling the despatch of the division that had not yet departed and recalling the 5th Division. The War Cabinet agreed.[38] This meant the British force in Italy would, for the time being, stand at four divisions.

At a conference on 22nd November, Generals Diaz, Foch and Plumer agreed that the French and British troops would move forward from their current positions on what had become known as the Vicenza Line, so that they could be in supporting distance of the Italians on the Piave. This followed a half-hearted Austro-German attack, first in the Monte Tomba area and then

---

34  TNA WO 79/67: Cavan to CIGS correspondence 10th November 1917.
35  Harrington's appointment was Major General General Staff (MGGS).
36  C Harrington, p.135.
37  J E Edmonds, Instructions by the Chief of the Imperial General Staff to General Sir Herbert Plumer When Leaving for Italy, Appendix X, p.424.
38  TNA CAB 23/4/63: War Cabinet Minutes, 3rd December 1917.

on the whole front from the Piave to the Brenta, which continued from 17th November to 25th November. Monte Tomba itself was captured, but the advance was held everywhere else. While this fighting was still going on, and clearly still concerned for the security of his line, Diaz called a further meeting with Plumer and General Fayolle (who had replaced Foch as commander of the French contingent) on 26th November. The Italians were very anxious that the British and French should occupy some portion of the line both to relieve some of their exhausted troops and also to demonstrate to the army and the Italian people that their allies were fighting alongside them.[39]

Reporting on the discussion to CIGS, General Plumer explained that an early proposal for the British and French to take over a section of line on the Asiago Plateau was found to be impracticable. There were two main reasons for this: first it would have been impossible to provide the necessary winter equipment in time; and second, neither the British nor the French had any experience of mountain warfare. Although the plateau is not a mountainous area in itself, it is 3000 feet above sea level, and, in the winter, is generally under a blanket of snow for months at a time. It would certainly have been very hard on the British and French soldiers who were not equipped for that environment. Instead, it was agreed that the British would take over the Montello sector, overlooking the Piave River, and the French would assume responsibility for the Asolo sector, immediately to the north.[40]

Consequently, Plumer issued orders to XIV Corps at 1000 on 23rd November to move quickly east from the Vicenza Line and locate itself astride the Brenta, south of Cittadella, no later than the night of 24th November, preparatory to taking over a seven-mile section of line between Nervesa and Rivasecca. The orders noted that Plumer's intention was for the XIV Corps to hold the front with two divisions in the line and a third in reserve around Castelfranco. The XI Corps, when complete, would be concentrated in the Castlefranco, Camposampiero, Montegalda area.[41]

There was some delay because the Italians could not clear the area east of the Brenta in time to allow the British and French troops to cross the river on the 24th. However, by the evening of the 25th, Plumer was able to report that the leading French and British Divisions were just west of the Brenta and by the next day he expected to have portions of two divisions across the river with a third closing up.[42] On the 28th XIV Corps (23rd and 41st divisions) began to relieve the Italian I Corps (Fourth Army) between Nervesa and Ciano. Meanwhile, 7th Division detrained in the area between Legnago and Isola della Scala, west of the Adige, and began moving up to the Bacchiglione River between Montegalda and Longare, as XIV Corps reserve.[43]

On 28th November the 23rd and 41st divisions moved north-east from the Brenta towards the Montello. The weather was cold but dry, and the frozen roads made for reasonably easy marching conditions. By the morning of 30th November, elements of the 41st Division began to relieve the Italian 1st Division, facing east, completing the process on 2nd December, whilst the 23rd Division had taken over from the Italian 70th Division, facing north, two days later. With the two reliefs complete, the British divisions now held the Piave Line between Pederobba

---

39  TNA CAB 24/33/90: Plumer to CIGS correspondence, 27th November 1917.
40  TNA CAB 24/33/90: Plumer to CIGS, 27th November 1917.
41  TNA WO 79/67: British Expeditionary Force (Italy) Operation Order No. 1, 23rd November 1917.
42  TNA CAB 24/33/56: Plumer to CIGS, 25th November 1917.
43  J E Edmonds, p.102.

in the north-west and Nervesa in the southeast. Lt Gen Cavan took command of the sector at 1000 on 4th December, his headquarters located at Fanzolo, about four miles north-east of Castlefranco.[44] Each division held their section of the front with two brigades forward, each brigade putting two battalions into the line.

The Montello is a loaf-shaped area of high ground which lies along the western bank of the Piave. In late 1917 it was of considerable tactical and strategic importance to both sets of combatants. It provided the British with excellent observation over the enemy positions to the east and north whilst forming a significant geographical speed-bump against any attempt by the Austro-Germans to continue their push to the west or to take Venice by a thrust from north to south. In his first official despatch from Italy, General Plumer described it as "a hinge to the whole line, joining, as it does, that portion facing north from Monte Tomba to Lake Garda with the defensive line of the Piave".[45] It was, in short, the key to unlocking the new Italian front line, along the river, and it is, therefore, unsurprising that Diaz was keen to make use of strong, well-rested British and French divisions there, to relieve his battle-weary forces in this vitally important sector.

The Montello position had been constructed by the Italians and, as the Official History explains, it consisted of three lines of trenches, running parallel to the Piave river. The forward or front-line trench was generally dug into the sand and shingle along the river bank, with numerous machine-gun emplacements (mostly not very well hidden), and shelters that would not have looked out of place in 1914, but were now very dated by western front standards, with few shellproof dugouts.[46] In places where the bank consisted of steep cliffs, the trenches ran along the foot of the rocks, relying on trees and scrub to hide them from the enemy's observation. Above the front position towered the flat-topped, wooded Montello hill, pock-marked with deep depressions, not unlike very large shell-holes. These proved to be handy cover for howitzers, their high elevations allowing them to fire over the lips of the "craters" to engage positions on the enemy side of the river, although getting guns in and out of them must have been a challenge. The whole area was criss-crossed by a series of narrow dirt tracks, enclosed by hedges. The Allies had the advantage of overlooking the Austro-German positions close to the river, but, opposite the Montello, to the north and east, the ground rises gradually until it eclipses the hill, giving the enemy uninterrupted, if longer-distance views over the British positions. The wooded slopes opposite the British positions provided dense cover for enemy artillery units.

The Piave itself, hereabouts, runs in a gravel bed that can extend up to a thousand yards from bank to bank – not a single stream but a series of separate channels, punctuated by sandbanks or islands. In normal conditions, the river channels are seldom more than three or four feet deep, but in heavy rainfall or in times of rapid snow-melt, the individual streams can swell to become a single, swiftly-flowing torrent, hence the need for strong flood banks that extend up to six feet above the normal river height. At low water the river can be easily forded, but in spate conditions, the deep, ice-cold and fast-flowing water can make wading or swimming a much more difficult proposition, as soldiers of both sides found to their cost.

---

44  The divisional artillery completed the reliefs by 7th December.
45  Plumer's First Despatch, *Sixth Supplement to the London Gazette*, 9th April 1918, p.4430.
46  J E Edmonds, p.104.

By the time the British troops arrived on the Piave Line, the fighting there had died down and the sector was regarded as 'quiet', at least in comparison with France and Belgium. The German 12th Division and the Austrian 13th Division seemed more interested in preparing their positions for the winter than in taking the fight to the Allies. An exception to this occurred on 8th December, when the artillery of the German division, on learning they were to be withdrawn, decided to fire off all their ammunition, creating a bombardment that was certainly on a par with those experienced on the western front.[47]

After the Caporetto rout and the long, hard fighting retreat to the Piave, the tired and battle-scared Italians had been content to hold the line on a live-and-let-live basis, reluctant to do anything that was likely to prompt a significant response from the Germans and Austrians opposite. However, with the British now in the line, that was about to change. As the Official History notes, the British artillery soon became active, putting down bombardments and counter-battery fire, and setting an example for the Italians in a bid to foster an offensive spirit.[48] Before long, a programme of night-time patrolling was also commenced, with small groups of men, usually under the command of a junior officer, seeking to dominate No-man's Land, and gather intelligence, as had been the standard approach in France and Flanders. As Plumer himself admitted, the river represented a "very serious obstacle" at that time of year, with a current running at 14 knots. Every form of raft and boat was tried in an attempt to work out the best method of getting across. In the end, however, it was found that wading was the most successful approach, even though the icy, fast-flowing water added to the difficulties.[49]

One soldier with first-hand experience of this was Northumberland Fusilier, Pte Norman Gladden, who describes an attempt to cross the river in his book, *'Across the Piave'*. On 8th January 1918, with the banks of the river blanketed in snow, Gladden and fellow Lewis Gunner, Pte Westgarth were detailed to take part in a patrol, by elements of B Company, 11/Northumberland Fusiliers, which was tasked to probe the enemy defences on the north bank. The soldiers, under command of a 2/Lt, were ordered to strip off their khaki and replace it with white canvas overalls, which would provide a degree of camouflage in the snow. Steel helmets and gas respirators were left behind, and while most of the other members of the patrol carried only their rifles and a bandolier of extra ammunition, Westgarth carried the Lewis Gun and Gladden had the spare ammunition. This was held in a number of heavy drum magazines, carried in specially-designed webbing pouches – definitely not the kit in which one would choose to go swimming in the icy waters of an Italian river, swollen by winter rains.

Crossing the front-line trench, they waded out into the stream, "a gliding torrent of icy water, not more than a foot deep". The water, coming from the snow-covered hills to the north, was very cold and soon the soldiers' feet and legs were numb, as they continued forward, surprised at the noise their boots were making as they kicked against the stones in the river-bed. Here and there, patches of stunted bushes sprouted up where the ground was higher, forming small and raised islands in the shingle. The roar of the fast-flowing river seemed to be coming from all around them, and they were, quite literally, surrounded by the angry waters. They had now reached one of the main channels, a much wider stream, some 30 yards wide:

---

47  J E Edmonds, p.115.
48  J E Edmonds, p.115.
49  Plumer's First Despatch, p.4430.

We began, with little thought, to wade across. It was shallow at first, like the previous streams, but deepened towards the middle. The water was now swirling towards our waists. Now, surely, it would get shallower, but as we approached the opposite bank the water continued to rise, and the current rushed upon us in a terrific spate. *Taken* completely by surprise, I found myself struggling, up to my neck. The man just ahead had been swept off his feet and had only just managed to strike the shore where it jutted out into the torrent. I had a similar experience. For a few moments I completely lost my balance and felt myself swirling along helplessly like a cork. It was touch and go, for I was no great swimmer. I saw the bank coming towards me, and then, when right in the grip of the eddy, a hand shot out and I found myself scrambling up the shingle to safety.[50]

Westgarth had dropped the Lewis Gun in his struggles, but it was close to the bank, and they managed to recover it, allowing the patrol to continue, although more cautiously after their dice with death. With the noise of the main channel growing louder, the patrol commander went forward with an NCO and a runner, to check the route. They discovered that the primary stream, was so swollen that it formed an impassable barrier. With their way blocked, the young officer decided that the best course of action was to head back to their own lines. They retraced their steps, this time forming a human chain to aid crossing the deepest channels. Completely soaked, the men had lost all feeling in their limbs, and Gladden found himself in a daze, conscious, but only just aware of his surroundings. He remembered crossing the trench, climbing up some steps to a road and then coming to a room where he "glimpsed paradise" in the form of tanks of steaming hot water which helped to restore their circulation, slowly bringing them back to normality with the aid of an issue of new, dry clothes.[51]

The 48th Division was not introduced to the Piave Line until February 1918. With its final elements arriving from France on 4th December, the division was ordered to concentrate southwest of the Bacciglione River. The initial GHQ plan was for the South Midlanders to be in reserve behind the Montello feature. However, Austrian successes in the mountains to the west of the Asiago Plateau reignited Commando Supremo concerns of a possible break-out into the plains and the division was instead diverted north, as a precautionary measure, establishing its headquarters at Montegaldella, between Padua and Vicenza, before moving to Piazzola, with units billeted in Villafranca, Camisano, Gromolo and Presina. By now the XI Corps headquarters and its commander, Lt General Sir Richard Haking, had arrived and established themselves at Campo San Piero. Together with 5th Division, which was still in the process of detraining, the 48th became part of the XI Corps order of battle.

On 13th December, the division was once again on the move, relocating to an area west of Citadella, astride the Brenta River, tasked to reinforce the mountain front north of Marostica in the event of further Austrian aggression. The Divisional Assistant Adjutant and Quartermaster General, Lt Col George Barnett, was not impressed with his new surroundings. The billeting accommodation was poor; there was little land or facilities for sport; and the local villages were crowded with Italian troops. It was only by "some hard pushing and a good deal of firmness" that the division managed to squeeze itself into the allocated area, dispersed in Brigade groups. 145th

---

50 N Gladden, *Across the Piave*, p.50.
51 N Gladden, p.50.

Brigade was at Tezze, 143rd Brigade at Pozzoleone, together with Divisional Headquarters, and 144th Brigade at Sandrigo. The divisional artillery was at Longa and Maragnole and the Pioneers found space for themselves at Schiavon.[52] The move was competed on 23rd December, just in time for Christmas, and although there were supply problems during this period as the Italian railway system struggled to handle all the extra train movements, most units managed to have a good festive season. Turkeys and pork were purchased from local farmers and, according to Barnett, the troops enjoyed "possibly the best Christmas dinner of the war".[53] The men of the Bucks Battalion, based at San Croce, would certainly have agreed. Spending their third Christmas away from home, and despite constant hard field training, the battalion managed to ensure that "every man was able to eat turkey and plum pudding to his tummy's content, helping it down with more than sufficient vino".[54] Indeed the local vino was proving to be the cause of much extra business for the battalion orderly room. As Capt. Philip Wright recalled, "it was not so much that it was a potent beverage, as that the men were unaccustomed to it, and thought it could be treated in the same manner as the French wine". Only when a number found themselves undergoing 28 days of Field Punishment No 1, was vino "shown the respect to which it had proved itself entitled".[55]

In late January, the division was ordered to move to an area about 10km west of Treviso where, with the weather beginning to improve, the men spent an enjoyable month – except for the supply column, based at Treviso, who had to put up with nightly bombing raids. On 23rd February, new orders were received instructing the South Midlanders to relieve 7th Division in the right sector of the Montello.[56]

---

52   G Barnett, p.19.
53   G Barnett, p.21.
54   P L Wright, p.96.
55   P L Wright, p.96.
56   The 48th Division was originally scheduled to relieve 41st Division in the left sector, but this turned out to be a staffing error and was quickly rectified.

8

# Battle of Asiago Origins

In his account of the Italian campaign, Lord Cavan states that the Austrian attack on 15th June 1918, was undertaken 'to show the loyalty of the Austro-Hungarian Army to the cause of the Central Powers'.[1] This may have been so. The Emperor certainly had some fence-mending to do with his German ally after it was found out, courtesy of Clemenceau, that he had secretly sought peace terms in spring 1917. Karl was forced to apologise to Kaiser Wilhelm II for his treacherous act and promised to 'prove by deeds that Austria would fight to the last.'[2] Whether or not it was an act of contrition on the part of the Austrians, planning for an offensive in Italy began following an agreement between the Austrian and German high commands regarding the roles of their respective armies during 1918.

According to the Austrian Official History, in the autumn of 1917 the General Staffs of the two Central Powers discussed the way ahead and concluded that rather than joining hands and concentrating their forces for a single attack on the allies, they would act separately. The Germans would launch a major attack on the Western Front in the second half of March, while the Austrians would 'strike a decisive blow' against Italy 'several months later'.[3] The Austrians saw their offensive as a means of driving Italy out of the war. Conversely, in Field Marshal Paul von Hindenburg's mind, the role of Austria in 1918 would be to pin down the Italian, British and French divisions in Venetia, stopping them from interfering with the planned German offensive to the north. By attacking on the Italian front, the Austrians might even draw entente forces away from the path of the German offensive, increasing the likelihood of success.[4]

The German situation at the beginning of 1918 was precarious but perhaps not yet disastrously so. At home, the impact of the British maritime blockade was starving the civilian population and constraining the nation's ability to supply and sustain its fighting men in the field. Casualties continued to mount. Losses at Verdun and the Battle of the Somme in 1916, and Passchendaele in 1917, had taken a heavy toll, creating a dire shortage of manpower. But despite the difficulties, the average German soldier was still up for the fight, although popular support for war was waning and realists among the German leadership could see that with

---

1 TNA WO 79/70: Cavan Papers.
2 TNA WO 79/70: Cavan Papers.
3 E Glaise-Horstenau and R Kiszling, *Osterreichs–Ungarns Letzter Krieg – 1914-1918*, Vol. 7, p.23.
4 E Glaise-Horstenau and R Kiszling, Vol. 7, p.22.

failing industrial output, increasing public unrest and America's eventual entry into the war, opportunities to bring the conflict to a conclusion in Germany's favour were beginning to move out of reach.

However, all was not yet lost. The Russian Revolution of October 1917, and the subsequent Treaty of Brest Litovsk, signed in early March 1918, provided some grounds for cautious optimism. It took Russia and Rumania out of the conflict and gave the German High Command what it had always wanted – an opportunity to prosecute the war on a single front in France and Belgium. At the same time, it allowed German commanders to shift over 50 divisions from the east to the west. Until this point, following the battles of 1916-17, the opposing sides along the 440 miles of the Western Front, were in relative equilibrium in terms of fighting strength. But with the injection of the troops from the East, the Germans would outweigh the allies by 192 divisions to 178. This was a significant, but perhaps not an overwhelming advantage, although it occurred at a time when the French and British armies were also suffering acute manpower shortages and America had not yet entered the fray on land in any meaningful sense.

Meanwhile, the Germans had developed an important tactical innovation, which, when combined with their numerical superiority, could, it was believed, create the conditions for strategic success. By early 1918 the Germans had perfected a new set of offensive tactics, based on the principle of strength against weakness and infiltration, bypassing strongpoints to penetrate deep into enemy territory, attacking rear areas and supply lines. These Hutier tactics (named after their originator, Gen Oskar von Hutier), coupled with a new cadre of specially-trained and equipped *Stosstruppen* (shock troops) to carry them out, could, Ludendorff calculated, allow Germany to launch one last, decisive blow, that would knock Britain out of the war and force France to sue for peace before America could become fully engaged and swing the pendulum the other way. But they would need to act quickly before Germany's ability to go on sustaining its forces in the field was finally exhausted.

Operation Michael, opening on 21st March 1918, was the initial large-scale manifestation of this thinking. Designed to breakthrough the British Fifth Army and push across the old Somme battlefield of 1916 towards the channel coast, the Germans, having made stunning early advances, lost momentum and halted. In an effort to generate operational tempo, they attacked in Flanders on 9th April, on the River Lys (Operation Georgette), driving for the important rail hub of Hazebrouck and then the vital ports of Calais, Boulogne and Dunkirk. Again, this made only limited progress. This was followed by a further advance to the south on the River Aisne (Operation Blucher-Yorck), on 27th May, and again in the Noyon-Montdidier area (Operation Gneisenau) on 8th June. A final offensive, the Friedensturm (Peace Offensive) was launched in mid-July.

## Austrian and Allied Attack Plans

While the Germans planned and executed their Spring offensive, the Austrians too began to sketch out how they might fulfil their end of the bargain, although on a slightly less urgent timeline. According to Edmonds, former Chief of Staff of the Austrian Army, Field Marshal Conrad von Hotzendorf, now commanding the Trentino Group of Armies, drew up a scheme for an attack between the Adige and Piave rivers and submitted this to his High Command at Baden, near Vienna.[5] This is corroborated by *Letzter Kreig*, which notes that Conrad set out his plan on 30th January, 1918, while the Austrians were engaged with the Italians at Mont de val Bella and Col del Rosso. Conrad was clear that the centre of gravity for the attack should be across the Asiago Plateau. He did not discount the possibility of an attack across the Piave towards Treviso, recognising the benefits of a 'pincer' manoeuvre, but he believed that the Treviso option, on its own, would merely drive the Italians back on their lines of communication. Only a thrust across the Asiago Plateau and down on to the Venetian Plain offered the chance of a decisive victory.[6] A quick glance at a map of the region will show the soundness of the military thinking behind this conclusion.

A large proportion of the Italian Army was deployed along the line of the Piave River, to the east of Venice, with supply lines running back along the Venetian plain towards Verona, Milan, and the port of Genoa, and then down the length of the Italian mainland. Here, an attack, while possible, would be made very difficult by the need to conduct multiple, opposed crossings of a fast-flowing river, and also by the strong allied position on the high ground of the Montello, which dominated the Piave valley between Pederobba and Nervesa. Meanwhile, the allied position on the Asiago Plateau was a precarious one. The plateau itself is only a few miles wide, enclosed on all sides by the jagged peaks of the Dolomites or deep ravines, worn out over millennia by fast-flowing rivers. From Asiago, the ground rises steeply through dense woodland to the south before falling precipitously several thousand feet to the plain below. This sector was served by two main supply routes and several mule tracks which snaked up the sheer face of the escarpment, the steep gradient and the sharp hair-pin bends making it difficult to get men and material up but almost impossible to allow for a managed, deliberate withdrawal in the face of a successful Austrian advance. If the Austrians could penetrate the allied line at Asiago, break through the narrow band of defences – only three miles deep before the edge of the mountains – there was very little to stop them from breaking out into the Venetian Plain below, where they could cut off the Piave defenders from their supply lines, forcing them to choose between withdrawal, surrender or annihilation. Following on from Caporetto, an advance across the plateau and down into the plain might well have been enough to force Italy to seek an armistice, taking them out of the war and allowing a transfer of Austrian resources to the north, where they could have threatened the French southern flank and reinforced German forces on the Western Front.

But not all Austrian generals were as offensively-minded as Conrad. Facing the Italians across the Piave River, Field Marshal Svetozar Boroevic, commanding the Isonzo Army, had no such attack plans. He favoured sitting tight on his current position, allowing the Germans to do the heavy lifting to win the war on the Western Front, thus keeping his elements of the Austrian army intact for whatever might follow.[7] There had already been signs of significant political unrest in some parts of the fading Hapsburg Empire and the army might be required for internal security duties once the war was won. The Russian Revolution and the subsequent peace treaty had been good news for Germany, but for Austria-Hungary, it was a double-edged sword. On the one hand it released large numbers of troops to reinforce the Italian and Western fronts. On the other, the collapse of Russia began to soften the glue that had helped to hold the multi-cultural, multi-racial, multi-national Dual Monarchy together – the powerful expedient

---

5   J E Edmonds, p.187
6   E Glaise-Horstenau and R Kiszling, Vol. 7, p.211.
7   J E Edmonds, p.188.

of mutual defence. Russia had been perceived by the Austro-Hungarian peoples as a common, existential threat, but that concern had now been alleviated to a large extent and the shackles of collective defence began to strain. Among the Slavic nationalities the Czechs took the lead in completely renouncing the Monarchy and the ruling house; in the so-called Epiphany Resolution (6th January 1918) they demanded unrestricted independence for themselves and the Slovaks. Among the South Slavs the idea of a federal union of the Serbs, Croats and Slovenes had been gaining strength since the Pact of Corfu in spring 1917. Even the Magyars, whose international standing was so closely connected with the fate of the Danube Monarchy, began to turn away once pressure from Russia subsided.[8]

At the beginning of 1918, the Dual Monarchy's food shortages were a significant cause for anxiety among the leadership as a cut in the flour ration set off a wave of strikes that turned into anti-war demonstrations. As notable 20th century historian, J M Roberts has observed: "The situation was disquietingly similar to that in Russia the year before."[9]

Despite Boroevic's misgivings about an offensive, at the headquarters of Austria's High Command, at Baden, the idea of a decisive attack in Italy was beginning to gain momentum, fanned by Emperor Karl's need to placate the Kaiser. As Operation Michael delivered early success in France, the Austrian planning effort was stepped up and on 23 March, orders were issued for a concerted attack between Asiago and the lower Piave. *Letzter Kreig* contains a direct quote from the Operation Order: "The main thrust will be delivered from the area between Asiago and the Piave, powerfully supported by artillery and trench mortars on both sides of the Brenta (river). It will reach the foot of the mountains as quickly as possible and force the Italians to break up their front along the Piave. The goal of this operation is to reach the Bacchiglione sector." This would be called Operation *Radetsky*.[10] A second attack, codenamed Operation *Avalanche* would take place in the Tonale sector of the Tyrol front and in a third advance, Boroevic and his Isonzo Army would cooperate with the main attack by thrusting over the Piave towards Treviso. This would be known as Operation *Albrecht*.[11]

This basic plan underwent a number of revisions over the next two months. The Tonale operations were reduced in scope, ultimately becoming nothing more than a 'feint', and an unsuccessful one at that. However, something of a stand-off developed between Conrad and Boroevic, over which arm of the pincer represented the main effort. Conrad continued to argue that only his attack, threatening to cut off the Italians in Venetia, could be decisive, while Boroevic now claimed that his operations represented the best chance of strategic success. At the end of April, he wrote to High Command to report that his plan was ready but added: "I must finally once again assert my conviction that the decisive thrust should be made from the Piave and will be decisive."[12]

---

8   E Glaise-Horstenau and R Kiszling, Vol. 7, p.5.
9   J M Roberts, p.247
10  Field Marshal Joseph Radetsky von Radets was an Austro-Hungarian soldier who had served as Chief of Staff during the latter part of the Napoleonic Wars. He oversaw the reform of the Dual Monarchy's army between 1809 and 1812. Best known for his victories at Custoza (1848) and Novara (1849) during the First Italian War of Independence.
11  Field Marshal the Archduke Albrecht, Duke of Teschen was the grandson of Emperor Leopold II and a senior military advisor to Emperor Franz Joseph I. He was made Commander in Chief of the Austro-Hungarian monarchy in 1866.
12  E Glaise-Horstenau and R Kiszling, Vol. 7, p.217.

Faced with a tough decision, in the face of two heavy-hitting Field Marshals, the High Command opted for a compromise. Instead of declaring a 'main effort' and ensuring it was properly resourced, they decided that both attacks should have equal weight. They distributed the available resources evenly between them, creating two relatively strong attacking forces. However, as *Letzter Krieg* openly admits, these dispositions meant that neither formation would have an overwhelming superiority over the enemy on their respective fronts[13] and thus the opportunity to concentrate force at a single point was lost. Conrad was allocated 23 divisions while Boroevic was given 23.5 divisions, although these included the High Command's strategic reserve, which was to be based close to the fighting front, but not engaged in the initial attack. Boroevic was unimpressed, complaining that "reserves in the rear are useless; only available [units] have value."[14] But the decision had been made and it was not revisited.

A change in German fortunes on the Western Front added a new impetus to the Austrian preparations. In On 2 April, as Operation Michael was beginning to lose momentum, Hindenburg wrote to Austrian Chief of Staff, General of Infantry Freiherr von Arz: "I believe Your Excellency's planned offensive of the k.u.k Army against Italy will enhance the overall situation, especially if it starts soon."[15] By the end of April, with the Michael and Georgette offensives now clearly failing to live up to early promise, Ludendorff noted in his war memoirs that "…Italian troops had appeared in the Argonne. British and French troops who went to Italy the previous autumn had stayed there." He demanded that the Austrians do something to try to weaken the allied forces in France and Belgium.[16]

Meanwhile, the Italians, British and French were planning their own offensive on broadly the same ground.

Despite the drubbing inflicted on the Italian Army at Caporetto and the subsequent pell-mell retreat first to the Tagliamento and then the Piave, by the time the British and French contingents arrived in northern Italy in late November 1917, what had been a fairly desperate situation was beginning to stabilise. But it was a close-run thing. Reporting to CIGS shortly after his arrival in Italy, Gen Plumer voiced his concern that 'one or two further local reverses would mean a general abandonment of the line now held," but, he added more hopefully: "…if the Italians can hold their present line (Piave) until we and the French are on the Vicenza Line, we should be able to hold that for some time and cover the retirement of the Italians if one is made…"[17] The one blessing of the retreat from the Isonzo was that it had shortened the Italian line by 170kms, which meant it required fewer men to hold it.[18]

In Plumer's second report, a month later, the situation was better, but still 'critical'. The Italians were beginning to recover from the shock of the Caporetto retreat, and their confidence was returning. While not entirely free from anxiety, the situation was now "distinctly hopeful." The Italian defensive line along the Piave was holding, and there had been no longer any need to rush the newly-arrived divisions into the fight. By the time Plumer submitted his third update, in January, the first snows had begun to fall in the mountains, reducing the likelihood of any

---

13  E Glaise-Horstenau and R Kiszling, Vol. 7, p.218.
14  E Glaise-Horstenau and R Kiszling, Vol. 7, p 218.
15  E Glaise-Horstenau and R Kiszling, Vol. 7, p.217.
16  E Ludendorff, *My War Memoirs*, Vol. II, p.609.
17  J E Edmonds, pp.95-96.
18  M Thompson, p.328.

significant Austrian attacks there before the Spring.¹⁹ On 2nd February, General Emile Fayolle, Commander-in-Chief of the French forces in Italy, felt able to report to his superiors that "The [Italian] armies in the line are practically complete in effectives and equipment. Their morale has risen considerably since the retreat, aided by the arrival of Allied troops, and is now good in the quiet sectors… Training has been neglected."²⁰

With the Austrian-German offensive clearly running out of steam, and the onset of winter bringing some relief for the Italians, General Diaz and his senior commanders felt they had the space they needed to restore discipline, rebuild disintegrated units and morale, and restructure their forces into six armies, all of a size that could be easily managed. This latter point was a hard-learned lesson of Caporetto reflecting General Luigi Capello's inability (or the inability of his staff) to control his huge Second Army in the face of the Austro-German onslaught. While that was going on, and as the situation grew ever more stable, thoughts began to turn to the possibility of moving once more onto the offensive. Although Diaz's strategic priority at this point was still very much on defence,²¹ by January he felt able to test the mettle of his reorganised army with minor attacks at Monte Asolone, and on the eastern end of the Asiago Plateau. Both of these achieved no more than partial success, but the fact that the Italian troops had not hesitated to go forward was taken as a signal that some of the old bravura had indeed returned. In addition, the transfer of the German guns back to the Western Front during November, followed in mid-December by the German divisions drafted in for the Caporetto offensive, meant that the Austrians were once more on their own while the Italians now had the assistance of 130,000 French and 110,000 British soldiers, and their artillery.²² The fortunes of war seemed to be swinging slowly in favour of Italy and her allies. But while Diaz was now prepared to consider offensive operations, he was determined not to be pushed into attacking before he was properly ready.²³ The strength of his conviction on this point was demonstrated in May. Hard-pressed by the German Spring offensives, Foch, now the Allied Supreme Commander, implored Diaz to launch a diversionary attack. He refused.²⁴

From a British perspective, there were a number of drivers that made offensive action in Italy important at this time. Some of these were set out in a paper written for the British Section of the Supreme War Council in Versailles by E (Enemies) Branch, dated 22nd February 1918. The un-named author, a Staff Officer just returned from General Headquarters in Italy, pointed to several critical factors that demonstrated why a strong offensive against the Austro-Hungarians might "produce results of considerable importance".²⁵ First, it was believed that the people of Austria-Hungary had a greater desire for peace than any of the other belligerent countries. A series of heavy defeats in the field might well bring matters to a crisis. Second, the morale of the Austro-Hungarian Army was "distinctly bad". The troops were thoroughly tired of the war and large numbers would desert "to anyone but Italians". In defence, "surrenders on a considerable scale may confidently be looked for, particularly after an effective artillery preparation". Thirdly, and according to the author, most importantly, the enemy lacked any kind of military

19  J E Edmonds, p.132
20  J E Edmonds, p.145.
21  M Thompson, p.330.
22  M Thomson, p.328.
23  M. Thomson, p331.
24  M Thomson, p.330.
25  TNA CAB 25/69: Supreme War Council Secretariat, Italy, Situation Report, 1917-1919.

efficiency. "A study of their methods of defence shows them to be of a most elementary description. Although adequate to meet the Italian methods of attack to which the Austrians have hitherto been accustomed, Austrian tactics would break down completely before an attack carried out in accordance with modern principles by French or British troops. The Austrian defence is organised in the manner current on the Western front in the early days of trench warfare and they have never passed the stage where continuous trench lines are held by lines of men crammed closely together. The principles of a defensive zone organised in depth, evolved with such success by the Germans on the Western Front, has never been adopted by the Austrians…" The author concluded that in a carefully-prepared attack, using British methods, with the necessary preliminary reconnaissance, counter-battery work and preliminary bombardment, followed by an infantry assault, well supported by artillery fire, the Austrians "would stand no chance whatever." The author cites as proof of this the highly successful attack at Monte Tomba on 30 December, by the French 47th Chasseur Division, in which the summit was recaptured, leaving over 500 Austrian dead and 1564 prisoners taken, at a cost of only 249 French fatalities.[26]

But there was one other important reason why British involvement in offensive operations was felt by some to be necessary. Encouraged by clever Austro-Hungarian propaganda, Italian public (and military) opinion was beginning to wonder if the British had any intention of shouldering any of the fighting.

The British and French contingents' arrival in Italy had come as a major tonic for the war-weary Italian people in general, and the army in particular. Lt Hugh Dalton, refitting with his Battery near Genoa, after the long withdrawal from the Isonzo, was delighted to bump into a group of Northumberland Fusiliers at Arquata railway station who told him of "…the wonderful welcome on the way through Italy and…all the hospitality shown to their officers and men at the stations where they had stopped."[27] Pte Norman Gladden recalled that his unit had been told they were to "create an impression to inspire confidence in the people, who were to see and hear about the Allied contingents marching with drums beating and fifes playing in smartly uniformed and well-aligned columns of four, towards the field of battle."[28] But by the time they had arrived in sufficient strength, with their supplies and support organisation, the tactical situation had changed and Plumer ordered that their role, for the time being, should be to provide a mobile reserve that could be quickly deployed to block the exits from the mountains in the now unlikely event that the Austrians broke through the Italian line.[29] However, Diaz was keen to begin to relieve some of his battle-weary troops in the front line and it was agreed with Plumer and Fayolle that British and French troops would assume responsibility for holding a section of the front along the Piave. Some Italian soldiers and politicians considered that their country's entry into the war in 1915 should have been subject to an agreement that British and French troops would be sent to the Italian front from the start.[30] Their deployment now was perceived as being 'better late than never'. On completion of the relief, Plumer reported: "There is no doubt

---

26 TNA CAB 25/69: Supreme War Council Secretariat, Italy, Situation Report, 1917-1919.
27 H Dalton, p.151.
28 N Gladden, p.17.
29 J E Edmonds, p.113.
30 H Dalton, p.152.

that the entry of French and British troops into the line at this time had an excellent moral effect, and it enabled the Italians to withdraw troops to train and reorganise."[31]

But at the British Section of the Supreme War Council, some staff officers were concerned that the morale boost created by the arrival of the British and French forces could be undone unless the British were prepared to do more than sit in a quiet sector, conducting the odd patrol across the Piave, but avoiding any serious offensive action.

Although not everyone in the British Section of the Supreme War Council agreed with this report's conclusions, there was considerable support for the idea that the British contingent needed to be seen to do more than hold the line in a relatively quiet sector of the front. "It is undoubtedly the wrong policy to let five good fighting divisions get stagnant by remaining continually in a quiet sector," wrote one. "I quite agree…as to the desirability of the British contingent taking, if possible, a more active part," commented another.[32] However, no-one at E Branch was really arguing for Britain to 'go it alone' as the French at done at M Tomba. It is clear that the overriding view at Versailles was that any significant offensive operation would need to be a tri-lateral effort, but where should the next major thrust be focused?

The Allies in Italy could read a map just as well as Field Marshal Conrad, and they too recognised the danger of a successful Austrian attack across the Asiago Plateau and down onto the Venetian Plain.[33] The Austrians had already highlighted this weakness earlier, only just failing to break the Italian line here and debouch out onto the Plain. By creating new depth to the Allied position on the plateau, General Diaz declared, such an offensive would "free the Italian front from the dread of this possibility"[34]

No doubt with all of the above in mind, General Fayolle, (soon to be recalled to the Western Front), put forward proposals for a joint offensive north across the Asiago Plateau in the direction of Trent, including the valley of the Upper Brenta, known as the Val Sugana. Fayolle's outline plan called for an attack by three groups of forces. On the right, five British and 2 Italian divisions would attack Primolana by the valley of the Brenta. In the centre, four French and 6 Italian divisions, under Gen Maistre, would attack Levico up the Astico valley. On the left, two French and six Italian divisions, under an Italian commander, would thrust up the Adige valley and capture Rovereto.

Fayolle's proposal found favour with the Italian Commando Supremo. In agreeing to the French plan, however, the Italians demanded that the attack should be carried out by the newly-formed Italian Sixth Army, under General Luca Montuori, reinforced by a French and a British Corps. On 28th February, the outline plan was agreed between Generals Diaz, Maistre (who had just taken over from Fayolle) and Plumer, and they also approved the re-distribution of forces necessary to facilitate it.[35] This involved handing the Piave front back to the Italians, thus freeing up French and British forces to relocate to the Asiago sector to prepare for the battle.

Even as the Allies were agreeing to the offensive in principle, however, events to the north were about to cast a heavy shadow over the detailed planning. On 4th January 1918, according

---

31  Plumer's first despatch, *The London Gazette*, 9th April 1918, p 4430.
32  TNA CAB 25/69: Supreme War Council Secretariat, Italy, Situation Report, 1917-1919
33  The Austrians had reinforced this thinking by attempting an identical, unsuccessful attack earlier in the war.
34  J E Edmonds, p.160.
35  JE Edmonds, p.158.

to the Official History, information was received from a 'high neutral source' that Germany was planning a formidable offensive in France.[36] In London on 15th February, the British War Cabinet considered a proposal by Marshal Foch, now the Supreme Allied Commander, to withdraw two British divisions from Italy to reinforce Haig's armies in France. In a letter to the CIGS (Robertson), Foch pointed out that since the British reserves in France were smaller than those of the French and the British front was more immediately menaced, it would be sensible to recall two British divisions from Italy to France at once, followed by two French divisions. Robertson told the War Cabinet that he agreed with Foch's assessment. Maj Gen Harrington, Plummer's Chief of Staff, who happened to be attending the War Cabinet that day to brief the members on the situation in Italy, said that in his opinion the task now being performed in Italy with five British divisions could just as easily be done by three. In addition, the Italians could well afford to send up to 10 good divisions to the Western Front. Robertson was instructed to find out if Haig would prefer to be reinforced by two British Divisions or four Italian divisions. Unsurprisingly, Haig opted to have back his two British divisions and Robertson immediately ordered Plummer to despatch two divisions to France. The Foreign Secretary was directed to inform the Italian Government.

The British Force in Italy now having been reduced to a single Corps of three divisions, it was also decided that Plumer should hand over command to Cavan and return to France with most of his own headquarters staff and that of XI Corps. On the evening of 22nd February, Plumer issued orders to XIV Corps that 41st and 7th Divisions would leave for France as soon as possible, replaced in the line by 23rd and 48th Divisions.[37] It was later decided that three, rather than two, French divisions (46th, 64th and 65th) would also return to the Western Front and they began to leave on 24 March. General Maistre was ordered home to command a new Tenth Army and his place as Commander-in-Chief of the French forces in Italy was taken by General Graziani, formerly commanding XII Corps.

The Italians were unhappy with losing five Allied divisions, but they were even more unhappy about the way in which the British decision had been made, without reference either to them or to the Supreme War Council in Versailles. The decision was reconsidered by the War Cabinet, on 1st March when General Smuts reported a discussion with Baron Sonnino, the Italian Foreign Minister. Sonnino felt strongly that if any allied divisions should leave Italy, they should be French rather than British "because the [British] troops were so popular and their presence had exercised so good an effect on the Italian morale".[38] But there was no going back. In the face of the expected German attack, the needs of the Western Front would have to come first.

With five divisions struck off their Order of Battle, the Italian Sixth Army began the detailed planning necessary to ensure a successful attack, recognising that it would be May at the earliest before the preparations could be complete. In March they submitted an initial draft of their plan to the Commando Supremo, maintaining Fayolle's original objective of striking towards the valley of the Upper Brenta (Val Sugana), but the scale was reduced, and two intermediate objectives were identified. This still represented a highly ambitious proposal. In order to achieve success, the allies would have to advance about 13 miles over very mountainous country while

---

36  J E Edmonds, p.146.
37  J E Edmonds, p.150. This decision was amended on 24th March and 5th Division rather than 7th Division was ordered to return to France. See Edmonds, p.154.
38  J E Edmonds, p.152.

the Austrians would be withdrawing back on their own supply lines and towards their own border, which was likely to make the defence all the more stubborn.

Sixth Army planners proposed that the attack would be carried out by 17 divisions rather than the original 25 as in Fayolle's outline – eight in the front line, nine in the second line, with the Italian XX Corps on the right, the French XII Corps in the centre and the British XIV Corps on the left.[39] Fayolle's original plan had the British on the right.

Lt Gen the Earl of Cavan, assumed command of British Forces in Italy on 10 March, taking over responsibility for organising the British contribution to the mountain offensive, which, at this time, he strongly supported. On 2nd April, he wrote to the new Chief of the Imperial General Staff, Gen Sir Henry Wilson:

> The Asiago offensive … in which we are to take part, should, I think, meet with considerable success and is necessary both to raise the Italian morale, and to give great depth to the defence in this area. I think it ought to be given every encouragement and will, I hope, be carried out by May 1st at the latest.

However, he also intimated that he was not entirely happy with the proposed scope of the attack, adding:

> I feel, however, very strongly that it should not be carried beyond the line – M Meletta–M Mosciagh–M Erio–M Campolongo, and on this I think the Versailles Conference ought to insist.[40]

Cavan was indicating that in his opinion, the ambition of the planners outweighed the capability of the available resources – strong evidence that Cavan, like Plumer at Messines in 1917, had learned one of the key lessons of the Battles of the Somme and Passchendaele and was determined not to try to bite off more than his force could chew.

On 12th April, however, as the German Operation Georgette was raging along the River Lys in Belgium, Wilson placed a significant caveat on British involvement in any offensive action in Italy. On the day after Haig had issued his "Backs to the Wall" Order of the Day, Wilson sent a telegram to Cavan stating that while there was no objection to a plan that could be carried out at a small cost to improve local conditions, that might lead to economy of men in the longer term, in view of the situation in Belgium, "in all other circumstances the offensive should be postponed"[41]. In a hand-written note to Cavan, the following day, re-enforcing the contents of the telegram in which he had "rather deprecated the attack in Italy unless it could be done cheaply", Wilson added: "The drain on men in France has been, is and will be very heavy."[42] As well as providing firm direction and guidance on the conditions in which Cavan should consider offensive operations, Wilson was also sending Cavan a strong message about the need to do everything possible to protect his force. There were precious few replacements available, and Haig would have first call on them. Cavan should not expect large drafts of men to replace any casualties he might sustain. This point

---

39  J E Edmonds, p.161.
40  TNA WO 79/68: Cavan Papers
41  J E Edmonds, p.176.
42  TNA, WO79/68, Cavan Papers.

is important because it is likely to have influenced the British approach to holding their line at Asiago as well as Cavan's perception of events on the plateau on 15/16th June.

## Defence or Attack? 48th Division Moves to the Mountains

The British 48th Division had taken over positions on the Montello, an area of high ground overlooking the Piave, on 2nd March. They had originally been ordered to replace the 41st Division in the left sector, but this turned out to be a mistake and they ended up relieving the 7th Division instead. The relief took place over three days – 27th, 28th February and 1st March, with the divisional headquarters being established at Selva, and the General Officer Commanding, Maj Gen Fanshawe, assuming command of the sector at 1000 the following morning. Although this was now a quiet sector, Fanshawe quickly identified that the position had a number of fundamental weaknesses, and set his men to work to tackle these, improving camouflage, repairing supply routes, constructing strong points and generally making the sector more resilient in the event of an Austrian attack.[43] Their stay there was short-lived and largely uneventful, being described by one staff officer as "the most quiet and comfortable sector ever held by the division during the war".[44] After just over a week in the line, on 12 March, the divisional headquarters was warned of a forthcoming move, and subsequent orders followed for the entire XIV Corps to replace the Italian XXVI Corps on the Asiago Plateau. Divisional staff and unit commanders were instructed to begin immediate reconnaissance related to future offensive operations.[45]

The Division assembled at first on the Venetian Plain between Cittadella and Padua before moving to the Agno valley (Val D'Agno), about 10 miles to the west of Vicenza, at the end of March. The pioneers were ordered to go straight up into the mountains to help with the construction of a new road. As a result of the early reconnaissance visits to the plateau, senior commanders considered that the troops would need to develop some basic mountain warfare skills. The engineers, in particular, were faced with a sharp learning curve, quickly having to acquire proficiency in new skills such as rock drilling and blasting and in maintaining and operating the telefericas, the Italian electrically-powered cable-ways used to transport stores up and down the mountainside. The infantry used their time on the plain to build up their fitness for the task ahead. The Bucks Battalion history records that practice attacks were delivered on all the neighbouring hills and the unit transport was increased by the arrival of 25 additional pack mules.[46]

After three weeks of intensive training on the plain, it was time for the 48th Division to make the 3000 feet ascent of the Dolomite foothills to fighting positions in woods on the plateau. A lucky few were able to make the climb in small Fiat trucks, which were better suited to the conditions than their British counterparts, while others slogged up on foot using mule tracks that zig-zagged their way ever upwards – 20 minutes marching, followed by 10 minutes rest until they reached the top. At a rate of one hour's march for every thousand feet of altitude, it

---

43 Barnett, p.31
44 G Barnett, p.31.
45 K W Mitchinson, p.201.
46 P L Wright, p.100.

took lightly equipped troops about five hours to climb from the foothills to the divisional rear areas at Grenezza (right sector) and Carriola (left sector).[47]

What they discovered there was a situation in many ways unlike anything they had known on the Western Front. The plateau itself can be regarded as a bowl, about seven miles long and three miles wide. The allies were sited around the southern rim with the Austrians to the north. No Man's Land could be anything up to 1500 yards wide, although it was much narrower towards the two flanks, particularly on the left. The positions occupied by the British in the Spring of 1918 had been constructed by the Italians after heavy fighting there in May 1916, during the Austrian *Strafe-expedition*,[48] and again in November 1917, after Caporetto. The Italians had originally held the peaks of the mountains to the north but had been forced out of these and back across the plateau. As the fighting stagnated, both sides dug in, the Austrians on the northern side of the plateau, in front of the town of Asiago, the Italians opposite, mostly on rising ground to the south. Being in the mountains, the terrain here consists of a very thin layer of soil, below which is solid limestone. Unlike France and Belgium, where it was relatively easy to dig deep trenches or construct breastworks in the clay soil and soft chalk, most of the work being done with the trusty shovel or pick, here, in the Dolomites, defenders and attackers had to drill and blast their trenches and dugouts out of the solid rock, making much use of noisy rock drills powered by compressed air, which, when used, often drew enemy artillery fire. One benefit of the ground was that neither side had to worry about their trenches falling in when it rained (although they could flood) or blown in by artillery fire (as happened frequently on the Western Front). On the other hand, high explosive shells and the local limestone combined to create an additional hazard for defenders and attackers alike – flying slivers of rock which could cause injuries just as terrible as shrapnel. The modern-day visitor to the battlefields benefits from the Italian method of trench-building, experiencing little trouble in tracing the trench lines, even 100-plus years after the conflict. Unlike in France and Belgium where most of the trenches were filled in after the war to allow recultivation, in the Italian mountains they are generally still there if one knows where to look, permanent scars on the landscape and timeless reminders of the fighting that took place there.

Italian military engineers were highly experienced in this environment after three years of mountain fighting. But even for them, the geography and geology of the plateau brought significant challenges. The British Official History describes the ground thus:

> From the Marginal Line (along the southern mountain ridge), the ground drops gradually over three miles to the plateau, which sits at around 3,300ft. This downhill slope is not an even incline, but a confusion of rugged pine-clad hills and valleys, bare rock where there are no trees, with spurs projecting towards Asiago. The only large open spaces are around the village of Cesuna and a clearing on the slopes of M Kaberlaba. At the bottom of the slope sits the plateau…undulating cultivated land sprinkled with villages … To the North the plateau is bounded by another range of high peaks including M Longara and M Mosciagh (both 5000ft-plus) and the ground then rises steadily to

---

47 F MacKay, *Touring the Italian Front*, p.35.
48 Punishment Expedition.

the old frontier with Austria before falling down into the Val Sugana in the valley of the Upper Brenta."[49]

## Sustaining the Force

Apart from a surplus of timber, there were few natural resources on the plateau with which the British could sustain themselves. This meant that pretty much everything necessary to maintain a fighting force of two divisions – troops, food, water, ammunition, artillery pieces, clothing, tools, building materials – had to be transported up the steep escarpment from the supply depots on the plains. The Italians, undoubted experts at military engineering, had constructed two good-quality roads that wound their way up to the plateau from the plains, emerging at Grenezza on the right and Carriola on the left, but these were reserved for artillery and transport vehicles. Men and pack animals were expected to travel up on foot using the numerous mule tracks that also zig-zagged their way up the near vertical rockface. On arriving in the mountains, the British found their standard motorised transport – the ubiquitous 3-ton truck – was unable to cope with the gradients and the hairpin bends. The temperamental engines overheated in the semi-tropical heat of the plains, and their wheelbase was too long and the steering lock too narrow to easily cope with the sharp twists and turns of the mountain roads.[50] As part of an early contingency plan for sending British troops to Italy, Brigadier-General JHV Crowe had conducted a reconnaissance in 1917 and signed an Anglo-Italian Convention designed to facilitate the arrival of reinforcements in the event of need. Under this agreement, the Italians provided 300 30cwt Fiat lorries and 200 Fiat 2-ton trucks, the former of which proved ideal for the mountains. British staff cars suffered from some of the same shortcomings as the trucks for mountain work and these were replaced with 18 35hp Lancias, while Talbot Motor Ambulances proved satisfactory for use in the hills.[51] Hugh Dalton observed some amusing differences between the drivers of different nations on these difficult mountain roads:

> The scared faces of some of the British the first time they had to come up the hundred-odd corkscrew turns on the mountain roads, taking sidelong glances at bird's eye views of distant towns and rivers on the plain below, were rather comical. Even the self-consciously efficient and outwardly imperturbable French stuck like limpets to the centre of the road and would not give an inch to Staff cars, hooting their guts out behind them. The Italian drivers, on the other hand, accustomed to the mountains, dashed round sharp corners at full speed, avoiding innumerable collisions by a fraction of an inch, terrifying and infuriating their more cautions Allies. But I only once saw a serious collision here in the course of many months."[52]

Another unusual form of transport was provided by the cable-ways, originally erected by the Italians, known as *teleferiche*. Powered by electricity, these were very similar to modern-day

---

49  J E Edmonds, pp16-68.
50  J E Edmonds, p.171.
51  J E Edmonds, p.171.
52  H Dalton, p180.

ski-lifts. They consisted of a number of small, flat trucks, suspended from a continuous steel cable, which was itself supported several metres above the ground by a series of steel girders. The British experimented with a number of different types of loads before deciding that these would mainly be used for transporting ammunition. Rations carried by this means were apt to go missing as some enterprising soldiers and locals found ways of removing them from the trucks as they passed through unobserved lower sections of the route.[53]

The supply system is well-documented in the Official History. The railhead for the division holding the left sub-sector was at Chiuppano, about two miles east of Rochette at the foot of the mountains. Supplies for the reserve division were unloaded at Chiuppano while those for the division in the line went on to Rochette where they were transferred to a narrow-gauge rack and pinion railway. From there they made their way uphill to Campiello, but only after dark when the train could not be observed by Austrian gunners. Unloading at Campiello had to be conducted with some speed in order to allow the train to head back down the mountain before daylight. At Campiello, unit first-line transport collected their stores in trucks and GS and Limbered GS waggons and moved them to wherever they were needed. A similar system operated for the division on the right, using a railhead at Villaverla, north-west of Vicenza.

To ensure continuity of supply, it was decided early on in the deployment that a considerable addition to first-line transport would be required. As a result, 400 extra mules and 200 pack saddles were provided by GHQ. The extra transport was mostly divided proportionately among the fighting units, while some was kept under the control of the OC Divisional Supply Train to be used as a pool where necessary.[54]

Despite its location in the mountains where there was often deep snow-cover during the winter months, water was a scarce commodity at Asiago. Ponds that held some water during the Spring had dried up by summer and water for the troops and supply animals had to be pumped up via a pipeline from the Astico River. Great pains were taken to provide water holding facilities, reservoirs, tanks and catchments while the Royal Engineers provided standpipes at various locations. However, because the pipeline was vulnerable to enemy shellfire, water was never guaranteed and thus had to be limited to a gallon-per-man-per-day for all purposes.[55]

Pack animals were critical to the British supply operation and great care was taken to ensure their safety and well-being, particularly in the winter and early spring, when horses and mules suffered as a result of having to move from the relative heat of the plains to the intense cold of the mountains. In addition, the journey itself was so long and energy-sapping that it was considered too cruel, and unproductive, to expect the animals to do this day after day. Although it was found that the mules could make the journey up and down in a day, it took 10 hours of hard work to complete, and animals used in this way needed a complete rest every third day. To resolve this, it was decided to split the mules and the journey into two. One group, based on the plain, would make the trip from there to a transfer point about half-way up the mountains at a hamlet called Schiessere, where there was space for outspanning[56], grazing, feeding and watering. From here, the loads would be moved across to a second group, kept in the mountains, to complete the journey. The number of horses and mules kept in the mountains was strictly

---

53   J Wilks, *The British Army in Italy 1917-1918*, p.72.
54   G Barnett, p.39.
55   J E Edmonds, p.173.
56   Outspanning means removing the harness from a horse or mule.

limited to 1,500[57], and for those animals required to haul the artillery's guns, the waggon lines were established well behind the batteries.

For all the difficulties posed by the mountains, the process of supplying the soldiers at the front seemed to function effectively – most of the time. Hand-over notes prepared by 144th Brigade provide an insight into how things actually worked. The nearest Expeditionary Forces Canteen, where troops could purchase the little luxuries – chocolate, eggs, HP Sauce – that made life in the line a bit more bearable, was located at Thiene at the foot of the mountains. The Brigade Canteen Sergeant lived there, and his job was to purchase stores and send them up to Campiello by the supply train. From there 1st Line transport delivered them to branch canteens at Handley Cross and Carriola. Beer was delivered in the same way. There was also an excellent Italian canteen at Campiello where eggs, tinned fruit and other 'goodies' could be purchased. Transport in the mountains was restricted to 40 animals per battalion and was controlled by the Brigade Transport Officer. Hard standings had been constructed by 144th Brigade and all horses had cover from the sun. It had been the practice to water the horses from local ponds but new water troughs, fed from a pipe, had just been completed and watering from ponds was being dispensed with.[58]

## Medical Services

A detailed description of the British medical services in Italy is found in John Dillon's volume.[59] At the tip of the medical lance was the unit Medical Officer (MO) and his small team of stretcher-bearers at the Regimental Aid Post (RAP). There were eight RAPs spread across the British lines at Asiago. Their job was to recover casualties in their area, dress their wounds, administer pain relief if appropriate, and, if necessary, move the casualty along the evacuation chain to the Advanced Dressing Station (ADS). There were two of these on the 48th Division sector – one at Boscon, known as Swiss Cottage on account of its likeness to an Alpine lodge, and the second at Magnaboschi. There were two more in the 23rd Division area at Barenthal and Grenezza. The locations of all four are close to the Commonwealth War Graves Commission cemeteries that now bear their names. From the ADSs, wounded soldiers were moved down the mountainside to the Casualty Clearing Stations at Dueville and Montecchio Precalcino, and from there, back to 'Blighty'. Due to the difficulties of moving casualties down to the CCSs on the plains, and after some deaths in transit, the Director of Medical Services in Italy, took the unusual step of creating an Advanced Operating Station in the mountains, near Cavaletto, where casualties with serious wounds could receive emergency surgery and be stabilised before being moved down the escarpment by motor ambulance or train.[60]

57  J E Edmonds, p.171.
58  TNA WO 95/4250: 145th Trench Mortar Battery War Diary,
59  J Dillon, *Allies are a Tiresome Lot: The British Army in Italy in the First World War* (Solihull: Helion, 2015), Chapter 4.
60  F MacKay, p.107.

## Communications

Although wireless communication was available by 1918, it was generally considered to be difficult to use and unreliable. However, in Italy the British immediately recognised its possibilities in the mountain theatre. Telegraph and telephone lines, running overland, were very vulnerable to shellfire and could be easily cut, even when buried deep under the earth, which was not possible in the Dolomites. Wireless did not suffer from that weakness. As former First Sea Lord, Admiral Sir John (Jackie) Fisher is reported to have said, in favour of wireless, as early as 1912: "You can't cut the air".[61] Wireless did, however, have other problems, such as the size and weight of the equipment, which limited its mobility. This meant it was of most utility at Divisional and Brigade level where headquarters tended to be relatively static. The equipment itself, once in place, was handed over to the incoming headquarters during reliefs rather than being dismantled and removed with the other divisional or brigade stores. Below that, power buzzers and field telephones continued to be the main links between battalion headquarters and units in the line. Power buzzers, sometimes known as 'ground wireless' worked by transmitting electrical impulses through an electrode (often a bayonet) stuck into the ground, to a receiving amplifier. With a range of about 4000 yards, the equipment was big, bulky and heavy, especially the amplifier and power generator, so it was not easy to move about, and it could be intercepted or even jammed by the enemy. The buzzers used Morse Code, and to ensure security, each message had to be encoded before sending and decoded upon receipt, making it difficult and slow to send anything other than brief reports or simple orders. Field telephones were very unreliable for the reasons set out above, working satisfactorily in quiet periods, but failing almost immediately in the face of any sort of artillery bombardment as shells cut the cables or brought down the trees on which they had been strung. When this happened, the troops fell back on visual signalling, using lights (Lucas signalling lamps) or flags. But given the dense woodland, the broken nature of the ground, the often-poor visibility caused by low cloud, rain, snow, mist or smoke, visual signalling was just as unreliable as the telephone, leaving runners or carrier pigeons as the communication channels of last resort. The passage of information was destined to be a major shortcoming in the battle to come. A lack of information or "ground truth" often made command and control impossible at division and brigade levels. As a result, there were times when neither the GOC nor his brigade commanders were in possession of sufficient detail to allow them to make effective decisions and thus influence the course of the battle. This meant the fight became the responsibility of unit commander and below. The outcome would be a test of how well the GOC had trained his subordinates, how well they understood his intent, and the effectiveness of his defence scheme.

## Asiago British Sector

The sector allocated to the British on the plateau was on the extreme left of the Italian Sixth Army front, sandwiched between the Italian First Army, defending the western end of the

---

61  Admiral Sir R H Bacon, The Life of Lord Fisher of Kilverstone, Vol 2, Hodder and Stoughton, London, 1929, p144.

plateau and the Val d'Astico on their left, and the French XII Corps on their right. The British front ran for about three miles as the crow flies, but the actual line extended for over five miles because of the way it snaked along the 3000ft contour.[62] The sector was divided into two sub-sectors, each held by a division. The right one, about 5,500 yards long, and held in June 1918 by 23rd Division, ran from the junction with the French overlooking the hamlet of Pennar, along (or just in front of) the San Sisto Ridge, past the foot of a long strip of open ground known as Malga Fasso, then coming out of the woods and extending for 1000 yards on the open, bare hillside above the villages of Kaberlaba and Roncalto before meeting the left sector back in the woods above the Ghelpac stream. The left sector ran through heavily wooded, undulating terrain, in front of Roncalto towards the Ghelpac Gorge, tracing the line of the river as it twists and turns through the rocks, passing in front of the village of Cesuna before meeting the Italian line near Cavrari. The Ghelpac flows east to west through no-man's land, shallow in the east but deepening to become a very significant obstacle on the western flank, and actually an impassable ravine as it entered the Italian sector before merging with the Val D'Assa. This meant there was little risk of the British left flank being turned.

Immediately behind the front line, troops were accommodated in poorly-constructed shelters of wood or tin, built into the sides of the ridges. Further back were the divisional base areas at Grenezza (right) and Carriola (left), where the accommodation was better, mainly consisting of log huts. At Grenezza, which, like Carriola, was hidden from direct observation and (at least until 15th June), rarely shelled, there was a church, a theatre, a football pitch and an outdoor gymnasium. Both areas had similar facilities and were also home to the reserve brigades, RE Field Companies, most of the first-line transport, elements of the divisional ammunition columns, and ammunition and ration dumps. The wooden huts were not in great condition when the British arrived, but the pioneers and Royal Engineers set about improving them until, for the most part, the men were "warm and comfortable there" when out of the line.[63]

At Grenezza, the road up from the plains continued north towards Asiago via a junction known as Pria del Acqua and the Barrenthal valley to the front line. Lateral movement between the two sub-sectors was along a good-quality military road running east-west from Pria del Acqua. It was just to the north of this road, about 100 yards to the left of Pria del Acqua, that the right-hand gun of Hugh Dalton's battery of 6in howitzers was located. Signs of the battery's gun pits can still be seen there today among the trees. There were two more roads leading across the British front here. One ran just in front of the reserve line and the other about 1000 yards further back. Artillery positions were mainly on the southern slopes of Kaberlaba and M Torle with some of the heavies further back near the reserve line. Marching south, back from the front line, past Pria dell Acqua, Norman Gladden described the scene as follows:

> At length we reached a large clearing where the hills parted to create a miniature plain on which a camp of crude hutments, now somewhat dilapidated in appearance, had been established. This was Grenezza, our new temporary home, looking dreary enough on our arrival … I discovered the military theatre, a neat, all-wood building constructed by

---

62   F MacKay, p.104.
63   G Barnett, p.43.

the Italian Army, where the band of the West Yorkshire Regiment provided a concert of popular music, which was well appreciated by an audience of all ranks.[64]

The base theatres were used for other entertainment too, including well-attended performances by the divisional concert parties, 'The Dumps' (23rd Division) and 'The Curios' (48th Division).

On the left sub-sector Carriola base was similar to Grenezza, although lacking the large, relatively flat area of open ground. Running from front to rear (north to south) there were two good roads, one from the reserve line at Monte Pau past the Divisional Headquarters at Carriola towards a major junction, known as Handley Cross and on to meet the front line, close to the divisional boundary on the right near Boscon. The second also ran from Monte Pau, but then through Campiello and Caprari, reaching the front line about 1000 yards north of the village of Cesuna. Laterally, a road ran from Pelly Cross (just behind Hill 1021) initially north into no-man's land before turning sharp left (south-west) towards Cesuna and on to the left divisional boundary near Fondi. To the rear, about 2000 yards back, another road wound its way from Grenezza through Handley Cross to Magnaboschi and on to Campiello. In addition, there were numerous tracks that criss-crossed the sub-sector and a metalled road that ran down-hill from Magnaboschi to Cesuna. Most of these routes still exist and can be navigated, with care, although in some places they have been interrupted by the marble quarrying that has become widespread in the area.

Links with the plain in this sector were "wretched" and far more difficult than at Grenezza.[65] The only road ran from Caltrano through the area of the Italian division on the left, with 14 hairpin bends and very steep gradients, to Campiello where it forked, the left section carrying on to Fondi and the right towards Monte Pau and then Carriola. There was also a rack and pinion railway in this part of the front, which climbed up the mountains from Rochette to Campiello. Both villages were under Austrian observation and were shelled fairly rigorously and regularly. Lt Col Barnett described Campiello as "an absolute death-trap, situated as it was in a narrow valley and in easy range of many of the enemy batteries on the hills to the north."[66] Here, the supply system looked sound on paper but in practice it was "thoroughly bad" and "likely to break down at any moment".[67]

## The Woods – Dark and Deep and Dangerous

It was not only the supply system that was 'thoroughly bad'. Parts of the British line in both sub-sectors could qualify for a similar description. A walk through the wide space that was no-man's land provides an indication of some of the difficulties for defenders – and for attackers – in this sector. Away from the trees on the southern slopes, the ground in front of Asiago is characterised by numerous, deep undulations that create large areas of dead ground in which attacking troops could gather unobserved from the British (or Austrian) front lines. In daytime they might be seen from observation posts high on the slopes behind or by aircraft if the cloud

---

64  N Gladden, p.87.
65  G Barnett, p.59.
66  G Barnett, p.60.
67  G Barnett, p.60.

base allowed. However, darkness, thick mist or a well-laid smoke screen would allow groups of infantry massing for an attack or raid to remain largely undetected, at least to troops in the front line. The same is true for the wooded areas. As Charles Carrington has pointed out:

> All the spurs of the hills and the ravines were covered with dense pine forests; elsewhere there were naked slopes of broken rocks so rough that what was open to the observer on the mountain top was invisible to sentries a few yards away among the boulders.[68]

Constructing basic trenches was difficult enough on the plateau. Building complex systems that mirrored those on the Western Front was a much greater challenge, and although the Italians managed this in other parts of the mountains (e.g. on Monte Ortigara to the north-east of Asiago) here they did not. As a consequence, the Allied defences on the plateau when the British took over in the Spring of 1918 bore little resemblance to those they had left behind in France. The front line snaked from east to west for about 10,000 yards, roughly following the 3000ft contour. The reserve line, also known as the Marginal Line, ran about three miles to the rear, along a row of mountain summits – Monte Corno, Cima di Fonte and Monte Brusabo. There were no traverses in either the front or reserve line trenches. Instead, the Italians had dug or cut short saps, (MacKay describes them as 'sprigs')[69] leading forward and to the rear from the main lines, which housed machine gun or trench mortar emplacements. Thick, high belts of barbed wire had been placed in front of the trenches but there were fewer dugouts than the British were used to, and those that had been excavated were not well-regarded as they were often sunk into the rear walls of the trenches. This meant their openings faced the enemy, leaving the occupants susceptible to in-coming artillery, mortar and machine gun fire. The dug-outs that did exist, in many cases suffered from a geological weakness common in the Dolomites, which rendered them liable to collapse under bombardment. Apart from a few caves there was no shell-proof cover behind the line, no strong-points, and very few communication trenches. As Pte Norman Gladden, of 11th Northumberland Fusiliers, part of the 23rd Division recalled:

> The pine-clothed slopes rendered communications trenches both impracticable and unnecessary on this part of the front.[70]

Edmonds also claims there were no communications trenches,[71] but there appears to have been at least one, which the author has seen, that still runs from the southern slope of Monte Lemerle to Carriola base.[72] According to Carrington:

> In the line there was no field of fire, no dug-outs and no strong-points. In case of attack everything depended on [two] unfinished trenches … Cesuna Switch and Lemerle Switch.

---

68   Carrington, Defence of Cesuna Re-entrant, *Army Quarterly*, No. 14, July 1927, p.309.
69   F MacKay, p.32.
70   N Gladden, p.97.
71   J E Edmonds, p.170
72   F MacKay, p.91.

Royal Artillery subaltern, Lt Hugh Dalton, whose battery's alternate battle position was in the woods just behind the San Sisto Ridge, appraised the allied trenches from an artilleryman's perspective:

> … our line was very strong, and the trenches, particularly on the eastern (right) side, very good, deeply blasted into the rock. The wooded ridge (San Sisto), running close behind our front line all the way, completely hid from the enemy all movement in our rear… Even movements in our front line, owing to the trees, were largely invisible at a distance…Our system of transport, supply and reliefs of the troops in the line could, therefore, be carried out at any hour of the day or night with almost complete disregard of the enemy.[73]

But Dalton was a gunner, not an 'infanteer', and he did not have to fight in the trenches (although as a Forward Observation officer (FOO), he might have had to visit them from time to time to direct the fire from his guns). If he had been required to live and fight there, he would perhaps have recognised that the same lack of observation that made it difficult for the Austrians to interfere with day-to-day business on the British side of the line, would also prove to be a hindrance for the British infantry when it came to defending against a concerted Austrian attack. He might also have recognised that in many parts of the front line it was impossible for defenders to see and thus provide support for their neighbours, or, because of the steepness of the ground running down to the plateau, to observe or cover with fire the wire obstacles to their front. The line may have had the appearance of being strong, but in reality, it was badly sited, often at the cost of preventing mutual support, and, in places, quite vulnerable. Comparing the two divisional sub-sectors, Lt Col George Barnett, a 48th Division Staff Officer, who had served as an Infantryman (King's Royal Rifle Corps), had this to say about his division's sector:

> On the debit side must be placed poorer observation, worse communications with the plains, and the unfortunate situation of the front-line trench. The latter was a real danger. Following as it did the south side of the Ghelpac, it twisted and turned in such an exaggerated zig-zag that many of the front-line posts were completely isolated from view and covering fire from adjacent ones on the right and left.
>
> To make matters worse, the very weakest part was the junction between the two forward brigades. The remedy, of course, was a series of strong points immediately to the rear and although they were sited and commenced as soon as we took over the sector it was quite impossible to make any real progress with them in the time available.[74]

Here, again, we see evidence that the indecision of the Commando Supremo about whether the force should be in defence or attack mode had real and serious consequences in terms of its ability to respond to the forthcoming Austrian attack.

It should also be remembered that since the line here had been created by the Italians, it had been constructed with their line-holding doctrine in mind. The Italian way was to pack the front trench with large numbers of troops, creating a single, continuous line of humanity. Whilst

---

73  H Dalton, pp.181-82.
74  G Barnett, p.62.

this, at least in theory[75], made for a very strongly defended front trench, which might be more difficult to penetrate, the main down-side was high numbers of casualties caused by an attacker's preparatory bombardment. And if it was penetrated, there were few, if any reserves. The 48th Division, with strict orders to keep casualties to a minimum, and a doctrine that preached 'thinning the line' in order to concentrate on defence in depth, chose to reduce the number of soldiers in the front line and to defend the position via a series of posts. In these circumstances, the shortcomings in the construction of the line identified by Lt Col Barnett and others were to have significant implications for the defenders on 15th June.

A glance at a map will demonstrate why the most vulnerable section of the whole British front was the portion extending from 48th Division's boundary with its neighbour on the right, in the woods above Roncalto, to the open ground to the north of Cesuna. Most of the line here was sited in dense pinewoods, which in June 1918 were largely intact and not much different from what one observes there today. This was where the Austrians had forced their way through the Italian line in a previous attack (November 1917), before finally being stopped with great losses on both sides, on the slopes of Monte Lemerle. As a result of this hard-learned lesson, the Italians had recognised the vulnerability and had strengthened the defences here with the construction of a second line, about 800-1000 yards back, running along the forward (northern) slopes of Lemerle, and connected to the front line by the Lemerle Switch on the right and the Cesuna Switch on the left. These two switch lines, which were substantially incomplete, were designed to create a pocket into which an attacker who broke through the front line could be channelled, held, and then counter-attacked.

The doctrine of elastic defence accepted that a well-motivated, well-supported enemy that achieved local numerical supremacy and therefore concentration of force, would almost certainly succeed in penetrating the front line, particularly in dense woodland where mass is often decisive. This approach relied on the initial penetration being held up by depth positions until the enemy's attacking momentum was drained. The attacker might 'break-in' but would not be allowed to 'break-through' and any ground lost would be regained by counter-attack, usually from a flank. As Charles Carrington has explained, the 48th Division had adopted the principles of elastic defence as early as the winter of 1915-16, challenging the British Army's received wisdom of the day on trench warfare. At that time, the division was in the line at Hebuterne, in front of Gommecourt Wood in the Somme region, where their trenches had been caving in due to prolonged rain. Under these circumstances, the South Midlanders opted to leave their sodden trenches and hold the line in depth behind a series of outposts. If attacked, forward posts were to be held to the last and the supports were trained to move forward early to be ready for immediate counter-attack. Throughout that period and later on the Somme, in front of the Hindenburg Line and at Passchendaele, the division never lost a defensive line or failed to hold its objectives once taken. However, on several occasions their forward positions were over-run but quickly retaken by immediate counter-attack. There is a period of inertia in every attack when the assaulting force has spent its strength, stretched its communications and probably out-run its artillery. This is the point at which it becomes very vulnerable to counter-attack.[76]

---

75 The Italian approach was not infallible in preventing penetrations. This was proved during the battle when a section held by the Italian troops, having been breached in three places, was seized by the attackers. See J E Edmonds, pp.217-18.
76 C Carrington, Defence of Cesuna Re-entrant, p.307.

The 48th Division's defensive plan in front of Asiago was based on exploiting that moment of weakness, using the switch lines and the Lemerle defences to sap the attacking momentum, setting up the Austrians for the coup de grace counter-stroke.

Neither of the switch lines had been fortified to Western Front standards: each consisted of not much more than unconnected stretches of trench fronted by barbed wire.[77] As Barnett has pointed out, however, whilst the two switches were "nothing like complete"... they nonetheless were "of the greatest value in the subsequent fighting".[78]

The defenders were aware of the weakness of the positions, and had begun to strengthen them, but this work had not been completed by the time the Austrians attacked due to the disruption caused by preparations for the "on-again...off-again" Allied offensive. As Maj Gen Fanshawe said, some years after the battle:

> The competition between 'Attack' and 'Defence' Plans ... caused me a great deal of thought at the time, as a Divisional Commander, as to how best to combine [them].[79]

To give depth to the position, the British had also created an outpost line consisting of a number of lightly-wired positions on areas of high ground in no-man's land, just in front of the enemy line. These posts were held in platoon strength during the hours of darkness, backed up by standing patrols. During the day the garrisons were reduced to a section under an NCO. As well as creating depth, the idea behind these posts was to demonstrate offensive intent on behalf of the Allies, to dominate no-man's land, making it more difficult for the enemy to launch surprise raids on the British line, and to help to disrupt any Austrian movement by day or night. Interestingly, although some of the posts were quite close to the enemy front line, they were little bothered by the opposition.[80]

XIV Corps' standard approach to holding this sector was to have two Divisions 'up" with a third in Reserve, usually down on the plain around the village of Trissino as there was insufficient accommodation above. Each forward division would occupy one of the two sub-sectors, usually with two Brigades in the line and a third in Reserve, close enough to respond to an enemy attack if required. On first moving into the mountains, 48th Division had been allocated the eastern (right) sector, with its headquarters at Grenezza at the end of the Barenthal Valley, while 7th Division held the left, from its base at Carriola. However, as British planning for the proposed offensive matured, it was decided that the attack in this sector would be carried out by the 7th and 23rd divisions, with 48th Division in reserve. To facilitate this, on 19th May, the 48th Division was relieved in the right sub-sector by 23rd Division. However, Cavan then decided that the assault would be conducted by 23rd Division and 48th Division, so on 31st May the latter took over from 7th Division on the left. The 48th Division was now in a new sector of the line, with which it was not familiar, and in a state of uncertainty regarding whether it was preparing for attack of defence.

---

77  J E Edmonds, p.170.
78  G Barnett, p58.
79  TNA CAB 45/84: Cabinet Office Historical Section: War Histories Correspondence and Papers – Original Letters, Comments and Personal Accounts.
80  F MacKay, p.87.

## Mountain Warfare?

It has already been stated that the British, on arriving on the plateau, found the environment quite different from that which they had left behind on the Western Front. Certainly, the snow-capped mountains, solid rockfaces and rudimentary trenches bore few similarities to the muddy plains of Flanders or the low, rolling countryside around Arras and the Somme region. Pte Norman Gladden says that only those soldiers "from Cumberland, Wales or the Highlands would have experienced anything with which to compare this precipitous territory".[81] Edmonds emphasises that "the British had no experience of mountain warfare in Europe".[82] But, to be clear, the main differences associated with this theatre of operations – at least during the June 1918 fighting – were largely the altitude at which the combat would take place – 3000ft above sea level, which is the equivalent of fighting on the summit of Scafell Pike or Mount Snowdon – and the associated difficulties this presented in sustaining and supplying the force. As Barnett explained:

> The nature of the terrain was, however, so totally different from anything we had previously experienced during the war that most of us felt a certain amount of anxiety as to the result, more especially those who were responsible for the supply of the division with food, ammunition, and other necessities.[83]

The British would be fighting in the mountains, but they would not be conducting the sort of mountain warfare that the Italians and Austrians had experienced in other parts of the Dolomites since 1915. Gladden had it about right when he identified an important characteristic of Asiago as its "uniqueness in affording territory over which the normal methods of attack could be employed." This is reinforced by Charles Carrington who also identifies the plateau as being the only area on the mountain front that "allowed space for the ordinary operations of war".[84] But Gladden was stretching the description when he went on to add that the plateau "could be regarded as the Ypres of the Italian line." Ypres it certainly was not, and it is surprising that someone like Gladden, who had fought at the Third Battle of Ypres, should make that comparison. The Asiago plateau had little in common with the low, muddy, shell-scared, treeless wasteland along the Menin Road, at Polygon Wood and in front of Passchendaele where the 23rd Division had fought in 1917…but neither was it a true mountain battlefield such as Monte Grappa, Monte Ortigara, Monte Pasubio… or the Marmolada[85].

In addition to the obvious problems associated with moving men and materiel up and down the steep and winding roads and mule tracks, the plateau itself presented other challenges for the British, particularly the gunners of the Field and Garrison Artillery. Gun

---

81  N Gladden, p.85.
82  J E Edmonds, p.217.
83  G Barnett, p.38.
84  C Carrington, Defence of Cesuna Re-entrant, p.309.
85  The Marmolada is the highest mountain in the Dolomites, located about 60 miles north-west of Venice. Until the Armistice, the border between Austria-Hungary and Italy extended over this mountain, so it formed part of the front line during the conflict. Austro-Hungarian soldiers were quartered in deep tunnels bored into the northern face's glacier, and Italian soldiers were quartered on the south face's rocky precipices. As the glacier retreats, soldiers' remains and belongings are occasionally discovered there today.

positions had to be blasted out of the rock. This meant batteries had to remain fairly static. It was impossible to move guns at short notice unless it was to a pre-prepared position. This would have been a serious problem during an attack, when the guns would need to move forward to cover the advancing infantry, or, during a withdrawal, when they would need to relocate further back. It also meant that the guns were sometimes located irregularly on a battery position, making controlled fire more difficult. The 'heavies' had particular problems. As Lt Dalton explained, his guns were not designed to fire at elevations greater than 45 degrees. This meant that batteries with gun pits cut into the reverse slope of a hill (as many of them were) had to chop down trees in front to create sufficient clearance to fire.[86] The gunners faced other challenges in the mountains, caused by large differences in levels between a gun and its target. This, according to Dalton, presented them with "one of the most intricate problems of theoretical gunnery, or for that matter, theoretical mechanics."[87] They eventually overcame these difficulties, at least to some extent, by adopting Italian range tables, modified to take account of the British guns.

By this stage of the war, British artillery methods had improved considerably from those of 1914 or even 1916. Better, more accurate mapping and surveying, and more reliable ammunition, together with new techniques such as sound-ranging and flash-spotting now allowed batteries to "shoot off the map". This meant the guns were able to engage a target simply by locating it on the map and avoided the lengthy "ranging and registration" process that had been common earlier in the war when the gunners would use observed trial and error to fix their fire on a given point. However, even with their new techniques, they still needed to observe the fall of shot to ensure pin-point accuracy. This was achieved by a Forward Observation Officer in a front-line trench or in an Observation Post (OP) high up in the mountains, who could also identify targets of opportunity and call down fire on them. There were a number of OPs on the southern slopes above the plateau, including a wooden platform built in the tree-tops near the summit of Cima del Taglio to the East of Grenezza, known as 'Claud' and another, tunnelled into the northern slope of M Kaberlaba, called "Ascot". A third was located further up Kaberlaba, which was known as the "Dress Circle" as it always seemed to be full of visitors, military and civilian. Francis MacKay records that these included the Duke of Connaught, the Lord Mayor of London, the Maharajah of Patiala and the Belgian and Japanese military missions.[88] However, for counter-battery shoots the gunners relied most often on observation from the air, using aircraft or tethered balloons:

> Most of our pre-arranged counter-battery shoots were carried out with aeroplane observation against enemy batteries situated in the thick woods on the slopes of the northern ridge, the airman flying backwards and forwards over the target and sending us his observations by wireless [using Morse].

However, the weather over the plateau is notoriously changeable and air observation was often impossible due to thick cloud or mist. Added to this, the closest airfields were on the plains and the flight to and from these used up a lot of fuel, leaving the aircraft with limited time on task.

86  H Dalton, p187-88
87  H Dalton, p.216.
88  F MacKay, p.121.

This became an issue when it was often necessary to spend half of a 400-shell bombardment targeting an area around a tree cover target so that the pilot could obtain a good enough view to correct the fire.[89] On the other hand, firing from a reverse slope, in heavy tree cover, meant the flashes of their guns were more difficult to see and therefore to locate, which in turn left them less susceptible to the enemy's counter-battery fire.

---

89  H Dalton, p.184.

# 9

# Battle of Asiago: 15–16th June 1918

Battles are rarely, if ever, neat and tidy occurrences. In fact, they are more often than not the opposite – chaotic and confusing, the product of a clash of opposing wills and military philosophies. That is certainly the case in relation to this battle, both in terms of its conduct at the time, and in trying to piece together the various elements of the fight today, 100-plus years after the fact. As the British Official Historian has pointed out, "the exact relation in time of events, even in adjoining battalion sectors, is not always certain".[1] This remains as true today as it was back when the Official History was published in 1948. For although the fighting on the plateau lasted for only a little over 24 hours, the challenge faced by Edmonds in trying to make sense of the various accounts, and reconcile one with another, has not lessened with the passage of time, as the following pages will demonstrate. Edmonds makes use of the official records, produced contemporaneously, as well as personal reminiscences, to tell the story of this battle – a mixture of primary and secondary sources. The weakness of the latter is that they were mostly written a long time after the events they describe and are thus at the mercy of individual memories and specific agendas. For example, Captain Charles Carrington produced the regimental war history of his battalion, the 1/5th Royal Warwickshires, which includes a detailed account of the Italian campaign. He also produced an account of the battle in an article he wrote for *Army Quarterly* in which he mounts a vigorous defence of his old division and its commander.[2] But Carrington was not there. He had left the battalion after Passchendaele (he received the MC for his actions in that battle), and in June 1918 he was helping to train recruits at Cramlington in Northumberland. After the war he actively campaigned to repair the reputation of Fanshawe, and the division, both badly treated, he believed, by Cavan. So, Carrington is neither a neutral observer nor an eye-witness, and we must take the post-facto accounts by him and others for what they are – interesting contributions to the historiography but not necessarily accurate or objective. It should be remembered, also, that contemporaneous accounts compiled by units and formation headquarters, may not be entirely objective. These accounts, although often prepared by junior staff officers, would have been signed off by individual commanders, who would have had an interest in ensuring that their unit, brigade or division was seen in a positive light. That

---

1   J E Edmonds, p.201
2   C E Carrington, The Defence of the Cesuna Re-entrant in the Italian Alps by the 48th (South Midland) Division, 15th June 1918: A Study of Minor Tactics in the Defensive, *Army Quarterly*, Vol XIV (1927).

is not to suggest that commanders deliberately sought to 'big up' their own roles or the roles of those under command, or to deliberately obscure unhelpful or unflattering facts, but it is human nature to wish to focus on the positives and this should be remembered when considering these accounts 100+ years after they were written. This description of the events of 15-16th June 1918 makes use of secondary material, including the views of Carrington and others, but it relies almost exclusively on the divisional, brigade and unit narratives, produced at or very close to the events described, to situate these events in time and space. As stated above, these accounts do not always align with each other, for a variety of reasons, not least of which is what Clausewitz called "the fog of greater or lesser uncertainty", and which military scholars have since paraphrased as "the fog of war".

## Divisional Disposition of Forces

On the night of 14/15th June 1918, the division was disposed in its usual configuration with two brigades holding the front line. 145th Brigade was on the right, and responsible for the sector from the boundary with the 11th Northumberland Fusiliers, on the left of the 23rd Division's area, to a point above the Ghelpac, just to the right of the hamlet of Perghele. 143rd Brigade held the sector from Perghele to the boundary with the Italians, near Cima Tre Prezzi, north-west of Cesuna. 144th Brigade, together with the divisional Pioneer battalion (1/5th Royal Sussex Regiment) and 48th Machine Gun Battalion (less 2 companies) were in divisional reserve, around Carriola base, but two of the 144th Brigade's infantry battalions, 1/6th Gloucesters and 1/7th Worcesters, were billeted at the foot of the mountains due to a shortage of accommodation in the hills. The division would normally be able to count on its own organic artillery support in the form of 240th[3] and 241st Brigades, Royal Field Artillery.[4] However, in view of the planned allied offensive, it had also been 'loaned' 35th Brigade, Royal Field Artillery, from 7th Division. Many of these batteries had been pushed well forward, in some cases beyond the front line. In addition, Fanshawe could, in theory, call on support from the 'heavies' of the Royal Garrison Artillery if required, although these were under Corps control and were supporting the whole of the British sector. Commanded by Cavan's CRA, Brigadier-General A E Wardrop, the heavy artillery consisted of five British brigades, totalling 25 batteries,[5] together with 19 Italian batteries (and eight batteries of heavy mortars). 21 batteries had been detailed for counter-battery work, with 23 (plus the eight Italian mortar batteries) allocated for bombardment.[6] The front infantry brigades each had a company of 48 Machine Gun Battalion attached – C on the right and D on the left – and these had sections of guns – in depth – widely spread across the whole of the divisional area, covering likely avenues of enemy advance and potential weak points in the line.

The British line here was usually held by three battalions – two on the right sector and one on the left – each battalion holding their part of the front with two companies in the line, one

---

3    Artillery Brigade numbers were usually given in Roman numerals at this time, so, for example, 35th Brigade, RFA would have been described as XXXV Brigade, RFA.
4    18-pdrs and 4.5-in howitzers.
5    6in howitzers, 60-pdrs and 9.2in howitzers.
6    J E Edmonds, p.197.

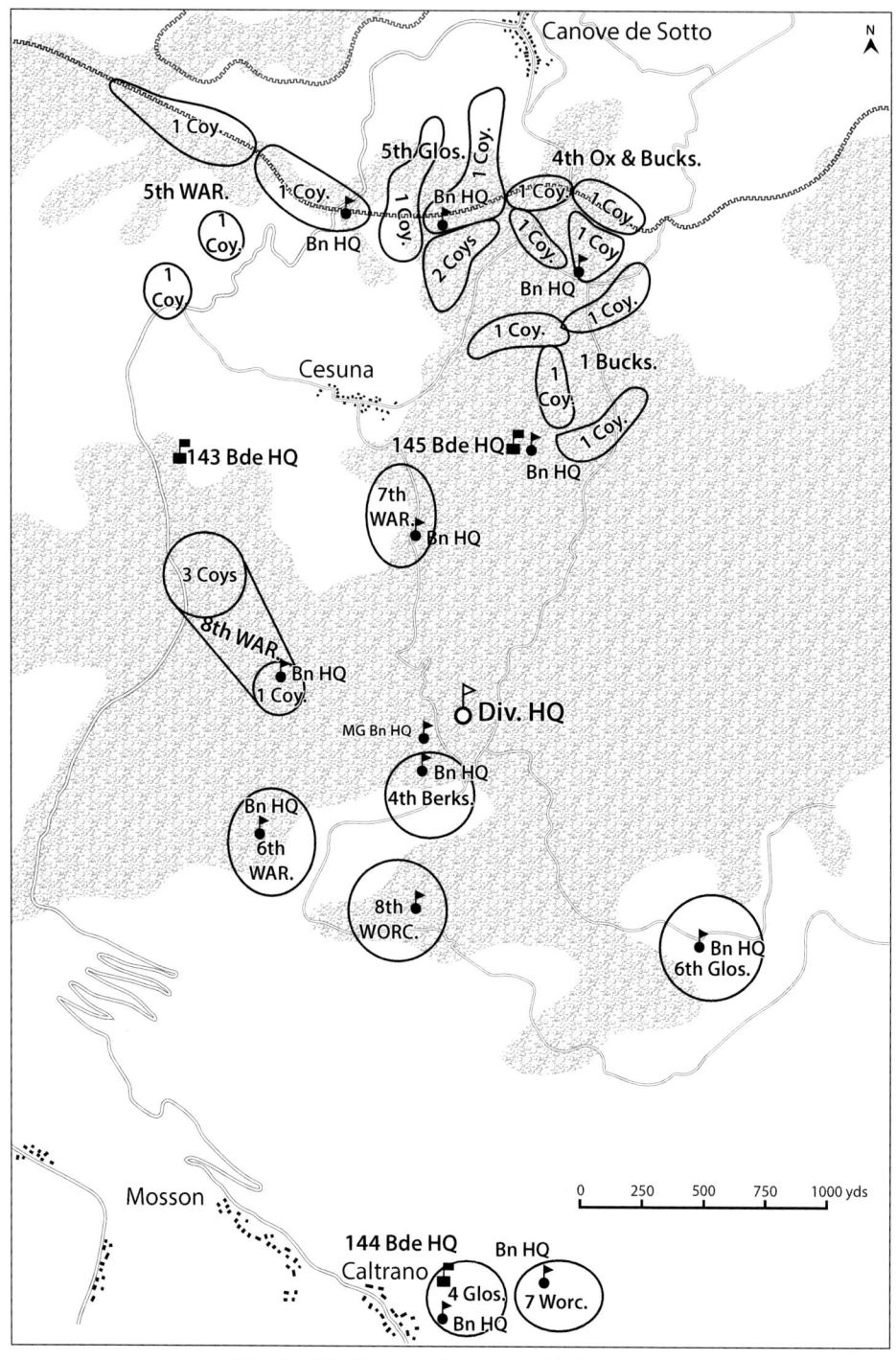

Map 5  48th Division dispositions 15 June 1918.

in support, just behind the front, and one in reserve a bit further back. The line was not manned continuously from left to right. It was held by posts – small groups of infantrymen, perhaps in section or half-section strength, holding short lengths of trench with gaps in between. In theory, these gaps should have been covered by those posts to the right and left, providing mutual support. But in practice, on this section of front, mutually supporting posts were not always possible due to the geography. The line here did not run straight. On the broken ground it weaved in and out of re-entrants and small salient and this meant that some individual posts were unable to see, and therefore unable to support, their neighbours. Some of the posts were not even able to cover their own wire, due to the steepness of the forward slope and the way the trench parapet and fire step had been made. Beyond the main line, in some cases quite close to the enemy front, ran the British outpost line, which on the night of 14/15th June was strongly held in order to protect dumps of ammunition and equipment and forward artillery positions that had been prepared in No-man's Land ahead of the now-postponed Allied offensive.[7]

In 145th Brigade sector, the 1/4th Oxfords held the right section from the boundary with 23rd Division, above Roncalto, to just west of where the light railway crossed the track leading to Pelly Cross. The left was held by 1/5th Gloucestershire Regiment, from the railway to the boundary with 143rd Brigade. The Buckinghamshire Battalion was in support on the slopes of Monte Lemerle, nearby, and 1/4th Royal Berkshire Regiment was in Brigade reserve at Carriola. In the 143rd Brigade sector, the commander, Brigadier-General Sladen, was holding his portion of the line with a single battalion, again on a two-company front. That meant the 1/5th Royal Warwickshire Regiment was responsible for the whole of the brigade position, stretching for about 2500 yards. In addition to the two companies in the line, a third was at Contra Graser and the fourth was at Cavrari. 1/6th and 1/8th Royal Warwickshires were 5000 and 3000 yards behind at Monte Pau and Monte Busibollo respectively, although one company of 1/8th Warwickshires was providing a thinly-spread garrison in the Cesuna Switch. The supporting Trench Mortar unit had five guns in the line and five more in reserve at 1/5th Royal Warwickshires' battalion headquarters. 1/7th Royal Warwickshires were in Divisional Reserve at Handley Cross. So, although two of the brigade's four infantry battalions were well back, Sladen could call on a strong local reserve if required.

On paper, it might be considered that two companies is quite a small force with which to hold 2500 yards of trench. By comparison, the French held 3300 yards of front with four battalions.[8] However, a look at the geography of this section of front shows why this was not as irresponsible as it might at first appear. The left flank of the 143rd Brigade area overlooked a deep ravine with sheer, scrub-covered rock faces on each side, and this was considered impervious to an infantry assault from the front. This proved to be the case on 15th June. The enemy did not even attempt to attack this flank. A sizeable portion of line enjoyed an excellent field of fire, running as it did over open, treeless ground, making it easier to defend. However, on the extreme right, the Warwickshires' line wound through the same dense scrub and woodland as that of the Gloucesters and the Oxfords, which made observation, and thus defence, much more difficult. With his left flank secure, Sladen could focus his troops on the weakest sections of his line, at Perghele, and on the right boundary with 145th Brigade, also in the trees. To hold his

---

7   TNA WO 95/4244: Fanshawe After Action Report, 48th Division General Staff War Diary.
8   J E Edmonds, p.196.

front securely, he only needed to ensure that the centre and right flank remained intact, thus preventing an attacking enemy from penetrating and then swinging to their right to envelope his line from the rear. The left would take care of itself. And even if his front was penetrated, the Cesuna Switch Line should provide protection from envelopment.

Taking account of the ground to be held and the likelihood of a heavy opening bombardment, and the emphasis on keeping casualties to a minimum, this was a reasonably sound disposition of forces. However, it should also be remembered that the 1/5th Royal Warwickshires, like every other British battalion in the line that day, was considerably under-strength at this time, as a result of the influenza epidemic which had swept through the force in recent days, and this would undoubtedly be a factor in the coming hours. According to Barnett and the 48th Division narrative of the engagement, the battalions' maximum fighting strengths on 15th June were as follows:[9]

| 143rd Brigade | | 144th Brigade | | 145th Brigade | |
|---|---|---|---|---|---|
| 1/5 R Warwickshires | 436 | 1/4 Gloucesters | 466 | 1/5 Gloucesters | 466 |
| 1/6 R Warwickshires | 379 | 1/6 Gloucesters | 538 | 1/4 Oxfords | 552 |
| 1/7 R Warwickshires | 380 | 1/7 Worcesters | 548 | 1/4 R Berks | 497 |
| 1/8 R Warwickshires | 450 | 1/8 Worcesters | 617 | 1/1 Bucks Battalion | 566 |

## Joining the Dots

Although by early June Diaz and Cavan were reasonably sure that the Austrians were about to attack somewhere between the Val d'Astico and the sea, by 13th June they still did not know for certain exactly where or when the offensive would take place. Then, on 14th June, Diaz received some new intelligence and the final piece of the jigsaw slotted into place. The Commando Supremo informed his army commanders, who in turn passed the details down to their Corps. During that same morning Cavan convened a conference of his divisional commanders at Lonedo, at the foot of the mountains, to put them in the picture, and to confirm that the allies' planned offensive was now 'off', at least for the time being.

Returning from the conference to his headquarters at Carriola, Fanshawe called together his brigade and unit commanders and his key staff officers during the afternoon and repeated the information, which, according to Lt Col Barnett, the divisional Assistant Adjutant and Quartermaster General, was regarded as being "absolutely reliable". The Austrians would attack "on a huge scale" the following morning on a front that stretched some 90km "from the Altopiano (Asiago Plateau) to the sea"[10]. The intelligence, which was very precise, put the western boundary for the attack at the French sector, in front of Monte Sisemol, but assessed that the preparatory artillery bombardment was likely to extend as far west as the British sector,

---

9   G Barnett, p.70 and TNA WO 95/4258: The Ghelpac Battle – 15th and 16th June 1918, 48th Division War Diary.
    *The normal fighting strength of an infantry battalion at that time was 900-1000 men. These strengths were reduced further by men who were still with their units but not yet fully recovered from the effects of influenza.
10  G Barnett, p.66.

although no infantry attack was expected there. Accepting the veracity of the intelligence, Fanshawe was clear with his subordinates that his division "would probably not have an infantry attack" on its front, but they were certain to get their share of the preliminary bombardment. In the circumstances, he directed, "the safest thing to do is to hope for the best and prepare for the worst".[11] In other words, even though the intelligence suggested otherwise, his force was to assume that an infantry attack was likely and take the appropriate measures. This is reinforced by the fact that he then went on to discuss the Divisional Defence Scheme in some depth, laying particular stress on the roles of the troops in the counter-attack, the time for the withdrawal of the outpost lines, and arrangements for the artillery to open fire on SOS lines and also their counter-battery work. Overall, Fanshawe concluded that the Divisional Defence Scheme held good. As Barnett recalled:

> When the conference broke up, I don't think that most of those present thought in their heart of hearts that an attack was likely. However, the General had given his preliminary orders, and everyone hastened to carry them out…We lay down for the night fully dressed.[12]

Hoping to gain further intelligence on the Austrian intentions, at dusk on the 14th, a patrol from 1/4th Oxfordshire and Buckinghamshire Light Infantry, led by 2Lt T. Moore, crept out of their front-line trench, through a gap in their wire and into the dense tree cover in front of their position. The men were nervous but confident. Most of them had done this before, some of them many times, and they knew that the Austrians rarely bothered to patrol their own wire or sought to dominate no-man's land as the British did. Continuing through the pines, they reached the edge of the woods and moved out across the now bare, open landscape, two men scouting ahead to make sure the route was clear. Moving in silence through the darkness, they eventually came to a halt in some dead ground just in front of an enemy position on the Vaister spur, a finger of raised ground jutting out towards the British trenches, just south-east of the village of Canove. At midnight, they heard the report of an 18-pounder field gun, located on the reverse slope of a hill just behind the lines, and almost immediately the enemy position was lit up by a series of explosions as 18 shrapnel shells exploded in the air over the trench. Pistol in hand, 2Lt Moore sprang up and waved his men forward, relieved to see the line of figures follow him towards the enemy trench. Leaping over the parapet and down into the trench, the raiders were just in time to see the garrison scuttling away, but not before one of their number was snatched and bundled back across no-man's land to the British lines, pursued by half-hearted bursts of machine-gun and rifle fire.

Arriving at battalion headquarters, dug into the bank in a sunken lane just behind the line, the prisoner seemed happy to talk, but an attempt by the battalion Intelligence Officer to converse in German brought no response. The prisoner was Hungarian, from 23rd Honved Regiment, and Magyar was not a common language amongst the Allies. However, "chiefly by signs" the prisoner managed to communicate that an attack was expected in that sector, beginning at 0300, with a heavy artillery bombardment that would include gas. Battalion staff were "a little sceptical"[13]: enemy prisoners were inclined to say whatever they thought would please

---

11 G Barnett, p.67.
12 G Barnett, p.67.
13 TNA WO 95/2764: 1/4 OBLI War Diary, 15th June 1918.

their captors and ensure a hot meal. And this prisoner, knowing an attack was imminent, was probably keen to get as far away from the front as possible. However, they decided to send him back to Carriola by car where the divisional Intelligence Officer could assess the strength of the information provided and report it up the chain of command. The officer tasked with seeing the prisoner to Carriola was Maj Percy Pickford, the battalion second-in-command. Writing in his personal diary for that day, Pickford noted that he took the prisoner to the Advanced Dressing Station, which was located along the Boscon Road. There he borrowed an ambulance (the only available vehicle) and driver and left for divisional headquarters.[14] It was now 0230.

In reporting on the events of 15/16th June to his superior headquarters, the commander of 143rd Brigade, Brigadier-General Sladen, chose to break down the action into three phases. Phase one was the preparatory bombardment; phase two the infantry assault and break-in; and phase three included holding and driving back the enemy. Given the complexity of the fighting, this seems a sensible structure that helps to divide up the action into distinct and manageable blocks. The same structure is employed below.

## Preparatory Bombardment – 0300-0700

At Carriola, a slumbering but fully-clothed Lt Col Barnett was awakened by the sound of someone stumbling along the corridor in his hut, asking for the Intelligence Officer.[15]

> Shouting out that he was in the next hut, I looked at my watch and saw that it was 2.58am. I was just going to sleep again when I heard a most extraordinarily weird and impressive sound, apparently coming nearer and nearer. I can only compare it to the sound of a heavy sea breaking on a rocky coast, intensely magnified, a quite continuous roar, not very loud but very insistent, giving the impression of some tremendous force let loose. For a few seconds, I wondered idly whether the noise really was the much-advertised attack, but any doubts were dispelled almost immediately by the sound of the swish-swish of gas shells overhead, followed shortly by the whine and bang of HE shells arriving."[16]

Maj Pickford, witnessed the arrival of a salvo of high explosive shells on divisional HQ at 0300 and, deciding that "the front line was pleasanter", he started back with the ambulance. However, they only managed to travel about 250 yards before running into gas shells. The driver could not see to drive whilst wearing his gas mask, so Pickford left the vehicle and went on foot through the "terrific bombardment" of gas and HE on all roads and batteries, especially Handley Cross, "where a dump of shells was blowing up and had to be widely circumvented". It was, he wrote, "a very exciting and unpleasant trip in a gas mask, by bounds, diving into [the] roadside ditch on seeing the flash of each salvo".[17]

---

14 TNA CAB 45/84: Extract from diary of Maj P Pickford DSO, MC correspondence attachment, Pickford to Edmonds, 30 May 1944.
15 This was almost certainly Maj Pickford searching for the IO to hand over the prisoner.
16 G Barnett, p.68.
17 TNA CAB 45/84: Excerpt from diary of Maj P Pickford correspondence attachment, Pickford to Edmonds, 30 May 1944.

Battle of Asiago: 15–16th June 1918 205

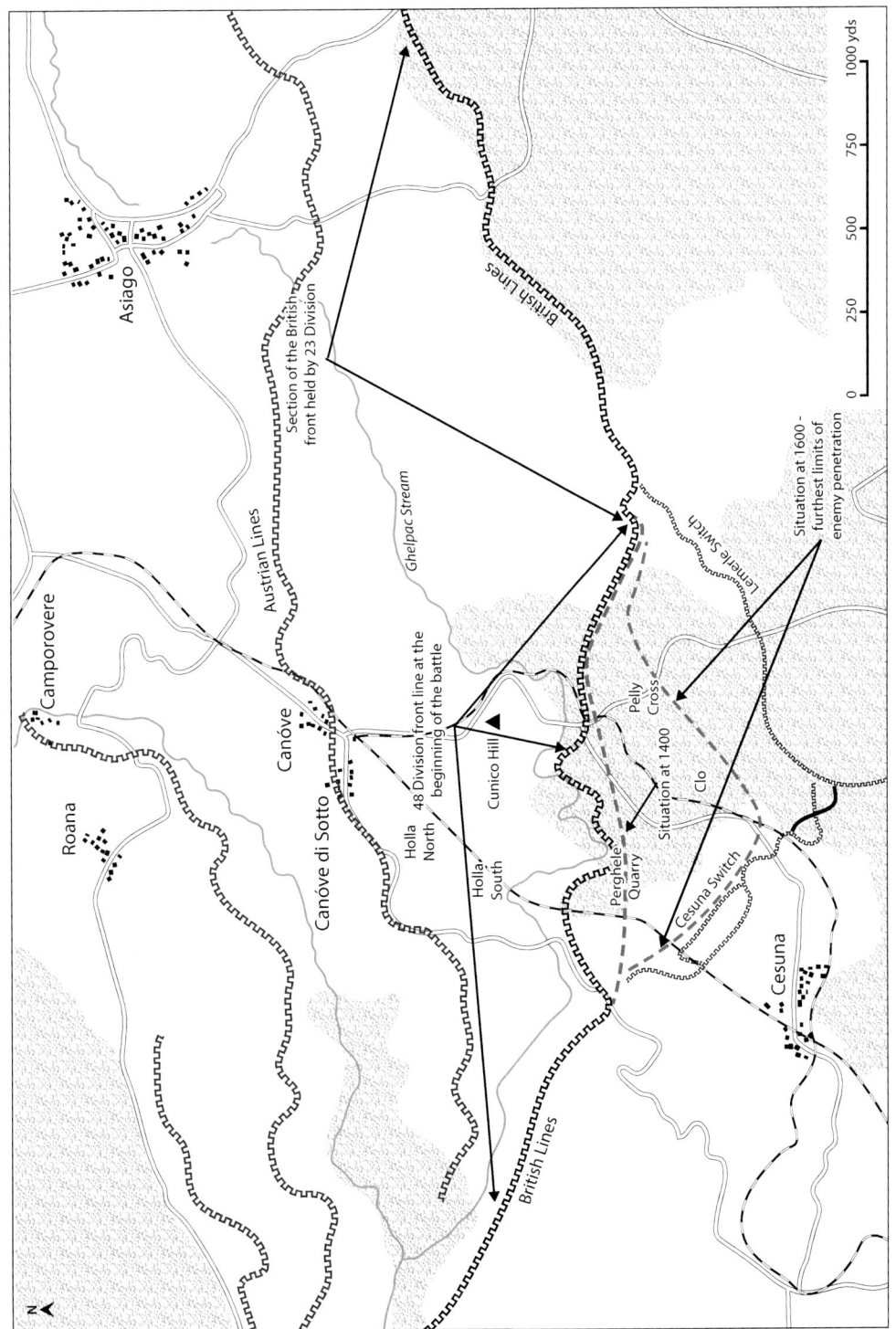

Map 6 Asiago 15-16th June 1918.

Several thousand yards north-west of Carriola, in 23rd Division's sector near the Pria del Acqua cross-roads behind San Sisto Ridge, Lt Hugh Dalton was up late. He was the duty officer in his artillery battery's command post, and although suffering from the effects of influenza, had just received orders to conduct an elaborate, two-part counter-battery shoot, using gas shells, part one between 11pm and midnight and part two between 2 and 3am. But there were no gas shells for his 6-inch howitzers on the battery position, and although informed by Brigade that they were on their way, they did not arrive in time to fire the first phase of the shoot. Dalton's guns were able to join in for the second part though, and when that was nearly complete, he received further orders to fire 10 rounds of HE at "Archibald", a particularly troublesome Austrian searchlight on the summit of Monte Mosciagh on the far side of the plateau. By the time that was done it was nearing 0330, and, as his flu symptoms were growing more severe, he decided to retire, leaving an NCO to oversee the unloading of gas shells that had arrived too late for the earlier shoot. He had just fallen asleep when the NCO came in and asked if the men should "go on unloading during the shelling".

Stumbling to the door of the Command Post, Dalton looked outside:

> Not only the road but the whole battery position and apparently the whole area for some distance around, was being bombarded very violently. So, I ordered everyone to take cover. It was 3.45am.[18]

In a front-line trench a few hundred yards east of the boundary with 48th Division, Private Norman Gladden, and the other members of his Lewis Gun team, part of B Company, 11th Northumberland Fusiliers, muffled in their greatcoats, were huddled on the fire step, too cold to do more than doze. Ordered to 'stand-to' just before daybreak (which was around 0300 in the mountains at that time of year), Gladden and his mates could hear guns firing out to their front. Flashes lit up the hills on the far side of the plateau and the roar of artillery rolled along the whole of their line:

> There was a crescendo of sound and then the storm burst upon us. Screaming shells rushed to earth amidst the wire and behind us, or further over in the woods. Lumps of rock were hurled about by the explosions. The trench soon became swathed in a cloud of acrid smoke ...[19]

The opening bombardment included shells of all calibres, gas, shrapnel, High Explosives and even solid shot.[20] The enemy gunners were hitting key locations throughout the depth of the British positions. Targets included front line trenches, gun batteries, battalion, brigade and divisional headquarters, supply depots, ammunition dumps, tracks leading to and from the front line, and key road and track junctions, such as Handley Cross and Pelly Cross. Some shells even cleared the southern peaks and exploded on the plain below. In his memoir, Cavan notes that a shell landed in the garden of his headquarters at Lonedo, at the foot of the mountains, but failed

---

18  H Dalton, p.206.
19  N Gladden, pp118-19
20  J E Edmonds, p.199.

to explode.[21] According to Edmonds, it was the opinion of artillerymen that the bombardment was unregistered and 'not a success'.[22] He also claims that the fire was "very dispersed and it had neither the volume nor the accuracy that the troops had been accustomed to on the Western Front in 1917".[23]

Lt Graham Greenwell, of 1/4th Oxfords, who, unlike Edmonds or the gunners quoted above, was actually in the front line that morning, had a different view. Writing to his mother on 17th June he described the shelling as:

> … the most intense I have ever known, even in the worst days of the Somme or Ypres … they shelled at the most intense pitch for four and a half hours without a stop and continued it for miles behind the lines …[24]

Norman Gladden, who had also been under German bombardments during the Third Ypres offensive, would also have disagreed. Cowering in his trench as the bombardment began, he later wrote:

> Here was a real slap-up barrage on the Western Front pattern.[25]

However, Capt S F Gedye, of A Battery, 240th Brigade, Royal Field Artillery, noted in his personal diary on 17th June:

> Bar cross-roads and roads, no particular targets seemed to be engaged, but the whole was a gigantic area strafe with every calibre and with assorted HE and gas. A bombardment in these districts is pretty beastly; in addition to the shell fragments there are falling trees and lumps of boulder flying about and the row of the explosions is magnified [by the mountains].[26]

Identifying lessons learned from the battle, a GHQ report claims the enemy artillery fire was:

> Very accurate on roads but not on trenches in woods. Too light to really damage front-line trenches or wire, which were intact and fightable on 90% of their extent. Enemy counter-battery work [was] ineffective and owed such results as it obtained from shelling obvious valleys and hollows, not batteries themselves.[27]

But Hugh Dalton, in his deep "caverne', remarked that:

---

21  CCC Cavan unpublished memoir.
22  J E Edmonds, p.199.
23  J E Edmonds, p.199.
24  G Greenwell, p.226.
25  N Gladden, p.119.
26  *Battery History, A Bty, 240th Brigade, RFA written by Capt S F Gedye MC* <http://www.google.com/url?q=http%3A%2F%2Fweb.archive.org%2Fweb%2F20160315162050%2Fhttp%3A%2F%2Fwww.thebristolgunners.webspace.virginmedia.com%2Findex.htm&sa=D&sntz=1&usg=AFQjCNFjuHS2n_U6cCA0uv_i6cx1Zf5nUg> (accessed 1 November 2023).
27  TNA WO 95/4194: GHQ After Action Report to Sixth Italian Army.

> We were wonderfully lucky to get off as lightly as we did. It is one of the most extraordinary phenomena of war, how many shells can fall in a position of no great size and yet do very little damage. It is estimated, and I think quite soberly, that at least 2000 rounds were pumped into our battery position that morning.[28]

It is certainly the case, from the Austrian official history and from British documents reporting on the questioning of prisoners, that some enemy batteries were only brought into their firing positions in the early hours of the morning and had no time to register,[29] and that some artillery units that were intended to take part in the offensive did not arrive in the area until after the 15th. This was due to transport difficulties, including a shortage of horses, poor coordination of traffic on the main supply routes, and congestion on the railways.[30] As a result, the total Austrian artillery strength on the southwestern front on 15th June was 6833 guns – roughly 76 guns per kilometre. But the planned allocation of ammunition had not been met due to the same logistical problems listed above. The Austrian account also complains that the supply of gas shells, which were intended to form a key element of their counter-battery work, had not met the stated requirement. The Austrians produced their own Green Cross (Chlorine/Phosgene/Diphosgene) and Yellow Cross (Mustard) shells, but they relied on the Germans for Blue Cross (Diphenychloroarsine)[31] and the Germans had failed to provide it.[32] In addition, the use of Mustard was problematic for the Austrians because they lacked the necessary protective clothing.[33]

It is also the case that the enemy artillery had remained silent in the days running up to the offensive in order to conserve ammunition stocks and to stay undetected by British observers. By doing so they hoped to avoid falling victim to counter-battery fire, at which the British, using air observation, excelled. However, many of the Austrian batteries had been in the area for some time and would certainly have had earlier opportunities to register. Notwithstanding the views of Edmonds and his "artillerymen" sources, the accuracy with which the Austrian gunners picked out the front line, supply routes, cross-roads and key command and control locations, including unit, brigade, and divisional headquarters, supports the conclusion that this was not entirely a 'blind' bombardment.

One place where significant damage was done by the Austrian artillery fire, was at Handley Cross, about half-way between the 48th Division headquarters at Carriola and the front line. As Maj Pickford recalled, within minutes of the bombardment commencing, a large artillery ammunition dump near this critical junction was hit and set alight, creating explosions that continued for much of the morning, badly hampering the movement of men, ammunition and equipment to the front. Trees brought down by shellfire blocked tracks and roads, adding to the problems of reinforcing, and resupplying the front line.

---

28 H Dalton, p.209.
29 E Glaise-Horstenau and R Kiszling, H Dalton, et al and GHQ artillery LL narrative.
30 E Glaise-Horstenau and R Kiszling, p.228. E Glaise-Horstenau and R Kiszling
31 A chemical irritant designed to force men to remove respirators and thus become susceptible to chlorine or mustard agents.
32 E Glaise-Horstenau and R Kiszling, p.231.
33 E Glaise-Horstenau and R Kiszling, p.231

Hugh Dalton believed the shells that struck close to his command post were a mixture of high explosives, shrapnel and gas, the latter mostly lachrymatory (tear gas), but mixed with "a certain quantity of lethal".[34] But it was hard to tell. The all-pervading smell of High Explosives and the burning pine trees made detection of gas very difficult, although it was clear that gas shells were being fired, due to their particular detonation characteristics: they exploded with a 'plop' rather than a 'bang'. As a result, troops right across the force were required to wear their respirators almost from the start, causing great discomfort for all, making breathing much more difficult, and, more alarmingly for the men at the sharp end, degrading the wearers' ability to observe what was happening around them. The glass eye-pieces tended to steam up due to condensation as the wearer breathed, making it almost impossible to see, identify and select targets and then engage them with their weapons. The gas being used was not persistent and tended to disperse quite quickly, especially if there was a breeze blowing. However, being heavier than air, it could 'pool' at the bottom of trenches, ditches and areas of low-lying land, and in dug-outs if it managed to get past the rudimentary gas-proofing systems in use (usually an airlock constructed of two gas blankets with a gap between them). But artillery observers on high ground would have been less affected and may not have had to wear gas masks for very long:

> ... the acrid fumes of a shell-burst close by caused me to imagine that the gas was already upon us. I adjusted my box respirator excitedly, taking more time than was usual on parade, and, my companions having done likewise, we crouched round in our weird garb puffing through our rubber mouthpieces and looking like other-world creatures from a novel by H G Wells.[35]

Telephone communications were disrupted almost as soon as the bombardment began. Shells cut wires running overground (they could not be buried in the hard limestone) and brought down trees on which cables had been strung over the branches. The divisional record says communication by wire and telephone was quickly "much broken" and messages came by wireless and visual (flags or lights). Visual was delayed and frequently interrupted by cloud, mist and smoke.[36] At 145th Brigade, the lines to the two forward battalions were reported disabled at 0326. The wireless set at 145th Brigade also became an early victim of the shelling, but on the left, 143rd Brigade's wireless link with division functioned throughout the day. Early on, division received short "all well" messages from the right and left battalions. However, the centre battalion, 1/5th Gloucesters, did not communicate at all at this stage. There are a number of possible reasons for this: their telephone link may have been cut close to the outset; their ground buzzer set may have failed; and their visual signalling station may not have been functioning effectively due to the thick mist that had blanketed the forward areas throughout the night and early morning.

Whilst there are many uncertainties regarding the failure of communications at the beginning of this battle, it is clear from the evidence of the post-action reports that before long, runners, and in some cases, cyclists, became the most reliable way of passing orders and information back and forth on much of the front. But with the ground between the front line and the brigade and divisional headquarters being heavily shelled, this method was by no means infallible. Runners could be injured or killed by the shellfire, or simply find themselves unable to

---

34  H Dalton, p.207.
35  N Gladden, p.120.
36  TNA WO 95/4244: 48th Division War Diary.

move due to the intensity of the bombardment. Thus, messages could take hours to get through. For example, an important despatch sent by 1/4th Oxfords, reporting enemy infantry activity on their front, timed at 0700, did not reach Brigade headquarters, only about half a mile away, as the crow flies, until 0945.[37]

By good fortune, however, the telephone lines held up just long enough for the order to withdraw the outposts – issued by GHQ at 0320 – to get through to the forward battalions. At 0335, the 48th Division's signals officer was on the phone, passing this message to 143rd Brigade when the line was cut as he was in mid-sentence, although he had managed to convey the key detail: the posts must be in by 0500. This timing was meant to ensure that the personnel manning the forward positions were able to make their way back, unmolested by the British counter-preparation barrage. Although the outposts came in, picquets and a few well-placed machine guns were left out beyond the British wire, with orders to disrupt the approaching enemy in the event that an infantry attack was launched.[38]

On the right, 145th Brigade headquarters repeated the order to pull in the outposts to its front-line battalions at 0340.[39] The right-hand battalion, 1/4th Oxfords, reported the outposts had withdrawn at 0430, but as they made their way back, those on the left front found enemy troops between them and the front line and they could not get through until much later. Two mortar teams of 145th Trench Mortar Battery, set up on the reverse slope of Hill 1002, covering the approaches to the right outpost line, did not receive the withdrawal order and remained at their posts until almost cut off. At the last safe moment, with the enemy all around them, they hid their mortar tubes, base-plates, and ammunition, and made their way back to the front line where they attached themselves to the infantry.[40]

Without waiting for further direction from above, as soon as the enemy artillery bombardment commenced, 145th Brigade directed the Bucks Battalion to move to its battle position with 2 companies in the Lemerle Switch Line, and 1 company each in Polderhoek Trench and Jargon Trench, on the slopes of Monte Lemerle. This order was timed at 0319. At the same time, the 1/4th Royal Berkshires were 'stood to' in their billets, awaiting orders to move.[41]

The left battalion's (1/5th Gloucesters) narrative shows that their outpost company returned at about 0430 to the low hills north of the Ghelpac. From there, at about 0630, they engaged and drove back enemy scouts, and later withdrew across the river, some of them heading towards the left of the battalion line and others to the right. The 145th Brigade record reveals that a Gloucesters soldier, claiming to have been on outpost duty, arrived at Lemerle at 0730 and stated that upon withdrawal he could find no trace of the battalion in the front line.[42] By that stage, this garrison had been penetrated and most of the posts had withdrawn, although there is evidence that one post from this battalion on the extreme right, held on in the front line for some time before being forced out. This post subsequently joined up with 1/4th Oxfords and continued the fight with them.[43]

37   TNA WO 95/4250: 145th Brigade War Diary.
38   J E Edmonds, p.200.
39   TNA WO 95/4250: 145th Brigade War Diary.
40   TNA WO 95/4250: 145th Trench Mortar Battery War Diary.
41   TNA WO 95/4250: 145th Brigade War Diary.
42   TNA WO 95/4250: 145th Brigade War Diary.
43   TNA WO 95/4250: Lt Col Reynolds personal narrative.

On the left, 143rd Brigade's narrative does not record the receipt of the order to withdraw their outposts, but, as stated above, it was passed on at around 0335. However, the narrative does report that all telephone lines were cut by 0400 with the exception of one to the left group of artillery batteries, which remained intact all day except for a single break of a few minutes.[44] At 0445, orders were received from division for the Cesuna Switch Line to be reinforced and this directive was passed on to 1/8th Royal Warwickshires at Busibollo and 1/6th R Warwickshires at Monte Pau. Both battalions moved forward in accordance with the Divisional Defence Scheme, except that the commander of the in-lying picquet company[45] of 1/8th R Warwickshires, Capt Bridges, intercepted the message and, acting on his own initiative, started his company forward at once. The head of this company passed Brigade headquarters at Val di Maso at 0535. This meant that reinforcements arrived in Cesuna Switch earlier than might have been expected, no doubt to the relief to the men of the single company of 1/8th R Warwickshires who were already there. General Fanshawe highlights this "prompt action" by Capt Bridges in his own After-Action Report to GHQ, dated 21st June 1918. This act of individual initiative may have been partly responsible for ensuring that the Cesuna Switch garrison was able to withstand early Austrian pressure.[46]

At this stage, it was still not clear if the enemy intended to launch a serious infantry attack on the British sector, but, in accordance with the Divisional Defence Scheme and Fanshawe's orders, the division had organised itself so as to be able to deal with an assault if it came. At GHQ, with not much information to go on, Cavan took the precautionary decision at 0350 to reduce 7th Division's notice to move, requiring them to take the necessary steps to be ready to start up the mountain at two hours' notice from 0500.[47] Receipt of this order would have sparked a flurry of activity down on the plain as the divisional headquarters, the three infantry brigades and supporting troops brought themselves up to high readiness, while staff officers made contact with 48th and 23rd Divisions to try to find out what might be awaiting them in the mountains.[48] Cavan's decision was later criticised by some 48th Division officers as 'precipitate' and evidence that he panicked. However, this was not an unreasonable move in the circumstances and does not indicate panic at GHQ level, but a prudent contingency. When the decision was taken, Cavan had no way of knowing how the attack was going to go and he needed to ensure his reserves were going to be available if he required them.

Although the front line itself remained lightly held, as per the defence doctrine of the day, the two switch lines – Cesuna and Lemerle – and the trenches on the forward slopes of Monte Lemerle itself, including Polderhoek Trench and Jargon Trench – which were key elements of the Divisional Defence Scheme, were now manned and ready to repel attackers. The outposts had retired as directed, some personnel taking up new positions just short of the British line in order to disrupt the vanguard of an infantry attack if it came. The brigade, divisional and GHQ reserves were warned-off for action, and unit Liaison Officers had arrived at divisional

---

44 TNA WO 95/4250: 143rd Brigade War Diary.
45 This picquet was probably located to provide force protection (cover) for Battalion headquarters, which was located at Monte Ceramella, situated slightly to the west of divisional HQ at Carriola.
46 TNA WO 95/2745: 48th Division After Action Report.
47 TNA WO 95/4194: Record of Messages, GHQ General Staff War Diary.
48 The 48th Division war diarist recorded a telephone call from 7th Division seeking a situation update at 0516.

headquarters to keep in touch with the situation as it developed so that they could brief their commanders ahead of any move forward. Individual units in the line were taking steps to ensure they were in contact with those on their flanks and in the switch lines. All of this had been achieved despite the disrupted communications, which is evidence that Fanshawe had trained his divisional staff well and that brigade and unit commanders were very familiar with the Divisional Defence Scheme and their parts in it.

The early failure of the communications systems was a critical weakness in terms of how the battle would be managed by senior officers, certainly in the initial stages, although there is evidence that front-to-rear links improved during the course of the day, even if lateral contact between individual units remained poor or, in some cases, non-existent. With the passage of information degraded, gaps were created in the situational awareness of commanders at all levels, particularly at division, brigade, and GHQ. This left senior officers at times frustrated and almost powerless to influence the developing situation. As Edmonds rightly says, the fighting very quickly became "a battalion commanders' and soldiers' battle".[49] In 48th Division, this was not a problem because the GOC had made sure his subordinates understood how he intended to fight the defensive engagement, and he was confident they would be able to act purposefully, even in the absence of further direction from above. The defence scheme was well-practiced. However, without a clear picture of the situation at the front, commanders could not be sure they were putting the reserves in the right places, at the right time, and could only hope that the scheme, as designed and practiced, would stand up to the test.

Fanshawe, his staff and his brigade commanders knew from the start that they were going to have to 'fight' for information. One example of this proactive effort was the approach taken by Brigadier-General Sladen of 143rd Brigade. By 0345, already frustrated by the lack of situational updates coming from the front, Sladen sent forward the Brigade Intelligence Officer and six observers to the headquarters of 1/5th Royal Warwickshires. The observers were dropped off at intervals to form a relay system and subsequent communications by this method worked satisfactorily for a time.[50] Fanshawe, too, achieved some degree of situational awareness by sending trusted officers to the forward Brigade headquarters to learn what they knew and report back.[51] One of these was Capt Foster, who was despatched to 145th Brigade at 0555. He made it there through the bombardment, arriving at 0650. Lt C T H Harrison was sent to 143rd Brigade, again dodging Austrian shells, to arrive at 0910, sending back his first situation report at 1030. Officers' patrols went out from the battalions already committed to make contact with flanking units, assess the situation and pass this back up the chain of command. But the information that flowed by these means was slow to materialise, and by the time it made its way back to brigade or divisional headquarters, it had often been overtaken by subsequent events. At Brigade and Division, commanders had to use their experience, and knowledge of the enemy's tactics, techniques and procedures, to assess the available information, decide, sometimes on the basis of probability, what was actually happening, and then employ their military judgement to work out what to do about it. Meanwhile, units in reserve sent Liaison Officers to Divisional Headquarters to gain their own battle picture and pass this on to their battalions so that they would be as well-informed as possible, should they be required to enter the fray.

49  J E Edmonds, p.201.
50  TNA WO 95/2754/5: 143rd Brigade War Diary.
51  TNA WO 95/4250: 48th Division War Diary.

The role played by the British artillery during the early stages of the action caused consternation and confusion at the time and since. The GHQ narrative records that the order to withdraw the outposts was transmitted at 0320, and at the same time the divisional artillery was directed to commence counter-preparation fire within the outpost line at 0500. This meant shelling targets or potential targets between the British front line and the outpost line. The 48th Division record shows that Fanshawe informed his gunners at 0410 that there should be no SOS shooting (within the outpost line) before 0500 (the time by which the outposts should be withdrawn), and that they were not to fire on SOS lines without orders. At 0445 the division received a message from the Brigadier-General, General Staff (BGGS) at GHQ, Brigadier-General Francis Gaythorne-Hardy, asking if the division would be satisfied with the SOS barrage coming down at 0500. Gaythorne-Hardy was informed that Fanshawe had told the gunners not to fire at 0500 unless ordered. At 0450, Brigadier-General Strong, the divisional Commander Royal Artillery (CRA), noted that GHQ wished to sweep Corps artillery fire across No Man's Land at 0500 and to switch some heavies[52] to engage Austrian guns in the open near Roana.[53] Fanshawe had no objections to this, and his agreement was passed up to Brigadier-General A E Wardrop, CRA at GHQ, at 0455. Edmonds says that Wardrop, ordered counter-preparation beyond the outpost line at 0330 and the defensive barrage (by definition within the outpost line) at 0500. 240th Brigade RFA's War Diary records that orders were received from Divisional Artillery to commence counter-preparation beyond the outpost line at 0335, and this was passed on to C and D Btys (the only btys with which they still had communications).[54] Hugh Dalton claims he did not receive orders to fire on his counter-preparation target until around 0600 and then the orders arrived, not from his brigade headquarters, but by proxy from a battery nearby.[55]

Defensive artillery fire at that time was divided into two stages. The first was the counter-preparation bombardment. This was aimed at disrupting the enemy as they were preparing to attack. It included counter-battery work, and also targeted likely areas of concentration/assembly, avenues of approach, supply routes, and command and control locations such as headquarters, signal stations and Observation Posts (OPs). The second element was the defensive barrage. This involved dropping a curtain of fire directly ahead of the front line to catch the enemy as they advanced from their jumping-off points in the assault. During the Division's time in the line in front of Passchendaele in September and October, 1917, there are many accounts of German attacks being stopped in their tracks by the accuracy and ferocity of the British defensive artillery fire, brought down either by direct observation from an artillery OP, a Forward Observation Officer, in or near the front line, or a call for fire from the units holding the line, by telephone, or, more likely, and usually more reliably, by coloured rockets fired by the defenders. This fire was also known as the 'SOS barrage'. At Asiago, a number of units would later report that there was no response to their rockets calling for SOS fire. Either the rockets themselves failed to burst, or they burst behind the trees, or they were obscured by cloud or smoke. Whatever the cause, they were not spotted by the artillery and thus, as Gladden has testified, the guns did not fire on SOS lines during the initial Austrian assault. With a paucity

---

52   Artillery pieces above 4.5in calibre, operated by the Royal Garrison Artillery – e.g. 60-pdr (5in).
53   This is counter-preparation fire.
54   TNA WO 95/2749: 240th Brigade RFA War Diary.
55   H Dalton, p.209.

of information coming back to the gunners, battery commanders "had to a great extent to act on their own initiative"[56], at least in the early stages.

Whatever Brigadier-General Wardrop ordered, the SoS barrage certainly did not occur at 0500. In the front line just to the right of 48th Division, Norman Gladden recalled: "The enemy's bombardment continued unabated, but our guns remained silent."[57] In any case, the Austrian infantry assault did not begin until sometime later so an SOS barrage at 0500 would have achieved little, apart from using up ammunition and giving the line-holding troops a bit of a morale boost.

As Edmonds has stated, there was "evidently some misunderstanding at GHQ".[58] This is a good example of the "fog of war" with which commanders through the ages, have had to deal. As the operational tempo increases it becomes more and more difficult to maintain a clear situational picture. Events and messages are misreported or missed altogether. Record-keeping becomes more challenging as information flows fluctuate, and this, in turn, can lead to confusion, even in well-trained, well-led and highly motivated headquarters. It still occurs today, even though the modern commander, in a digitally-enabled headquarters, has access to a sophisticated, reliable, three-dimensional[59] situational picture, fed by an array of electronic sensors and imagery, the likes of which a First World War general could not have dreamed. The problem for today's commanders is that there is often too much information, rather than too little, but the "fog of war" persists, nonetheless.

The artillery would make a significant contribution as the day went on, but it seems clear that the Austrians were able to make their initial advance to and through the British front line, little troubled by the shell-fire that should have been a key element of the Defence Plan. As Cavan himself admitted in his report on the day's fighting, despatched to CIGS that evening: "The enemy did not suffer much from our SOS barrage and the brunt of the attack had to be borne by the infantry".[60]

## Enemy Infantry Assault and Penetration

The Official History puts the beginning of the Austrian infantry assault at about 0700,[61] and this is also the time recorded by GHQ in its post-battle report to the Commando Supremo.[62] However, there were earlier indications of an infantry attack, and the initial contact occurred before 0700. The first combat indicator that an infantry assault was imminent came at 0400 as members of the outpost garrison in front of 1/4th Oxfords were withdrawing across No-Man's Land. The troops who had been occupying the outposts on the left found their way back blocked by parties of enemy infantry, who had been held up by the British wire. The Oxfords were unable to by-pass these parties and consequently, this sighting of the enemy went unreported to

---

56  J E Edmonds, p.200.
57  N Gladden, p.119.
58  J E Edmonds, p.200.
59  Four-dimensional if you include cyberspace.
60  TNA WO 100/852: Cavan-Wilson correspondence, 15th June 1918.
61  J E Edmonds, p.205.
62  TNA WO 95/4194: GHQ after-action report to Commando Supremo.

division until after the battle, when it was included in the battalion narrative.[63] On the left of the Oxfords, the 1/5th Gloucesters' outpost garrison (B Company), who had established themselves on the north bank of the Ghelpac after their initial withdrawal, engaged enemy scouts to their front at about 0630 and drove them off. They then retired across the river to avoid envelopment by the enemy's main body, joining the two companies holding the front line (A Company on the right, D Company on the left). Again, this is included in the Gloucesters' narrative, but there is no evidence that it was reported up the chain of command at the time. It does not appear in either the Brigade or Divisional records. Meanwhile, at 0640, a platoon from the Gloucesters' support company (C Company), acting on orders from Brigade Headquarters, had moved up towards the front line, intending to push on to Hill 964. However, on arriving at the line, this platoon was surprised to find itself being heavily engaged by Austrian troops attempting to get through the wire. It was here that Pte Bertie Pegler, from Tetbury, Gloucestershire, distinguished himself doing "great execution" with his Lewis Gun to help to break up the attack.[64]

At 0700 the 1/5th Gloucesters' battalion headquarters reported sighting some enemy on Hill 972, in front of their left company, due west of Cunico Hill. This was 145th Brigade's first news of the enemy infantry, and it is noted in the brigade narrative as being received at headquarters at Carriola at 0930. However, the battalion narrative also mentions the enemy first being observed on a hill at map reference H.287.365, overlooking the left front company headquarters. This party then extended east across the valley and attacked the Gloucesters' left front company from the rear, cooperating with a second group who had broken through at the boundary between the Gloucesters and the Oxfords, and turned west. Together, these two enemy groups formed the left and right arms of a pincer movement, a classic infiltration and envelopment manoeuvre that was straight from the German "Stosstruppen" tactical doctrine.

As soon as the enemy were first sighted, on Hill 972, a second platoon from the Gloucesters' support company[65] was sent up the valley in an attempt to reinforce the front-line troops. However, in the face of very heavy machine gun fire the whole of the platoon's Lewis Gun section was knocked out and the enemy then pushed along the ridge to the north of the valley in some strength. The left platoon was extricated from a difficult position by the quick thinking of 2Lt G F Churchill, who was later awarded the Military Cross for his bravery and leadership at this time.[66] The withdrawal of the Gloucesters' right front company was covered by 203325 Pte G H Oliver[67] and his Lewis Gun, holding up the advancing Austrians long enough to allow his

---

63  TNA WO 95/2763/1: 1/5th Gloucester Regiment War Diary.
64  13773 Pte Pegler was later awarded the Military Medal for his part in this action. Pte Pegler survived the fighting on the Asiago Plateau but was killed in action in France on the night of 5-6 October 1918, during an attack to capture the village of Beaurevoir. Pegler now lies in the Beaurevoir Communal Cemetery British Extension, between Cambrai and St Quentin, one of 10 men from 1/5th Gloucestershire Regiment killed that night. He is referred to in the 1/5th Gloucester narrative as Pte S Pegler, but his CWGC entry shows that his name was Bertie. He was just 23 years old when he died.
65  In this context a support company was a rifle company being held behind the front line to support the garrison if required. This is not the same as the Second World War grouping that saw support companies providing specialist anti-tank, machine gun and mortar platoons.
66  E Wyrall, *The Gloucestershire Regiment in the War, 1914-1918*, p.338.
67  203325 Pte G H Oliver (as he is referred to in the battalion narrative) was 21 years old when he died. According to the Commonwealth War Graves Commission database, he was actually Pte Gilbert Norman Oliver, a son of John and Martha Oliver, Cheltenham, Glos. His body would

comrades to escape. Pte Oliver was eventually overrun and killed, probably by a combination of grenades and small-arms fire. The remnants of these two platoons, together with the remaining platoon of the support company (C) and survivors of the left and right front companies (D and A), then organised themselves on a defensive line from the ridge above Perghele, across the valley to the right and up the next ridge above battalion headquarters. A platoon from the outpost company and a few details from the right front company, formed a defensive flank, facing north-east, with their right on the Cesuna–Canove Road. This line was formed at about 0730. There was then a sizeable gap between the Gloucesters and the left of the Oxfords.

In an unpublished memoir of his service in the war, how held at the Imperial War Museum, Sgt T C Bodington of 1/5th Gloucesters, described the Austrian attack on his section of the line:

> After some considerable time, the barrage lifted, and the enemy attack commenced. This was about 0700. Sgt Broughton shouted to me: "Can you see them?" to which I replied "They're coming through the trees. He said: "Hold on and I will send reinforcements." I waited until the first wave was about 50 yards when I gave the order to fire. On our left a gap was blown in the wire where many men fell from our fire. We continued firing on on-coming Austrians until they got into dead ground in front of our post, when we made use of our bombs …
>
> On our right … the fighting seemed to be in our rear. At this point, an Austrian had gained a footing on our little plateau. This man I shot as I felt we were being closed in on three sides. I sent Lyons off to get some assistance. He returned with the news that company headquarters was surrounded… At this point everything happened so quickly, and we were immediately surrounded. I received a bullet wound to by right upper arm, which severed an artery, and I was bleeding profusely… I remember no more until I came around to find myself kicked in the buttocks by an Austrian who pulled me up from the bottom of the trench on to my feet [and] led me to a point where prisoners were being collected."[68]

Observing from the right flank, Norman Gladden described the Austrian assault tactics:

> The attackers, appearing to enjoy charmed lives, then put something into the wire and ran back quickly. The bomb or torpedo exploded with considerable concussion, blowing a complete section of the wire into the air and clearing a passage through the belt. It was an amazing feat.
>
> A party of enemy then rushed the gap under cover of the dense smoke from the explosion and were in the trench in a matter of seconds. Almost simultaneously, a stooping figure appeared above the brow about 25 yards in front of us, an enemy soldier, bowed down with the weight of some infernal contrivance, a flame-thrower as we subsequently discovered.

---

have been recovered after the battle but was not identified and as a result he probably lies in Boscon or Magnaboschi British Cemeteries under a headstone marked "Known Unto God". He is commemorated on the Giavra Memorial to the Missing.

68  IWM: Boddington Papers. See also Cassar, *The Forgotten Front*, pp.156-57.

The trench belched fire from end to end and the poor, brave devil fell forward on the skyline, riddled by dozens of bullets."[69]

On the left of the 1/5th Gloucesters, 1/5th R Warwickshires reported to 143rd Brigade headquarters at 0650 that shelling had increased and become intense, especially on their left. According to the brigade narrative, this was the last message received from that battalion. This is incorrect. It may have been the last message received from the Commanding Officer, but there were other messages sent and received from battalion headquarters later in the morning. At 0755, an unconfirmed message arrived at the brigade visual signalling station saying that the battalion visual station at Perghele had been bombed (attacked with grenades). Five minutes later, the Brigade Intelligence Officer arrived back at Carriola from 1/5th R Warwicks, with the news that the enemy had launched an infantry assault. Parties were seen coming out of the woods and entering Perghele and shortly afterwards, large numbers of enemy were observed "swarming down the slopes of Ambrosini Hill and Hill 975". This was confirmed by the Brigade OP, which was by now functioning more effectively as the early-morning mist began to lift. Capt Gedye, A Bty, 240th Artillery Brigade, in an artillery OP high up in the pines on the slopes of Monte Lemerle, also spotted this advance. The Battery War Diary notes that "A/240 engaged and dispersed three Coys of enemy infantry seen advancing towards our lines from Ambrosini".[70]

There is no 1/5th R Warwicks battle narrative for this action in the files of the National Archives so, apart from some fairly cursory notes in the battalion war diary, written after the fact, and some entries in the brigade account of the fighting, there is no official contemporaneous record of what actually happened to this battalion at the start of the battle. Lt Col Barnett, who conducted an inspection of the Warwickshire and Gloucestershire sections of the line, after the front had been re-taken on the 16th, pieced together how he thought the Austrians had attacked:

> One or possibly two posts close to the junction [between the two battalions] were destroyed, together with the whole of their garrisons, during the preliminary bombardment and barrage, by direct hits from heavy shells. The attackers, taking advantage of this, filtered in, and immediately turning outwards, were able to take the next posts in flank or even reverse.[71]

In 1922, Lt Charles Carrington, tasked with producing the battalion's published war record, also created an account, presumably drawing on the scant details in the war diary and some individual recollections. According to his version, an Austrian attack against D Company, holding the right front, developed at around 0700. The company was quickly overwhelmed by the initial assault, "with large numbers killed or taken prisoner". The Company Commander, Capt J B Florance was captured before he could report the enemy's arrival to battalion headquarters.[72] Interestingly, on casualties, the battalion war diary has this to say:

---

69  N Gladden, p.124.
70  TNA WO 95/4246: 240th Brigade RA War Diary.
71  G Barnett, p.73.
72  C E Carrington, *War Record of 1/5th Royal Warwickshire Regiment*, p.70.

The enemy's losses during his attack were severe. It is estimated that 200 enemy dead were lying in our lines. About 150 prisoners were captured … **But our losses were light.**[73]

The battalion's losses were actually recorded as totalling 79 over the course of this battle. Of these, 17 (2 Officers, 15 ORs) were killed in action. 29 (2 Officers and 27 ORs) were wounded, and 31 (3 Officers, 28 ORs) were missing (many of the missing were later found to be prisoners). To put this into perspective, during an earlier action by this battalion, when it attacked east of the Steenbeek, near St Julien, on 5-7 October 1917, losses amounted to 243 – 4 Officers and 55 ORs killed in action with a further five officers and 177 ORs wounded and 7 ORs missing. Obviously, losses in an attack are likely to be greater than in defence. However, the total killed on 15th June, although tragic for the families of all those concerned, did not amount to 'large numbers' by Great War standards, although the number of "missing" at 31, seems high for an action of this sort, given that the battalion was in defence, within its own lines, rather than attacking over muddy, shell-torn ground such as in the Ypres salient, where soldiers could disappear into the mud and shell holes, never to be seen again.

Carrington believes the first news of the penetration came from the team manning the battalion OP near Perghele, who reported that the enemy were approaching them along a ravine. Maj Bindloss, the acting commanding officer, sent forward the Adjutant, Capt E P Q Carter MC, and the Intelligence Officer, 2Lt T L Foode, to try to find out what was happening, but they ran straight into a party of enemy soldiers and were surrounded, Foode being killed, and Carter taken prisoner. B Company, high up on a spur on the left, with good observation over the line and the enemy's avenues of approach, was not attacked.[74] Shortly after this, Maj Bindloss was himself killed, apparently "rifle in hand", leading an attack to re-capture the battalion visual signalling station.[75] The circumstances surrounding Bindloss's demise are not included in the Brigade narrative, nor in the short account in the battalion's war diary. However, Fanshawe's after-action report records that Bindloss:

> … had been killed, actually using a rifle, and the second-in-command, Maj Watson, wounded leading a local counter-attack to re-take the Visual Signalling Station.[76]

There is no other primary evidence within the National Archives files to support this statement relating to Bindloss. The battalion War Diary simply notes that "Maj Bindloss was killed and Capt Watson wounded shortly after the attack opened". It is possible that Fanshawe received the information regarding Bindloss from a survivor.

Acting Commanding Officer of 1/8th R Warwicks, Maj Whitehouse, who, with his headquarters group and a rifle company had moved up into the railway tunnel at Cesuna as part of the Divisional Defence Plan, was struggling for situational awareness until the commander of the 143rd Trench Mortar Battery, Capt Wales, appeared, at around 0800, with news of the enemy break-in. Whitehouse immediately ordered his rifle company to take up defensive positions in front of the local church, facing north-east towards the front line, down the valley from

---

73  TNA WO 95/2756/2: 1/5th R Warwickshire Regiment War Diary.
74  C E Carrington, p.70.
75  G Barnett, p.74.
76  TNA WO 95/4244: Fanshawe AAR.

which the enemy were likely to approach. This provided additional support for the north end of the Cesuna Switch.[77]

On the right of the British line, at 0510, the left front company of 1/4th Oxfords, reported that the road and railway arch, just behind their front, was being heavily shelled and that there had been no communications along the front line since 0410. At 0550 the right front company messaged that it too was being heavily shelled. Battalion headquarters despatched a scouting patrol towards the right to try to gain some 'ground truth'. Returning at 0700, the patrol reported that the right front company headquarters could not be reached due to the intensity of the bombardment and that the enemy appeared to be attacking in force.

In fact, the Oxfords' first contact with the Austrian infantry was just before 0700 when they reported the enemy attacking their "tree posts"[78] just inside the woods in front of the main line, the message being received by 145th Brigade headquarters at around 0945.[79] This is probably the scene that was witnessed by Norman Gladden, from his position just to the right of the Oxfords:

> The barrage was lifting… Over to the left, where a tongue of forest stretched forward, along the far side of the depression, through the dividing mists, I saw a remarkable sight. An officer in strange uniform on horseback was galloping up and down marshalling a column of enemy troops into the woods, where they were quickly lost to view.
>
> A crackle of rifle fire came from among the trees on our left front; a red light shot up in the valley. And still our artillery maintained their extraordinary silence. The rifle fire developed into an unbroken rattle, and it was obvious that the enemy were working their way through the woods towards the front line.[80]

At 0710 the Oxfords fired their SOS rockets from battalion headquarters. There was no response from the artillery. At 0715, the battalion commander learned that the enemy had penetrated the line on the right, at the inter-divisional boundary, and was advancing towards his headquarters. HQ company, cooks, clerks, orderlies, was quickly pushed out, under Maj Pickford, to provide additional protection. At 0750, the Bucks Battalion in the Lemerle Switch reported to brigade that the enemy was heavily attacking both front line battalions. At the same time, the Oxfords told brigade the enemy was close up to their front-line trench. Then, at 0821, they reported that the line was broken, but that they were holding a position around Hill 1021, preventing a further advance. Meanwhile, although brigade received a report a few minutes after 0900 that the Oxfords were in touch with the 1/5th Gloucesters on their left, this turned out to be a mistake and arose from the fact that the Gloucesters' right post had joined up with the Oxfords as the enemy had broken in. In reality, the Oxfords' left flank was in the air and they were dangerously exposed.

---

77  TNA WO 95/2756/2: 1/8th Royal Warwickshire Regiment War Diary.
78  The 4/Oxfords had prepared rifle and Lewis Gun posts in the trees just inside the edge of the woods, 3—400 yards in front of their main front line, designed to disrupt and hold up an enemy advance. These posts were manned by some of the outpost company, who took up the positions as they withdrew earlier in the morning.
79  TNA WO 95/4250: 145th Brigade War Diary
80  N Gladden, pp,121-22.

At divisional headquarters, General Fanshawe received three messages in quick succession, the third one finally confirming the Austrian infantry attack. The first, at 0755, was from the GHQ OP, and reported increased shelling in Squares 23, 33 and 43 (the whole of the divisional front). This meant the enemy guns were being brought back to hammer the front line, hoping to keep the defenders' heads down as the assaulting infantry approached. At 0806 an Artillery Observation Group (recorded as 24th Artillery, but more likely 240th or 241st Brigade, RFA[81]) reported rifle and machine gun fire and heavy shelling on the 48th Division's front. This small-arms fire was an indication that the infantry were engaged. Five minutes later, a Sixth Italian Army OP reported seeing SOS flares going up from Square 23 and very heavy machine gun fire. Square 23 includes the frontage held by 143rd Brigade's 1/5th R Warwicks. At 0825 the Italians also reported seeing Austrians in the front line at Perghele. Between these last two messages, Fanshawe ordered Brigadier-General Strong, the divisional CRA, to put down the SOS barrage in front of Square 23 and, for good measure, included Square 33. By the time the artillery opened fire on SOS lines, however, it was too late to help the battalions in the front line to repel the assault. Enemy infantry had already penetrated the British line and were pushing forward into the woods in front of Monte Lemerle, where, for the time being, they were relatively unscathed by the British defensive barrage – but not, as it happened, from a few individual artillery pieces and their gunners, who would play a significant part in the next phase of the fighting.

## Situation at 0900

From a division and brigade perspective, by 0900 the situation along the front was beginning to clarify after some early confusion. On the right, it was known that the Oxfords' line had been penetrated at the junction with 11th Northumberland Fusiliers of 23rd Division, and on their left at the junction with 1/5th Gloucesters. The Oxfords were holding the enemy on a new line, but their flanks were in the air. Likewise, in the centre, the Gloucesters had been penetrated on both flanks and the enemy had then pushed through the gaps and swung right and left to attack the line from the rear, forcing a fighting withdrawal. The surviving Gloucesters had worked their way back, some to Cesuna Switch and some to Lemerle Switch, or just in front of it. On the left, the 1/5th R Warwicks' right front company had been over-run and the survivors had established a defensive position, a little way back from the original front line. Their left front company had not been engaged. The Divisional Defensive Scheme had been put into operation. Reinforcements had started to move up. The switch lines had been manned, along with the defences on the northern slopes of Monte Lemerle. The break-in had not yet become a break-through and preventing this from happening now became Fanshawe's main priority.

---

81  There was no 24th Artillery in the XIV Corps order of battle.

## Holding and Driving the Enemy Back

There is some evidence that for a short period around 0900-1000, Fanshawe was worried that the situation was about to deteriorate. The enemy appeared to be building up their strength in the pocket: an Italian OP reported seeing machine gun teams moving up. Austrians were still advancing from Perghele to Villa Brunialti, threatening the centre of Cesuna Switch, 1/5th R Warwicks' battalion headquarters, in Square 33, was believed to be surrounded. Over on the right, the Oxfords messaged at 0935 that the enemy was in possession of Hill 1021, threatening battalion headquarters nearby. At 0950 143rd Brigade's Brigade Major returned from a personal reconnaissance and reported that the southern end of the Cesuna Switch, near its junction with Polygon Trench, was also under pressure.

In response, Fanshawe ordered his reserve brigade, 144th, to move the two battalions still on the plain up to Carriola and called forward both the 144th brigade commander (Lt Col Tomkinson) and 48th Machine Gun Battalion commander (Lt Col Clarke) to divisional headquarters for briefings and orders. He also gave instructions for 144th Brigade to be prepared to move the battalion already at Serona to garrison the defences at Monte Pau, well to the divisional rear. This latter move, whilst a sensible precaution in the circumstances, suggests that there was some concern that the Divisional Defence Scheme might be under strain.

Having conducted a quick appreciation of the situation, based on the information he had available, at 0950 he issued orders for 1/7th R Warwickshires to counter-attack to clear the Cesuna Switch and hold the northern end including Guardiano.

The most comprehensive and detailed account of the action on the 143rd Brigade front during this period is provided by Lt Col Knox, Commanding Officer of 1/7th R Warwicks, in his personal narrative, reported up through the chain of command on 17th June. According to this, at 10.10am he received the following from division, under Fanshawe's signature:

> Enemy reported advancing from Perghele to Cesuna Switch and at 0900 to near Villa Brunialti. Drive them back and hold Cesuna Switch, especially the south end.[82]

With his company commanders already at his headquarters, Knox issued the following orders:

- D Company (Capt E B Mitford MC) to recapture and re-establish the Cesuna Switch from Brunialti to the front line and then to retake Perghele. Maj A S Alabaster, the Bn second in command, was despatched to take charge of operations on the left.
- B Company (Capt Reynolds MC) to establish his company in Cesuna Switch from Brunialti to the road south of Guardiano and to assist in recapture of Brunialti if lost.
- A Company (Capt Anthony MC) to garrison Cesuna Switch from the road south of Guardiano to the Lemerle Switch and get in touch with the garrison of this switch (Lemerle).
- C Company – in reserve.

---

82  TNA WO 95/2756/1: Lt Col Knox, CO 1/7th Royal Warwickshire Regiment personal narrative.

The companies were on the move within a few minutes, heading down the valley. Knox accompanied the leading company. This move, and the subsequent counter-attack, were exactly as practiced by this battalion a few days earlier. On reaching the valley floor, south of the hamlet of Valle, he encountered two 18-pdr guns firing over open sights, up the valley, towards a building marked on contemporary maps as Clo.[83] This is located just to the east of the light railway, where it crosses the track known as Pine Avenue on the outskirts of Cesuna. The guns, of 12 Battery, 35th Brigade (belonging to 7th Division) were under Maj Colin Jardine, covered by a party of gunners led by Lt Col Hugh Oldham, the Commanding Officer. These guns were continuing in action despite being under heavy fire from Austrian machine gun teams near the road, south of Guardiano, supported by personnel from D Bty, 240th Brigade RFA.[84] Oldham and Jardine briefed Knox on the local position, pointing out parties of enemy crossing the railway at Clo and making for the Lemerle Switch.

As Knox's centre company (C) got into position to mount the first phase of their counter-attack, they came under fire from the woods around Guardiano and the enemy could be seen attempting to cut the wire in front of Brunialti. The Austrians made three attempts to get through the wire and each time they were driven back by fire from two 1/7th R Warwicks' Lewis Guns. The left (south) end of the Lemerle Switch seemed to be thinly garrisoned at this stage so Knox sent a platoon from his right company (A) to reinforce the position until other troops came up. In the meantime, the Officer Commanding the right company (Capt Anthony), had collected some 1/5th Gloucesters men, together with small groups of Royal Engineers, and Royal Artillery personnel who were in the area, totalling about 50, and put them into the junction between Polygon Trench (a continuation of Polderhoek Trench and Lemerle Switch) and Cesuna Switch before getting in touch with the Bucks Battalion, further up Polygon Trench. This meant there was now a continuous British line stretching from the right of the Lemerle Switch across Polderhoek and Polygon Trench and down Cesuna Switch towards Brunialti. Knox placed two platoons from his reserve in strong positions among the rocks south of Valle and two more around the junction of the Valle-Cesuna track. The centre and southern portions of Cesuna Switch were now reasonably secure, providing Knox with a firm baseline from which to mount his attack.

One of the 1/7th R Warwicks reserve platoons helped to pull an 18-pdr onto the high ground near Valle and the gunners immediately began to bombard Guardiano, Clo and the slopes of Monte Lemerle, south-east of Clo, over open sights. According to Knox, this fire "considerably checked the enemy", and Knox was convinced that the part played by Jardine and his gunners, who stuck to their task under withering enemy machine gun fire, was largely responsible for clearing up a potentially dangerous situation, buying him time to establish a firm garrison in the Cesuna Switch between the railway and Polygon/Polderhoek Trench.

D Company 1/7th R Warwicks now launched their counter-attack. A platoon advanced to the ridge at Traverso South and established a post, 100 yards south of Traverso, where they were held up. A second platoon was pushed down the Cesuna Switch (north) to drive out any enemy who were there, reaching as far forward as the 1/5th R Warwicks cookhouse, just behind the original front line. On the way they had launched a series of bombing attacks, forcing the enemy

---

83   Clo is not a name in itself, although it was used as such in some British accounts. Clo is, in fact, an abbreviation of *Casello*, which is Italian for toll booth, or in connection with railways, a signal box.
84   TNA WO 95/2749: 240th Brigade RFA War Diary.

to withdraw, killing about 30 and capturing 7. Another platoon took up position on a hill in front of Brunialti. At 1315 Knox received a message that the switch line was now secure up to Brunialti and also from there to 100 yards south of Traverso. However, the enemy continued to hold Perghele with a strong force and his left company was unable to make further progress, being enfiladed by machine guns in the woods overlooking the northern end of the switch. D Company was later ordered to hold this position until the morning.

Knox then decided to attack Guardiano, commencing at 1400. He had an 18-pdr repositioned to provide artillery support for the assault and at 1355 the gunners slammed several rounds into the building. Following close behind the short bombardment, Knox and a platoon 'rushed in", capturing a machine gun and establishing strong-points, before pushing on up the Cesuna–Canove Road and the railway to drive the enemy out of Clo. According to the 143rd Brigade record, Maj Corsan, Officer Commanding, D Bty, 240th Artillery Brigade, RFA, was bringing back the personnel of his battery, which had been surrounded and over-run by the enemy, losing their guns. He was told the situation on the left and asked to garrison Guardiano, which he immediately did. The 240th Artillery Brigade war diary records:

> OC D/240 reported enemy holding woods about H33 Central, some 800 yards from the battery. D Bty was assisting to hold Cesuna Switch, firing first charge…[85]
>
> D/240 continued to man their guns until the position became untenable owing to enemy machine gun fire. Personnel then retreated with breech blocks and dial sights and assisted personnel of 12 Bty to man two of their guns which were in rear of D/240.
>
> After evacuating his position, Maj Corsan armed his men with rifles and assisted to hold Cesuna Switch.[86]

From here the Warwickshires advanced up the Cesuna–Roncalto Road (Pine Avenue) to the junction with C Track. By this stage, his right flank was exposed and heavy machine gun fire from the Cesuna-Canove road and to the north-east of it, had checked his momentum. Pulling forward reinforcements from Cesuna Switch, he sent a platoon to his right to cover his open flank and sent two others to the left to try to outflank the machine guns holding up the advance. He also ordered B Company, holding the line from the Brunialti to Cesuna Road, to move forward, which they did, in the face of a heavy machine gun barrage. The line now ran from Brunialti due east to the Cesuna–Canove Road and then on to the junction at the southern end of the track connecting Cesuna–Roncalto Road with the Cesuna–Canove Road.

Meanwhile, at around midday, as it was becoming clear that there was no attack developing south of Ambrosini, the CO of 1/6th R Warwicks sent Capt Linfoot forward with his company with orders to reinforce the 1/5th Battalion's headquarters party, under Regimental Sergeant Major Townley, who were surrounded but continuing to hold off the enemy amongst the headquarters buildings to the south of Perghele. Linfoot was also instructed to try to work east along the front-line trench and counter-attack the enemy from the west. Before committing his force, Linfoot decided to conduct a personal reconnaissance. Leaving his company at Contra

---

85   The "firing first charge" in this instance refers to a 4.5in howitzer, which operated with variable propellant charges, depending on the range to the target. First charge was the smallest of these, suggesting that the target was very close.
86   TNA WO 95/2749: 240th Artillery Brigade War Diary.

Graser, he went forward, accompanied only by his orderly, along the Cavrari–Canove Road and then by a short length of trench to the battalion headquarters. There he found RSM Townley continuing to command the defenders, with large numbers of enemy on the bluff, north of the HQ buildings, and snipers on Perghele Ridge. Having viewed and assessed the situation, Capt Linfoot returned to Contra Graser and sent two platoons to reinforce Townley while he deployed the remainder of the company from Casa Traverso, north-west towards the front line, in touch with 1/7th R Warwicks on the right. Making their way east along the front-line trench, Linfoot and his party bumped into the enemy, and he shot three with his pistol before being forced back along the trench. A bombing team was sent forward and established a block.

By 1730, 144th Brigade was ready to get into the fight. Parties of men from 1/6th Gloucesters came up and were pushed in on the right of Knox and the R Warwicks but made little progress through the woods in the face of a determined Austrian defence, which was supported by heavy machine gun fire. At 1930 they tried again, this time with help from 1/7th Worcesters, but once more, little was achieved, although at 1936 Lt Col Tomkinson reported to division that one of his companies had reached Pelly Cross, quite close to the Oxfords. At 2130, the three commanding officers – Knox, Lt Col H St G Schomberg, 1/4th Gloucesters, and Maj J F Bate, 1/7th Worcesters, held a council of war. They decided that they were unlikely to make further progress that evening, and that they should, therefore, consolidate on their present positions, with a view to resuming their attack in the morning.

On the left, meanwhile, 143rd Brigade decided to attack Perghele at 2100 intending to clear the enemy from this area and relieve the remaining pressure on the Cesuna Switch. A second company of 1/6th R Warwicks was sent forward to undertake this advance, arriving at 1930. Arrangements were made for a short, sharp, creeping artillery barrage, including Trench Mortars, located near Guardiano, to be put down on Perghele in conjunction with Vickers and Lewis Gun support. However, this attack failed as the Warwicks' routes into their objective were covered by enemy machine guns firing from the south and they could not make progress.[87]

Over on the right, the Oxfords were engaged throughout the day in a swaying fight which raged to and fro between the railway and the divisional boundary on the right as attack and counter-attack took place. At 0950 the Oxfords reported that they had regained nearly all of their old front line. But this was a short-lived success. Twenty minutes later they were forced out again as the Austrians mounted machine-guns in trees overlooking the position. Being fired on from above, they had little choice but to pull back into better cover. At 1035 145th Brigade ordered a company of 1/4th R Berkshires to move up as reinforcements. At 1115 the Oxfords' CO called for a protective barrage to be put down 200 yards in front of the original front line, probably to disrupt the enemy machine guns in the trees. However, when this request was received at brigade it was decided that without a clear picture of what was happening on their left, it would be inadvisable to fire on SOS lines in the area at that time. In addition, the brigade was rightly concerned that with the 1/7th R Warwicks advancing over on the left, it would be unwise to bring back the barrage on the right as this would have "broken the continuity of the barrage line". Without the SOS fire, the Oxfords and Berkshires clung on and by midday they were on a line that now ran from the railway arch on the left, across the Roncalto track north of Pelly Cross, around the front slopes of Hill 1021, to the raised ground above

---

87  TNA WO 95/2754/5: 143rd Brigade War Diary.

battalion headquarters. At 1230 1/5th Gloucesters reported that they had about 100 men in a line running west to east on the forward slope of Monte Lemerle, in front of Polygon Trench, with both flanks open, but holding their ground.

Around 1500, the enemy made another concerted effort to break the Oxfords. At about 1445 143rd Brigade reported that large numbers of enemy were advancing from Canove di Sotto towards the Oxfords' line, and just after 1500 that Austrians were massing in dead ground between Holla and Holla South. This information was passed on to the artillery and to GHQ, where BGGS, Gaythorne-Hardy, expressed concern that the division's guns were not bombarding the pocket between the two switch lines. He was worried that the Austrians would mass there and then punch their way through the support line by sheer force of numbers. Given that the situation in the pocket was still somewhat confused and that 143rd Brigade was counter-attacking from west to east in line with the Divisional Defence Scheme, the lack of shelling between the switch lines is perhaps not altogether surprising, since there would have been a danger of firing on friendly troops. When Gaythorne-Hardy's views were reported to Fanshawe (who was at 144th Brigade headquarters at the time), he ordered the pocket to be shelled, but this was limited to the division's own field-guns – 18-pounders and 4.5in howitzers. The use of these light guns would have struck a balance between attriting the enemy and minimising friendly casualties. An hour later, Gaythorne-Hardy called back, presumably after receiving reports of the shelling from the GHQ OP, to ask why only light guns were being used, and suggested that 6-inch howitzers should be employed instead. A divisional staff officer, his patience no doubt being sorely tested by this further intervention from above, had to explain that with two companies of 1/7th R Warwicks currently working their way towards the British bombardment, the use of heavy guns would increase the risk of 'blue-on-blue'[88] casualties. Faced with this unassailable logic, Gaythorne-Hardy backed down.[89] The incident is included here as an example of what modern soldiers would call "long screwdriver" syndrome, which occurs when a superior headquarters – usually with a less granular picture of what is happening on the ground – tries to interfere in how a more junior headquarters is fighting its bit of the battle. In this instance, it may also be evidence of some doubts at GHQ about Fanshawe and his staff and their ability to manage the situation, perhaps a manifestation of the misunderstanding and mistrust that sometimes existed between regulars and their territorial counterparts. Or it may simply have been an attempt, without having all the details, to add some senior thinking to a divisional headquarters that was short-handed due to the 'flu outbreak.

Meanwhile, with the Austrians pressing hard against the Oxfords' line, the left-hand company was eventually compelled to withdraw from the railway arch to just north of Pelly Cross and then south to the Lemerle Switch where they consolidated again and sent reinforcements to strengthen the position above battalion headquarters. The Oxfords continued to hold this line throughout the rest of the day and overnight, the Austrians making no further attempts to break through on this flank. The survivors of 1/5th Gloucesters remained spread among the garrisons of the Lemerle and Cesuna switch lines, with a small number still attached to the Oxfords.

---

88 The 'term blue-on-blue' is a relatively modern military term, but it has its genesis in the First World War. Friendly and enemy forces were identified as blue and red respectively, and this is often seen in trench maps with the allied lines marked in blue and the enemy in red. Blue-on-blue means inadvertently engaging one's own forces.
89 TNA WO 95/4258: 48th Division War Diary.

At about 2300 the enemy opened up a heavy machine gun barrage, within the pocket, which was maintained for much of the night, presumably as a form of defensive fire, designed to keep the British heads down and to make it difficult to move up stores and equipment in preparation for the next phase of operations. According to Edmonds, the Austrian fire did make movement more difficult, but, being directed high and into the pines, it caused comparatively few casualties.[90] However, rather than allow the fire to go unanswered, Lt Col Knox ordered a large amount of small-arms ammunition to be sent up and instructed his men to keep up a similar heavy fire with rifles and machine guns. The 143rd Brigade narrative noted that the result of this was "satisfactory".

## Situation at midnight 15th June

By midnight, the situation on the 48th Division front was relatively stable. After a day of hard fighting, the Austrians had advanced up to 1000 yards into the pocket formed by the Cesuna and Lemerle Switches and Polderhoek/Polygon trenches, but were being held, as per the Divisional Defence Scheme. The Cesuna Switch had been cleared and secured, although the enemy continued to hold Perghele. The enemy had attempted to consolidate the pocket and reinforce their gains, presumably in preparation for the next stage of the attack, but this had come at a heavy cost in terms of men and materiel. Reinforcements moving south from Canove towards the pocket had come under a relentless artillery bombardment once the early-morning mist had cleared, and gun batteries sited in the open had been neutralised by the counter-battery fire of British, Italian and French gunners who had enjoyed a target-rich environment for most of the daylight hours. The Austrian pause to regroup, whilst understandable, had blunted their early momentum. This reflected their failure to properly learn the lessons of Germany's Hutier tactics, which were to infiltrate to depth, by-passing strongpoints, which could be dealt with by follow-on forces, recognising that once an attack bogs down it is notoriously difficult to get it going again, as the defenders recover from the initial shock.

The 143rd Brigade, with some support from 144th Brigade and 145th Brigade, had counter-attacked from west to east, making some ground before being held up, and were now firm for the night. On the eastern flank, although the Oxfords, had been put under considerable enemy pressure, their line had flexed back and forward, but had not been broken, largely thanks to the judicious employment of cooks, clerks and orderlies from battalion headquarters, under Maj Pickford, and support from 1/4th Berkshires, 1/5th Gloucesters and the Bucks Battalion, as well as 11th Northumberland Fusiliers on their right. Pickford was awarded the DSO for this part in this action, the citation stating that he was constantly moving between battalion headquarters and the front line. "When the situation was critical, he personally took a handful of men and placed them exactly where they were required. But for his courageous example and quick initiative the battalion might several times have been surrounded."[91] At divisional headquarters, Fanshawe and his staff could afford to heave a small sigh of relief before getting

---

90  J E Edmonds, p.214.
91  *The London Gazette*, 24 September 1918, Col 11278.

down to the business of planning their next move, which would involve the deployment of the uncommitted element of his reserve brigade – 1/8th Worcesters.

## Final Push

Thirty minutes after midnight, Fanshawe issued verbal attack orders, which were circulated on paper at 0230, with Zero set for 0430. Although the Official History and other accounts, including the GHQ narrative, treat this early-morning attack on 16th June as a separate event, it is clear from Fanshawe's after-action report that he conceived it as a continuation of the counter-attack that had begun the previous afternoon. As Fanshawe himself wrote at the time:

> The final general counter-attack, which commenced … on the evening of 15th, was suspended during the night, and renewed again at daylight on the 16th, and not only cleared all our own line but led to the capture of many prisoners and much material in no-man's land.[92]

The 144th Brigade battle narrative sets out the Scheme of Manoeuvre for the resumption of the attack. 1/8th Worcesters had moved from Brusabo to Carriola during the early evening, their place in the Monte Pau defences being taken over by the 21st Manchesters of 91st Brigade, 7th Division, who had arrived in the mountains from the plains. The Worcesters received verbal attack orders at about 2200, followed by written orders as stated above. These were a model of simplicity and brevity: "The battalion will move into a position in front of Lemerle Switch and at 0430 on 16/6/18 will advance and clear the area up to our front line and make touch on the flanks."[93] Other units in the pocket were ordered to conform to the Worcesters' movement and advance in line.

Upon reaching Handley Cross, B and A Companies and Battalion HQ turned right while D and C moved to the left, both proceeding to their forming up point. B and D deployed on a line 200 yards in front of Lemerle Switch, B on the right and D on the left, with A and C companies behind them in support. The move up through the woods to the front line had been challenging, their progress being slowed by the darkness and the numerous trees that had fallen across the tracks, brought down by the enemy artillery barrage. Indeed, B and A companies only just made it in time, finally shaking out into their attack formation with just five minutes to spare.

At 0430, D Company set off to their front, gaining touch with 1/7th Worcesters on their left and passing through posts manned by 1/4th R Berkshires. They immediately ran into heavy machine gun and rifle fire but were able to make progress, driving the enemy before them as they advanced. The left platoon became detached, having moved too far to the left, where they joined forces with 1/7th Worcesters. The right platoon reached the railway line where they went firm and began to re-organise themselves while the platoon sergeant, Sgt Fox, going forward on his own, entered the original front line, finding only a few enemy snipers and stragglers. Returning, he briefed his platoon commander who then ordered a further advance, retaking

---

92  TNA WO 95/4244: Fanshawe AAR.
93  TNA WO 95/2760: 1/8th Worcesters War Diary.

the front line near the Ghelpac Fork at about 0610. Meanwhile, C Company and the remainder of D Company were formed up on Pine Avenue with elements of 1/7th Worcesters, 1/4th R Berkshires, 1/6th Gloucesters and 1/7th R Warwicks, and at 0730 this force advanced, with little opposition, through the woods to the front line, capturing several prisoners, most of them wounded, on the way. This section of the original front line, held by 1/5th Gloucesters, was soon firmly back in British hands.

On the right, B Company moved forward behind a screen of scouts, hardly troubled by the Austrians until they were within 20 yards of the Oxfords' former front line, where they came under machine gun and rifle fire from positions to the north. They continued to push forward, however, and re-occupied the front line by 0525. Bombing patrols were sent out to the left, to make contact with D Company and on the right, they quickly gained touch with 11th Northumberland Fusiliers of 23rd Division.

On the far left, in the 143rd Brigade sector, D Company, 1/8th R Warwicks attacking at around 0815, captured Perghele, at their second attempt, taking 17 prisoners and 8 machine guns, before advancing down to the old front line where a further 40 prisoners and three machine guns were captured. They then linked up with 1/6th R Warwicks, who had bombed their way along the line from the opposite direction. Further to the right, two platoons crossed the Ghelpac and captured approximately 100-150 Austrians and two machine guns, handing the prisoners over to the 1/6th Gloucesters before recovering a battery of 18-pdrs, a battery of 4.5-in Howitzers and a battery of Italian trench mortars that had been lost during the initial attack.

At this stage, enemy troops could be seen falling back, along the road to Roncalto and in the village itself and patrols were ordered to occupy Roncalto and the hill to the west. The patrols came under heavy artillery and machine gun fire as they advanced but they got into the enemy positions and killed or captured the garrisons, sending back two mountain guns, one machine gun and 19 prisoners. To the west, 1/8th Worcesters despatched a patrol of two platoons towards Canove, entering the enemy lines in front of the village and advancing north until they ran into large numbers of Austrians and were forced with withdraw. 145th Trench Mortar Battery troops managed to go back to the outpost line and recover two of the three tubes that had been hidden when the Austrians advanced the previous morning.

It quickly became clear that the Austrians were retreating in some disarray, and Cavan sensed an opportunity to exploit the situation. GHQ Chief of Staff, Gathorne-Hardy issued the following on his behalf:

> Daylight patrols today have taken prisoners and material from Ave (23rd Division) and have occupied Ambrosini (48th Division). It appears probable that the enemy on our front are largely demoralised and many are ready to surrender. C-in-C wishes arrangements made on receipt of this telegram to send out strong patrols and occupy the line given for the proposed operations on the 18th (i.e. no farther than the southern edge of the Val d'Assa and the southern exits of Asiago), except that from Ave it will be drawn back from our present front line. C-in-C does not wish these patrols to start until they are thoroughly organised but considers rapidity is essential. He wishes all patrol commanders firmly impressed with the following principles:
>
> 1. That if strong opposition is met with or opposition likely to cause considerable casualties the patrols are not to proceed.

2. The line [above] is not to become the line of resistance; our [original front] line remains the line of resistance.
3. The operation is not to be pushed beyond the objectives given for the 18th. Heavy artillery and neighbouring units must be informed of time of departure.

Reporting to Wilson on the result of these orders, Cavan said that during the following few hours his men "had the time of their lives". However, the Austrians were not as ready to surrender as he had hoped. They were already reorganising themselves and as the patrols moved forward, they were, in some cases, met by quite stubborn resistance, as the Austrian commanders brought up two brigades from their 24th Division to reinforce their line, clearly anticipating Cavan's move. The British troops were well-controlled, however, and as soon as stiff opposition was encountered, they withdrew as ordered, bringing with them many more prisoners and war booty, including artillery pieces and machine guns, which were recovered back across no-man's land in broad daylight, practically unmolested by artillery fire. Cavan attributed this to his own artillery's counter-battery work, which had neutralised many Austrian guns and may have discouraged others from opening fire and thus sharing the same fate.[94]

On the left, 143rd Brigade sent a platoon-sized patrol up to Ambrosini, covered by Vickers and Lewis Guns from the front line. They entered the enemy trenches without opposition. Three further platoons were quickly sent after them, supported by riflemen of 1/5th R Warwicks. The leading troops reached Ambrosini House and captured two officers and 10 other ranks from two dugouts there. Two machine guns and their teams were found near the top of Hill 975 and a third gun was discovered abandoned nearby. However, the enemy soon realised what was happening and opened fire from depth. In view of the clear instructions from GHQ not to incur significant casualties, the troops in Ambrosini were ordered back and Lt Col Pryor of 1/6th Gloucesters went forward and managed the withdrawal.[95]

The 48th Division sustained the following manpower losses. The casualty return below, collated by XIV Corps HQ, reflects loses between 15th and 18th June 1918:[96]

| Division | Killed | | Wounded | | Missing | |
| --- | --- | --- | --- | --- | --- | --- |
| | Off | OR | Off | OR | Off | OR |
| 7th Division | 0 | 9 | 7 | 53 | 0 | 47 |
| 23rd Division | 8 | 84 | 22 | 418 | 1 | 46 |
| 48th Division | 16 | 134 | 42 | 446 | 9 | 256 |
| GHQ Tps | 2 | 15 | 10 | 90 | 0 | 2 |
| Totals | 26 | 242 | 81 | 1,007 | 10 | 351 |

British casualties totalled 1717, including 117 Officers and 1600 Other Ranks, of which 903 were from 48th Division. Of the two divisions that had been in the front line during the battle, 48th Division clearly had the higher total number of casualties by some way.

94 TNA WO 100/852: Cavan-Wilson correspondence, 19th June 1918.
95 TNA WO 95/2754/5: 143rd Brigade War Diary.
96 TNA WO 95/4194: GHQ Italy (GS) War Diary.

Reporting on the action to the 6th Italian Army, on 30th June, GHQ identified the following units who had particularly distinguished themselves:

> Infantry: 11th Northumberland Fusiliers, 11th Sherwood Foresters (23rd Division); 1/7th Royal Warwicks, 1/4th Oxfordshire and Buckinghamshire Light Infantry (48th Division).
> Artillery: 35th Battery, 22nd Brigade, RFA, 12th Battery, 35th Brigade, RFA (7th Division); A Battery, 102nd Brigade, RFA (23rd Division); and a number of Italian batteries.[97]

The total number of prisoners captured was 19 Officers and 1060 Other Ranks while war booty amounted to seven Mountain Guns, 72 Machine Guns, 20 Flammenwerfers and one Trench Mortar. The same report noted that the battlefield was covered with enemy dead and Austrian casualties were estimated to have been "at least 6,000". Overall, it is hard to argue with the view that this was a massive victory for the British and a very heavy defeat for the opposition.

---

97  TNA WO 95/4244: 48th Division (GS) War Diary.

# 10

# Fanshawe 'Degummed'

Despite 48th Division's hard-fought but successful defence of its position in front of Asiago, just three days later, on 19th June 1918, the divisional commander, Major General Sir Robert Fanshawe, was ordered by Cavan to hand over command and return to England, his place being taken temporarily by Brigadier-General Julian Steele. The dismissal came 'out of the blue' and was a massive blow to Fanshawe personally, and to the 48th Division. In his farewell message he wrote: "I wish to thank all units for their devotion. I feel the parting so deeply that I will not say more than wish the Division collectively every success …"[1] Lt Col George Barnett described the news as "…certainly the hardest blow to the division which it received during the war", and that it was "received with the greatest consternation by all ranks".[2] Fanshawe had become something of a talisman to his troops, and his sudden removal would undoubtedly have been disconcerting for them, the loss made all the more difficult to bear since there was a general view among officers and men that his sacking was entirely unjustified. The division had performed well in difficult circumstances, they felt, and the action had been fought and won on the basis of Fanshawe's carefully worked-out defensive scheme, which had been practiced in advance and implemented largely as he had intended. His removal was perceived not just to be a slight against the man himself, but also as an unwarranted stain on the hard-won reputation of the division as a whole. As Lt Col Tomkinson, in temporary command of 144th Brigade during the battle, remarked in a letter to the editor of the Official History, Brigadier-General James Edmonds, afterwards, "48 Div were for some time mud to GHQ Italy".[3]

Was Fanshawe sacked with good cause? Can Cavan's action be vindicated on the basis of Fanshawe's performance at Asiago? Or was Fanshawe simply an unfortunate but necessary casualty incurred in the pursuit of some greater objective? The fate of the divisional commander was the subject of considerable debate among military men at the time, and in the years before the publication of the Official History in 1948. Some, particularly those who served with the division and who had known Fanshawe during his time in command, were of the view that he had been treated very unfairly and that his removal had been without justification. Writing to Edmonds, in 1944, Charles Carrington (by then back in uniform with the rank of Lt Col, acting

---

1   G Barnett, p.97.
2   G Barnett, p.95.
3   TNA CAB 45/84: Carrington to Edmonds correspondence, 28 June 1944.

as army liaison officer to Headquarters Bomber Command at Naphill, near High Wycombe), probably spoke for many divisional officers when he noted:

> We all thought … and I still think that the action of 15-16th June was a brilliant little victory.[4]

Others took a different view. Lt Col G W Howard, GSO1, head of the Operations branch at 7th Division headquarters, felt Cavan had been right to sack Fanshawe, "which put an end to the Divisional Commander feeding his troops with pieces of chocolate when inspecting the front lines early in the morning".[5] This is an interesting comment, because it appears to focus on Fanshawe's humanity and interest in the welfare of his troops, rather than his generalship. Howard seems to be saying that Fanshawe's dismissal was somehow justified because of his habit of handing out chocolate to cold, tired, frightened young soldiers during his frequent visits to the front line. Whatever it says about Fanshawe, it certainly says something about the attitude of Howard, and may be reflective of a particular section of the officer class at that time. If he had been considered to be "too soft" on his soldiers, or, perhaps, too popular with the rank and file, could that have been considered to be sufficient cause to have him removed? Fanshawe may have cared about his soldiers, and they liked and respected him for it, but that was not the same as being 'soft' on them. As those who had assaulted Poziéres or held the line at Le Sars on the Somme, or who had crossed the Steenbeek to capture the Springfield, Genoa and Hubner Farm strongpoints during Third Ypres would no doubt have testified, despite his popularity with the rank and file, he was a hard charger and not known for sparing his men when the situation demanded it.

Regrettably, there is no formal record that explains why Fanshawe was sent home after this battle. There is nothing specific in Cavan's regular reports to his superior, Sir Henry Wilson (Chief of the Imperial General Staff), nor in his personal papers, nor, indeed, in the War Office or War Cabinet files at the National Archives, that details the case for Fanshawe's fall from grace. This absence of a 'smoking gun' has left historians to attempt to piece together the case for the prosecution – and for the defence – from the limited evidence that remains. It is unsurprising, therefore, that the outcome of this scholarly enquiry is not a clear, indisputable conclusion but a lengthy list of possibilities, all of which can be refuted in one way or another. As a result, Fanshawe's reputation has been left in limbo. Thus far, it might be said, history has neither wholly convicted nor wholly acquitted him, and thus his reputation continues to bear the stain of his dismissal.

At a range of more than 100 years, and with such a dearth of source material, it may never be possible to reach an unequivocal view on this controversy that is sufficient to satisfy all sides in the debate. However, in the interests of doing justice to Fanshawe and Cavan, the case is revisited in the following pages.

Any reappraisal of Fanshawe's sacking must surely be based not only on the attitudes of today, but on the values and standards of the time. It would be grossly unfair to all concerned, and poor

---

4   TNA CAB/45: Carrington to Edmonds correspondence, 28th June 1944.
5   TNA CAB/45: Carrington to Edmonds correspondence, 28th June 1944. Also quoted in Cassar, *The Forgotten Front*, pp.162-63.

historical practice, to form an opinion on this matter by applying modern norms without also considering what was militarily acceptable in the second decade of the 20th century.

## Cavan and Fanshawe

If the decisions that led to Fanshawe's downfall are to be judged in a reasonable and even-handed way, this must be done on the basis of an understanding of the two men at the heart of this controversy and how they had been shaped and conditioned by their social status, education and military experience, alongside the prevailing circumstances on the Asiago plateau that day in June 1918, and the strategic situation across the main battle fronts.

So, who exactly were the two main actors in this drama? Born within a year of each other, Fanshawe and Cavan came from quite different social backgrounds, but they were both military professionals – products of the Victorian era of colonial soldering – who had shared many of the same experiences and followed broadly similar career paths. Like their peers, after commissioning into their respective regiments, they had each served in a range of regimental and staff appointments, broadening their experience as they moved up through the ranks. Neither's assent was meteoric until the outbreak of the First World War, when a rapidly-expanding army created a demand for commanders at all levels. Both achieved brigade and divisional command at roughly the same time, but while Fanshawe remained a Major General, Cavan, well-connected and highly-regarded at GHQ, was promoted to Lieutenant General after just six months, during which he had commanded the 50th Division and then the new Guards Division.

Fanshawe had more actual combat experience, having fought in India and also in South Africa, where his contribution was recognised with the award of the Distinguished Service Order. Cavan arrived in South Africa later than Fanshawe, missed the early actions, and although Mentioned in Despatches, was not thought to have done enough to warrant further honours. Fanshawe was a graduate of the Army's Staff College, although his course there had been cut short by the Second Boer War. He had held a key staff post with 2nd Division during the retreat from Mons and at the Marne and the Aisne. Cavan, conversely, had not attended Staff College, and had less operational staff experience. But he enjoyed links at the highest levels of society. He was, for example, one of a small number of senior officers – Haig was another – who maintained regular contact with the King through his Assistant Private Secretary, Major Clive Wigram.[6] In addition, it has been argued, because Cavan was a man of some financial means and thus not entirely reliant on his Army pay, he was prepared to be outspoken and contrary when the occasion demanded it, traits which could have been a double-edged sword, but which seem to have worked in his favour on most occasions.

Until his arrival in Italy, Fanshawe had never served under Cavan, but both would have been known to each other, certainly by reputation. The son of a clergyman, Henry Leighton Fanshawe and his wife, Ellen, Robert Fanshawe was born at South Weston, a tiny hamlet to the west of Chinnor in Oxfordshire, on 5th November 1863. He was the youngest of three soldier

---

6    G Sheffield and J Bourne (eds.), p.4.

brothers. The eldest, Lt General Sir Edward Fanshawe, and the middle brother, Lt General Sir Hew Fanshawe, both – uniquely – commanded V Corps during the First World War.

Educated at Marlborough College, Robert was commissioned into the 2nd Battalion, the Oxfordshire Light Infantry (formerly the 52nd Regiment of Foot) in 1883, serving in various regimental appointments in India, where he enjoyed polo and pig-sticking as well as seeing active service with the Mohmand Field Force and the Tirah Expeditionary Force. In early 1899 he was selected to attend Staff College at Camberley, Surrey, where, according to his obituary in The Times, he proved to be a student of exceptional ability. In November of that year, his Staff College course cut short, he left for South Africa.

Initially a staff officer to the Assistant Inspector-General of Communications, he was subsequently appointed adjutant of the 6th Battalion, Mounted Infantry, seeing operational service leading up to the Relief of Kimberley. He then took part in the successful pursuit of Boer General, Piet Cronje, and his force, as they withdrew from Magersfontein to Bloemfontein. Wounded at the Battle of Paadeberg in February 1900, he was back in action in time to take part in the fighting at Poplar Grove, Karee Siding (March 1900) and Houtnek (April 1900), after Bloomfontein had been captured. He was also present for the advance on Pretoria (May-June 1900) and fought at Diamond Hill (June 1900). He was then given command of a mobile column, serving in the Transvaal, Orange River Colony and Cape Colony until the end of the conflict.

Having been promoted to Major in September 1900, in August 1902 he was given the brevet rank of Lieutenant Colonel and in September of that year he was appointed Deputy Assistant Adjutant General on the staff of 4th Division. He married the former Miss Evelyne Katherine Isabel Knox, 11 years his senior, in October 1903. She was the daughter of Rev Robert Knox, (a Church of Ireland clergymen who became Archbishop of Armagh and the Lord Primate of All Ireland in 1886), and Mrs Catherine Delia Knox (nee FitzGibbon), and the sister of Second Boer War veteran, Lt Gen Sir Charles Edmond Knox. She died in 1943, aged 91 years.

Fanshawe returned to regimental duty in December 1903, taking command of his battalion in September 1907. Gazetted as a brevet colonel in March 1908 he was promoted substantively in 1911 and went to Aldershot in the post of General Staff Officer Grade 1 of 1st Division. It was in this role that he deployed with the British Expeditionary Force on the outbreak of war in August 1914, part of Haig's I Corps. He was present with the division at Mons and throughout the subsequent withdrawal south of the Forest of Mormal, all the way to the Marne, near Meaux, and then during the advance to the Aisne. As GSO1 he would have acted as the divisional Chief of Staff, coordinating all the activities of the General Staff branch within the divisional headquarters. In addition to overseeing training and intelligence he would have assisted his divisional commander, Major General Samuel Lomax, to plan operations and draft orders for issue to the division's infantry brigades and supporting arms and services, as well as directing operations as they progressed. There are examples of Operation Orders and other documents signed by him during this period in the divisional War Diary.[7]

On 20th September 1914, just after the successful attack at the Aisne and the following "race-to-the-sea", he was promoted to the rank of Brigadier-General and given command of 1st Division's 6th Infantry Brigade for the First Battle of Ypres. At the Battle of Festubert (May

---

7   TNA WO 95/1227: 1st Division War Diary.

1915), Fanshawe's brigade took part in the successful night attack, capturing the German first and support lines. After Festubert he was promoted to Major General and moved north to take over command of the 48th (South Midland) Division, then in the line near Ploegsteert Wood in Belgium. In the opening year of the war Fanshawe was Mentioned in Despatches three times. The first was in Sir John French's Despatch of October 1914. The second was in February 1915 and the third was in May, just after Festubert. Throughout the course of the war, Fanshawe was mentioned in despatches a total of eight times, including by successive Commanders-in-Chief, French and Haig, and by General Herbert Plumer in his final despatch from Italy in April 1918. He was created a Companion of the Order of the Bath (CB) in 1915, recognising his contribution to the war effort up to that point. In the King's Birthday Honours List for 1917 he was advanced to Knight Commander of the Order of the Bath and was knighted "in the field" by King George V at Albert, alongside his elder brother, Edward. In December 1918, together with Cavan and a number of other senior officers, he was awarded the Croce de Guerra by the King of Italy.[8]

On returning to the UK from Italy, he took over command of the home-based 69th (2nd East Anglian) Division from November until his retirement in August 1919, when he moved back to Oxfordshire to live at Lobbersdown near Milton Common. He retained his military links by taking up the chairmanship of the Oxfordshire Territorial Association and becoming the Honorary Colonel of the 1/7th Battalion, The Worcestershire Regiment, a unit that had been part of the 48th Division. He also served as a member of the Special Constabulary. A keen horseman, he rode with the South Oxfordshire Hounds.

Robert Fanshawe died, aged 83 years, at the Victoria Cottage Hospital in Lower High Street, Thame, not far from his home at Lobberstown, on 24th August 1946, the result of injuries sustained in a riding accident.[9]

Frederick Rudolph Lambart, the 10th Earl of Cavan, was born at Ayot St Lawrence in Hertfordshire on 16th October 1865, into an Anglo-Irish family. He could trace his roots back to Sir Oliver Lambart, the son of a London goldsmith, who was knighted by Elizabeth I for his contribution to the storming of Cadiz in 1596 and was subsequently appointed to be Governor of the Irish province of Connaught in 1601.

Rudolph or Ru, as he was sometimes known to friends, was the eldest son of the 9th Earl of Cavan, the long-serving Liberal MP for South Somerset, and a former naval officer who had served at Sevastopol, at the bombardment of Canton and at the storming of the Pei-Ho forts in 1860 during the China Wars (1856-60).

Educated at Eton, the young Rudolph was destined for military service. He joined the Eaton College Rifle Volunteers Corps in 1881, serving until 1884 and achieving the rank of Colour Sergeant before going up to Christ Church, Cambridge and thence on to the Royal Military Academy Sandhurst. Commissioned into the Grenadier Guards in 1885, his "short and stumpy" build soon earned him a rather unflattering soubriquet. During his first parade in "blue"[10], at Chelsea Barracks in London, the senior subaltern remarked that his trousers "were far too short

---

8   *The Edinburgh Gazette*, No. 13360, 2nd December 1918, p.4350.
9   Obituary, Maj General Sir Robert Fanshawe, *The Times*, 26th August 1946.
10  No. 1 Dress Uniform.

and a yard too broad in the seat".[11] From then on, he was known as "Fatty" in regimental circles, which, understandably, he felt was "a rotten nickname".[12]

During his early years with the regiment, Cavan found himself with gambling debts amounting to £1,300 (£116,000 in 2022 prices), which might have cost him his commission had his father not agreed, with some reluctance, to meet the liabilities.[13]

When his father succeeded to the family title in 1887, Rudolph took on the courtesy title of Viscount Kilcoursie. In 1890 he went to Canada as Aide de Camp to the Governor General, Lord Stanley (afterwards the 16th Earl of Derby) and in August 1897 he returned to the Grenadiers as regimental adjutant, being promoted to the rank of Captain in October 1898. When the war in South Africa broke out in 1899, he was given command of a company (No 7 Company) and embarked for the Cape with his regiment's 2nd Battalion, which was attached to the 16th Brigade of 8th Division. Although he missed the war's early engagements, he participated in the final stages of the march to Pretoria and was present at the actions at Biddulphsberg and Wittebergen in July 1900. He went with his battalion to the Transvaal for a time in 1901 before returning to the Orange Free State and remaining there until the end of the war. He was mentioned in despatches during his time in South Africa.

His father died in 1900 and Viscount Kilcoursie assumed the title the Earl of Cavan. On his return to Britain, he continued his regimental service, promoted to Major in October 1902 and Lt Colonel in February 1908, assuming command of the 1st Battalion. After four happy years as Commanding Officer, Cavan decided to leave the army.

> In January 1912 I walked out of Chelsea Barracks very sad in spirit, but quite resolved that such a command was a fitting ending to my military career. I sent in my papers, retired to Wheathampstead, and took the Hertfordshire Hounds.[14]

Recalled to the colours on the outbreak of war in August 1914, at the age of 49 years, he was given command initially of the 2nd Brigade of the 1st London Division of the Territorial Force, which had been mobilised for home defence. After just five weeks in that role, he was sent to France to assume command of the 4th (Guards) Brigade, replacing Brigadier-General Robert Scott-Kerr, who had been wounded during the retreat from Mons. Cavan took over the brigade on 19th September, during the last days of the Battle of the Aisne, before moving to Flanders with the 2nd Division for the First Battle of Ypres where he distinguished himself on the right of Haig's I Corps front. His brigade was further heavily engaged during the Battle of Festubert in May 1915. That month he was gazetted as Companion of the of the Order of the Bath (CB) in the same honours list as Fanshawe.[15]

Promoted to Major General on 29th June 1915, in recognition, no doubt, of his sterling work at Ypres and Festubert, he took command of 50th Division. He was recalled to London to receive his CB from the King at Windsor on 19th July. During a private audience, after the inauguration, he was told informally by the King – and formally later by Lord Kitchener – that he had

---

11  CCC Cavan unpublished memoir.
12  CCC Cavan unpublished memoir.
13  CCC Cavan unpublished Memoir.
14  CCC Cavan unpublished memoir.
15  *The London Gazette* ???

been selected to command the new Guards Division.[16] He took the division to France in time to participate in the Battle of Loos in September 1915. By January 1916, Haig had promoted him to Lt General and put him in charge of the newly-formed XIV Corps for the Battle of the Somme, initially as part of Rawlinson's Fourth Army (Delville Wood, Guillemont, Ginchy, Flers-Courcelette, Morval and Le Transloy). He and his corps moved to Allenby's Third Army for the advance to the Hindenburg Line, and then to Gough's Fifth Army for the Third Battle of Ypres (Pilkem, Langemarck, Menin Road, Polygon Wood, Broodseinde, Poelcapelle and Passchendaele 1 and 2).

Described as one of the outstanding Corps Commanders of the war,[17] Haig certainly had a high regard for Cavan[18] and his proactive approach to Corps Command, which involved giving his divisional commanders firm, clear direction without stifling their creativity and initiative. He had considered Cavan as a potential replacement for General Sir Charles Monro, to command First Army, but opted to keep him at XIV Corps and appointed his protege, Horne, instead.[19] CIGS, Sir William Robertson, was also a fan. Writing to Haig in April 1917, about Cavan as a potential successor for Gen Sir Archibald Murray in Palestine, Robertson noted: "You won't like losing him, but we need a good man."[20] In the end, Murray was replaced by General Sir Edmund Allenby.

Cavan's accomplishments during the Somme operations and at Third Ypres had marked him out as a talented and tenacious leader who was quite prepared to "push back" against higher direction if he thought it was wrong. As the Somme offensive concluded in November 1916, Rawlinson, acting on direction from GHQ, ordered Cavan to attack Le Transloy, largely to ensure that the French, attacking to the south, would have their left flank protected. The ground conditions were appalling, and Cavan felt he was being forced into an attack that had little hope of success. On 5th November 1916, he wrote to Rawlinson:

> I assert my readiness to sacrifice the British right rather than jeopardise the French…but I feel I am bound to ask if this is the intention, for a sacrifice it must be. It does not appear that a failure would much assist the French, and there is a danger of this attack shaking the confidence of the men and officers in their commanders. No-one who has not visited the front trenches can really know the state of exhaustion to which the men are reduced.

Rawlinson having visited the front, agreed with Cavan and reported this to Haig. However, under considerable pressure from the French, Haig overruled Rawlinson and Cavan and the attack went ahead as originally ordered.[21]

On 5th November 1917, as the fighting for the Passchendaele Ridge was coming to a close, Cavan was ordered to Italy with two divisions – 41sth and 23rd – the initial British contribution to bolster the Italian army in the aftermath of the Caporetto disaster. He had requested

---

16 CCC Cavan unpublished memoir.
17 Andy Simpson, British Corps Command on the Western Front, 1914-1918 in Sheffield and Todman (eds.), *Command and Control on the Western Front*, pp.97-118.
18 G Sheffield, *The Chief*, p.193.
19 G Sheffield and J Bourne (eds.), p.218.
20 D R Woodward (eds.), *The Military Correspondence of Field Marshal Sir William Robertson*, p.175.
21 G Sheffield, p.193.

that his force should include his "beloved Guards Division", but Haig, already deeply unhappy about losing a well-regarded corps commander and a number of infantry divisions, would not countenance it.[22] On arrival at Mantua, Cavan assumed the dual roles of corps commander and Commander-in-Chief of British Forces Italy. However, as the force was expanded by a further two divisions (7th and 48th), with two more (5th and 21st) to follow, together with a second Corps headquarters (XI Corps) under Lt General Sir Richard Haking, he was obliged to hand over command of the British Contingent to General Sir Herbert Plumer, who had been moved from Second Army to assume the role of Commander-in-Chief, Italy. The arrival of 21st Division was subsequently cancelled due to concerns about the German counter-attack at Cambrai. By the following March, with the post-Caporetto situation well-stabilised, and a large-scale German offensive on the Western Front becoming more likely by the day, Plumer was recalled to the Western Front, together with 41st Division, Haking's XI Corps headquarters, and later, 5th Division. On 10th March, Cavan reverted once more to Commander-in-Chief and Corps Commander.

Following the Battle of the Piave (15-24th June 1918), and after weeks of behind-the-scenes manoeuvring, mainly by the new CIGS, Sir Henry Wilson, Cavan was promoted to full General and given command of a new Italian Tenth Army of two corps – one Italian (XI Corps) and one British (XIV Corps – 7th and 23rd Divisions), now under Major General J M Babington, for an Italian offensive, later known as the Battle of Vittorio Veneto. This attack, led by Cavan's Army, commenced on 24th October and routed the Austrians on the Piave front, leading to an armistice on 3rd November.

With the war over, Cavan returned to Great Britain in 1919 and went onto half-pay as a General without a post. He was appointed to head Aldershot Command in early 1921 and the following October he was sought by the Prime Minister, Mr David Lloyd George, to go to the US as Head of the British Military Mission, attached to Arthur Balfour's staff for the Washington Limitation of Armaments Conference. As the conference was closing in December, he received a telegram from the Secretary of State for War, Sir Laming Worthington-Evans, offering him the position of CIGS in succession to Sir Henry Wilson, an unusual appointment for an officer who was not a Staff College graduate. He held the position for four years, overseeing a period of significant reduction in the Army's budget and manpower, as required by the Geddes Report of February 1922. Cavan eventually retired back to Wheathampstead in 1926, having served under three different Secretaries of State including Lord Derby and Mr Stephen Walsh, the first Labour MP to hold that post, in Ramsay McDonald's short-lived administration of 1923-24.

Appointed to the honorary rank of Field Marshal in 1932, on the outbreak of the Second World War, in 1939, and the subsequent establishment of the Local Defence Volunteers, which became the Home Guard, Cavan donned uniform once more to command the Hertfordshire contingent.

Lord Cavan died, after a short illness, at the London Clinic, on 28th August 1946 at the age of 80, leaving behind his second wife, the former Lady Joan Mulholland, daughter of the Fifth Earl of Stafford, daughters, Elizabeth and Joanna and step-daughter, Daphne, together with an unfinished and unpublished memoir, entitled *"Recollections Hazy But Happy"*.[23]

---

22  CCC Cavan unpublished memoir.
23  CCC GBR/0014/CAVN 1/1: Cavan Papers.

## Importance of Divisional Command

Effective command at divisional level was critical to overall success on the battlefield. As Haig himself explained: "much ... depends on the fighting spirit of the GOC Division since the division is our real battle unit." Commanders had to be able to "inspire the unit with their own personal energy and fighting spirit".[24] In this diary entry, Haig is pointing out that the division was essentially the main building block of his army, able to function as a self-contained, self-supporting formation. In addition to their three infantry brigades, divisions had their own organic artillery, engineer, medical, transport and supply elements. It follows, then, that the men who commanded at this level had to be at the top of their game, otherwise the ability of the force to prosecute the conflict was likely to be compromised. This placed a considerable weight on divisional generals and also meant that their jobs were often precarious and risky.

First, there was the ever-present danger to life and limb posed by enemy action. For despite the myth that generals sent their men to die while they remained in relative safety, well behind the fighting front, in reality, it was not unusual for senior commanders to be in or near the front line. Good generals knew they needed to understand the ground over which they were required to fight, and the conditions under which they expected their men to operate. Although they had access to detailed maps and aerial photography, for many there was no substitute for "walking the ground". As a result, eight divisional commanders and many more brigade commanders were killed in action or died of wounds during the conflict.[25] Robert Fanshawe was well-known for his visits to the trenches. Lt Charles Carrington claimed that every soldier in the division got to know that "Fanny spent more days in the front line than any of them".[26] He liked to "drift into a trench wearing an old raincoat over his rank badges so that the men were not intimidated".[27] Lt Edwin Campion Vaughan, 1/8th Royal Warwickshires, recalled meeting Fanshawe in early April 1917, "standing alone on a little knoll" observing a cavalry charge on enemy positions in front of Epehy, during the German withdrawal to the Hindenburg Line.[28] On the morning of 16th June 1918, while his counter-attack was under way and before the area between the Cesuna and Lemerle Switch Lines had been fully cleared and secured, Fanshawe, accompanied only by his ADC, conducted a personal reconnaissance of the ground.

A second significant hazard, and, for some, a fate just as awful as being killed or suffering a life-changing injury, was being sacked and sent home in disgrace – "degummed"[29] or "Stellenbosched"[30] in the vernacular of the time. As John Bourne has pointed out, there was considerable turn-over at the top of divisions over the course of the conflict. The Army's 84

---

24  TNA WO 256/6: Haig Diary, 7th November 1915.
25  The fatalities were: Broadwood, 57th Division; Capper, 7th Division; Feetham, 39th Division; Hamilton, 3rd Division; Ingouville-Williams, 34th Division; Lipsett, 4th Division; Lomax, 1st Division; Thesiger, 9th Division' and Wing, 12th Division.
26  C E Carrington, *Soldier From the Wars Returning*, p.103.
27  C E Carrington, p.103.
28  E C Vaughan, p78
29  From the French verb dégommer, meaning to de-gum (unstick), to unseat, to dismiss or to sack.
30  The term Stellenbosch was used as a verb meaning to be removed from a position of authority or command. During the Second Anglo-Boer War in South Africa officers who were considered to have been ineffective on the battlefield were typically sent to the military remount camp at Stellenbosch, near Cape Town.

divisions were commanded by 222 officers. Of these, 44 commanded 2 divisions, 11 commanded 3, 2 commanded 4 and one commanded 5. Throughout the war, 40 divisional commanders went on to take charge of Corps and six were promoted to head Armies.[31] However, while these statistics demonstrate many success stories, the historiography of the Great War is also littered with accounts of senior commanders – at all levels up to including the Commander-in-Chief – being dismissed for real or imagined failings.

It was, of course, a commander's duty to ensure that his subordinates were "up to the job", and to take appropriate action, including removing them from command, if they were not. For example, many of the officers who were "dug out" of retirement to take command of battalions, brigades and divisions as the army expanded during 1914-1915, were subsequently removed from their posts as younger, fitter officers, with more recent experience of fighting a modern conflict, began to emerge from the mud and blood of northern France and Flanders. This was a reasonable policy, aimed at ensuring fighting effectiveness, maintaining morale, and keeping casualties down, although some generals were more inclined to it than others. Haig criticised General Herbert Plumer, the Second Army supremo, for being "too kind to his subordinates".[32] This was in regard to his supposed failure to take sufficiently firm action against two of his divisional commanders, Major General Thomas Pilcher (17th Division) and Major General Aylmer Haldane (3rd Division) in the winter of 1915.[33] Pilcher was described by journalist, Philip Gibbs, as "a fine old English gentleman and a gallant soldier, but modern warfare was too brutal for him".[34] Lt General Henry Horne, who commanded XV Corps during the Somme battle, and later replaced General Charles Munro at the head of First Army, had no such reluctance. He unceremoniously sacked Pilcher, together with Major General Ivor Phillips (38th (Welsh) Division) after their divisions' poor performance during attacks on Mametz Wood in July 1916.[35] Haldane managed to survive at 3rd Division and was later promoted to command VI Corps.

Major General Sir George Forestier-Walker (21st Division) was removed – somewhat harshly, some felt – by his Corps Commander, Lt General Sir Charles Fergusson (XVII Corps), due to his "unpopularity with the troops".[36] Major General the Hon Edward Montagu-Stuart-Wortley, 46th Division, aged 58, found himself out of a job after his formation's disastrous assault on the Gommecourt Salient on 1st July 1916. This was followed by a strongly unfavourable report from his Corps Commander, Lt General Sir Thomas Snow (VII Corps), who wrote that the 46th Division "showed a lack of offensive spirit in the recent operations" which he attributed to the fact that "Stuart-Wortley was not, on account of his physical condition, able to get about the trenches as much as was necessary for a Divisional Commander to do in this sort of war".[37] Snow was himself dismissed by Haig, together with fellow Corps Commanders, Pulteney (III Corps)

---

31  J Bourne, *British Divisional Commanders During The Great War* <https://www.westernfrontassociation.com/world-war-i-articles/british-divisional-commanders-during-the-great-war-first-thoughts/> (accessed 20 July 2022).
32  Sheffield and Bourne (eds.), p.181.
33  Sheffield and Bourne (eds.), p.181.
34  P Gibbs, *Now It Can Be Told* <https://www.gutenberg.org/files/3317/3317-h/3317-h.htm#link2H_PART> (accessed 21st December 2022).
35  Sheffield and Bourne (eds.), p.201.
36  IWM DS/MISC2: Lt Col K Henderson, Memoirs, pp.178-79, Henderson Papers.
37  Holmes, p231

and Woollcombe (VII Corps), after the British failure at Cambrai in 1917. Major General Henry Rycroft, 32nd Division was sacked by General Sir Hubert Gough (Fifth Army), a man feared and hated by many of his subordinates, after a failed attack on 18th November 1916, as the Somme offensive closed.

The practice of removing incompetent generals for committing serious tactical errors, was a reasonable one, providing it worked properly. However, this was not always the case. One example of where it failed involved Major General Charles Barter, who commanded the 47th (London) Division during the Battle of the Somme. After a particularly bloody fight, Barter's 47th (London) Division's Territorials successfully captured High Wood on 15th September 1916. But despite his victory Barter was despatched back to Britain "at an hour's notice" a few days later, for "wanton waste of men". The division had actually achieved a great victory, overcoming the enemy's stubborn resistance where several others had failed. However, in doing so, it had suffered 4500 casualties, for which the Corps Commander, Pulteney (and Haig) held Barter responsible. Barter was indignant at the charge and challenged the decision, believing that the measures which led to the losses were "either in opposition to my representations, or I was not responsible for them". Denied an official investigation, he was, nonetheless, exonerated by an internal enquiry. He was subsequently knighted and sent on an important military mission to Petrograd.[38]

It is also clear that some commanders were sent home for reasons that were not solely or even vaguely connected with their own military inefficiency or incompetence. In 1916, Major General Sir Aylmer Haldane (3rd Division) was of the opinion that: "There are several Generals in our Army who, the moment anything goes wrong search for a scapegoat". This, he added, inevitably led to "a general feeling of insecurity".[39] General Snow noted that in 1915, when he was in command of 27th Division: "There was a great epidemic of Stellensboching in which the higher commanders were determined to whitewash themselves for the unsatisfactory state of affairs by making scapegoats of subordinates."[40] Snow added that throughout the war it was "often difficult to know how one's actions would be viewed by one's superiors…one was never sure whether for some particular action one would be promoted or Stellenbosched."[41]

There are also examples of generals at all levels being sacked simply because they did not get on with their superior, or even, incredibly, to settle old scores. General Sir Edmund Allenby, now feted for his spectacular defeat of the Turks in Palestine, believed Haig had removed him from command of the British Third Army after the failure of the Battle of Arras in the Spring of 1917. Although the battle had not delivered on its early promise, it is more likely that Allenby – The Bull, as he was known – was sacked because he was irascible and perhaps too willing to stand up to Haig and question his orders. Allenby was undoubtedly a difficult man, whose short temper frightened his staff, but he was also an effective senior commander who, later in the war, seized the cities of Damascus and Jerusalem, leading to the collapse of the Ottoman Turks.[42]

Lt General Horace Smith-Dorrien, commanding II Corps, whose rearguard action at Le Cateau on 26th August 1914 saved the BEF from being over-run by the pursuing enemy during

---

38  T Norman, *The Hell They Called High Wood*, pp.235-236.
39  NLS A Haldane War Diary, 24-30th June 1916, Haldane Papers.
40  IWM 76/79/1: T D Snow Memoir: 27th Division November 1914-June 1915, p.25, Snow Papers.
41  IWM 76/79/1: T D Snow Memoir: 27th Division November 1914-June 1915, p.25, Snow Papers.
42  M Gilbert, *The First World War*, p.325

the retreat from Mons, was sent home, somewhat vindictively, by Sir John French, during the Second Battle of Ypres, the following April.[43] The relationship between French and Smith-Dorrien, had been difficult for some time before the latter was appointed to command II Corps vice Lt General Sir Jimmy Grierson, who died of a heart attack on his way to the front. It was exacerbated when Smith-Dorrien told French that the King had asked him to report directly on the activities of his corps and made even more difficult when Smith-Dorrien ignored French's orders to withdraw and made his stand at Le Cateau. French never forgave Smith-Dorrien for Le Cateau. The Field Marshal was "as bad an enemy as he was a good friend" and "he lavished the full force of his hatred upon Smith-Dorrien".[44] A down-beat assessment of the situation at Ypres in April 1915, provided French with the excuse he sought to have him replaced.[45] French did not have the courage to wield the knife in person. Instead, he sent his Chief of Staff, then Major General Sir William Robertson, to do his dirty work. Robertson, known for dropping his aitches, despatched the luckless Smith-Dorrien with the words "'Orace, you're for 'ome".[46]

It is clear from the above that senior commanders served at the pleasure of their superiors, and they could be removed for many reasons, ranging from old age and infirmity, weak generalship, tactical failure, lack of fighting spirit, and unpopularity, to something as random as a clash of personalities. Can Fanshawe's removal be explained by one or more of these causes?

Major General Sir Robert Fanshawe was 51 years and six months old when he was first appointed to command the division in May 1915. He was 54 years and seven months old in June 1918.[47] That puts him squarely in line with the average age for divisional commanders on initial appointment during the First World War.[48] His replacement, Major General Sir Harold Walker, was 56 when he assumed command of the division. Fanshawe appears to have been in strong physical condition throughout his time in charge, during which he was seldom ill enough to be away from his headquarters. He had managed well in the hard winter of 1916/1917 and the physically-draining period of mobile warfare during the pursuit to the Hindenberg Line and was one of the few officers to remain at his post during the 1918 influenza epidemic that ripped through his division, laying low many of his staff officers and younger, fitter soldiers in the fighting brigades. It cannot be argued that his removal was justified either by his age or his physical condition.

There is no doubt that Fanshawe was well-liked by his men. In the words of Lt Col Tomkinson, they were "devoted" to him[49], while Lt Charles Carrington described him as "the kindest-hearted old swashbuckler in the army"[50]. He had commanded the division since May 1915, moulded the men to his way of fighting, and led them through the dark days and bitter fighting of the Somme, the Hindenburg Line and Passchendaele. In Lt Col Barnett's estimation, he had

---

43 L MacDonald, *1915*, pp.256-257.
44 R Holmes, *The Little Field Marshal*, pp.224-225.
45 R Holmes, *The Western Front*, p.128.
46 A J P Taylor, *The First World War: An Illustrated History*, p.83.
47 These biographical details are primarily gleaned from Fanshawe's *The Times* obituary.
48 J Bourne, *British Divisional Commanders During The Great War* <https://www.westernfrontassociation.com/world-war-i-articles/british-divisional-commanders-during-the-great-war-first-thoughts/> (accessed 20 July 2022).
49 TNA CAB 45/84: Carrington to Edmonds correspondence, 28th June 1944.
50 TNA CAB 45/84: Carrington to Edmonds correspondence, 28th June 1944.

been the "soul and inspiration of his command" during the whole of the three years.⁵¹ During their time on the western front the division sustained heavy casualties, but under Fanshawe's leadership, gained a deserved reputation for steadiness under fire. Capt Gedye of 240th Brigade, RFA, had this to say:

> He has had the division practically from the time it first went overseas and there is no doubt his is the credit for a lot of the reputation that the 48th has. He worked his division hard, but not harder than he worked himself, and the old man was a familiar sight in the trenches at all hours, complete with chocolate and soup squares, which he used to distribute if he went home to a meal earlier than he expected. The whole division was proud of the old fire-eater, and he was a very fine type of British Regular soldier.⁵²

Certainly not a 'chateau general'⁵³, Fanshawe, as stated above, was a frequent and familiar figure in the front line, gaining the respect of his South Midlanders by being prepared to go into the trenches and see things for himself rather than relying on second-hand reports from his staff. It has never been claimed that Fanshawe's demise was due either to a lack of physical or moral courage or to unpopularity amongst his troops.

By June 1918, Fanshawe was among the Army's most experienced divisional commanders, having led the 48th from mid-1915. He had survived the hard-fought and costly offensive battles of 1916-17, holding on to his job while many others were dismissed in the purges that followed the failures of the Somme and Passchendaele battles. Like Cavan, he was quite prepared to stand up to his superiors if he thought they were wrong. On the first day of the Somme, he persuaded Hunter-Weston (VIII Corps) that a follow-up attack by the 48th Division near Serre would be pointless, and it has been suggested that he came close to resigning after an argument with Gough over an order to attack during the fighting to the west of Poziéres on 25th August 1916.⁵⁴

There is clear evidence that he was a capable, competent and courageous leader, who was quite prepared to put his men in harm's way when the circumstances demanded it – but not at any cost. His abilities were confirmed by one of his Corps commanders. Lt General Sir Ivor Maxse was not a man to be overly-generous with his compliments. However, reporting to Fifth Army on his divisional commanders in 1917, as the Third Battle of Ypres raged, Maxse described Fanshawe as "a good average divisional commander and trainer".⁵⁵ But not everyone saw him in the same light, especially some of his fellow-regular officers at GHQ and in other divisions, who felt he was too familiar with his men. As Charles Carrington commented in a letter to the Official Historian, Fanshawe was "incapable of bearing malice but by no means incapable of making enemies".⁵⁶

---

51 G Barnett, p.95.
52 *Capt. S F Gedye MC* <http://www.google.com/url?q=http%3A%2F%2Fweb.archive.org%2Fweb%2F20160315162050%2Fhttp%3A%2F%2Fwww.thebristolgunners.webspace.virginmedia.com%2Findex.htm&sa=D&sntz=1&usg=AFQjCNFjuHS2n_U6cCA0uv_i6cx1Zf5nUgb> (accessed 21st November 2022).
53 Chateau General: A pejorative term for senior officers who have been accused of fighting the war from the safety of chateaux miles behind the lines.
54 LHCMA: PHP IV/D/13, N Malcolm Diary, 25th August 1916.
55 S Robbins, PhD Thesis, British Generalship on the Western Front 1914-1918, KCL, 2001, p175.
56 TNA CAB 45/84: Carrington to Edmonds correspondence, 28th June 1944.

In his book, *The Forgotten Front* George Cassar concludes that Cavan sacked Fanshawe for two main reasons. The first was allowing the line to be penetrated. To support this, he draws on a letter written by Cavan to Sir Henry Wilson on the evening of 15th September, in which Cavan hinted that Fanshawe's deployment of his forces may have been to blame for the enemy break-ins. Cavan felt the line was held too thinly and that this had directly resulted in the enemy penetrations. Cassar also suggests that Cavan may have been influenced by the fact that the French on the right of the British line, with a higher density of men in the front trench, had managed to prevent the attackers from even reaching their line through the effective application of defensive fire. The second reason relates to Fanshawe's conduct of the counter-attack. As evidence for this he quotes from Cavan's correspondence with Edmonds in which he states:

> Privately, I think Fanshawe could have 'softened' the pocket with TMs (Trench Mortars) for some hours before his first counter-attack, which was unprepared. I looked at the position from about Magnaboschi late on the evening of the 15th and told Gathorne-Hardy that the triangle with apex at Clo should be well-plastered and a counterstroke by the reserve brigade should follow – but Fanshawe had already given other orders and a counter-order then would have made confusion.[57]

Aimee Fox-Godden, in her thesis on British learning and innovation during the First World War, states Cavan claimed he "dismissed Fanshawe due to the latter's decision to man the front line thinly and the fact that he gave way too easily".[58] This is not correct. Reporting to Wilson on the evening of the 15th, before the final outcome was known, Cavan wrote: "The 48th on the left held the front line very thinly. This was done for economy in men, and to avoid the destructive bombardment, but I think it was too thin – the result being that in two or three places the enemy were able to get through the wire unopposed."[59] There is no evidence to prove that this was the cause of Fanshawe's dismissal.

John and Eileen Wilks in *The British Army in Italy 1917-1918*, also point to the supposed ease with which the Austrians were able to penetrate the British line. In addition, they include:

- The scale of the casualties sustained. They point out that in 1918 there was a great shortage of manpower and add that there was little prospect of further drafts being sent out to Italy.
- The result of the battle was a 'rather a close-run thing". As well as drawing heavily on the Official History, they add their own view that "certainly, when the Austrians first broke into the British positions, there was quite insufficient strength in the second line to resist a determined attack, as the bulk of the reinforcements were still on their way up to the front".[60]
- The disappointing performance of the British artillery. They note that the Austrians "appear to have made their initial penetration not greatly hindered by the British guns" (unattributed in the book, but, in fact, a direct quote from Cavan, writing to Sir Henry Wilson on

---

57 TNA CAB 45/84: Carrington to Edmonds correspondence, 28th June 1944.
58 A Fox-Godden, PhD Thesis, Putting Knowledge in Power: Learning and Innovation in the British Army of the First World War, 2015, University of Birmingham, pp.80-81.
59 TNA WO 100/852: Cavan Papers.
60 J and E Wilks, p.113.

the evening of 15 June),[61] and that Fanshawe himself had directed the divisional artillery not to fire on SOS lines unless ordered.[62]
- Too much reliance by Fanshawe on the intelligence reports that the enemy infantry assault would not extend as far west as the British sector.
- Fanshawe's apparent loss of grip at the height of the battle.
- Cavan learned of the Austrian penetration from the Italians, rather than from Fanshawe.

John Dillon, concurs with most of the above points in his analysis, and adds that in sacking Fanshawe, Cavan may have been following the policy of his old Commander-in-Chief, Field Marshal Sir Douglas Haig, who had removed his 'favourite', Gen Sir Hubert Gough, from command of the British Fifth Army following the German breakthrough in March 1918. In addition, he considered the sacking may have been intended to assuage British embarrassment over allowing their line to be penetrated by an enemy they regarded as being inferior to the Germans they had faced on the western front.[63]

KW Mitchinson, in his excellent divisional history, published in 2017, adds that, with hindsight, Fanshawe may have been guilty of a "lack of situational appreciation", but points out that he believed that even if his front were assaulted, his practiced divisional defence scheme and the faith he had in his senor commanders' capacity to implement it, would contain and then repel any penetration.[64] Mitchinson also points out that with only three miles between the British front line and the edge of the escarpment, this may not have been a suitable area on which to practice elastic defence as there was little space in which the elastic could be allowed to stretch.[65]

Edmonds, although referring to a long list of factors that "had militated against the British in the Asiago fight", completely ignores the fate of General Fanshawe in his reflections on the battle. There is no mention of Fanshawe's removal or the circumstances surrounding it. Instead, 34 pages after the section dealing with the fighting on 15-16th June, Edmonds simply records that on the 23rd July, "the 48th Division (Maj Gen H B Walker, who had taken over command on 4th July) relieved the 23rd Division …"[66] Lt Col George Barnett does likewise, simply noting that: "On 19th June[67], Maj Gen Sir R Fanshawe was ordered to hand over command of the division and proceed to England for duty there".[68]

The list of alleged failings levelled at Fanshawe, if justified, could be considered to amount to a "failure of generalship", a term used by Cassar to explain Cavan's decision.[69] But with a paucity of primary evidence to analyse, and at a range of over 100 years, modern historians have struggled to reach a categorical conclusion about whether Fanshawe's performance did actually amount to a failure to meet the standard required of a general officer at that time, and whether his dismissal was fair and reasonable in the circumstances. Most recent accounts appear to

---

61 TNA WO 100/852: Cavan Papers
62 J and E Wilks, pp.113-14.
63 J Dillon, p.163.
64 K W Mitchinson, p.226.
65 KW Mitchinson, p.224.
66 J E Edmonds, p.252.
67 Wednesday, 19th June was the date Fanshawe handed over to temporary GOC, Brig-Gen J Steele. Maj Gen H B Walker took command on 4th July 1918.
68 G Barnett, p.95.
69 G Cassar, p.162.

demonstrate a degree of sympathy for the man himself, and the circumstances surrounding his removal from command, whilst sitting firmly on the fence regarding the rights and wrongs of the decision.

John and Eileen Wilks conclude that it was a judgement that involved balancing several factors.[70] Dillon points out that Cavan made a success of his time in Italy, eventually being promoted to command an Army, which he led at the successful crossing of the Piave River in October 1918, but suggests that his treatment of Fanshawe "was not his finest hour".[71] Mitchinson deduces that Cavan's decision may have been driven by something as basic as a desire to appoint someone who was more in sympathy with his own views and he used the temporary penetration of the line as an excuse to do so.[72] Edmonds in private correspondence with Carrington, agreed that Fanshawe was "very badly treated" and that "Cavan was too stupid to understand elastic defence".[73] This latter view seems unreasonable, given that Cavan has been described as "a highly gifted commander" and "rated the best Corps Commander in France".[74]

Whatever the reason for the sacking, it was highly controversial at the time and has remained something of an enigma ever since. In a letter to Edmonds, written on 30 May 1944 the then Lt Col Pickford, who, as a Major, had been second-in-command of 4/Oxfords during the battle, referred to "a controversy that had better not be revived", although he does not say exactly what constituted the controversy.[75]

## Bad Generalship?

Generalship is often defined as the skill or practice of exercising military command. In the First World War, this would have been considered to apply to command at Brigade level and above. For a charge of a "failure of generalship" to stand, the facts would need to point to serious weaknesses in Fanshawe's planning for and conduct of the battle within his area of responsibility. We would need to see evidence of – among other things – consistently poor decision-making resulting in ineffective application of defensive principles and/or deployment of resources, particularly the positioning and use of reserves; significant loss of territory; poorly-trained, badly-led troops; a failure of subordinate commanders to understand his intent and their part in the overall plan, and to act accordingly and an unacceptably-high casualty rate.

Before considering these factors, however, it is worth setting out the British defensive doctrine of the time, and, in particular, the concept of elastic or flexible defence, of which Fanshawe was such an ardent and enthusiastic adherent. On the more open battlefields of France and Flanders, the British had paid a high price to learn that by packing the front line with troops to fight off an enemy attack they risked losing large numbers of men to the preliminary barrage. As a result, they adopted German tactics of holding the front line relatively lightly, keeping the bulk of their men further back, out of the way of the opening bombardment, but close enough to

70  J and E Wilks, p.115
71  J Dillon, p.162
72  KW Mitchinson, p.230.
73  TNA WO 100/852: Cavan Papers.
74  CCC C Bonham-Carter Papers, Autobiography, Chapter VII, p.21.
75  TNA CAB 45/84: Pickford to Edmonds, 30th May 1944.

be available for counter-attack when required. This defensive doctrine was set out in pamphlet SS210 *The Division In Defence*, disseminated by the General Staff in May 1918. Under this approach, much reliance was placed on artillery and machine guns firing from depth to break up an attack before it reached the front line. However, it was also accepted that if the enemy could generate sufficient mass at a decisive point, and if their soldiers were sufficiently well-motivated, well-led, and supported by an effective creeping barrage, using smoke and gas to blind or incapacitate the defenders, it was always possible that they would penetrate the front line. In that event, the defenders would seek to create strong defensive flanks on either side of the breach, preventing the attackers from manoeuvring laterally and forcing them to try to move forward against successive lines of wire and other barriers. The defence was designed to flex like an elastic band, giving some ground but forcing the attackers to use up men and ammunition until their initial momentum was lost. At that point, before the enemy had an opportunity to consolidate any gains, the defenders would counter-attack to drive out the invaders and re-occupy the ground temporarily won by the enemy.

On his arrival in Italy in November 1917, General Herbert Plumer was surprised to discover that the Italian method of holding the line was to put nearly every man and machine gun into the front with no supports or reserves. This meant they sustained heavy losses in every bombardment, and it placed an unnecessary strain on the men. Reporting on the state of the Italian army on Boxing Day, 1917, General Fayolle explained that their defence was not properly distributed in depth. There was a lack of defensive works behind the front, and troops were massed in the front line in excessive numbers with insufficient reserves behind. As well as leading to heavy casualties from enemy artillery fire, this also meant that immediate local counter-attacks were delivered too late or not at all owing to the lack of reserves.[76] The British and French expended a lot of capital in trying to persuade the Italians to follow their approach instead. When the British first took over a stretch of front on the Montello in December 1917, Plumer ordered that every effort was to be made to organise their sector as a model to demonstrate to the Italians how few men needed to be kept in the front line.[77]

Although flexible defence-in-depth was the British army's settled doctrinal approach by 1918, not every general was comfortable with it in practice. Charles Carrington, wrote:

> For two-and-a-half years Fanshawe had imbued his division with the doctrine of elastic defence – to the dismay of more than one higher commander. So bad was the tactical doctrine and wooden the leadership of Kitchener's armies that the temporary loss of a muddy ditch was regarded by most generals as a disgraceful failure to be avoided at any cost in bloodshed. We had never thought or behaved so in the 48th Division but always followed the true doctrine…of elastic and mobile defence behind a lightly-held front line. We were often thought to be taking chances, but, in fact, we never lost a defensive position in any action throughout the war.[78]

One influential critic of flexible defence was Lt General Sir Richard Haking, commanding XI Corps. In his view, such an approach "does not agree with the system of defence which is

---

76  J E Edmonds, p.144.
77  J E Edmonds, p,107.
78  G Cassar, pp.163-64 and TNA CAB 45/84: Pickford to Edmonds, 30th May1944.

in accordance with our native characteristics, i.e. the defence of the front line at all costs…our experience has been that counter strikes to regain lost trenches are more costly in casualties than the stubborn defence of the front-line system."[79] Haking later wrote to Edmonds: "We would have no truck with the 'defence-in-depth idea at Givenchy (in 1918) and we should have lost the battle if we had." Another nay-sayer of defence-in-depth was the commander of III Corps, Lt General Sir Richard Butler, even though his formation fought next to Sir Ivor Maxse's XVIII Corps during the German Spring Offensive and saw the benefits of a well-organised defensive zone demonstrated at first hand.

However, there is no evidence that Cavan was uncomfortable with the general principle of elastic defence, and whatever the views of Haking or Butler, this defensive approach was approved British doctrine and Fanshawe was entirely justified in applying it to the circumstances he faced at Asiago. Having been practising the approach for nearly all of his time in command of the division, Fanshawe had conceived and drawn up an effective defence scheme, based on this concept, even though the division had only been holding the left sector of the line for 10 days, during which time most of his focus had been on preparing for an attack rather than defence. We can see evidence of this in the pages of the 474th Field Company, Royal Engineers' War Diary, which notes work on dugouts for a battalion headquarters and advanced dressing station, re-commencing work on a dug-out in the Cesuna Switch, preparation of new forward battery positions and headquarters dugouts and accommodation for 240th Brigade, RFA, as well as improving the local water supply, fitting electric lighting in Cesuna Tunnel and preparing to renew a bridge over the Ghelpac "for the proposed offensive".[80]

The obvious evidence for the effectiveness of Fanshawe's planning and his abilities as a senior commander is that the enemy, attacking under a heavy supporting artillery barrage, with massive numerical superiority, from deep cover, in poor light conditions, although able to break-in at several points, failed to break through anywhere on the divisional front. They were held by the Monte Lemerle defences and the Cesuna and Lemerle Switch Lines, and were ejected by counter-attack, the status quo being restored in a little over 24 hours. As Carrington later observed:

> We did exactly what we set out to do. There was much ill-feeling [within the division] against GHQ when we got no credit for it. The ill-feeling still rankles in my breast a quarter of a century later. On 15th June, the attacking enemy were contained in a pocket between two switch lines prepared for that express purpose and were counter-attacked according to the plan which had been rehearsed. The 48th Division, using only its own resources, defeated the enemy on this chosen ground, chased them back to their own lines, and occupied the enemy's outposts until ordered by GHQ to withdraw.[81]

In writing about this in June, 1944 – over two decades years after the event – Carrington appears to have overlooked the support provided by the Italians on the 1/5th R Warwicks' left, both in taking over a section of British line to allow the garrison to support the later counter-attack if

---

79  M Senior, *Victory on the Western Front: The Development of the British Army, 1914-1918*, passim.
80  TNA WO 95/4246: 474th Field Company RE War Diary.
81  TNA CAB 45/84: C E Carrington to J E Edmonds and G Cassar, pp.163-64.

required,[82] or the role of the Italian artillery in helping to bombard the attackers during their initial assault and while they attempted to reinforce the pocket during the day. However, his general point, that Fanshawe fought the battle exactly as he had planned it, with the expected result, holds good. Fox-Godden agrees. In her view, "Fanshawe had fought a model defence in depth battle as laid out in SS210."[83]

Looking at this in more detail, Fanshawe, had obviously considered the ground, identifying the potential weak spots (ie the sections of line running through the woods, particularly on the 1/4th Oxfords' and 1/5th Gloucesters' front, and other areas with poor forward visibility and limited fields of fire, such as the right-hand sector of the 1/5th R Warwicks' front, and the inter-divisional boundaries). He had noted the likely enemy avenues of approach, and the 48th Machine Gun Battalion had placed Vickers machine gun teams to cover these routes. The divisional artillery brigades had drawn up fire-plans to hammer the likely enemy concentration areas as part of their counter-preparation barrage. He had considered the high likelihood of an enemy penetration at one or more of the weak points and taken steps to prevent a break-in becoming a breakthrough. This can be deduced from the fact that he had begun to fortify the Lemerle and Cesuna Switch Lines, linked into the Monte Lemerle defences (Polygon Trench, Polderhoek Trench and Jargon Trench), creating a pocket in which the attackers could be contained, reduced, and counter-attacked. These two switch lines were fundamental to the defence scheme, and the attention paid to fortifying them, although limited by the time available, is proof that Fanshawe correctly identified the most likely area in which the enemy might penetrate, ignoring the left flank because the deep ravine there meant this section was unlikely to be breached by a frontal assault. The left could, potentially, be taken if the line was penetrated elsewhere and the enemy was able to move laterally to attack the position from the flank or the rear. However, the Cesuna Switch was, in part, designed to prevent that from happening, and on the day, it did its job. He had also identified the need to create strong-points between the first and second lines, providing rallying points for defenders if the front line was broken, and from which reserves could counter-attack. Sites for these had been located and work had commenced on one or two but had been held up by having to prioritise preparations for the allied attack, scheduled for 18 June.[84] He had ensured that his subordinate commanders understood how he intended to defend his sector, and the part each would play in this, and that the infantry battalions were aware of, and had practiced, their defensive roles. This is clear from the fact that he had located key support battalions within easy reach of their battle positions, namely the Lemerle Switch (First Bucks Battalion) and the Cesuna Switch (1/8th R Warwicks), and they had moved into these positions almost as soon as the enemy bombardment opened up. 145th Brigade, without waiting for further direction from Division, ordered the Bucks Battalion to move to the Lemerle Switch at 0319.[85] 143rd Brigade already had a company of 1/8th R Warwicks in the Cesuna Switch and this was augmented by the remainder of 1/6th R Warwicks, (to the switch itself), and 1/7th R Warwicks (to a supporting position in the rear of the switch), whose movements

---

82   J E Edmonds, p.208.
83   A Fox-Godden, PhD Thesis, Putting Knowledge in Power: Learning and Innovation in the British Army of the First World War, 2015, University of Birmingham, pp.80-81.
84   G Barnett, p.92.
85   TNA WO 95/4250: 145th Brigade War Diary.

were "in accordance with the brigade defence scheme".[86] In addition, as Fanshawe pointed out in his After-Action Report, the move forward and subsequent counter-attack on Guardiano and Clo by 1/7th R Warwicks, were both well-practised. The battalion had "previously rehearsed the very situation with which it was confronted in battle".[87]

Cavan was critical of Fanshawe's handling of the early phases of the counter-attack, as can be seen from the quote above relating to the use of Trench Mortars to soften-up the pocket before the attack went in. However, if we consider the tactical situation at this stage of the fighting, Cavan was perhaps wrong to make this suggestion, and apparently indifferent as to the potential consequences for friendly troops in the area. The operational picture in the pocket at the time of the initial counter-attack was not entirely clear. In fact, to use Fanshawe's own words, quoted by Lt Col Tomkinson (Comd, 144th Brigade), who was briefed at divisional headquarters around 1230 on the 15th, it was "very obscure".[88] There were small groups of British troops scattered throughout the area, in front of the two switch lines and around Pelly Cross. Some of these were in close-contact with the Austrians. The use of Trench Mortars to 'soften the pocket' could have put at risk friendly troops, whose exact whereabouts was not always known with pinpoint accuracy at brigade or division. It might have been possible to order British troops to withdraw while a Trench Mortar bombardment took place, but there could be no guarantee that such an order would have reached the intended recipients, and if it had, the Austrians would almost certainly have spotted the withdrawal and reacted accordingly, at the very least potentially gaining further territory. The risk to friendly forces had been explained to Gathorne-Hardy earlier when he suggested using 6-in Howitzers to shell the pocket. Although the use of Trench Mortars rather than field or heavy artillery would have reduced the danger of friendly casualties, there would still have been some risk.

There were three types of trench mortars in service with British forces at this stage of the war. The 3-in Stokes Light Trench Mortar, operated by the infantry battalions themselves, was designed to provide intimate local support to units in the line. The 6-in Newton Medium Mortar, operated by the Royal Artillery, was chiefly used against enemy trenches and for cutting wire. The 9.45-in (240mm) Heavy Trench Mortar (also known as The Flying Pig) was also operated by the RA, and was intended for use against fixed positions, strong-points and bunkers. Mortar bombs with contact fuses would have been much less effective in woods and forests where they were likely to have been detonated by hitting trees, causing air-bursts, or knocked off course before they could find their intended targets. The mortars available at the time were effective in dealing with fixed positions, but would have been less useful attacking small, dispersed enemy groups within thick woods. In addition, mortar fire could not be directed at specific targets due to the lack of observation: it would have been very difficult to identify specific targets in the dense woodland, and impossible to direct the fire against those targets without functioning communications between the Forward Observation Officer and the mortar teams. In GHQ's own report on the battle, the Lessons Learned annex states that:

> In wood fighting, rifle grenades and Stokes Mortars were of little use owing to trees.[89]

---

86 TNA WO 95/4250: 143rd Brigade War Diary.
87 TNA WO 95/4244: Fanshawe AAR.
88 TNA CAB 45/84: Tomkinson-Edmonds correspondence, 3rd July 1944.
89 TNA WO 95/4194: GHQ Italy (GS) War Diary.

In short, a Trench Mortar bombardment of the pocket would have been random and undirected and is unlikely to have made a significant difference to the outcome of the initial part of the counter-attack. It would, however, have posed a significant risk of injuring friendly forces scattered across the area between the two switch lines. In addition, switching the mortars to that task would necessarily have diverted them from striking the enemy attempting to cross the Ghelpac in front of Perghele to reinforce the pocket, a roll for which they were much better suited and in which they were very successful. As the 240th Brigade RFA battle narrative records: "the effect of the 6-in TMs was most discouraging to the enemy. Several parties had bombs [dropped] right into them and one machine gun was knocked right out by a direct hit".[90] Good use was made of the 18-pounders and 4.5in howitzers of 240th and 241st Brigades, Royal Field Artillery, for close support, as has already been described, but only against clearly identifiable targets at short ranges, over open sights, in direct-fire mode[91], when the risk to friendly troops would have been much reduced.

Cavan's comments to Edmonds could be read as an effort to justify his decision to remove Fanshawe – an oblique attempt to question his abilities as a divisional commander. If Cavan felt so strongly about the use of mortars, he could have said so when he visited the divisional headquarters earlier in the day and they could have discussed the matter face to face. It is inconceivable that the commander-in-chief would not have enquired about the plan to deal with the penetration. As the Official History records, Cavan visited Fanshawe's headquarters during the afternoon to see if he could be helpful; his presence was encouraging and he did not interfere with the arrangements which had been made.[92] Cavan later told Edmonds that changing Fanshawe's orders then "would have made confusion".[93] This is a valid point, but only if he had done so after the initial orders had been issued. Cavan had opportunity to influence Fanshawe's plan before the orders had been despatched but chose not to. Could it be that Cavan was actually content with the plan when it was briefed to him, and only changed his mind subsequently when he needed a reason to justify the sacking?

## Austrian Penetration

It is true that the Austrians were able to break in to the British position at several points, but how much of the blame for this can reasonably be placed at the door of the defending divisional commander or his front-line troops? First, it is important to point out that the Austrians also broke in to the 23rd Division's front away on the right of the British position, at San Sisto ridge, close to the boundary with the French. This penetration, on the sector held by 11th Sherwood Foresters, again in densely-wooded ground with poor observation from the line over the enemy's avenues of approach, was minor and very short-lived, the small group of attackers

---

90   TNA WO 95/4246: 240th Brigade RFA War Diary.
91   Mortars and field artillery can fire in direct or indirect mode. Direct fire occurs, usually at short ranges, where the gunners can see the target, they are firing on and make adjustments themselves. Indirect fire means the target cannot be seen by the men serving the gun (or mortar), and adjustments have to be made by an observation officer situated between the target and the gun.
92   J E Edmonds, p.212.
93   TNA CAB 45/84: Cavan to Edmonds correspondence, n.d.

being driven out by a local counter-attack, led by the Foresters' Commanding Officer, Lt Col C E Hudson, for which he was awarded the Victoria Cross. The Austrians made a half-hearted and unsuccessful attempt to breach the British line on the open ground on the slopes of Monte Keberlaba, held by 23rd Division's 68th Brigade, where there was a clear field of fire dominating the approaches. They also attacked the French line opposite Capitello Pennar in some strength, but failed here, due to the weight of fire brought to bear on them by the French garrison and its supporting artillery, who also enjoyed a clear field of fire along most of their line except for a small section on the extreme left, next to 23rd Division. However, the Austrians did manage a more serious break-in on the whole of the front held by the Italian XIII Corps, between the Brenta and the boundary with the French, penetrating to a depth of up to three miles. This demonstrates that defence 'en masse', as per the Italian policy, did not necessarily guarantee that the line would be secure. Although the French line was held more densely than the British, the two key factors in preventing a penetration there was the poor quality of the attackers – even the Austrian official account was critical of the 16th Honved Division, composed of Hungarian and Rumanian troops, who, it claimed, panicked and withdrew after receiving a few casualties[94] – and the open "killing zone" in front of the line, which allowed the French infantry and artillery to cut the attacking Austrians to pieces.

In the British sector, the break-ins all occurred in areas where the line ran through dense pine woods. On sections where the line was in open ground, the Austrians either chose not to attack, or were stopped well beyond the front line by the effective application of artillery, rifle and machine gun fire. This suggests that local geography was an important factor in facilitating the penetrations. As Cavan pointed out, in a letter to CIGS:

> The enemy attacked selected points only, each point being attacked on a two-company front with supports in great depth. He chose his ground well, which is, of course, easy in the broken country of the plateau …[95]

The Austrians knew this ground better than the British. They had attacked here seven months earlier, and had similarly penetrated the line, then held by the Italians, advancing to Monte Lemerle before running out of steam and being forced back. The British line was badly sited and as a result it was not always possible for the posts to provide mutual support. Nor, in some cases, were the defenders able to cover their barbed wire obstacles with fire. This was a fundamental problem and broke a key defensive principle – obstacles must be covered by fire. These weaknesses cannot be attributed to Fanshawe, who was not responsible for siting the line, and had little time to do anything about it. As Cavan later admitted, in an article on leadership for Army Quarterly, he had been around the line the day before the attack (14th June) but:

> I had neglected the precaution of ensuring by questions to the Brigadiers, that every man could use his rifle to cover all the ground. The result was that the enemy got into some dead ground and made a break in our line. It is true that he was checked at the second line and

---

94  J E Edmonds, p.217 and E Glaise-Horstenau and R Kiszling, p. XXX.
95  TNA WO 100/852: Cavan to Wilson correspondence, 15th June 1918.

pushed back by a counter-stroke, but the breach should not have occurred. Dead ground must be covered from a flank or flanks.[96]

This is somewhat disingenuous. If Cavan had made a personal reconnaissance of the line, surely, as an experienced infantryman, he would have seen the weaknesses, including the thin manning, for himself. He would not have required individual brigade commanders to point out the obvious. Cavan chose not to highlight the manning of the front line as the cause of the break-in in this article, but he did focus on it in an earlier piece, written for the same publication in 1920, in which he observed:

> Owing to the situation in France, the conserving of manpower was all important… We had taken the precaution of keeping as many men as possible out of the front line in order to avoid the bombardment. In places this policy was over-done, and the temporary success of the enemy in getting through the wire on the British left was due to this cause.

To give him his due, he continues:

> On the other hand, the strength of the reinforcements in immediate support [as a result of holding the front line thinly], made it possible for us to launch a vigorous counterstroke at dawn on the 16th of June and restore the whole line to its former position.[97]

Edmonds states that had the 48th Division's line been held more strongly, in the Italian fashion, there might have been no break-in.[98] But this is surely a failure to appreciate the ground on which this action took place. The thickly-planted woods allowed the attackers to approach to within tens of yards of the British line before they could be effectively engaged by aimed rifle and machine gun fire – and in some cases not even then. The broken 'dead' ground in front of the line provided cover, in some cases right up to the wire. From that distance, particularly in the absence of the SOS barrage, it is entirely possible that a well-motivated attacking force with sufficient numerical superiority, would take only minutes to move from cover, breech the barbed wire (if it had not already been destroyed by the bombardment), assault the front line, and overwhelm the defending garrison, irrespective of how thinly or thickly the line was held. Mass matters in an assault, and it matters doubly in assaults in woods and forests. The enemy force that attacked the much-weakened 48th Division on the morning of 15th June, consisted of two strong divisions of Austrian regulars, the 6th and 52nd KuK divisions, using their own versions of Bangalore torpedoes to breach the wire entanglements in front of the line where necessary, and flame-throwers to deal with the defending posts. In addition, many of the 23rd Honved Division infantrymen who were supposed to attack the left of the 23rd Division, ended up in the 48th Division sector, apparently veering into the woods on their right in a bid to get away from the open ground in front of the Northumberland Fusiliers. Lt Col W H Middleton, Commanding Officer of 10th Northumberland Fusiliers of 68th Brigade, wrote:

---

96  FM The Earl of Cavan, *Army Quarterly*, Vol. XL, April-July 1940, pp.56-60.
97  FM The Earl of Cavan, *Army Quarterly*, Vol. 1, October 1920-January 1921, pp.11-18.
98  J E Edmonds, p.217.

> ... a large proportion of the enemy infantry edged off to their right – i.e. away from the open country on the 68th Brigade front – into the wooded country on the 145th Brigade front, there bringing a great weight (of numbers at any rate) on the OBLI.[99]

## Reliance on Bad Intelligence

The charge levelled by John and Eileen Wilks that Fanshawe relied too heavily on intelligence reports that there was unlikely to be an infantry assault on his section of the line, does not stand up to detailed scrutiny. Although the intelligence passed on by the Italians suggested that the Austrian infantry attack would not extend as far west as the British line, and Fanshawe himself felt an infantry assault on his sector was "by no means certain", as Lt Col George Barnett has pointed out, when Fanshawe briefed his brigade and unit commanders on the afternoon before the attack, he went out of his way to emphasise that whatever the intelligence suggested, they must prepare for the worst-case scenario. To reinforce this point, he then went through the Divisional Defence Scheme in some detail. This is not the act of a general who has allowed the available intelligence to blind him to all possibilities. Fanshawe and his subordinate commanders may not have believed they would be attacked, but they were under no illusion that they needed to take all precautions to meet such an attack if it came.[100] The fact that the Divisional Defence Scheme was put into operation so smoothly on the morning of 15th June suggests that this order had been obeyed.

## Loss of Grip

It has been claimed by the Wilks's and by Mitchinson that Fanshawe may have lost his grip on the battle. This fails to recognise the reality of divisional command in the First World War. It is a fact that Fanshawe was operating in something of an information vacuum for long periods of time, particularly during the early stages of the battle. With the telephone lines down, radio sets knocked out, power buzzers failing, poor visibility caused by smoke and low clouds reducing the effectiveness of signalling using lights and flags, and heavy shelling making life difficult for runners, information was without doubt a scarce commodity. However, this was not an unusual situation for commanders at that time. As John Lee has pointed out, after three years of experience, the British Army was well aware that the modern battle was a thoroughly chaotic affair and had developed ways of coping with the chaos.[101] They knew that communications were generally fragile and could break down at any moment, even taking account of built-in redundancy, designed to increase the reliability of critical links. They also knew that the best antidote to this was detailed planning and preparation. A sound, well-understood and frequently-rehearsed plan with built-in contingencies, based on a common doctrine and training and mutual trust across the various levels of command, could help to ensure that subordinates were able to act

---

99 TNA CAB 45/84: Middleton to Edmonds correspondence, 14th July 1944.
100 G Barnett, p.67.
101 J Lee, British Divisions on the Menin Road Ridge, 20 September 1917 in Sheffield and Todman (eds.), *Command and Control on the Western Front*, p.119.

purposely in the absence of further direction from above, thus reducing the likely impact of a failure of communications. Fanshawe had created a robust plan for defending his area of responsibility. He had ensured that this was very familiar to all of his subordinates, and that each unit had practiced its part in it, in some cases on several occasions. This approach would also have helped to reduce the number of decisions that would be required by the divisional commander in the absence of accurate, up-to-date information.

To back up their 'loss of grip' theory, the Wilks's point to the following:

> On one occasion, when Fanshawe had no news on the situation at the front, information was obtained by the initiative of Col Tomkinson who himself suggested that he should go forward and talk with Col Reynolds (Acting Commander, 145th Brigade).[102]

This is a paraphrased quote from a letter Tomkinson wrote to Edmonds on 3 July 1944. There are two problems with this. The first is that Tomkinson was about to bring his formation into action to counter-attack the enemy, and whilst he was understandably keen to know the latest situation, it was not his job to put himself at greater risk by going forward to look for it through a heavy artillery bombardment. Whilst no doubt a courageous act on Tomkinson's part, it was really a task for someone else, and if Fanshawe is blameworthy in this example, it is for allowing Tomkinson to go forward in the first place. The loss of a brigade commander at that stage of the fighting would have been problematic in several ways.

To grasp what was actually happening in this episode, it is worth quoting the whole of what Tomkinson wrote about it:

> When I went to H.Q. at 12.30pm I was told that the situation was very obscure. Div HQ had most of their personnel down with 'flu. All forward lines were cut and the woods between Div H.Q. and M. Lemerle were under continuous shell fire. I asked the General to let me go to M. Lemerle as I was confident that if Reynolds, the a/Bde Cdr was not a casualty he would have an accurate idea of the position on his front and flanks. So, I went there and saw Reynolds, who had the position well in hand, returned to Div. and reported to the General who told me to attack... I think I had only been away for about 1 hour – I knew all the ground well."[103]

It seems clear from this that it was Tomkinson who was desperate for information, not Fanshawe. Although there is evidence that GHQ was worried about the situation, there is no evidence that Fanshawe, closer to the actual fighting, was unduly concerned at that point. By about 0930-1000 he was reasonably sure that the most significant threat to his position, the loss of the Cesuna Switch, was no longer likely, and his attention was now focused on the counter-attack. As Tomkinson himself pointed out:

> I had no anxiety that we would not push them out and we did so without any outside assistance ...[104]

---

102 J and E Wilks, p.114 and TNA CAB 45/84: Middleton to Edmonds correspondence, 14th July 1944.
103 TNA CAB 45/84: Tomkinson to Edmonds correspondence, 3rd July 1944.
104 TNA CAB 45/84: Tomkinson to Edmonds correspondence, 3rd July 1944.

To support the "loss of grip" theory there would need to be evidence of some significant mistake, contradictory orders being issued, or a general sense of panic in the headquarters. There is no sign of any of this. Instead, we see a divisional commander who is confident in his defence plan, knows it is being put into operation, comfortable (perhaps more comfortable than some of his subordinates and seniors) about operating in an uncertain environment, and who is focused on the next phase of operations.

## Victory – but too close for comfort?

Cavan, in his initial report to CIGS, admits that he had "a nervous half-hour about 0930 when Cesuna might have been captured and a serious breach made in the Lemerle defences". He also points out that although the four divisions opposed to the British fought bravely, they "did not take instant advantage of their changes (sic) as the Germans would have done".[105] Lt Col Pryor, 1/6th R Warwicks, suggested that:

> If the Austrians had had any initiative at all I think the official history would be very difficult to write![106]

Neither Cavan's nervousness nor Pryor's views about the fighting qualities of the Austrians, are sufficient to make the case for the result of the battle being "a close-run thing", and even if it had been, would that have been sufficient grounds for sacking the divisional commander who had apparently snatched victory from the jaws of defeat? Similarly, the Wilkses' claim that when the Austrians first broke into the British positions, there was "quite insufficient strength in the second line to resist a determined attack" is not credible and fails to understand the concept of flexible defence. It is true that at around 0930 the Austrians were pressing hard on the northern end of the Cesuna Switch, had occupied Guardiana and were attempting to pierce the Lemerle defences. It is also true that at around 1000 Fanshawe ordered the 144th Brigade to have one of its battalions stand by to man the rear defences at Monte Pau – a prudent contingency but not evidence of panic.

The key point that stands against all of these claims is surely that there was no break-through. This may have been due, to some degree, to the quality of the Austrian forces, who were clearly not Germans, and had their own way of doing things. Cavan noted, for example, that when the Austrians over-ran a British battalion headquarters, they instantly set about looting, thus stopping their attack and losing their momentum. There are, of course, examples of German troops doing exactly the same thing during the 1918 Spring offensive. One of the most important factors in determining victory and defeat in this encounter was undoubtedly the dogged determination of Fanshawe's troops and their officers, who, operating within the broad framework of the Defence Scheme, were able to use their experience, skill and initiative to identify potential problems and deal with them, using the resources at hand. As Cavan admitted: "Our local commanders showed the better initiative, and the situation was restored."[107] Those

---

105  TNA WO 100/852: Cavan to CIGS correspondence, 15th June 1918.
106  TNA CAB 45/85: Pryor to Edmonds correspondence, 4th June 1944.
107  TNA WO 100/852: Cavan to CIGS correspondence, 15th June 1918.

local commanders were the product of Fanshawe's leadership and training. The Lemerle Switch had been manned by the Bucks Battalion on receipt of orders from 145th Brigade at 0319. The Cesuna Switch was already garrisoned by a company of 1/8th R Warwicks, and this was augmented by the remainder of the battalion, who were ordered to move at around 0415 and were in place before 0700. Pryor's own battalion, 1/6th Royal Warwicks was standing by in the Cesuna Tunnel to provide further support if required and later deployed forward to create a line of resistance looking north-west towards the likely direction of enemy advance.[108] The second-line defences were strongly held before the initial Austrian attack, and they resisted, despite the repeated attentions of the enemy. The Austrian pressure on the northern end of the Cesuna Switch was relieved when Lt Col Knox, supported by individual field guns, attacked and cleared Guardiana and Clo, while another of his companies assaulted and drove the enemy from the small toe-hold they had established in the Switch itself. The threat to the Lemerle defences was neutralised, in part, by artillery fire coordinated by Maj Colin Jardine and his men, engaging the enemy as they attempted to move across the Cesuna–Canove Road in the direction of Monte Lemerle. As Knox himself stated in his battle narrative:

> We pulled an 18-pdr gun onto the high ground and the gunners kept up a fire over open sights around Guardiana, Clo Station, and the slopes of Lemerle Hill, SE of Clo Station, my men carrying ammunition. This fire considerably checked the enemy, and I consider the magnificent work done by this battery (X/240), especially Maj Jardine, under very heavy machine gun fire, saved [an] at one time very serious situation and gave us time to establish the Cesuna Switch from the railway to Lemerle Switch.

Notwithstanding Lt Col Knox's reference to a 'very serious situation', even if the Austrians had managed to break out of the pocket, they were still nearly three difficult, uphill miles from breaking through the rear defences and debouching onto the Venetian Plain. Indeed, with another two defensive lines to cross, that was scarcely even a remote possibility. With their rear areas being pulverised by British and Italian guns, much of their artillery support being neutralised by effective counter-battery fire as visibility improved during the day, and their re-supply and reinforcements being seriously interdicted by a combination of artillery, mortar and machine gun fire from depth, it was obvious by mid-afternoon that the attack had failed. Once the initial thrust had been blunted, the Austrians were simply unable – or unwilling – to resume the offensive. As Pryor subsequently remarked:

> They were determined not to come out from the shelter of the woods and, on the morning of the 16th, began straggling back past our companies…even before the counter-attack began.[109]

The Austrians were not the Germans. Fanshawe and the 48th Division could only fight the enemy in front of them. If the Austrians did not possess the same drive and determination as their German allies, that is hardly Fanshawe's fault. Perhaps if the enemy had been Germans

---

108 TNA WO 95/4248: 143rd Brigade War Diary.
109 TNA WO 45/84: Pryor to Edmonds correspondence, 14th June 1944.

the result would have been different. Perhaps, facing German opposition, Fanshawe would have planned his Defence Scheme differently, and put more men into the front line. We will never know, and it seems pointless to dwell on "what-ifs". The final result is not in dispute and it was a clear victory for Fanshawe and his division.

## Casualties

The British Army was facing a manpower crisis in 1918. In April, Sir Henry Wilson had warned Cavan that he should avoid doing anything that might result in heavy casualties, for which he was unlikely to get replacements. In these circumstances, as Sandilands has said, it would have been considered 'criminal' to risk casualties lightly or without good reason. According to the GHQ report on the action to the Italian Sixth Army, dated 30th June, the casualty returns for 15th-18th June were as follows:[110]

| Division | Killed | | Wounded | | Missing | |
|---|---|---|---|---|---|---|
| | Off | OR | Off | OR | Off | OR |
| 7th Division | 0 | 9 | 7 | 53 | 0 | 47 |
| 23rd Division | 8 | 84 | 22 | 418 | 1 | 46 |
| 48th Division | 16 | 134 | 42 | 446 | 9 | 256 |
| GHQ Tps | 2 | 15 | 10 | 90 | 0 | 2 |
| TOTALS | 26 | 242 | 81 | 1,007 | 10 | 351 |

There is no disguising the fact that the 48th Division's casualties were greater than those of the 23rd Division, (or 7th Division, which had some troops in the mountains providing working parties but was mostly held in reserve). However, to put these numbers into context, first, the 48th Division was attacked by two strong, good-quality KuK regular divisions (plus an element of a third division which ended up assaulting the 1/4th Oxfords' line rather than the 10th Northumberland Fusiliers which was their target). The Oxfords later reported that they had found evidence of at least seven different battalions attacking on their front.[111] The KuK divisions pressed hard for a time before losing heart. The serious fighting on this sector also lasted longer than on the right. In addition, the 23rd Division's opposition was inferior Honved divisions, whose attack appears to have been somewhat less than whole-hearted, and quickly petered out, with large numbers of enemy troops pulling back during the course of the first day. Second, the casualties sustained by the 48th Division, although not insignificant in themselves, were not substantial by the standards of the day. For example, when 1/8th R Warwicks attacked near the village of Serre on 1st July, 1916 at the opening of the Battle of the Somme, this single battalion lost a total of 12 Officers and 223 Other Ranks dead.[112] A less extreme example occurred during the crossing of the Steenbeek, north-east of the village of St Julien, during the Third Battle of Ypres on 16 August 1917, when the 1/1st Bucks Battalion alone lost 56

---

110 TNA WO 95/4194: GHQ Italy (GS) War Diary.
111 G Barnett, p.72.
112 K W Mitchinson, p.90.

killed and 200 wounded.[113] They were certainly nowhere near the 4500 casualties that cost Maj General Barter of 47th (London) Division his job, despite capturing High Wood, back in 1916.

Lt Col H.R. Sandilands observed that at this stage of the war, "to risk incurring casualties lightly or with insufficient reason would be more than ever a crime".[114] The 48th Division casualties were certainly not "incurred lightly nor with insufficient reason". They were sustained in a gallant defence against an attack by a stronger and initially a fairly determined enemy, in order to ensure that the Austrians were unable to break through in the mountains and threaten the rear of the Italian forces on the Piave Line. If Fanshawe had manned his line more thickly, it is most likely that he would have suffered a greater number of casualties as a result of the opening bombardment and would still have had to deal with a penetration. In addition, the various unit war diaries for the period show that in many cases the wounded were quickly patched up and were back 'at duty' within a few days. The last word on losses in this action goes to Cavan and puts the impact of the casualties into proper perspective. Writing to Sir Henry Wilson on 19th June, he observed:

> All ranks have been filled up now and about 1700 reinforcements remain at the camps and base …[115]

This shows that the gaps caused by the fighting on 15-16th June had quickly been made good and there was still a healthy reserve available in the rear areas to support future operations. The losses, whilst tragic for the individuals, their families and their pals who survived, had not placed a significant stress on the manpower supply and there is nothing in the files to show that Cavan was forced to seek additional troops from the Great Britain. Indeed, the opposite was the case. As the manpower situation became more dire on the western front, and the War Office decided in September 1918, to reduce all infantry brigades in Italy from four to three battalions (as it had already done on the western front at the beginning of the year), nine battalions were actually sent back from Italy to augment Haig's forces in France and Belgium.[116]

## Cavan Embarrassed?

The Wilks's claim that Cavan was embarrassed by the fact that he first heard of the Austrian break-in on his front from the Italians rather than from Fanshawe. For this they rely on the Italian Official History, published in 1980, which claims that Italian artillery observers of the 12th Division, on the left of 48th Division, saw large numbers of enemy moving across the Ghelpac and breaking into the British lines. On learning this, General Segre, the Commandante d'Artigliere of the Sixth (Italian) Army, telephoned Cavan, who was still without news from Fanshawe. The Italians subsequently opened artillery fire on the now-occupied British front

---

113 P L Wright, pp.78-79.
114 J and E Wilks, p.113 and H R Sandilands, *History of the 23rd Division*, p.240.
115 TNA WO 100/852: Cavan-Wilson correspondence, 19th June 1918.
116 J E Edmonds, p,260.

line.[117] This may all be true, but in no way could it be considered to be reasonable grounds either for Cavan to be embarrassed or for Fanshawe to be sacked.

The fact that Cavan may have learned of the penetration of the 48th Division front first from the Italians can be attributed to the "fog of war". As has already been explained, the communications systems between the front line and Brigade and Divisional headquarters were broken within the first few minutes of the preparatory bombardment, leaving Fanshawe almost blind during the initial phase of the battle. In addition, the British divisional and brigade staffs were busy fighting for information while the 12th (Italian) Division was not under the same pressure because there had been no infantry assault on its sector. According to the divisional battle narrative, at 0825, 48th Division HQ received a report from an Italian OP that the Austrians were in the British line about Perghele. This was followed at 0845 by a report from the right front battalion (1/4th Oxfords) that their line was broken. 48th Division passed on the news to GHQ at 0850 and GHQ told them that the Italians had also reported enemy machine guns being moved up near Perghele.[118] This does not seem like an undue delay in the passage of information between the two headquarters in the circumstances. Cavan may have been something of a martinet, but he was a very experienced soldier who had recent command experience at brigade, division and now corps level. Given the situation at that time, it is stretching credibility to accept either that he would have been embarrassed by the Italians knowing more than he did, or that he would have blamed Fanshawe for not passing on information promptly. He does not mention this as an issue in any of his private correspondence with Wilson. It is not identified as a "lesson learned". The incident is not highlighted in the GHQ report to the Sixth Italian Army. As Cavan himself admitted:

> The liaison with our allies was all that could be desired, our divisions working in perfect harmony with the French 24th Division on the right and the Italian 12th Division on the left.[119]

## The Gough Example

John Dillon has suggested that in sending Fanshawe home Cavan was following the example of Haig's sacking of General Sir Hubert Gough after the German break-through on the Fifth Army front that same spring. It is possible that Cavan may have believed any penetration of the line was a sacking offence. Edmonds, corresponding with Carrington in 1944, wrote: "It was said of him in France [that] 'his great heart doesn't pump the good red blood above his waist'. He sent other good men home."[120] But there is nothing in any of his correspondence with his superiors at the time, or in anything he wrote later, to suggest that this was his position. In his report on the events of 15th June to Wilson, penned that evening, Cavan simply explains that he

---

117 J and E Wilks, p.116 and R Isidoro (ed.), *Storia Della Grande Guerra*, Vol. 1, p.430.
118 TNA WO 95/4258: 48th Division War Diary.
119 TNA WO 100/852: Cavan to Wilson correspondence, 15th June 1918.
120 Edmonds to Carrington, quoted in G Cassar, p.164.

plans to hold a "careful enquiry into the exact reasons of the break into the 48th Division line, in order that we may benefit in the future and see how to strengthen our defence".[121]

The circumstances relating to Fanshawe, and those surrounding Gough's dismissal, are quite different. Gough had been skating on thin ice with Haig for some time before the Spring offensive. His performance at the start of the Third Battle of Ypres in 1917 had fallen short of what Haig had expected from his fellow-cavalryman, and responsibility for the main weight of the offensive was switched to Plumer and his Second Army. Haig's patience with Gough ran out on the morning of the 21st March 1918 when the might of 76 crack German divisions fell upon 28 tired British formations, punched a hole through their defences, and headed for the channel ports, a breakthrough that some suggested, perhaps unfairly, was on a par with the Italian rout at Caporetto.[122] The penetration of the British line at Asiago was neither a re-run of the Italian retreat to the Piave River in October, 1917, nor of the Fifth Army's debacle during the opening phase of Operation Michael. There was no break-through at Asiago and the penetration was pinched out in a little over 24 hours. As John Keegan has pointed out, in Gough's case, his army appeared to have "no cohesion of command, no determination, no will to fight and no unity of companies or battalions.[123] This was emphatically not the case with the 48th Division or Fanshawe.

## Artillery fire 'disappointing'…

John and Eileen Wilks also claim that the performance of the British artillery was 'disappointing' and that this may have been a factor in Fanshawe's dismissal.[124] It is a fact that the British artillery did not fire an SOS barrage at the beginning of the Austrian assault, and that this probably contributed to the ease with which the enemy managed to break in to the British line. Before considering this in more detail, however, in fairness to the artillery, it should be pointed out that the British batteries did sterling work in other ways throughout the day. Their counter-preparation fire, helped to disrupt the initial attack and the subsequent re-supply and reinforcement of the enemy in the pocket. Their counter-battery fire was highly successful, silencing many enemy guns, resulting in a significant reduction in artillery support for the attackers after the opening bombardment. This was achieved without the help of aerial observation as the bad weather prevented the Royal Air Force from flying over the plateau and they were diverted to support the defensive battle on the Piave Line. The Commander Royal Artillery (CRA) at GHQ, Brigadier-General Wardrop, wrote in his own after-action report: "One of the features of the day was the prompt action taken by batteries on their own initiative when all communications were gone."[125] As already stated, individual guns provided close support to the British infantry within the pocket, particularly in breaking up enemy attempts to pierce the Cesuna and Lemerle switch lines, and in the subsequent counter-attacks during the afternoon of the 15th. It is also the case that not all of the guns were under divisional command. Some were controlled at Corps level.

---

121  TNA WO 100/852: Cavan to Wilson correspondence, 15 June 1918.
122  J Keegan, p.430.
123  J Keegan, p.430.
124  J and E Wilks, pp.113-14.
125  TNA WO 100/852: Cavan to Wilson correspondence, 15th June 1918.

Fanshawe's CRA could have requested them to fire in support of the 48th Division if required, but there was no guarantee that they would be made available for that purpose.

The absence of SOS fire at the start of the infantry assault had two causes. The first was that, as he openly admitted, Fanshawe had instructed his gunners not to fire on SOS Lines unless ordered. This was because, due to the intelligence reports received from GHQ:

> I was not at all certain that the enemy would attack, and a premature SOS barrage would be a great mistake, using up our ammunition and energy uselessly and encouraging the enemy by making him think he had diverted our artillery from the real attack.[126]

The second was the failure of the SOS rockets fired by troops under attack as a signal for the artillery to commence firing on SOS lines. The rockets either failed to explode at all, or if they did explode, they were hidden from the view of the artillery observers, either by the trees or by the smoke and mist.

Employing the gift of hindsight, it might appear to be easy to find fault with Fanshawe's decision in this case. However, looking objectively at the matter, Fanshawe's direction to the gunners not to fire, which he issued at 4.10am, was not unreasonable in the circumstances that existed at that time. To be effective, the SOS barrage needed to be coordinated with an actual attack, otherwise it would be a waste of shells. However, this decision was undoubtedly predicated on the existence of communication between the front, brigade and divisional headquarters and the batteries, and, in the absence of this, the effectiveness of the SOS rockets. In the event, none of these methods of communication proved reliable on the day. However, in Fanshawe's defence, whilst he was aware that telephone and visual signalling was problematic, he had no way of knowing that the SOS rockets would go unseen. The system was well-tested on the western front and was, with good cause, considered to be reliable.

None of the criticisms set out above, either individually or collectively, appears to be of sufficient merit to justify Fanshawe's sacking, even by the norms of that time. Taking account of the circumstances in which he was operating, his overall generalship throughout the period in question was entirely effective as evidenced by the success of his defence plan. His troops had put the plan into action with minimal further direction; they had stopped the enemy in their tracks in the pocket designed for that purpose, preventing a breakthrough; the ground occupied was regained in just over 24 hours; and the casualty rate, whilst significant, would not have been considered heavy by First World War standards. If a penetration of the line was thought to be sufficient cause to dismiss a divisional commander, then surely the man in charge of 23rd Division would have suffered the same fate, as would every divisional commander whose front was breached during the opening day of the German Spring Offensive the previous March. That did not happen. There are, however, two further issues that might have influenced Cavan's decision.

The British were worried about the Italian army's performance. It had failed to learn and adopt the lessons either from its own efforts along the Isonzo and in the mountains since the start of the war, or those of its allies on the western front. As a result, its attacks too often failed, and its defences were too often pierced. Mark Thompson in his masterly work, "*The White War*",

---

126 TNA WO 95/4250: Fanshawe AAR.

described the Italian army at this time as "in doctrine and organisation, one of the most hidebound in Europe".[127] The overall impact of this was high casualty rates, particularly among the infantry, with little to show for them in terms of operational success. By November 1918, there was a genuine concern that the Italian army, and the public at large, were growing war-weary and that this, along with internal political pressures, would force the Italian government to seek an armistice. As Thompson noted, for weeks after Caporetto many Italian officials believed that revolution or sheer exhaustion would force Italy out of the war.[128]

The Caporetto rout came as a hammer-blow to the Italian nation. The scale of the retreat – 150kms from the Isonzo to the Piave in 26 days of fighting – and the eye-watering loss of men and equipment, represented one of the most comprehensive defeats of any army in the war up to that point. Whilst Italy was left reeling from the shock, British and French politicians fretted about their ally's ability, and willingness, to continue to prosecute the war against the Austrians. Russia appeared to be on the brink of signing a cease-fire.[129] If the Italians had also decided to seek an end to hostilities, this would have been a major blow to the Allies, allowing the Austrians to significantly reinforce the German army on the western front, and exposing the French to the threat of an attack through Italy against the southern end of their line. On 4th November, while the Italians were pulling back from the Tagliamento to the Piave, British and French delegations met bilaterally at Rapallo, near Genoa to discuss the situation, ahead of the conference proper, which was concerned with the provision of assistance, and was scheduled to commence on the following day. In the margins of this meeting, France's General Petain told British Prime Minister, David Lloyd George that he doubted whether the Italian army existed any longer and "if it did exist it was probably only in the shape of individual units and not as an army". Petain's solution was for the French and British to take charge, just as "the Germans had taken charge of the Austrians".[130]

As it happened, the Italian army, certainly battered and bruised by Caporetto and the retreat to the Piave, had not disintegrated in the way that Petain believed, and soon bounced back, demonstrating unsuspected powers of recuperation. But at the time, whilst there was great concern among the allies for the immediate future of the Italian front, neither Lloyd George nor Painlevé felt they could go as far as to step in and "take charge", as Petain had counselled. However, there was general agreement between the French and British that ways needed to be found to persuade the Italians to learn from the Caporetto debacle and put these lessons into effect in the coming months in order to improve their fighting performance, and in turn drive up military and civilian morale. This became a key element of British and French policy in Italy in the following months, alongside efforts to help the Italians to benefit from their allies' hard-won experience on the western front. These two linked objectives – in essence amounting to the need to gain influence over the Italian military in order to help them to modernise, improve their effectiveness, stand on their own two feet, stay in the fight, and thus allow the British and French forces to return to the western front – would be at the heart of British strategic thinking in Italy until the end of hostilities.

---

127 M Thompson, p.325.
128 M Thompson, p.326.
129 The Bolsheviks actually signed an armistice with the Central Powers on 15th December 1917.
130 J E Edmonds, p.80.

Writing to Chief of the Imperial General Staff, General Sir William Robertson (CIGS) on 10th November 1917, Cavan, then in temporary command of British forces in Italy, just ahead of the arrival of General Plumer, assessed the failure at Caporetto thus:

> I am quite sure that the dispositions [of the Italian army] for defence were extremely faulty, judged by our standards and our textbooks. The idea of defence in depth does not seem to be grasped, and foresight was completely lacking in the preparation of back lines of defence, though line upon line of trenches at a few hundred metre intervals from the front were given up without a struggle, no reserves, no idea of counter-attack. The happy-go-lucky, childlike spirit seems still to pervade everybody, much talk, little action, and even now not one spade has been put into the ground behind the Adige or the Mincio [to prepare new defensive lines in case of a further Austrian breakthrough at the Piave or in the mountains], though there are masses of troops available in every village. I can see a distinct feeling of anxiety in the higher command.[131]

General Plumer, reporting on the situation on 13th January 1918, identified a number of areas of concern in relation to his Italian allies. But the worst problem, he thought, was the lack of attention paid to training, and the failure to appreciate the necessity for it. He was also critical of Italian staff officers, who, although easy to work with and keen to help, had only a theoretical knowledge of staff work and did not understand the practical difficulties of their orders. "Paper is the ruling factor, and they agree to things and issue orders which cannot be carried out, and this has been the chief defect in their operations."[132] They needed to be helped to get better. But, Plumer warned, it was vital to tread carefully along this path. Although they deplored the behaviour of their Second Army at Caporetto, the Italians did not consider there was much wrong with the remainder of their forces and whilst they were willing to profit from the experiences of their allies, "any attempt to force foreign methods on them would result in nothing being done". He had issued instructions to all British officers that they were to avoid any appearance of superiority or of telling the Italians what to do. Everything was to be done by illustration and demonstration.[133]

Following his own direction, Plumer was careful to ensure that when the British took over a section of the Piave Line, it quickly became a model for how a modern defensive position should be organised and for how few men were required to hold the front line. He then invited General Diaz to visit the sector and was pleased to note that after the visit the Italians on either side of the British set about improving their very simple defences.[134] He also ensured that the British schools of instruction were open to Italian students. A GHQ training area with accommodation for up to an Infantry Brigade, was quickly established at Torreglia, south-west of Padua, with a central school set up at the nearby Praglia Monastery, opening in January 1918. Although this was primarily aimed at ensuring that British personnel were able to benefit from the latest tactical thinking, it was also hoped that by inviting Italian officers and NCOs to take part in

---

131 TNA WO 79/67: Lt Gen R F Cavan Private Papers, Italy.
132 J E Edmonds, p.135.
133 J E Edmonds, p.133-34.
134 J E Edmonds, p.107.

British training, it would help to instil good doctrine and practice into the Italian army.[135] All General Staff publications about the lessons learned in France were translated into Italian.[136]

By April 1918, the situation had stabilised. Plumer had gone back to France, Cavan had taken over as Commander in Chief of British Forces in Italy, and the Italian army seemed to have recovered from the shock of Caporetto. Its self-confidence was returning, and it had engaged in a number of small, largely-successful offensive operations. However, the British continued to seek influence over the Italians and Cavan still had concerns. Writing to the new CIGS, Gen Sir Henry Wilson, on 2nd April, he pointed to three principal issues – bad commanders, bad communications and dangerous zones. Of the latter, he highlighted the area between the Piave and the Astico, especially in the Grappa sector; the Pasubio area; and the Lake Garda area, principally the Judicaria and Val Lagarina passes. The British might have some influence between the Piave and the Astico but would have "little or no influence on either the Pasubio or Lake Garda zones. Responding to a question from Wilson, seeking views on how to "obtain an influence on a greater length of the line and a greater part of the Italian army", Cavan offered two proposals, one of which could have had a bearing on Fanshawe's sacking.

According to Cavan, the best way to gain influence over the Judicaria and Val Lagarina passes – the most important lines of advance into Italy for the Austrians – was to withdraw the French from their current sector at Asiago and assign them to the protection of the passes, whilst bringing the British divisions into a general reserve, ready to move as a corps to any threatened zone. This was intended to happen after the proposed allied offensive.

The most effective way to achieve influence over a wider swathe of the Italian army would be to create new British and French armies in Italy and incorporate Italian Corps and Divisions into them. Cavan suggested a British-led Army of three corps, each corps consisting of three divisions – one British and two Italian. One corps would be commanded by an English general and the other two by Italians. To assist the Italian Generals in their relations with the British divisions, a British staff officer should be attached to each Brigade and "thereby great influence would undoubtedly be obtained". These British and French divisions should be placed at the most vital points – Lake Garda and astride the Brenta. Nevertheless, Cavan was well aware that this was a high-risk strategy. He added:

> The Germans did it with the Austrians and undoubtedly increased their fighting efficiency, but it did not increase the love between the nations. Dare we try it?[137]

Although he does not say so in this document, the obvious implication is that Cavan himself would command the proposed British army, and this is confirmed in later correspondence. On 13th April, Wilson penned a hand-written note to Cavan, enclosing a letter from Major General Charles Sackville-West, the British Military Representative at the Supreme War Council at Versailles, "on the subject of your commanding three mixed corps…you will see that Giardino is not opposed to it…"[138] General Gaetano Giardino had been appointed, in the post-Caporetto re-organisation, as one of two joint deputies to Diaz, and was an Italian repre-

---

135 J E Edmonds, p.128.
136 J E Edmonds, p.134.
137 TNA WO 100/852: Cavan to Wilson correspondence, 2nd April 1918.
138 TNA WO 100/852: Wilson to Cavan correspondence, 13th April 1918.

sentative at Versailles. Sackville-West had obviously sounded him out about Cavan's proposal on Wilson's behalf.

On 28th April, Cavan again wrote to Wilson on the matter stating that he thought British influence was spreading but admitting that "It is slow and confined to certain keen commanders". Moreover:

> If we made an attack in which we were successful, or beat off a strong hostile attack, no doubt more attention would be paid to our teaching, owing to our success on the field.[139]

However, on 3rd June, Cavan was forced to report to Wilson that the Italians had decided to withdraw all their students, officers and men, from the British and French schools. The Italians offered three key reasons for the move – the need for all officers [to be] with their units in the coming time of stress; being trained on different lines to what they were accustomed to, the students emerged with a lessened faith in their own training and an incomplete knowledge of the British methods; and the intention of opening their own large training school in the future.[140]

Gaining and maintaining influence over the Italian army, and the way it fought, continued to be a high priority for Wilson and Cavan. Initially, under Robertson and Plumer, this had been focused on stabilising the situation post Caporetto, supporting the Italians until they had regained their confidence and fighting spirit, and thus allowing the British and French divisions to return to the western front at the earliest sensible moment to help to meet the expected German offensive. However, with the passing of time, and the failure of the Spring Offensive, the strategic objective became less about facilitating a return of British and French troops to the western front and more to do with the need to assure the security of two key danger zones – Pasubio and the mountain passes above Lake Garda. Achieving this was still highly dependent on being able to exert influence over the Italian military and political leadership. This, in turn, was going to be heavily reliant on the reputation of the British and French forces. On 11th July, Cavan wrote to Wilson to report that the British Military Attache in Rome (Lt Col Rorke, DSO), had speculated that:

> Society in Rome all say that the British line was broken on June 15th and that Italian reserves restored the situation. Two of my Staff who have just returned from leave in Rome confirm this as being the general view in that city and that it is based on the fact that the early newspaper reports on June 16th gave the British line as broken, while the whole Italian line was intact.[141]

Although the newspaper reporting is entirely wrong, and the report itself comes long after Fanshawe had been dismissed, the fact that Cavan thought to pass the information back to Wilson, shows that the reputation of the British military and how it was perceived in the eyes of the Italians, continued to be very important.

---

139 TNA WO 100/852: Cavan to Wilson correspondence, 28th April 1918.
140 TNA WO 100/852: Cavan to Wilson correspondence, 3rd June 1918.
141 TNA WO 100/852: Cavan to Wilson correspondence, 11th July 1918.

The other possibility is that Fanshawe was axed because of the poor performance of one particular battalion, 1/5th R Warwicks. There is no mention of this in the 48th Division battle narrative, except to note that the enemy was able to break in on the Warwicks' front. However, in a letter from GHQ to the Italian Sixth Army, dated 30th June, although not referred to in the actual account of the battle, the Lessons Learned annex states the following:

> There is every evidence to suggest that on one portion of the front, the whole of the garrison went into dugouts during the bombardment, left no sentries, and did not come out of the dugouts when the bombardment lifted.[142]

The note does not provide details of the 'evidence', nor does it name the battalion concerned. However, the 48th Division's battle narrative, noting key elements of the fighting, highlights:

> As regards the fighting in the front line in the centre and left of the division, when the enemy infantry first advanced, info is wanting owing to the garrison being killed, wounded or missing; but the counter-attacking troops report that they think they must have put up a good fight owing to the [number of] enemy dead in the line our men found on arrival.[143]

The 143rd Brigade's battle narrative had this to say:

> Investigation has shown that the garrison of the trenches which met the attack (1/5th R Warwicks), offered stout resistance and were not caught in their dugouts, as many enemy were found lying in and by the trenches attacked.[144]

In correspondence with Edmonds, Carrington does not specifically refer to the charge that the battalion was caught in its dugouts, but he does admit that:

> The 48th Division, and my battalion in particular, 1/5th R Warwicks, were thought to have done badly in this battle …[145]

Unfortunately, there is no battalion narrative for this battle in the National Archives files. This may be because the two men who would have been responsible for producing it were no longer available to write it. The adjutant, Capt Carter was a prisoner, and the CO, Major Bindloss, was dead.

Casualty figures for the battalion during this fighting show that it suffered the highest losses of the Brigade – 17 killed, 29 wounded and 31 missing. This, in itself, is unsurprising, given that the battalion faced the enemy's main infantry assault in that part of the line. However, an analysis of the brigade figures shows that the number of wounded is lower than for 1/7th R Warwicks, who led the counter-attack on the 15th (49). The number of missing also stands out when it is compared with the others who, together, were unable to account for only six soldiers.

---

142 TNA/WO 95/4191: GHQ Italy (GS) War Diary, Lessons Learned, 15th June 1918.
143 TNA WO 95/4244: 48th Division (GS) War Diary, Battle Narrative, 15th/16th June 1918.
144 TNA WO 95/4248: 143rd Brigade War Diary.
145 TNA CAB 45/84: Carrington to Edmonds correspondence 28th June 1944.

This figure could support the theory that the front-line company was caught in its dugouts, and a large number of men were thus taken prisoner, or it could simply relate to the speed with which they were overwhelmed, leaving them with no choice but to put up their hands.

This, then, is surely the controversy that Pickford felt should not be revived.

If GHQ really believed that this incident had occurred, it is possible that it tainted the reputation of the South Midlanders in the eyes of XIV Corps and was seen as a reflection on Fanshawe's leadership. The performance of individual battalions was, with good justification, considered to be a reflection on their commanders, who might bask in the glory of success, but also shouldered the responsibility for failure. However, it would have been very unusual for a divisional commander to be dismissed for the poor performance of a single battalion. It would certainly have been enough to cost the job of the relevant Brigade Commander – in this case Brigadier-General G C Sladen. But apart from the problems encountered by 1/5th R Warwicks, the other elements of 143rd Brigade had fought well during the 15-16th June, and Sladen's removal would have been equally unreasonable and hard to justify.

Looking back on the Asiago battle through an objective lens, it appears that Fanshawe was a sacrificial pawn in the game of military-political chess being played in Italy and London by Cavan and Wilson as they sought to gain influence over the Italian army and its way of fighting. While Cavan afterwards tried to make it look like he had sacked Fanshawe for military failure, this is not justified by the available evidence, even when considered against the standards of that time. It is possible that Cavan and Wilson took the view that by allowing their line to be penetrated at Asiago, the performance of the 48th Division, whilst a long way from being a military failure, had potentially undermined the reputation of British forces in the eyes of the Italians, and thus dented Italian confidence in British expertise. Fanshawe's sacking may have been a knee-jerk reaction born of bitterness and frustration at the possible impact of the Division's performance on the carefully-laid plan to create a new Anglo-Italian army with Cavan at its head. By removing Fanshawe, Cavan made himself look like a tough, no-nonsense commander who was quite prepared to take difficult and unpalatable decisions – including sacrificing one of his most experienced divisional commanders – for the greater good. Just the sort of man the Italians should want in command of a joint army. Cavan and Wilson's ultimate objective – keeping the Italians in the war in order to 'fix' the Austrians on the Italian front and prevent them from reinforcing the Germans in France – was reasonable and apposite. But some of the means by which they sought to achieve it, specifically in being prepared to obliterate the reputation of a good and able divisional commander and undermine the morale of his division at an already difficult time, reflects badly on the reputations of both.

# 11

# From Asiago to Austria

With the Austrians now, seemingly, in disarray at Asiago, Cavan was keen to launch the planned but previously postponed Allied offensive. To confirm the state of the enemy, he ordered 23rd Division to execute a raid east of Asiago on 16th June. This was highly successful, resulting in the capture of a number of prisoners, at the cost of only three British casualties. For Cavan this was proof positive of the demoralised state of the opposition, and he used the information gained to try to persuade Diaz to authorise the postponed attack across the plateau.[1]

Diaz, concerned about the progress of an Austrian penetration on the Piave Line, at the Montello, turned down the request, pointing to his need to hold his reserves in hand against the eventuality of further Austrian incursions there. However, on 23rd June, Cavan visited the Italian Sixth Army headquarters and was told by General Montuori that, in the event of the enemy withdrawing troops from the Asiago area, he might decide to attack, and, if the enemy renewed his offensive and was defeated, the Sixth Army was to be prepared to pursue.[2] Consequently, that evening, Cavan issued orders for the two British divisions holding the line to be prepared to advance at short notice and seize the objectives given in the Operation Order (dated 12th June, 1918) for the postponed attack.[3]

In his memoir, Cavan claims Diaz's decision not to attack led to a "long lull in operations … so boring for the troops concerned".[4] The XIV Corps General Staff War Diary supports that statement, noting in its summary for July that "no operations of importance have taken place during the month…"[5] However, for the men of the 48th Division (and, indeed, the 7th and 23rd Divisions), July, and the following three months, were anything but boring. Initially occupied with repairing battle damage and improving their defences on the plateau, the British soon found themselves conducting a series of raids, often in considerable strength, against the Austrian positions in front of the town of Asiago.

The South Midlanders were relieved by the 7th Division over the 24th, 25th and 26th June, and went down the mountains and into reserve in the Sacredo, Villa Verla and Montecchio areas, with divisional headquarters at San Rocco, moving to Tressino on 30th June and 2nd July.

---

1 CCC Cavan unpublished memoir.
2 J E Edmonds, p.217.
3 TNA WO 95/4194: GHQ Operation Order No. 35, 23rd June 1918.
4 CCC Cavan unpublished memoir.
5 TNA WO 95/4212: XIV Corps General Staff War Diary.

The King of Italy ordered an International Review at Marostica on 4th July, at which the 48th was represented by 1/7th Royal Warwickshires. On the same day, Major General Sir Harold B Walker, KCB, DSO, a veteran of Gallipoli and the Somme, arrived from France to replace Fanshawe. Over the next fortnight the division re-equipped, received and integrated replacements for the losses from the Asiago fighting and undertook a rigorous training package.

On 12th July, orders arrived to relieve the 23rd Division in the eastern sector. This was completed by noon on the 23rd, the troops making their weary way back up the mountain tracks to Grenezza and from there, into the line on the left of the French.[6] Although they did not know it at the time, they were destined to spend the next 17 weeks there, without relief, until hostilities had ceased and the war in Italy was at an end.

As the post-15th June situation stabilised, and the likelihood of a renewed Austrian attack receded, British intelligence officers, analysing captured documents and reports of interrogations of prisoners and deserters, began to identify the possibility of an enemy withdrawal to the northern edge of the Asiago plateau, where the enemy had constructed a new *Winterstellung* (winter position). Desperate to confirm the rumours, GHQ ordered an immediate step-up in patrolling of no-man's land, and a series of deliberate raids on enemy positions. These raids were primarily designed to identify any early signs that a retirement was in the offing, and, at the same time, to keep the Austrian garrison "on the alert" and, if possible, force him to conduct his withdrawal under pressure. They would also "fix" as many troops as possible in and near the front line, where they were more susceptible to harassing artillery fire and to being taken prisoner. At the same time, the frequent attacks, usually supported by heavy artillery bombardments, would have helped to undermine Austrian morale. According to Captain Philip Wright, these raids were "planned with the greatest care and worked out to the smallest detail".[7]

A good example of this raiding policy occurred on the night of 8th-9th August when no fewer than eight limited attacks took place, simultaneously, between Asiago and Canove. The 48th Division contribution to this involved 143rd and 144th Brigades, who were to conduct four raids. The divisional operation order, setting out the details, was issued on 6th August. 143rd Brigade's objectives were Santa Maria Maddalena and Ave, fortified hamlets to the south-east and south of Asiago, while 144th Brigade was to strike at Edelweis Spur and the railway near Gaiga South, located between Asiago and Cesuna. The strength of the raiding parties was left to the Brigade Commanders, but both attacks were to be pushed well through the enemy's front line and to clear the dugouts and shelters in the rear. The 143rd Brigade raiders were specifically directed to patrol right into the southern outskirts of Asiago itself.[8]

The assault on Santa Maria Maddalena was conducted by two companies of 1/5th Royal Warwickshires, B and C, who formed up half-way across no-man's land and moved forward, with C Company in the vanguard. At Zero, which was set for midnight, under a heavy artillery bombardment, the leading platoons of C Company entered the enemy trench system, established a bombing block and then worked their way to the right (east), reaching their objectives, a group of dugouts, where they took 24 prisoners. According to Charles Carrington, in his war history of the battalion, the raid did not go to plan. He claims that the remaining two platoons of C Company and the whole of B Company failed to go forward. Capt H P

---

6   TNA WO 95/4244: 48th Division General Staff War Diary.
7   P L Wright, p116.
8   TNA WO 95/4244: Operation Order No. 33, 6th August 1918, 48th Division (GS) War Diary.

Williams-Freeman (38), 3rd Royal Warwickshires, attached 1/5th Battalion, was killed and his place was taken by Capt H L R J Groom (DSO, MC and Bar), who ordered a withdrawal at around 0115, bringing the prisoners.[9] The divisional report of the raid states that the initial success achieved by C Company was "not adequately exploited" and notes that the circumstances were being investigated.[10]

Meanwhile, to the left of the 1/5th Royal Warwickshires, the 1/7th Battalion reached the enemy line at Ave at 0004, after overcoming strong resistance, including heavy machine gun fire, and severe hand-to-hand fighting, in which about 20 Austrians were killed, and three machine guns disabled. Having entered the line, the attackers used rifle grenades against enemy positions near Silvegnar, forcing a further 20 defenders to capitulate. The Warwickshires managed to reach the dugouts north-east of Ave and these were bombed. However, further heavy machine gun fire from depth prevented parties from reaching the southern edge of Asiago. In all, about 90 prisoners were captured, along with two machine guns. A further 70 Austrians were estimated to have been killed and seven machine guns destroyed, while the attackers' casualties amounted to 13 wounded, including one officer.[11]

In the 144th Brigade sector, three companies of 1/8th Worcestershires raided Edelweiss Spur. In this case, there was concern about a possible enemy post, located in no-man's land, and a party was detailed to go out in advance of the main body and clear the assembly area. Once this had been done, the raid progressed as planned. The enemy wire was cut under cover of a rifle grenade barrage and supporting Lewis Gun fire, and the attackers entered the Austrian position to the east of the spur and worked their way northwards along the communications trench until they reached a point just south of the railway line where they bombed dugouts and killed or captured the garrison. Another breech was made near the point of the spur, clearing the area right up to the railway, again killing or capturing the garrison and bombing the dugouts [author's note: this raid needs to be illustrated with a map, annotated to show the various points at which the attackers entered the line]. In all, 40 prisoners were taken, together with a single machine gun. About 60 enemy soldiers killed. The attackers suffered 2 other ranks killed, 14 wounded and two missing (one believed killed).[12]

In the fourth raid, three companies of 1/6th Gloucestershires (also 144th Brigade) attacked the railway cutting south of Gaiga South. One company engaged the enemy holding Norfolk Trench while the remaining two companies launched the main assault on Middlesex Trench, between Post Spur and Coda Spur. The troops targeting Norfolk Trench ran into an enemy patrol as they moved to their assembly area, and the ensuing fire-fight caused considerable delay and some confusion. This resulted in two platoons advancing straight at the main Coda Spur (which was not part of the plan). They were met with heavy machine gun fire and could not get forward. The remaining two platoons eventually managed to work along a section of the trench, but it was not possible to clear it all the way up to the railway cutting. Despite their efforts, the attackers suffered three other ranks killed and seven wounded. It was estimated that about 20 enemy were also killed.

9  C E Carrington, *War Record of the 1/5th Bn, Royal Warwickshire Regiment*, pp.72-72.
10 TNA WO 95/4244: Report of Raids on 8/9th August, n.d., 48th Division (GS) War Diary.
11 TNA WO 95/4244: Report of Raids on 8/9th August, n.d., 48th Division (GS) War Diary.
12 TNA WO 95/4244: Report of Raids on 8/9th August, n.d., 48th Division (GS) War Diary.

The raids had been broadly successful, but there was no conclusive evidence to support the suggestion that an enemy retirement was looming. In fact, if anything, the physical indications at this point suggested the reverse: the Austrians were continuing to hold their current line strongly, demonstrating a resolve not to allow the British to have easy access. On 12th August, Cavan called a conference with his Divisional Commanders at GHQ at Lonedo, during which it was stated that while an Austrian retirement remained possible, nothing showed that it was imminent.[13]

But the rumours of a withdrawal persisted and Cavan and Montuori needed to know for sure if the intelligence was sound. On 23rd August, Cavan noted that information received "over the past 24 hours" indicated that "the much talked of Austrian retirement is imminent and may, in fact, begin tonight …".[14] This proved to be an over-optimistic assessment of the situation. However, divisions in the line (48th and 23rd) were ordered to make every effort, "by means of patrols and any other methods that Divisional Commanders may select, to obtain prisoners during the next 48 hours".[15] On 25th August, two small patrols from the 48th Division hit the enemy front-line system between Ave and Sec, capturing six prisoners. Following on from this, Major General Walker ordered a brigade-level raid on the night of 26th-27th, again targeting the Austrian line near Ave. The task was given to 145th Brigade, the strength of the attacking party being restricted to "no greater than two battalions".[16] The operation was planned and overseen by Brigadier-General D M Watt, who selected 1/1st Bucks Battalion and 1/4th Royal Berkshires for the job. The Operation Order directed them to push forward as far as the Asiago–Clama Road, killing or capturing the garrison. Dugouts and shelters were to be searched. Normally, once searched, dugouts would be destroyed to deny them to the enemy. However, in this case, the orders specifically forbade their destruction.[17] No explanation for this is given in the papers, but it is likely that the British wished to be able to make use of them once the enemy had retired – providing they had not been demolished by the retreating Austrians.

Reporting to HQ 48th Division on the raid, newly-appointed brigade commander, Brigadier-General Walter Pitt-Taylor[18], who, on 27th August, had taken over from Brigadier-General D M Watt, noted that all objectives were achieved and "apparently the entire garrison was killed or captured"[19]. It was discovered that the Austrians were holding their front line in considerable strength and, after earlier raids, were very much on the alert. They defended stoutly at first but "gave up directly they were seriously tackled". However, a quarry that had previously held large numbers of troops was found to be empty. The houses on the southern outskirts of Asiago were

---

13 TNA WO 95/4195: Notes of C-in-C's Conference with Divisional Commanders, 12th August 1918, GHQ War Diary.
14 TNA WO 95/4195: GHQ Operation Order No. 40, 23rd August 1918, GHQ War Diary.
15 TNA WO 95/4195: GHQ Operation Order No. 40, 23rd August 1918, GHQ War Diary.
16 TNA WO 95/4244: Operation Order No. 36, 48th Division War Diary.
17 TNA WO 95/4244: Operation Order No. 36, 48th Division War Diary.
18 Brigadier-General Walter William Pitt-Taylor, another Boer War veteran, had previously been deputy to the XIV Corps Chief of Staff, Brigadier-General Francis Gaythorne-Hardy. After Cavan was appointed to command Tenth Italian Army, taking with him Gaythorne-Hardy, Pitt-Taylor assumed the post of Chief of Staff, XIV Corps. Post-war he was appointed to be Military Assistant to the Chief of the Imperial General Staff (Wilson).
19 TNA/WO95/4244, 48th Division GS War Diary, Report on raid by 145th Brigade on night 26/27 August 1918.

searched but no sign of occupation was found. The majority of prisoners were captured in the front line and in dugouts just behind and on the Sec road. Taken together, these were possible signs that the enemy was beginning to thin out the line preliminary to retirement. As a result, on 31st August, XIV Corps issued a warning order to prepare for an attack north-west across the plateau, to be led initially by 7th and 23rd Divisions, with 48th Division following up to capture Monte Erio and Cima di Campolongo.

This operation never took place. Instead, Commando Supremo, General Diaz, under pressure from the Supreme War Council to take the offensive, began to prepare for an attack across the Piave, to be launched before the year's end. In the autumn, as part of this planning, Diaz created two new Armies. The first of these, initially the Mobile Army of Reserve, later renamed the Tenth Army, was to consist of an Italian corps and a British corps, each of two divisions, under the command of the Earl of Cavan. The British contribution would be the XIV Corps, now formed of the 7th and 23rd divisions. The 48th Division was to remain in the Asiago sector, becoming part of the Italian XII Corps. As Cavan explained in his memoir: "In October, with every precaution of secrecy, we left the 48th Division in the hills and moved by rail to the Piave…"[20] Edmonds adds that the 48th, together with a French division, were left at Asiago, in an attempt to prevent the Austrians from discovering that French and British troops had been withdrawn.[21]

At Asiago, raiding increased in frequency until, on the night of 28th-29th October, with the Piave offensive under way, the Bucks Battalion, entering the area Sec – Santa Maria Maddalena-Cassodar, found the enemy positions deserted. A single soldier of 11/67th Infantry Regiment had been left behind to fire off rockets in an attempt to fool the British into thinking the line was still occupied. The Austrian retirement had begun.

48th Division immediately issued orders for the brigades in the line (144th and 145th) to each push forward one company to occupy the line Capitello Mulche-Camprovere and then to send patrols towards Monte Catz and Monte Razta and the line Mosciagh-Interotto. The right brigade's company (1/4th Royal Berkshires) established its headquarters in the old barracks in Asiago, sending troops towards Rodighieri, Costa and Bosco, only meeting resistance at the latter, where 16 prisoners and one machine gun were captured. A second patrol reached Costa and then continued along Dogs Trench and from there down the south-west slopes of Monte Catz through Du Ballon Trench. No enemy were encountered but a machine gun firing from depth, in the vicinity of Rodighieri, prevented them from continuing forward. A third patrol to the north of Hattala was held up all day by machine gun fire but was able to report that the enemy was occupying the *Winterstellung* near Bosco and at the foot of Monte Catz. On the left, a company from 1/7th Worcesters was pinned down in Camporovere village by fire from Goodwood Trench, while another Worcesters patrol suffered some casualties in a sharp exchange with the enemy to the west of the village at about noon. Throughout this period, Austrian artillery shelled the line it had just evacuated and, during the night, targeted roads and tracks in the area to make it difficult for the British to move men and material forward. By the morning of 31st October, however, 144th and 145th Brigades had established a line of observation as ordered.

---

20  CCC Cavan unpublished Memoir.
21  J E Edmonds, p.249.

That evening the commander of the neighbouring 24th French Division (General Odry) sent word that his patrols had also found the enemy trenches to their front deserted and that he planned to attack Monte Longara at 0500 the following morning (1st November). To protect the French left flank, Major General Walker immediately sought permission from XII Corps to conduct a coordinated assault on Monte Mosciagh and Monte Interotto, and orders were issued to that effect. However, given the short planning window, 144th Brigade asked for zero to be moved back to 0545. This was agreed, although the preliminary barrage remained timed to begin at 0500.

The attack was launched as planned, with the 1/1st Bucks Battalion and 1/4th Royal Berkshires of 145th Brigade on the right and 144th Brigade's 1/4th and 1/6th Gloucestershires on the left. Monte Catz was captured by the Berkshires by 0630, who then pushed on along the Catz ridge to Roccolo where, by 0815, they had joined up with the Bucks Battalion. On the left, however, 144th Brigade met with stiff resistance from Goodwood Trench and were forced back to Camporovere, having to evacuate Bosco. Walker now moved 1/7th Worcesters, 144th Brigade's reserve battalion, to the right to reinforce the success achieved by 145th Brigade, while 143rd Brigade, in divisional reserve, was moved forward, concentrating in the San Sisto-Asiago area.

At dawn on 2nd November the 1/7th Worcesters and 1/4th Oxfords flung themselves up the slopes of Monte Mosciagh and Monte Dorbellele, capturing both locations by 0730. 144th Brigade, attacking at the same time, found Goodwood Trench abandoned and were able to press forward to occupy Monte Interotto by 0845. 143rd Brigade moved up and took on the role of divisional advanced guard, with a section of 18-pounders and two 4.5in howitzers attached to provide intimate artillery support.

This formation entered the Val d'Assa at 1000, its right flank being protected by 145th Brigade while 20th Italian Division covered its left. Lt Charles Carrington described the brigade's part in the final phase:

> All that day, the three battalions pressed on through the narrow valley running between high mountains. There was little opposition. The 6th and 7th had the honours at first, for they cleared the mountains on either side and captured incredible quantities of material and many prisoners. The 5th marched along the road in the centre. They covered 14 miles that day on a road through the high mountains … The country was so wild, steep and rocky – they had climbed a thousand feet and were now 4,300 feet above sea level – that it was almost impossible to leave the road. At dusk they reached the abandoned camp of Osteria del Termine on the Austrian border, and halted for the night … By 5.30 the next morning the Brigade was on the move again. Crossing the frontier, they marched on, the first British troops to enter hostile territory …[22]

Although there was some sporadic resistance from isolated parties of Austrian troops, the leading elements of the advanced guard reached the junction between the Val d"Assa and Val Portule by 1300 and had passed Monte Porreche d'Avanti by 1500. By 1700 the line Vezzena – Marcia di Sotto had been reached and 143rd Brigade units were in touch with the enemy

---

22   C E Carrington, p.76.

rearguard. As they pushed forward, the Warwickshire Brigade found an Austrian battalion drawn up on the road, accompanied by its Divisional Commander, who insisted that an armistice had been signed and that 143rd Brigade had advanced beyond the agreed limits. Brigadier-General Sladen came up and disillusioned him. Giving the Austrians 10 minutes to surrender, he sent his Lewis Gun teams up the hills overlooking the road and threatened to destroy them if they refused. Although the Austrians outnumbered the small group of Warwickshires before them, they had no appetite to fight on. The divisional commander submitted and was marched to the rear with his men.[23] In the fighting up to 1800 that day, a total of 3000 prisoners and several hundred artillery pieces had been captured by 48th Division units. French and Italian units to the right and left had made equally spectacular advances.

With the French on the right advancing along Val Sugana, Major General Walker ordered 143rd Brigade to take Caldonazzo and Levico, blocking the valley to the west. If this could be achieved, the Austrians, pulling back in the face of the French onslaught from the east, would be trapped and forced to capitulate. By 0800 a force of 14 enemy battalions, together with the III Austrian Corps commander and three divisional commanders, had been surrounded and captured. Pressing on towards Caldonazzo, all opposition appeared to have ceased and Austrian troops surrendered in large numbers. They too were apparently under the false impression that an Armistice had been signed at 0300 that morning. The Austrian High Command had sent a message to the Trentino front at 0200 on the 3rd November, stating that all hostilities were to be stopped at once. This was premature, however, as the negotiators had agreed that the armistice would not come into effect until 1500 on the 4th.[24]

The following day (4th November), on orders from XII Corps, the advance was resumed while the 48th Division Chief of Staff, Lt Col H C Howard and the Intelligence Officer, Lt G J Eastman, were sent forward, by car, to the Austrian Third Army headquarters at Trent, with terms of surrender. These were accepted without significant alteration. By 1500 the division was concentrated in and around Caldonazzo, establishing a cease-fire line at Cima Brada – Baselga di Pine – Doss di Brusadi – Monte Calisio.

Recording the advance of the Bucks Battalion, Capt Philip Wright, described the trail of destruction in the wake of a defeated foe:

> Abandoned guns, waggon parks, ammunition dumps, lay by the side of the whole route; the roads were littered with articles of Austrian equipment. In their anxiety to travel as fast and as lightly as possible, the enemy had cast away all that encumbered him. Gas masks, helmets, packs, haversacks, and, finally, rifles lay scattered along the road, down which but a few hours before the routed army had passed in their helpless, panic-stricken flight. One's dream of the typical army rout of history days had come true, and indeed surpassed all imagination. As we neared Vezzena, we met whole battalions of the enemy marching to the rear, under the escort of a handful of British soldiers. In many cases an Austrian battalion commander led back his battalion complete, while in front of him walked a man with the white flag. Generals were permitted to ride, at footpace. It was a pathetic sight to see these

---

23   C E Carrington, pp.76-77.
24   J E Edmonds, p.378.

thousands of men trudging their weary way to our rear. Their spirit was broken, and tragedy was written plain on every officer's face.[25]

As General Walker noted in his after-action report, between 1st and 3rd November the 48th Division had advanced more than 60 kilometres through the mountains, sustaining less than 200 casualties[26] – a magnificent feat of arms, albeit against a now beaten and dejected enemy, attempting to retire back across the Austrian-Italian border. Walker was clearly pleased with the performance of his division in those final days. His report concluded:

> I would bring to notice the admirable manner in which the 145th Infantry Brigade, plus the 1/7th Worc. R. (Brig.-Genrl. W. Howard, C.M.G., D.S.O., Commanding) carried out the arduous operations against M. Mosciagh, the brunt of which fell on the 1/4th R. Berks R. (Lieut.-Colonel Whitehead, D.S.O. Commanding) and the Bucks Battalion (Lieut.-Colonel L.L.C. Reynolds, D.S.O., Commanding); also, the resolution of the 143rd Inf. Bde., as Advanced Guard, in pushing through the Val d'Assa as far as Vezzena without halting.[27]

The Duke of Braganza, surrendering to Major General Walker, paid the South Midlanders this compliment: "The advance of your 48th British Division will go down in history as one of the most splendid feats of the British Army."[28] Cavan agreed. In his official despatch, following the cessation of hostilities, putting the final advance into context, he explained:

> It must be remembered that this division was attacking very formidable mountain positions with only a fifth of the artillery that would have been at its disposal (due to the terrain and the difficulty getting the guns forward)… Its performance, therefore, in driving in the enemy's rear-guards so resolutely, while climbing up to heights of 5000 feet, is all the more praiseworthy. The infantry had been waiting for an opportunity to show that they could worthily emulate the performance of their comrades in France (during the last 100 days). When the opportunity came, they fulfilled my highest anticipations.[29]

While the captures of prisoners and guns made by the 48th Division during the final advance "cannot be accurately ascertained", Cavan estimated that they amounted to at least 20,000 prisoners and 500 artillery pieces.[30]

The fighting on the Italian front came to a conclusion at 1500 on the 4th November, 1918, bringing to an end three years and five months of bloody fighting in that theatre. On 6th November, the division was informed that it was to be sent back to Grenezza, and it was eventually agreed that it would retrace its route of advance. The retirement began on 8th November, and once the division had concentrated at Grenezza, it was directed to move down the mountains

---

25 P L Wright, p.132.
26 TNA WO 95/4244: Report of Operations, 8th November 1918, 48th Division War Diary.
27 TNA WO 95/4244: 48th Division (GS) War Diary, Report of Operations, 8th November 1918.
28 E Wyrall, *The Gloucestershire Regiment*, p.348.
29 Cavan Despatch, *The London Gazette*, Supplement 31049, December 1918, p.14412.
30 Cavan Despatch, *The London Gazette*, Supplement 31049, December 1918, p.14412.

to Thiene and then to Trissino, where it rejoined the XIV Corps. From there, arrangements were made for demobilisation. Although some small groups were sent back to the UK almost at once, the first "demob" train did not depart until 23rd December, and it would be many months before the last men of the division made it back onto home soil. The Bucks Battalion's final cadre of five officers and 50 other ranks, arrived back at their headquarters in Aylesbury on 31st March, parading in front of the Town Hall, from where they had departed to the war in August 1914.[31] The 1/6th Gloucesters drew a short straw and were detailed for garrison duty in Montenegro and Albania and then on to Egypt. It was not until 25th March 1920, that the cadre and colours reached Bristol, the battalion having been abroad on active service for five years and seven months – a record that not many Territorial battalions could boast.[32]

31   P L Wright, p.142.
32   E Wyrall, p.350.

# Select Bibliography

## Archival Sources

### The National Archives of the United Kingdom
CAB 45/84: Cabinet Office Historical Section: War Histories Correspondence and Papers – Original Letters, Comments and Personal Accounts
CAB 25/69: Supreme War Council Secretariat, Italy, Situation Report, 1917-1919
CAB 23/4/63: War Cabinet Minutes, 3rd December 1917
CAB 24/33/90: War Cabinet Minutes, 27th November 1917
CAB 24/33/56: War Cabinet Minutes, 24th November 1917
CAB 23/4/46: War Cabinet Minutes, 13th November 1917
WO 32/9192: Efficiency of Territorial Force Compared to Regular Army: Reports from Officers Commanding in Chief, 1911
WO 95/4194: GHQ Italy General Staff War Diary
WO 95/432: Fourth Army War Diary
WO 95/518: Fifth Army War Diary
WO 95/638: II Corps War Diary
WO 95/674: III Corps War Diary
WO 95/804: VI Corps General Staff War Diary
WO 95/820: VIII Corps General Staff War Diary
WO 95/4194: GHQ Italy (GS) War Diary.
WO 95/951/4: XVIII Corps War Diary
WO 95/2745: 48th (South Midland) Infantry Division War Diary
WO 95/4244: 48th Division (GS) War Diary.
WO 95/2756: 143rd Infantry Brigade War Diary
WO 95/2754: 143rd Infantry Brigade War Diary
WO 95/2757: 144th Infantry Brigade War Diary
WO 95/2760: 145th Infantry Brigade War Diary
WO 95/2763/2: First Buckinghamshire Battalion War Diary
WO 95/2763/1: 1/5th Battalion Gloucestershire Regiment War Diary
WO 95/2756/1: 1/7th Battalion Royal Warwickshire Regiment War Diary
WO 95/2758/2: 1/6th Battalion Gloucestershire Regiment War Diary
WO 95/2764/1: 1/4th Battalion Oxfordshire and Buckinghamshire Light Infantry War Diary
WO 95/2755/2: 1/6th Battalion Royal Warwickshire Regiment War Diary
WO 95/2756/2: 1/8th Battalion Royal Warwickshire Regiment War Diary
WO 95/2762: 1/4th Battalion Royal Berkshire Regiment War Diary

WO 95/2759/1: 1/7th Battalion Worcestershire Regiment War Diary
WO 95/2749: 240th Brigade Royal Field Artillery War Diary
WO 95/4250: 145th Trench Mortar Battery War Diary
WO 95/4248: 143rd Infantry Brigade, Italy War Diary
WO 95/4246: 474th Field Company Royal Engineers War Diary
WO 79/67: Lt Gen F R Earl of Cavan (XIV Corps) Private Papers, Italy
WO 79/68: Lt Gen F R Earl of Cavan (XIV Corps) Private Papers, Italy, 1 January 1918-30 April 1919
WO 79/70: Lt Gen F R Earl of Cavan (XIV Corps) Private Papers. Campaign in Italy, 1917-1918
WO 100/852: Lt Gen F R Earl of Cavan correspondence

*Australian War Memorial*
1/42/18: 1st Australian Division General Staff War Diary

*Unpublished Memoirs*
Cavan Papers, Recollections Hazy But Happy, Churchill College Cambridge (CCC)
Doc 3841, Private Papers of T C Boddington, Imperial War Museum (IWM)


## Memoirs and Autobiographies

Admiral Sir R. H. Bacon, *The Life of Lord Fisher of Kilverstone* (London: Hodder and Stoughton, 1929)
Vera Brittain, *Testament of Youth* (London: Virago Press, 2004)
Charles E. Carrington, *Soldier From the Wars Returning* (Barnsley: Pen and Sword Military, 2015)
Hugh Dalton, *With British Guns in Italy* (Uckfield: Naval and Military Press 2004 reprint of 1919 edition)
David Lloyd George, *War Memoirs* Vols. 1 & 2 (London: Odhams Press Limited, 1938)
Norman Gladden, *Across the Piave* (London: Her Majesty's Stationary Office, 1971)
Richard Burdon Haldane, *An Autobiography* (London: Hodder and Stoughton Limited, 1928)
General Erich Ludendorff, *My War Memories 1914-1918* (London: Hutchinson and Co, 1919)
Charles a'C Repington, *The First World War 1914-1918, Personal Experiences of C a'Court Repington,* Vol. II (London: Constable, 1921)
Edwin Campion Vaughan, *Some Desperate Glory* (London: Macmillan, 1994)


## Private Papers

*Imperial War Museum*
Doc 10814, F A Brettwell Papers
Doc 20614, C E Carrington Papers
Doc 17689, H W Turner Papers

## Biographies

Major General Sir C. E. Callwell, *Field Marshal Sir Henry Wilson, His Life and Diaries Vols 1 and 2* (London: Cassell and Company Limited, 1927)
General Sir Charles Harington, *Plumer of Messines* (London: John Murray, 1935)
Gary Sheffield, *The Chief: Douglas Haig and the British Army* (London: Aurum Press Ltd, 2012)

## Formation/Unit Histories

Lt Col G H Barnett, *With the 48th Division in Italy* (Edinburgh: William Blackwood and Sons, 1923)
Lt Charles E. Carrington, , *The War Record of the 1/5th Battalion Royal Warwickshire Regiment* (Worksop: SDU Publications 2017 reprint of 1922 edition)
K W Mitchinson, *The 48th (South Midland) Division 1908-1919* (Solihull: Helion, 2017)
Lt Col H R Sandilands, , *The 23rd Division 1914-1919* (Edinburgh: William Blackwood and Sons, 1925)
Capt. P L Wright, *The First Buckinghamshire Battalion 1914-1919* (Uckfield: Naval and Military Press reprint of 1920 edition)
E Wyrall, *The Gloucestershire Regiment in the War 1914-1918* (London: Methuen and Company, 1931)

## Journal Articles

Charles E. Carrington, The Defence of the Cesuna Re-entrant in the Italian Alps by the 48th (South Midland) Division, 15th June 1918. A Study of Minor Tactics in the Defensive, *Army Quarterly,* Vol XIV (1927)
Field Marshal The Earl of Cavan, Some Tactical and Strategic Considerations of the Italian Campaign in 1917-1918', *Army Quarterly*, Volume XL (1940)
Field Marshal The Earl of Cavan, Leadership, *Army Quarterly* Vol. I (1921).
Trevor Harvey, Biographical Notes on Sir Hubert Gough, *Journal of the Society for Army Historical Research* (2018)

## War Office Publications and Pamphlets

*Field Service Regulations*, 1909
*Notes For Officers on Trench Warfare, War Office*, 1916

## Official Histories

Brigadier-General Sir James E Edmonds and Major General H R Davies, *Military Operations Italy 1915-1919* (Uckfield: Naval and Military Press reprint of 1949 edition)

Edmund Glaise-Horstenau and Rudolf Kiszling, (trans. by Samuel Hanna), *Osterreich-Ungarns Letzter Krieg Vol. VII 1918* (Vienna: Veröffentlichungen aus der Militärwissenschaft, 1938)
Captain Wilfred Miles, *Military Operations France and Belgium, 1916*, Vol. 2 (Uckfield: Naval and Military Press, 1938 (facsimile reprint))

## Secondary Published Sources

Ian F W Beckett, *Riflemen Form: A Study of the Rifle Volunteer Movement* (Barnsley: Pen and Sword Military, 2007)
John Dillon, *Allies Are a Troublesome Lot: The British Army in Italy in the First World War* (Solihull: Helion, 2015)
Martin Gilbert, *The First World War: A Complete History* (London: Orion Books Limited, 2008)
Elizabeth Greenhalgh, *The French Army in the First World War* (Cambridge: Cambridge University Press, 2014)
Graham Greenwell, *An Infant In Arms: War Letters of a Company Officer 1914-1918* (London: Allen Lane The Penguin Press, 1972)
General Sir Charles Harrington, *Plumer of Messines* (London: John Murray, 1935)
Holger H. Herwig, *The First World War: Germany and Austria-Hungary, 1914-1918* (London: Hodder, 1996)
Richard Holmes, *Tommy: The British Soldier on the Western Front 1914-1918* (London: Harper Collins, 2004)
Richard Holmes, *The Western Front* (London: BBC Books, 2008)
H. A. Jones, *The War in The Air Vol II* (Oxford: Clarendon Press, 1928)
Spencer Jones, *From Boer War to World War: Tactical Reform of the British Army, 1902-1914* (Norman: University of Oklahoma Press, 1981)
John Keegan, *The First World War* (London: Pimlico, 1999)
Francis MacKay, *Asiago, Italy* (Barnsley: Pen and Sword Military, 2016)
Francis MacKay, *Touring The Italian Front 1917-1919* (Barnsley: Leo Cooper, 2002)
Martin Middlebrook, *The First Day On The Somme* (London: Penguin Books, 2001)
Robin Neillands, *The Great War Generals on the Western Front 1914-1918* (London: Magpie Books, 2004)
Robin Prior, and Trevor Wilson, *Command on the Western Front: The Military Career of Sir Henry Rawlinson 1914-1918* (Barnsley: Pen and Sword Military, 2004)
J. M. Roberts, *Europe 1880-1945* (Harlow: Pearson Education, 2001)
Michael Senior, *Victory on the Western Front: The Development of the British Army* (Barnsley: Pen and Sword Military, 2016)
Gary Sheffield, and John Bourne, (eds.), *Douglas Haig – War Diaries and Letters 1914-1918* (London: Weidenfeld and Nicholson, 2005)
Gary Sheffield, *The Somme* (London: Cassell, 2004)
Peter Simkins, *Kitchener's Army: The Raising of the New Armies 1914-1916* (Barnsley: Pen and Sword Military, 2007)
Mark Thompson, *The White War: Life and Death on the Italian Front 1915-1919* (London: Faber and Faber, 2008)

John Wilks and Eileen Wilks, *The British Army in Italy 1917-1918* (Barnsley: Pen and Sword Military, 2013)

## Unpublished Theses and Dissertations

Aimee Fox-Godden, PhD Thesis, Putting Knowledge In Power: Learning and Innovation in the British Army, University of Birmingham

R D Williams, MA Dissertation, A Social and Military History of the 1/8th Battalion the Royal Warwickshire Regiment, University of Birmingham

## Miscellaneous Sources

Buckinghamshire County Territorial Association Minutes Book, Buckinghamshire County Archives

Oxfordshire County Territorial Association Minutes Book, Oxfordshire County Archives

*Report of Royal Commission on the Boer War* (Elgin Commission)

## Electronic Sources

*Commonwealth War Graves Commission* <www.cwgc.org>

*London Gazette* <www.thegazette.co.uk>

Capt. S. F. Gedye, *History of A Battery, 240th Brigade, Royal Field Artillery* (unpublished) <http://www.thebristolgunners.webspace.virginmedia.com/Gedye%20Diary%20ITALY%20240%20bde.%20Unit%20war%20Diary.htm>

*National Library of Scotland Trench Map Archive* <www.maps.nls.uk>

*Pte Hutt VC Obituary* <www.earlsdon.org.uk/history/arthurhutt.html>

*The Long, Long Trail* <www.longlongtrail.co.uk>

*World War I Document Archive* <https://wwi.lib.byu.edu/>

# Index

## People

Boroević, Field Marshal S., 176–77

Cadorna, General L., 118–23, 126–27, 129–31, 165
Carrington, C.E., 22–23, 42, 75, 96, 158–60, 191, 198–99, 217–18, 231–32, 239, 242–44, 248, 260, 267, 274–75
Cavan, Lieutenant-General the Earl of, 165–67, 181–82, 211, 228–29, 231–33, 235–38, 243–46, 250–53, 256, 258–61, 264–66, 268–69, 272–73, 276, 279–80

Dalton, H. 127–28, 179, 185, 192, 196–97, 206, 208–9, 213
Diaz, General A., 130–31, 166, 168–69, 178–79, 202, 265, 269, 273

Fanshawe, Major-General R. 33–35, 42–44, 50, 56–57, 67–70, 73, 79, 83, 91–92, 99, 198–99, 201–3, 212–13, 218, 220–21, 225–27, 231–68

Gaythorne-Hardy, Brigadier-General F., 212-13, 225

Haig, General/Field Marshal Sir D., 48, 57–58, 61, 80–82, 84, 91, 94, 98–99, 101, 129, 131–32, 181–82, 233–41, 261

Hotzendorf, Field Marshal F.C. von, 121, 175–77
Hunter-Weston, Lieutenant-General Sir A.,

Jacob, Lieutenant-General Sir C., 72–73
Joffre, General J.C., 31, 37, 48, 82

Lloyd George, D., 21, 80, 82, 122, 129–32, 166–67, 263
Ludendorff, General E. von, 124–25, 174, 177

Nivelle, General R., 82, 98

Plumer, General Sir H., 132, 156, 166–69, 170, 177, 179–82, 238, 247, 261, 264–66

Rawlinson, General Sir H., 48, 52, 57–58, 61, 80, 83, 85, 87, 94–95, 99–100, 237
Robertson, General Sir W., 129–31, 166–67, 181, 237, 242, 266

Tomkinson, Lieutenant-Colonel F.M., 90, 162, 255

## Places

Amiens–Roye Road, 82–83
Arras, 84–85, 99–100, 122, 124, 163, 165, 195, 241
Asiago, 146–47, 151, 168, 171, 175–76, 178, 180, 183–84, 186–87, 189, 191, 195, 198–229, 231, 233, 261, 268–73, 275

Bainsizza Plateau, 123–24
Bapaume, 61, 64, 69–70
Beaumont Hamel, 49–51, 54, 57
Brenta, 168, 176, 180, 252, 265
Brunialti, 221–23

Cambrai, 124, 163, 167
Campiello, 186–87, 190
Caporetto, 115–31, 175, 177–78, 184, 261, 263–65
Carso Plateau, 119–24, 126–27
Cockcroft, The, 103, 109–11

Epehy, 87, 89–91, 93, 99, 239

Festubert, 32, 234–36
Fifth Avenue, 71–74
Fonquevillers, 37, 39–41

Goodwood Trench, 273–74
Gorizia, 119–23, 126–27
Grenezza, 145, 184–85, 187, 189–90, 194, 196, 270, 276
Guillemont Farm, 95–99

Hamelet, 87–88
Hebuterne, 37–41, 53, 79, 91, 193
Heidenkopf Redoubt, 51–53, 56
Hillock Farm, 104–7, 109
Hindenburg Line, 84–85, 87, 89–91, 95, 97–100, 114, 193, 237, 239
Hindenburg Trench, 76–77

Isonzo, 119–25, 127–28, 163, 177, 179, 262–63

John Copse, 46–47, 56–57

La Boisselle, 57–59, 67
Langemarck, 31, 101–3, 108–9, 112–13, 237
Le Gheer, 27–29

Lemerle Switch, 191, 193, 205, 219–22, 225–27, 249, 257
Lempire, 93–94

Mailly-Maillet, 53, 55, 57
Mantua, 164, 166, 238
Marquaix, 87–89
Maison de Hibou, 103–4, 106–7, 109, 111
Monte Catz, 273–74
Monte Kaberlaba, 184, 189, 196
Mouquet Farm, 58, 61, 69–71, 74, 79

Nervesa, 168–69, 175

Ovillers, 58–60, 63–64, 67–68, 71–72, 74, 76, 78, 91

Perghele, 199, 201, 205, 216–18, 220–21, 223–24, 226, 251, 260
Peronne, 82–113
Petit Priel Farm, 95–96
Piave, 125, 127, 129, 165–71, 175–77, 179–80, 183, 238, 263–65, 273
Ploegsteert, 26–30, 32, 34, 36–38, 40–41, 114, 134–36
Polygon Trench, 221–22, 225, 249
Pozières, 51, 57–58, 61–65, 67, 69–70
Pria del Acqua, 145, 148, 189, 206

Roisel, 87–89
Roncalto, 189, 193, 201, 228
Ronssoy, 89, 91–94

Serre, 38, 49, 51, 258
Sickle Trench, 59–60, 62–63, 65
Skyline Trench, 62, 70–77
Somme, 37, 41, 48–49, 52, 58, 61, 80–82, 84–87, 124, 126, 158, 241–43, 281
Springfield, 101, 104, 106, 110, 112–14, 232
St Julien, 101, 104, 106–7, 109–11, 113, 156, 158, 218, 258

Tagliamento, 127–29, 177, 263
Thiepval, 58, 61–62, 69–72, 76, 78–79
Tolmino, 118, 123, 125–26
Tombois Farm, 95–97
Touvent Farm, 38, 46

Trentino, 116–17, 119, 121
Triangle, The, 103, 106, 109, 244
Triangle Farm, 105–7, 109–10, 113

Vale House, 103, 158
Vancouver, 103–4, 110–13
Villa Brunialti, 221

Villers Faucon, 86, 89–90, 92
Vimy Ridge, 31, 82, 163

Winnipeg, 101, 104, 110, 112

Ypres, 25–26, 31–33, 37, 99–100, 102–3, 123, 156, 195, 234, 236–37, 242–43, 258, 261

## Formations/Units

*Armies*
British
British Expeditionary Force (BEF), 21, 25, 48, 132, 234
First Army, 83, 237
Second Army, 100, 110, 114, 132, 156, 238, 240, 261
Third Army, 4, 36, 41, 51, 83, 137, 241
Fourth Army, 48, 56-57, 59, 67, 70, 79, 83, 85, 87, 89, 94, 99, 237
Reserve Army/Fifth Army, 57, 59, 61, 70, 79, 80, 83, 99-102, 112, 114, 129, 132, 156, 174, 237, 241, 243, 245, 260-261

French
First Army, 100

Italian
First Army, 119, 121, 188, 240
Second Army, 119, 122-123, 178, 264
Third Army, 119, 121-123, 127
Fourth Army, 119, 168
Sixth Army, 180-182, 188, 258, 269
Tenth Army, 181, 238, 273

Austro-Hungarian
Third Army, 275

*Corps*
British
I Corps, 32, 234, 236
II Corps, 70-71, 77, 79, 241, 242
III Corps, 31, 32, 34-37, 48, 58-59, 61, 79, 80, 82-83, 85, 87, 90, 94-95, 99, 240, 248
IV Corps, 36, 37, 41, 99-100, 130
V Corps, 79, 163, 234
VI Corps, 240
VII Corps, 36-38, 42, 48, 51, 79, 240, 241

VIII Corps, 48-49, 56-57, 243
X Corps, 48, 57-59, 61, 129, 132, 167
XI Corps, 132, 168, 171, 181, 238, 247
XII Corps, 181-182, 189, 273-275
XIII Corps, 48, 79, 253
XIV Corps, 101, 102, 129, 166, 168, 181-183, 194, 229, 237-238, 268-269, 273, 277
XV Corps, 48, 240
XVII Corps, 240
XVIII Corps, 100-102, 108, 110, 113, 132, 156, 248
XIX Corps, 101-102, 110, 113
XX Corps, 182

Italian
I Corps, 168
XII Corps, 273
XIII Corps, 252
XX Corps, 182

French
XII Corps, 182, 189

*Divisions*
Austro-Hungarian
13th Division, 170
16th Honved Division, 252
23rd Honved Division, 203, 253
55th Division, 129

British/Dominion
Guards Division, 233, 237-238
1st Australian Division, 61, 67, 69
1st Division, 37, 41, 82, 85, 234, 239
2nd Australian Division, 71-72, 76
2nd Division, 34, 233, 236
3rd Division, 100, 239-241
4th Division, 28, 29, 37-39, 49, 51, 56, 234, 239

5th Division, 167, 171, 181, 238
5th Cavalry Division, 87
7th Division, 132, 168, 172, 181, 183, 194, 199, 211, 222, 227, 229-230, 232, 239, 258, 269
8th Division, 58, 236
9th (Scottish) Division, 239
11th (Northern) Division, 100-102, 109-110, 111
12th (Eastern) Division, 58-59, 69, 71, 129, 239
15th (Scottish) Division, 79-80
17th (Northern) Division, 240
18th (Eastern) Division, 79
19th (Western) Division, 58
21st Division, 167, 238, 240
23rd Division, 164, 166, 168, 187, 189-191, 194-195, 199, 201, 211, 220, 228-230, 238, 245, 252-253, 258, 262, 269-270, 273
25th Division, 59-60, 76-77
27th Division, 38, 241
29th Division, 49, 57
31st Division, 48-49, 51, 54, 56-57
32nd Division, 59
33rd Division, 79
34th Division, 58, 239
35th (Bantam) Division, 77
36th (Ulster) Division, 70
37th Division, 37
38th (Welsh) Division, 240
39th Division, 79, 94, 101, 239
41st Division, 129, 164, 166-168, 172, 183, 238
42nd (East Lancashire) Division, 99
46th (North Midland) Division, 127, 240
47th (London) Division, 37
48th (South Midland) Division, 26, 33-34, 37-39, 41-42, 48-52, 56-57, 59-61, 65, 67, 69-73, 76-77, 79-80, 82, 83-87, 89, 91, 94-95, 98-102, 104, 108-114, 135-136, 138, 149, 156, 163-164, 166, 171-172, 181, 183, 187, 190, 192-194, 200, 202, 206, 208, 210-214, 220, 226, 228-229, 230-231, 235, 243, 245, 247-248, 253, 257-262, 267-270, 272-273, 275-276
49th (West Riding) Division, 71, 79
51st (Highland) Division, 101
57th (2nd West Lancashire) Division, 239
58th (London) Division, 114
59th (2nd North Midland) Division, 85, 89

French
21st Division, 38

24th Division, 274
47th Chasseur Division, 179
56th Division, 39
152nd Division, 83

German
12th Division, 126, 170

Italian
1st Division, 168
12th Division, 259, 260
19th Division, 126
20th Division, 274
70th Division, 168

***Brigades***
British
2nd Brigade, 236
3rd (Ambala) Cavalry Brigade, 87
4th (Guards), 236
7th Brigade, 60
10th Brigade, 29
11th Brigade, 29, 51-53, 55
12th Brigade, 51, 56
16th Brigade, 23
68th Brigade, 252, 253-254
74th Brigade, 59-60
75th Brigade, 60
88th Brigade, 57
91st Brigade, 227
93rd Brigade, 57
94th Brigade, 57
116th Brigade, 101
118th Brigade, 101
143rd Brigade, 33, 38-39, 41, 46, 51-52, 57, 59, 60, 69, 74, 77-79, 83, 90, 96, 109-110, 112-114, 156, 160, 172, 199, 201-202, 204, 209-212, 217, 220-226, 228-229, 249, 267-268, 270, 274-275
144th Brigade, 38-40, 43, 46, 52, 57, 60, 64-68, 71, 76-77, 79, 83, 86, 89-90, 94, 97, 104, 106-107, 109-114, 160, 163, 172, 187, 199, 202, 221, 224-227, 231, 250, 256, 270-271, 274
145th Brigade, 33-34, 38-39, 41, 50, 52, 57, 61, 63-68, 71, 75, 77, 79, 85, 89, 92, 95-97, 99, 104, 108, 112-113, 156, 160, 163, 199, 201-202, 209-210, 212, 215, 219, 224, 226, 249, 254-255, 257, 272-274

Gloucestershire and Worcestershire Brigade, 19, 29, 31
South Midlands Brigade, 18, 19
Warwickshire Brigade, 17, 19, 22, 24, 29-32, 56, 60, 160, 275

Italian
Friuli Brigade, 126

*Regiments/Battalions*
British
1/7th Argyll and Sutherland Highlanders, 29
1/1st Buckinghamshire Battalion, Oxfordshire and Buckinghamshire Light Infantry, 19, 21-22, 24, 28, 30, 38- 39, 63-69, 72, 74, 77, 86, 92, 96-97, 104-106, 108, 111, 133-134, 138, 141-142, 160, 163-165, 172, 183, 200-202, 210, 219, 222, 226, 249, 257-258
1/4th Gloucestershire Regiment, 21, 23, 29, 76, 89, 97, 161-163, 202, 224, 274
1/5th Gloucestershire Regiment, 21, 29-30, 64-69, 74, 78, 86-87, 92-97, 104, 107, 156, 164, 201-202, 209-210, 215-217, 219, 220, 222, 225-226, 228, 249
1/6th Gloucestershire Regiment, 21, 46-47, 65, 68, 76, 90, 97, 112, 161-162, 199, 202, 224, 228-229, 271, 274, 277
1st Grenadier Guards, 32, 235
1st Hampshire Regiment, 29, 51
1st King's Own (Royal Lancashire) Regiment, 28
2nd Lancashire Fusiliers, 28
9th Lancashire Fusiliers, 157
1/5th London Regiment (London Rifle Brigade), 29-30
1/15th London Regiment (London Scottish), 25, 26
10th Northumberland Fusiliers, 253, 258
11th Northumberland Fusiliers, 170, 191, 199, 206, 220, 226, 228, 230
1/4th Oxfordshire and Buckinghamshire Light Infantry, 17, 21, 32, 35, 63-64, 68-72, 74, 77, 87-88, 92-94, 97, 104, 107, 156, 160, 201-203, 207, 210, 214-216, 219-221, 224-230, 246, 249, 258, 260, 274
2nd Oxfordshire and Buckinghamshire Light Infantry, 32
1st Rifle Brigade, 29, 51
1/4th Royal Berkshire Regiment, 22, 29-30, 65, 71, 75, 78, 92-93, 96-98, 104, 106, 111, 160, 163, 200-202, 210, 224, 226-228, 272-274, 276
1/5th Royal Sussex Regiment, 50, 199
1/5th Royal Warwickshire Regiment, 22-23, 26, 29, 46, 59-60, 74-75, 96, 109, 112, 156, 157, 159-160, 198, 201-202, 212, 217, 220-223, 229, 248-249, 267-268, 270-271
1/6th Royal Warwickshire Regiment, 19, 22, 29, 51-55, 74-75, 114, 156-160, 201, 202, 211, 223-224, 228-249, 256-257
1/7th Royal Warwickshire Regiment, 22, 23, 29, 33, 59-60, 75, 112, 156-157, 160, 201-202, 221-225, 228, 230, 249-250, 267, 270, 275
1/8th Royal Warwickshire Regiment, 22, 29, 30, 51-52, 54, 55, 78, 83, 86, 107, 113-114, 156, 160, 201-202, 211, 218, 228-239, 249, 257-258
11th Sherwood Foresters (Notts and Derby) Regiment, 251
1st Wiltshire Regiment, 76
3rd Worcestershire Regiment, 60, 77
1/7th Worcestershire Regiment, 29, 43, 52, 90, 91, 97, 107, 113-114, 162-163, 199, 202, 224, 227-228, 235, 273, 274
1/8th Worcestershire Regiment, 24, 64, 97, 106, 109-110, 113, 114, 162-163, 202, 227-228

*Miscellaneous British Units*
22nd Brigade, Royal Field Artillery, 230
35th Brigade, Royal Field Artillery, 222, 230
102nd Brigade, Royal Field Artillery, 230
240th Brigade, Royal Field Artillery, 199, 207, 213, 217, 220, 222-223, 243, 248, 251
241st Brigade, Royal Field Artillery, 199, 220, 251
94th Heavy Artillery Group, 123, 127
164th Company, Royal Engineers, 34
174th Tunnelling Company, Royal Engineers, 30
178th Tunnelling Company, Royal Engineers, 35
48th Machine Gun Battalion, 199, 221, 249
143rd Trench Mortar Battery, 218
145th Trench Mortar Battery, 210, 228